RICHARD STRAUSS IN CONTEXT

Richard Strauss in Context offers a distinctive approach to the study of a composer, placing the emphasis on contextualizing topics rather than on biography and artistic output. One might say that it inverts the relationship between composer and context. Rather than studies of Strauss's librettists that discuss the texts and his musical settings, for instance, this book offers essays on the writers themselves: their biographical circumstances, styles, landmark works, and broader positions in literary history. Likewise, Strauss's contributions to the concert hall are positioned within the broader development of the orchestra and trends in programmatic music. In short, readers will benefit from an elaboration of material that is either absent from or treated only briefly in existing publications. With its contextually rich approach, this book serves as a valuable and unique resource for students, scholars, and a general readership.

MORTEN KRISTIANSEN is Associate Professor of Musicology and director of the music program at Xavier University in Cincinnati, Ohio. In addition to conference papers and journal articles on Richard Strauss and fin-de-siècle German opera, he has authored program notes for the Salzburg Festival.

JOSEPH E. JONES is Associate Professor of Music at Texas A&M University-Kingsville where he also serves as director of an annual study abroad program in Vienna. His research areas include German opera and the fin de siècle, and he previously coedited *Genetic Criticism and the Creative Process* (2009).

D1127678

COMPOSERS IN CONTEXT

Understanding and appreciation of musical works is greatly enhanced by knowledge of the context within which their composers lived and worked. Each of these volumes focuses on an individual composer, offering lively, accessible, and concise essays by leading scholars on the many contexts – professional, political, intellectual, social, and cultural – that have a bearing on his or her work. Biographical and musical influences, performance and publishing history, and the creative afterlife of each composer's work are also addressed, providing readers with a multi-faceted view of how the composers' output and careers were shaped by the world around them.

Titles forthcoming in the series

Beethoven in Context, edited by GLENN STANLEY and JOHN D. WILSON

Liszt in Context, edited by JOANNE CORMAC

Mahler in Context, edited by CHARLES YOUMANS

Stravinsky in Context, edited by GRAHAM GRIFFITHS

RICHARD STRAUSS IN CONTEXT

EDITED BY

MORTEN KRISTIANSEN
Xavier University

JOSEPH E. JONES
Texas A&M University-Kingsville

CAMBRIDGE
UNIVERSITY PRESS

CAMBRIDGE
UNIVERSITY PRESS

Shaftesbury Road, Cambridge CB2 8EA, United Kingdom

One Liberty Plaza, 20th Floor, New York, NY 10006, USA

477 Williamstown Road, Port Melbourne, VIC 3207, Australia

314–321, 3rd Floor, Plot 3, Splendor Forum, Jasola District Centre, New Delhi – 110025, India

103 Penang Road, #05–06/07, Visioncrest Commercial, Singapore 238467

Cambridge University Press is part of Cambridge University Press & Assessment, a department of the University of Cambridge.

We share the University's mission to contribute to society through the pursuit of education, learning and research at the highest international levels of excellence.

www.cambridge.org
Information on this title: www.cambridge.org/9781108434461

DOI: 10.1017/9781108379939

First published 2020
First paperback edition 2022

A catalogue record for this publication is available from the British Library

Library of Congress Cataloging-in-Publication data
NAMES: Kristiansen, Morten, editor. | Jones, Joseph E., editor.
TITLE: Richard Strauss in context / edited by Morten Kristiansen, Joseph E. Jones.
DESCRIPTION: [1.] | New York : Cambridge University Press, 2020. |
SERIES: Composers in context | Includes bibliographical references and index.
IDENTIFIERS: LCCN 2020016728 (print) | LCCN 2020016729 (ebook) | ISBN 9781108422000
(hardback) | ISBN 9781108434461 (paperback) | ISBN 9781108379939 (epub)
SUBJECTS: LCSH: Strauss, Richard, 1864-1949–Criticism and interpretation. |
Strauss, Richard, 1864–1949–Friends and associates. | Musicians–Germany.
CLASSIFICATION: LCC ML410.S93 R497 2020 (print) | LCC ML410.S93 (ebook) |
DDC 780.92–dc23
LC record available at https://lccn.loc.gov/2020016728
LC ebook record available at https://lccn.loc.gov/2020016729

ISBN   978-1-108-42200-0   Hardback
ISBN   978-1-108-43446-1   Paperback

Contents

Contents

Figures

Notes on Contributors

KENNETH BIRKIN is the author of *Friedenstag and Daphne* (1989), *Richard Strauss: Arabella* (1989), and *Hans von Bülow* (2011), and is the editor and translator of *Stefan Zweig – Joseph Gregor: Correspondence 1921–1938* (1991). His work has appeared in journals and periodicals, including the *Richard Strauss-Blätter*, *Music & Letters*, *Opera Magazine*, *The Musical Times*, and *Tempo*. He has written and presented programs for BBC Radio 3 and is the librettist of British composer John Joubert's three-act opera *Jane Eyre*.

SEBASTIAN BOLZ studied musicology, German philology, and history in Hildesheim and Munich. He is a research assistant at the *Kritische Ausgabe der Werke von Richard Strauss* and is currently preparing a dissertation on German opera around 1900. He coedited the volumes *Richard Wagner in München* (2015), *Denkstrukturen der Musikwissenschaft* (2016), and *Richard Strauss: Der Komponist und sein Werk* (2017). In addition to nineteenth- and twentieth-century opera and song, his research focuses on the history, historiography, and teaching of musicology.

LEON BOTSTEIN is music director of The Orchestra Now and American Symphony Orchestra, artistic codirector of Bard SummerScape and the Bard Music Festival, artistic director of Campus Grafenegg and Grafenegg Academy in Austria, and conductor laureate of the Jerusalem Symphony Orchestra. He is a prolific author and editor of *The Musical Quarterly*. He has recorded Strauss's operas *Die ägyptische Helena* and *Die Liebe der Danae* and performed other less explored Strauss works. He has been president of Bard College since 1975.

JAMES DEAVILLE teaches music at Carleton University, Ottawa, Canada. He has published essays about Strauss and the Allgemeine Deutsche Musikverein (ADMV), as well as Liszt, Wagner, and Mahler. He has coedited the collections *New Light on Liszt and His Music* (1997) and *Liszt's Legacies* (2014) and contributed introductory remarks to the source anthology *Neudeutsche Schule* (2020). He has received funding from the Social Sciences and Humanities Research Council of Canada and the German Academic Exchange Service (DAAD) to conduct research in the Weimar ADMV archives.

PETER FRANKLIN has been an Emeritus Fellow of St Catherine's College, Oxford, since 2014. He writes on late nineteenth-century European musical culture, post-Wagnerian opera, and film music. Publications include *Mahler: Symphony No. 3* (1991), *The Life of Mahler* (1997), and *Seeing through Music: Gender and Modernism in Classic Hollywood Film Scores* (2011). *Reclaiming Late-Romantic Music: Singing Devils and Distant Sounds* (2014) was based on his 2010 Bloch Lectures at the University of California at Berkeley.

JASON GEARY is Professor of Musicology and Dean of the Mason Gross School of the Arts at Rutgers University. His research focuses on the intersection of music and Hellenism during the nineteenth and twentieth centuries, and he is the author of *The Politics of Appropriation: German Romantic Music and the Ancient Greek Legacy* (2014). He is currently at work on a book exploring the theme of childhood in music of the nineteenth century.

BRYAN GILLIAM is Professor emeritus of Music at Duke University. Gilliam has published five books on Strauss, including *Richard Strauss's Elektra* (1991), *The Life of Richard Strauss* (1999), and *Rounding Wagner's Mountain: Richard Strauss and Modern German Opera* (2014). He has published articles in *The Journal of the American Musicological Society*, *19th-Century Music*, *The Musical Quarterly*, and *The Cambridge Opera Journal*, among others. He serves as an associate editor of *The Musical Quarterly*.

PHILIP GRAYDON is a lecturer in music at the Conservatory of Music and Drama, Technological University Dublin, and the Royal Irish Academy of Music. His research interests center on music and culture in early twentieth-century Austria and Germany, and are particularly focused on German opera in its historical, political, and aesthetic contexts. He has published essays on Richard Strauss in *The Musical Quarterly*, *The Journal of the Royal Musical Association*, and *The Cambridge Companion to Richard Strauss*.

INGEBORG HAASE served for many years as copy-editor for the critical edition of Hugo von Hofmannsthal's works (Freies Deutsches Hochstift), the publishers S. Fischer and C. H. Beck, and the archive for the history of the German book trade (Börsenverein des Deutschen Buchhandels). Her publications include the critical edition of *Der Schwierige* (with Martin Stern, 1993), *Der Rosenkavalier: Textfassungen und Zeilenkommentar* (2016), and *Gisela Hemau – Lebensspuren einer Lyrikerin in unlyrischer Zeit* (2018), the latter two with Dirk Hoffmann.

CLAUDIA HEINE is a research staff member at the *Kritische Ausgabe der Werke von Richard Strauss* in Munich. She studied musicology and history in Zurich, Switzerland, completing her Ph.D. in 2009. At the Richard-Strauss-Institut in Garmisch-Partenkirchen, she has created and run the Richard-Strauss-Quellenverzeichnis (RSQV) with Adrian Kech. Currently, she is editing the *Salome* volumes for the critical edition, of which the first (Series I, Vol. 3a) was published in 2019.

DIRK HOFFMANN is Professor of German emeritus at Colgate University, Hamilton, New York. His main research interests are textology, German literature of the fin de siècle in Prague and Vienna, language instruction methodology, and cross-cultural learning. His book publications include the critical edition of *Der Rosenkavalier* (in collaboration with Willi Schuh, 1986), a monograph on and editions of Paul Leppin's work, a German textbook and survey of German culture, and a book on poetry.

RAYMOND HOLDEN has conducted many of Britain's and Europe's leading orchestras; has been published by Oxford, Cambridge, and Yale University Presses; and has appeared on BBC Television and Radio, Servus TV (Germany), RAI Television and Radio, ABC Classic FM, 3MBS FM, Vision Australia Radio, Classic FM (South Africa), and SRF (Switzerland). He is currently the Royal Academy of Music's Professor of Public Engagement and was appointed Member of the Order of Australia (AM) in the 2019 Australian Queen's Birthday Honours List.

KATHARINA HOTTMANN teaches at the University of Flensburg. She earned her doctoral degree in musicology with a dissertation on historicism and genre-awareness in Strauss's later operas. Her second book is titled *"Auf! stimmt ein freies Scherzlied an": Weltliche Liedkultur im Hamburg der Aufklärung* (2017). She has taught at several conservatories and universities in Hannover, Hamburg, Berlin, and Kiel, among others. Her research spans the seventeenth to the twentieth centuries and focuses on the intersection between cultural history and analysis.

JOSEPH E. JONES is Associate Professor at Texas A&M University-Kingsville, where he also serves as director of an annual study abroad program in Austria. His research interests include German opera, Viennese cultural history, and the fin de siècle, and he previously coedited a book with William Kinderman titled *Genetic Criticism and the Creative Process* (2009). Jones has presented papers at dozens of conferences, including meetings of the American Musicological Society, International Musicological Society, College Music Society, and Royal Music Association.

ADRIAN KECH studied musicology, philosophy, and European law at the Ludwig Maximilian University (LMU) in Munich. His dissertation *Musikalische Verwandlung in den Hofmannsthal-Opern von Richard Strauss* was published in 2015. He worked as an academic associate both for the Richard-Strauss-Quellenverzeichnis (RSQV) at the Richard-Strauss-Institut in Garmisch-Partenkirchen and for the Institute of Musicology at the LMU. In 2015 he moved to the *Kritische Ausgabe der Werke von Richard Strauss*, where he has since been responsible for editing the operas.

ULRICH KONRAD is Head of the Institute for Music Research at the Julius Maximilian University in Würzburg, Germany. He has published widely on music history from the seventeenth to the twentieth centuries, especially on Bach reception, Mozart, Schumann, Wagner, and Strauss. Konrad also serves as editor of the forthcoming *Richard Wagner Schriften (RWS) – Historisch-kritische Gesamtausgabe*.

JONATHAN KREGOR is Professor of Musicology at the University of Cincinnati, College-Conservatory of Music. His research interests include aesthetics, Franz Liszt, musical reproduction, music and memory, virtuosity and gender, and art song. He is the author of *Liszt as Transcriber* (2010), *Program Music* (2015), and articles and reviews in numerous academic journals; editor of keyboard works by C. P. E. Bach and Clara Schumann; coeditor of *Liszt et la France* (2012); and editor of *Nineteenth-Century Programme Music: Creation, Negotiations, Reception* (2019).

MORTEN KRISTIANSEN, a native of Copenhagen, is Associate Professor of Musicology and director of the music program at Xavier University in

Cincinnati, Ohio. He has presented papers at the national meetings of the American Musicological Society and many other conferences, contributed program notes to the Salzburg Festival, and published essays on Richard Strauss and Ernst von Wolzogen in the *Richard Strauss-Blätter*, *The Musical Quarterly*, *The Cambridge Companion to Richard Strauss*, and a number of other essay collections.

DAVID LARKIN is a senior lecturer in musicology at the University of Sydney. His scholarly writings have appeared in *The Cambridge Companion to Richard Strauss*, *19th-Century Music*, *The Musical Quarterly*, *Music and the Moving Image*, and various essay collections. At present he is working on a study of progressive composers and their audiences in the nineteenth century. He is also a regular pre-concert speaker at the Sydney Opera House and other local venues, and is active as a music critic.

ERIK LEVI is Visiting Professor of Music at Royal Holloway, University of London, an experienced professional accompanist, and regular contributor to *BBC Music Magazine*. He has published widely on the impact of Nazism and fascism on musical developments during the twentieth century, and his books include *Music in the Third Reich* (1994) and *Mozart and the Nazis* (2010). His latest publication is *The Routledge Handbook to Music under German Occupation, 1938–1945* (2020), co-edited with David Fanning.

JÜRGEN MAY received his Ph.D. from the University of Bonn in 1989. From 1999 to 2018 he was Research Fellow at the Richard-Strauss-Institut in Garmisch-Partenkirchen, and is currently Research Associate at the Beethoven-Archiv (Bonn). May has researched nineteenth- and early twentieth-century composers, particularly Beethoven and Richard Strauss, often focusing on the inter-relationship between creative output, biography, and socio-political contexts. May is a member of the advisory board of the Richard-Strauss-Edition (Munich) and Associate Professor Extraordinary at Africa Open Institute (Stellenbosch).

FRANZPETER MESSMER studied musicology, German philology, art history, and violin in Munich. His doctoral thesis was titled *Altdeutsche Liedkomposition: Der Kantionalsatz und die Einheit von Singen und Dichten*. He has published biographies of Orlando di Lasso, Richard Strauss, and George Frideric Handel. He is artistic director of Landshuter Hofmusiktage: European Festival of Early Music, and he designed and organized the Richard-Strauss-Jahre of the Bavarian State in 1999 and 2014. He is editor of the book series *Komponisten in Bayern*.

ANDREAS PERNPEINTNER earned his Ph.D. in musicology with a thesis on the German-Irish composer Aloys Fleischmann. He was an editorial member of the Deutsche Forschungsgemeinschaft project *Bayerisches Musiker-Lexikon Online*. Since 2011, he has served as a research staff member for the *Kritische Ausgabe der Werke von Richard Strauss* and is responsible for the edition of the Lieder. He offers seminars at the Institute for Musicology at Munich's Ludwig Maximilian University and has been a music journalist for the *Süddeutsche Zeitung* since 2003.

RYAN M. PRENDERGAST's dissertation research (Theatre Studies, University of Illinois at Urbana-Champaign) focuses on the history of opera production and is based in Munich with the support of the Deutsche Akademische Austauschdienst. His work reflects his experience as a stage manager and director and pays close attention to the visual and audio legacies of opera.

MICHAEL SAFFLE, recently retired as Professor of Music and Humanities at Virginia Tech, has published on rural American television music and *The Sopranos* television series as well as Liszt, Wagner, and Edward MacDowell. In addition to Rockefeller and Humboldt awards, in 2000–01 Saffle was the Fulbright Bicentennial Chair in American Studies at the University of Helsinki as part of the Fulbright Distinguished Chairs Program. In 2006, he was honored with a Festschrift published in *Spaces of Identity*: the first-ever e-journal Festschrift in the field of musicology.

GIANGIORGIO SATRAGNI holds a Ph.D. in Musicology from the Humboldt University of Berlin and in Comparative Studies from the University of Turin. He currently teaches music history at the G. F. Ghedini Conservatory in Cuneo. His main books are *Richard Strauss dietro la maschera* (2015) and *Il Parsifal di Wagner: Testo, musica, teologia* (2017). In 2018, he organized the exhibition *Richard Strauss e l'Italia* in Turin and wrote its catalog in three languages.

DIETMAR SCHENK received his Ph.D. from the University of Münster focusing on history, mathematics, and philosophy. He completed studies at the Archives School Marburg and has headed the Archives of the Berlin University of the Arts since 1991. In 2001, he curated the *Richard Strauss im kaiserlichen Berlin* exhibition at the Musical

Instruments Museum. He has authored books on the cultural history of Berlin, and his publications include *Die Hochschule für Musik zu Berlin* (2004) and *Kleine Theorie des Archivs* (2008, 2014).

STEFAN SCHENK completed an engineering degree (IT/Cybernetics) and a second degree in musicology and theater. His Ph.D. explored avant-garde electronic music from the Munich Siemens Studio, ca. 1960, which earned him the University Award of the City of Munich. Since 2011, he has served as a research staff member for the *Kritische Ausgabe der Werke von Richard Strauss* and is responsible for the edition of the tone poems. He also offers seminars at the Ludwig Maximilian University's Institute for Musicology.

MANUELA SCHMIDT is a judge at the Regional Court (*Richterin am Landgericht*) in Trier, Germany. She has published essays on copyright, tenancy, insolvency, enforcement, and inheritance law and on legal questions surrounding the termination of life-prolonging measures. Her academic publications focus on the annotation of the German rules of legal succession in the *juris PraxisKommentar*, an online annotation (9th edition published in 2020) which is part of *juris*, one of the leading legal databases in Germany.

CHRIS WALTON studied at the universities of Cambridge, Oxford, and Zurich, and was a Humboldt research fellow at the University of Munich. He ran the music division of the Zentralbibliothek Zürich for ten years before being appointed chair of music at the University of Pretoria. He currently teaches music history at the Basel University of Music, runs a research project at the Bern University of the Arts, and is an honorary professor at Africa Open Institute, Stellenbosch University.

SCOTT WARFIELD is Associate Professor of Music History at the University of Central Florida. He earned his Ph.D. at the University of North Carolina-Chapel Hill with a dissertation on Strauss's early years and the emergence of his mature style in his first tone poem, *Macbeth*. His essays and reviews on Strauss, his music, and related topics have appeared in the *Richard Strauss-Blätter*, *MLA Notes*, *The Richard Strauss Companion*, *The Cambridge Companion to Richard Strauss*, and *Ars Lyrica*, among other publications.

WALTER WERBECK is Professor emeritus of Musicology at the University of Greifswald in Germany. He is author of *Die Tondichtungen von Richard Strauss* (1996) and numerous other publications on the life and music of Strauss. Werbeck is a member of the Advisory Board of the *Kritische Ausgabe der Werke von Richard Strauss* and coeditor of *Macbeth* and *Don Juan*, and in 2016 he edited (with Marion Beyer and Jürgen May) the *Späte Aufzeichnungen* of Strauss.

MATTHEW WERLEY is lecturer in musicology and dance studies at the University of Salzburg and Mozarteum. His work focuses on opera and dance studies, especially their connections to political history and literary culture from 1700 to 1950. His publications have appeared in various academic journals and books, and he has presented on a broad range of subjects at conferences and universities throughout Europe, North America, and Australia. He is Secretary General of the Internationale Richard Strauss Gesellschaft and editor of the *Richard Strauss-Jahrbuch*.

BEN WINTERS is Senior Lecturer in music at The Open University, UK. He is the author of *Music, Performance, and the Realities of Film* (2014) and recently coedited *The Routledge Companion to Screen Music and Sound* (2017) and *Music, Modern Culture, and the Critical Ear* (2018). He is a coeditor of the *Ashgate Screen Music Series*, and of the journal *Music, Sound, and the Moving Image*.

CHARLES YOUMANS, Professor of Musicology at Penn State University, is the author of *Richard Strauss's Orchestral Music and the German Intellectual Tradition* (2005) and *Mahler and Strauss: In Dialogue* (2016), and the editor of *The Cambridge Companion to Richard Strauss* (2010) and *Mahler in Context* (forthcoming). He has published articles in *19th-Century Music*, *The Musical Quarterly*, the *Journal of Musicology*, and elsewhere, and contributed nine chapters on Strauss's tone poems to the *Richard Strauss Handbuch* (2014).

JEREMY R. ZIMA holds a Ph.D. in musicology from the University of Wisconsin-Madison. His dissertation, completed in 2016, explores the economics and aesthetics of early twentieth-century German artist operas. He is Assistant Professor of Music at Wisconsin Lutheran College in Milwaukee where he teaches courses in music history, theory, and composition. His current research focuses on the discourse surrounding music criticism in Germany during the 1920s and 1930s.

Preface

Morten Kristiansen and Joseph E. Jones

Nearly a half century elapsed after Richard Strauss's death in 1949 before the composer became the object of sustained musicological inquiry, in spite of his prominence in the concert hall and opera house. Not until the early 1990s, with the publication of two English-language essay collections edited by Bryan Gilliam, did Strauss scholarship experience something of a turn-of-the-millennium resurgence that has not since abated.[1] In addition to numerous articles, contributions from this period include a string of biographies,[2] three comprehensive "companions,"[3] several other essay collections published in 1999 in commemoration of the semi-centennial of Strauss's death,[4] and a more recent volume in 2014 stemming from the 150th anniversary of his birth.[5] The latest product is an English translation

---

[1] *Richard Strauss and His World*, ed. Bryan Gilliam (Princeton: Princeton University Press, 1992) and *Richard Strauss: New Perspectives on the Composer and His Work*, ed. Bryan Gilliam (Durham, NC: Duke University Press, 1992).

[2] Franzpeter Messmer, *Richard Strauss: Biographie eines Klangzauberers* (Zürich/St. Gallen: M&T Verlag, 1994); Veronika Beci, *Der ewig Moderne: Richard Strauss 1864–1949* (Düsseldorf: Droste, 1998); Tim Ashley, *Richard Strauss* (London: Phaidon Press, 1999); Matthew Boyden, *Richard Strauss* (Boston: Northeastern University Press, 1999); Bryan Gilliam, *The Life of Richard Strauss* (Cambridge: Cambridge University Press, 1999); Michael Kennedy, *Richard Strauss: Man, Musician, Enigma* (Cambridge: Cambridge University Press, 1999); Maria Publig, *Richard Strauss: Bürger–Künstler–Rebell, eine historische Annäherung* (Graz: Styria, 1999); Michael Walter, *Richard Strauss und seine Zeit* (Laaber: Verlag Laaber, 2000); Kurt Wilhelm, *Richard Strauss: An Intimate Portrait*, trans. Mary Whittall (New York: Thames & Hudson, 2000); and Raymond Holden, *Richard Strauss: A Musical Life* (New Haven: Yale University Press, 2011).

[3] *The Richard Strauss Companion*, ed. Mark-Daniel Schmid (Westport, CT: Praeger, 2003); *The Cambridge Companion to Richard Strauss*, ed. Charles Youmans (Cambridge: Cambridge University Press, 2010); and *Richard Strauss Handbuch*, ed. Walter Werbeck (Stuttgart: Metzler, 2014).

[4] *Richard Strauss und die Moderne*, ed. Bernd Edelmann, Birgit Lodes, and Reinhold Schlötterer (Berlin: Henschel, 2001); *Richard Strauss, Hugo von Hofmannsthal: Frauenbilder*, ed. Ilija Dürhammer and Pia Janke (Vienna: Praesens, 2001); *Richard Strauss: Essays zu Leben und Werk*, ed. Michael Heinemann, Matthias Herrmann, and Stefan Weiss (Laaber: Laaber-Verlag, 2002); and *Richard Strauss und das Musiktheater*, ed. Julia Liebscher (Berlin: Henschel, 2005).

[5] Richard Strauss: *Der Komponist und sein Werk – Überlieferung, Interpretation, Rezeption*, ed. Sebastian Bolz, Adrian Kech, and Hartmut Schick (Munich: Allitera, 2017).

(rare for composer biographies) of Laurenz Lütteken's 2014 monograph, *Richard Strauss: Musik der Moderne*, hopefully a sign of an expanding global interest in the composer.[6]

The volumes in Cambridge's *Composers in Context* series differ in approach from previous edited collections, in that they place the emphasis on contextualizing topics rather than on the composer's biography and artistic output. One might say they invert the relationship between composer and context. For instance, while both *The Cambridge Companion to Richard Strauss* (2010) and the *Richard Strauss Handbuch* (2014) contain essays with titles echoed in this volume, (e.g. Strauss as Conductor, the Allgemeine Deutsche Musikverein, Strauss's Librettists, and the Genossenschaft Deutscher Tonsetzer), these earlier publications appropriately center on Strauss himself. The equivalent essays in *Richard Strauss in Context* instead focus attention on the composer's orbit. Rather than essays on Strauss's librettists that discuss the texts and his musical settings, Chapters 5 and 6 foreground the writers themselves: their biographical circumstances, styles, landmark works, and larger positions in literary history. Similarly, while previous essays on Strauss's development as an opera composer concentrate on the genesis, style, and reception of the works, the larger picture of German opera after Wagner might be addressed only in passing. The corresponding chapter in this volume expands that discussion into a survey of post-Wagnerian operas by composers such as Max von Schillings, Hans Pfitzner, Wilhelm Kienzl, and Eugen d'Albert – important figures in Strauss's operatic environment who typically receive only cursory mention in the existing literature. And yet, not all chapters in this volume focus exclusively on context. Those of the final section (Part VI: *Artifacts and Legacy*) are by nature more Strauss-centric as are a few others, such as Chapters 1, "Family and Upbringing," 14, "Strauss as Reader," and 29, "Lateness." What all chapters share, however, is the elaboration of material that is either absent from or treated only briefly in biographies and journal articles. Through this supplemental and broader contextual approach, we aim for this book to serve as a valuable and unique resource for students, scholars, and a general readership.

Richard Strauss in Context features 36 essays divided into six parts. Part I, *Family, Friends, and Collaborators*, explores a range of figures who played central roles in Strauss's life and career. Chris Walton examines the composer's family and upbringing with respect to the wider culture of

---

[6] Laurenz Lütteken, *Strauss*, trans. Erik Butler (New York: Oxford University Press, 2019).

his native Bavaria, while David Larkin focuses on three figures who exerted significant influence over Strauss's development: his father Franz Strauss, Hans von Bülow, and Alexander Ritter. Katharina Hottmann presents a study of Strauss's wife, Pauline de Ahna, assessing their marriage relative to contemporary norms for domestic partnerships and compared to that for women with similar professional backgrounds. Walter Werbeck then discusses the lives of Ludwig Thuille and Friedrich Rösch, two of Strauss's closest friends. The next two chapters center on Strauss's librettists. Ingeborg Haase and Dirk Hoffmann survey the life and work of Hugo von Hofmannsthal, his longest and most significant collaborator, and Kenneth Birkin considers the careers of Ernst von Wolzogen (*Feuersnot*), Stefan Zweig (*Die schweigsame Frau*), Joseph Gregor (*Friedenstag, Daphne,* and *Die Liebe der Danae*), and Clemens Krauss (*Capriccio*). Ryan M. Prendergast investigates key stage collaborators, including Max Reinhardt and Alfred Roller, and touches upon the Salzburg Festival they cofounded with Strauss. Finally, Bryan Gilliam underscores the importance of several conductors, singers, and other composers who championed Strauss at various stages of his career.

Part II, *Career Stations*, includes studies of the seven cities most closely associated with Strauss, focusing both on the institutions where he pursued his professional activities as well as the cities' broader artistic milieus. Sebastian Bolz offers portraits of Munich, the city in which Strauss grew up and twice held conducting posts (1886–89 and 1894–98), and of Garmisch, where he built his mountainside villa in 1908. Strauss also spent time early in his career in Meiningen (1885–86) and Weimar (1889–94), and Michael Saffle's report on these two cities illuminates aspects of cultural life in pre–World War I Germany and its impact on the composer's professional development. Ulrich Konrad documents the city, institution, and phenomenon of Bayreuth that greatly influenced Strauss's career, including his relationship with Wagner's widow, Cosima. Dietmar Schenk writes on Berlin, the Prussian capital where Strauss spent the largest share of his conducting career, from 1898 until the abolishment of the German monarchy in 1918. Joseph E. Jones then contextualizes Strauss's difficult tenure as codirector of the Vienna State Opera (1919–24) through the lens of post-war politics and various social initiatives that impacted life in the city.

Part III, *Cultural Engagement and Musical Life*, explores Strauss's interests in literature, philosophy, and religion, as well as musical organizations in which he played a leading role. Matthew Werley examines the composer's lifelong consumption of literature with fascinating commentary on

the contents of his Garmisch library. Jason Geary traces the rich history of
German engagement with antiquity and the ways in which it informs our
understanding of Strauss's operas that are based on Greek myth. Charles
Youmans introduces Strauss's views on metaphysis and faith, specifically
his active engagement with Schopenhauer and Nietzsche, as well as the
composer's agnosticism, in their contemporary artistic contexts. James
Deaville's essay on the Allgemeine Deutsche Musikverein details not only
the legacy of Strauss's tenure as president (1901–09), but also the society's
four decades prior to Strauss's leadership and its eventual dissolution
during the Nazi era. Lastly, Manuela Schmidt discusses the complex
history of the Genossenschaft Deutscher Tonsetzer, the first successful
collective management organization in Germany, which Strauss helped
found in 1903.

The first two essays of Part IV, *Professional and Musical Contexts*,
compare his path as composer (Jeremy R. Zima) and conductor (Raymond
Holden) with those of the broader profession, drawing contrasts between
Strauss and his contemporaries with respect to education, career options,
income, repertoire, and more. Scott Warfield then focuses on the development and significance of the orchestra in the long nineteenth century as
a crucial backdrop for assessing Strauss's music. In an effort to better
situate Strauss's aesthetic orientations, Jonathan Kregor presents a broad
history of programmatic composition, outlining the absolute versus program music debate and its impact on concert life. Morten Kristiansen
explores new directions and challenges in German opera after Wagner,
highlighting many now-forgotten examples that formed the context of
Strauss's fin-de-siècle stage works. The section concludes with Jürgen
May's assessment of the historical and cultural backdrop of Strauss's
Lieder, a topic that has received limited scholarly attention despite the
composer's prolific output.

Part V, *In History*, covers a series of historical contexts that profoundly
affected the careers and reception of Strauss and his contemporaries. Pulling back the lens, Peter Franklin investigates the wider modernist narrative
that declared Strauss an irrelevant conservative after 1910, while Leon
Botstein offers a sweeping assessment of traditionalism in twentieth-
century music vis-à-vis Strauss, arguing that his "alternate formulation of
the modern" made him the century's most representative composer. Next
is another pair of essays, by Philip Graydon and Erik Levi, respectively,
that analyze the cataclysmic impacts of the World War I on German
musical life, and then the conditions of music creation and consumption
in Nazi Germany, including the role of the Reichsmusikkammer.

Giangiorgio Satragni's examination of Strauss's celebrated "Indian Summer" in the larger contexts of classicizing and aging is followed by Franz-peter Messmer's survey of contemporary Strauss reception within the context of contemporary developments in music, the visual arts, literature, philosophy, and science.

Lastly, Part VI, *Artifacts and Legacy*, considers the critical and scholarly reception of Strauss, the artifacts of his long and productive career, and his influence and legacy. Andreas Pernpeintner and Stefan Schenk discuss the composer's relationships with his publishers as well as the various editions of his works spanning from the late nineteenth century to the present, including the new critical edition begun in Munich in 2011. Claudia Heine and Adrian Kech document the enormous quantity of Strauss's correspondence and the process that continues to lead to the publication of letters, diaries, and other artifacts, with a list of these sources appearing as an Appendix. Raymond Holden studies Strauss's posthumous legacy of musical performances through programming, recordings (including Strauss's own), and conductors and performers closely associated with his oeuvre. Ben Winters adopts a more analytical approach in tracing Strauss's influence from contemporaries such as Erich Korngold to the film scores of John Williams. Charles Youmans then assesses the impact of the inclusion of *Also sprach Zarathustra* in Stanley Kubrick's *2001: A Space Odyssey* (1968), emphasizing the affinities between the tone poem and film. In the final chapter, Matthew Werley takes stock of trends in Strauss research, particularly from dissertations written over the past three decades, while pointing to potentially fruitful paths for future research.

Note on Translation

The names of major orchestras (e.g. Berlin Philharmonic) and performance venues (e.g. Vienna State Opera) that are well known in English appear as such, while the others (e.g. Danzig Stadttheater) remain in German. They all, along with the names of organizations (e.g. Allgemeine Deutsche Musikverein), are printed in standard roman type, with italics reserved for German terms (e.g. *Zeitoper*). Position titles such as Kapellmeister and Generalmusikdirektor, that are widely used in English or are almost identical in translation, are left in German. The titles of works (musical, literary, etc.) are translated parenthetically when relevant to the author's argument.

PART I

Family, Friends, and Collaborators

CHAPTER I

Family and Upbringing

Chris Walton

Richard Strauss's biography begins with a lie, at least in his own telling of it. Late in life, he wrote of how his father, Franz Strauss (1822–1905), was born the son of a watchman in Parkstein, north-east of Nuremberg.[1] In fact, as Richard later admits, the watchman was his father's uncle, Franz Michael Walter. Franz Strauss was illegitimate, though he kept the surname of the man who had abandoned him and his mother. By the time Richard committed his family reminiscences to paper in the 1940s, he had long been a dominant force in German music life. So, for a prince of music, such proximity to bastardy presumably had to be obscured. Strauss's progress as a musician was invariably determined in large part by his family circumstances and their socio-economic and cultural position in early Wilhelmine Germany. This chapter will look at the very different backgrounds of his parents, the impact of Strauss's humanistic schooling, his early music education, and then reflect on issues of mental health and how they might have co-determined the composer's socialization.

Music played a major role in Franz's family. Two cousins became professional violinists (Benno and Josef Walter), and music brought Franz to the Bavarian capital in 1837 as a guitarist in the folk music band of Duke Max in Bayern. Franz then switched his focus to the horn, joining the Munich Court Orchestra in 1847. In 1851, he married Elise Seiff, a daughter of a military music director. But their first child, a boy, died of tuberculosis in 1852, and then Elise and their second child, a daughter, died in the cholera epidemic of 1854. Franz married again nine years later, this time to Josepha Pschorr (1838–1910, also known variously as Josephine/Josefa/Josefine), the daughter of the wealthy Munich beer baron Georg Pschorr – a remarkably good match for an illegitimate musician.

---

[1] Richard Strauss, "Reminiscences of My Father," in *Recollections and Reflections*, ed. Willi Schuh, trans. L. J. Lawrence (London: Boosey & Hawkes, 1953), 127.

The city of Munich underwent immense changes in the mid-nineteenth century, not least thanks to the interests of its ruling family. Ludwig II (r. 1864–86) is justly famous as Richard Wagner's patron, but he was merely continuing a family tradition of supporting art, music, and architecture. The Bavarian education system was also one of the most advanced in Europe, with statutory schooling having been introduced in 1802, some 70 years before England. Although Bavaria was on the losing side of the Austro-Prussian War of 1866 and was compelled to join the German Reich on Prussian terms five years later, it retained considerable sovereignty and benefitted from the late-century upswing in the German economy. Munich itself acquired the trappings of modernity, from electric street lighting and trams to a municipal sewage system, with concomitant improvements in public health. The young Richard Strauss was thus doubly fortunate. Through his father, he profited from the vibrant music life of a thriving, modern metropolis, while his mother's rich family provided access to a superior education and entry into the upper echelons of society. The Pschorrs were music lovers too, and Richard would later play at many house concerts in their villa. Comparisons are generally fraught, but it can be instructive to consider that Strauss's early cultural and social environment had more in common with that of Mendelssohn than, say, with Mahler or Schoenberg.

Josepha's family, however, did not shower their wealth on their illegitimate son-in-law. Franz's first marital apartment belonged to the Pschorrs, but it was tiny and situated just behind their large brewery-cum-beer hall on the Neuhauser Strasse in the city center. It was here that their first child, Richard, was born on June 11, 1864. Not long afterwards, the Strausses moved to a nearby apartment without running water on the corner of Sonnenstrasse and Schwanthalerstrasse, where their daughter, Johanna, was born in 1867. Two years later, Franz and family moved back to the beer hall, into an apartment on the third floor provided by Josepha's brother Georg, now the head of the family firm. However, the walls were infested with bugs and had to be treated with the arsenic compound "Paris green" to kill them off. So Franz Strauss, although nominally head of his own family, was both dependent on the beneficence of his in-laws and aware that their generosity had its boundaries. Franz also followed the example of the Pschorrs in joining the *alt-katholische Kirche* (Old Catholic Church) in the 1870s, a breakaway movement from the Roman Catholic Church that disavowed the Pope's claims to infallibility. It remains moot whether Franz was acting out of conviction or to promote his familial and professional interests (his boss, Intendant Karl von Perfall, was also an open supporter of the anti-infallibles). It was furthermore thanks to the Pschorrs – more precisely, to an inheritance from Josepha's grandmother in 1874 – that Franz was able to buy a grand piano and take the family on summer holidays in the years thereafter. They later also funded the publication of Richard's early music.

It was Franz's orchestral colleagues who gave Richard his early music lessons (August Tombo for piano, cousin Benno Walter for the violin, then court conductor Friedrich Wilhelm Meyer for harmony and counterpoint), just as they provided Richard with his formative experiences of opera and concerts. Richard's school education formed a profound counterpoint to his father's purely musical environment. When he moved up to high school in 1875, to the Ludwigsgymnasium, Richard received a humanistic education with an emphasis on the German classics and the literature of the ancients that remained a source of inspiration throughout his life. This school was the second oldest of its kind in Munich and a place where the future intellectual, social, and military elites of Bavaria rubbed shoulders. Richard's affinity for all things Greek (he later delighted in calling himself a "Greek Teuton") was also kindled in high school, finding initial musical expression in a setting of a chorus from Sophocles' *Elektra* composed in 1881.

In 1882, Strauss enrolled at Munich University to attend lectures in philosophy, aesthetics, Shakespeare, and Schopenhauer, though these studies were soon abandoned when it became clear he would pursue a career in music. Strauss's educational background was thus very different from that of near-contemporaries such as Schoenberg, Wolf, Janáček or, further afield, Debussy and Elgar, all of whom came from less affluent families and whose general schooling ceased in their early to mid teens. Although Strauss later modestly downplayed his school achievements, it was clearly the Ludwigsgymnasium that helped to turn him into one of the most erudite, best-read composers of his generation. His teenage years were also significant for the friendships he established with men such as Friedrich Rösch, Arthur Seidl, and Max Steinitzer. As an adult, Strauss was notoriously reserved, remaining on formal, "Sie" terms with even his closest colleagues. By contrast, it seems he retained a deep affection for his male friends from early youth.

The music of Strauss's teens reveals none of the individuality of a Mendelssohn or a Schubert, but instead a remarkable gift for assimilation. Listening chronologically to his works of the 1870s and early 1880s is like getting a potted audio-history of his father's favorite Austro-German repertoire, starting with Haydn, Mozart, and early Schubert before moving swiftly through to Beethoven and ending with Mendelssohn. These were standard influences for a composer of Strauss's time and place, though he remained as yet immune to the teenage Wagner enthusiasm that we find in Hugo Wolf and others (probably because his father Franz would not have countenanced it anyway). Strauss was already writing notes "as a cow gives milk," to use his own later simile, and was also unencumbered by any trepidation towards his predecessors. Whereas Brahms had labored for years on his first symphony, Strauss wrote his at sixteen in D minor, the iconic key of Beethoven's Ninth, and it was given its world première by the Munich Court Orchestra under Hermann Levi in 1881. Strauss's Second Symphony, Op. 12, composed in 1883 and 1884, was his last big work before he left for Meiningen. The shadow of Brahms lies heavy on it but, while there are hints of the later Strauss, especially in the Scherzo, it is primarily fascinating for the passages that sound more like Mahler, Dvořák, Bruckner, or even foreshadow Sibelius's middle period. This symphony is like a crossroads from which Strauss could have gone in any one of several directions, with nothing here to suggest that its composer would soon become the leading composer of the progressive school.

Unlike Mahler, Wolf, or Debussy, Strauss never attended a conservatory, presumably because his father's professional circle could provide whatever learning opportunities he desired. The years between leaving full-time education and moving to Meiningen as Hans von Bülow's assistant in 1885 were mostly spent composing, performing, and networking. Strauss visited other major German-speaking centers including Leipzig, Dresden, Frankfurt, Vienna, and Berlin, taking care to become acquainted with all kinds of movers and shakers from the field of music and beyond. Fewer than 20 years had passed since Prussia and Bavaria had been at war, and Strauss's later correspondence leaves us in no doubt that he was acutely aware of his Bavarian background when among northern Germans (for a contemporary comparison, one might imagine a young man from Alabama negotiating the intellectual elites of post-bellum New York). But Strauss mixed easily with everyone, from the Berlin intendant Botho von Hülsen to Joseph Joachim, Philipp Spitta, the conductor Robert Radecke, the pianist Karl Klindworth, the composer Heinrich von Herzogenberg, the mathematician Alfred Pringsheim (Thomas Mann's future father-in-law), the publishers Bock and Spitzweg, and finally Bülow and Brahms. Strauss's gift for assimilation clearly extended well beyond the composing sphere and seems to have remained with him throughout his later years in Berlin and Vienna. Whereas Mahler worked his way up from one provincial theater to the next, Elgar made ends meet as a violin teacher, and Wolf worked as a hack journalist, Strauss moved effortlessly among the Central European elites as if he belonged naturally to their number (aided, no doubt, by the musical and business connections of his father and maternal uncle, respectively). When Bülow had an opening for an assistant in Meiningen, Mahler was desperate to be chosen; instead, the position more or less fell into Strauss's lap. Strauss was not alone in his immediate family in being so upwardly mobile; his younger sister Johanna married a lieutenant in the Bavarian army, Otto Rauchenberger, who was later ennobled by the Emperor and ended the World War I as a lieutenant general.

Altogether, the pre-Meiningen Strauss comes across as a thoroughly "normal" young man, who, despite being highly gifted and a bit nerdy, remains keen to enjoy the convivial aspects of a big city. He took dancing lessons with his peers, attended society balls, flirted with girls, enjoyed holidays in the countryside, had a circle of male friends who stayed loyal for years to come, and socialized easily with everyone including those much older than him. From 1883 to about 1885, he even indulged in an affair with a married woman, one Dora Wihan, the (purportedly unhappy) wife of the cellist Hans Wihan from the Munich Court Orchestra. Dora later ensured the destruction of Strauss's letters, so we will never know the details. But all in all, the young Strauss is almost unrecognizably different from the "aloof and phlegmatic" man described by later commentators.[2] The reason for the change in him might lie in family developments that first came to a head in April 1885.

The dominant influence on Strauss's early aesthetic was his father, whose virtuoso musicianship was coupled with a violent temper and a hatred of any music more modern than the early Romantics. In her later life, the composer's sister, Johanna, wrote that their father "was very strict and we had a holy respect for him ... if [Richard] became over-exuberant and Father became strict, my tears soon helped to calm him down and Mama in her gentleness poured oil on the troubled waters."[3] Richard himself wrote late in life of how his father was "an embittered character ... with a violent temper, tyrannical," and he too contrasted this with his mother's "gentleness." He recalled how she "frequently had to pay for visits to the theatre and concerts with sleepless nights ... she was

[2] Bryan Gilliam and Charles Youmans, "Strauss, Richard," *Grove Music Online*, accessed August 18, 2019, www.oxfordmusiconline.com.

[3] Johanna von Rauchenberger-Strauss, "Jugenderinnerungen," in *Richard Strauss Jahrbuch 1959/60*, ed. Willi Schuh (Bonn: Boosey & Hawkes, 1960), 9–10.

happiest when she was allowed to spend the summer afternoons alone and quietly, busy with her embroidery, in the beautiful garden of my uncle Pschorr's villa, where we children also used to go after school . . ."[4]

Since those concerts and theater visits were presumably coupled with her husband's orchestral engagements, perhaps Franz was the real cause of Josepha's sleeplessness. Franz himself once remarked on having suffered corporal punishment as a child, so when his daughter relates how he once battered his wooden desk because a horn pupil made a mistake, she seems to be intimating that Franz's violence was at times directed at more than just furniture. If Josepha and her children were happier in the garden of her brother's villa than with Franz in the insect-infested, arsenic-laced walls of their third-floor apartment, this could have exacerbated feelings of inadequacy that Franz's lowly background might already have engendered in him. To be abandoned by one's father, beaten by one's uncle, and then to lose a first wife and two children – all this would leave deep scars in anyone's psyche. So, if Franz indeed found release for his emotional baggage through physical violence, it is likely that Josepha was its principal object. When Richard writes that he "cannot say" if his father's violence affected his mother, he has already answered the question. Corporal punishment of one's children and even of one's wife was legally permissible in Bavaria at the time, but this does not mean that it was everywhere the norm, for it was a matter of contentious, contemporary debate across Germany.[5]

In April 1885, Josepha finally experienced a breakdown of some kind, was diagnosed with "melancholy," and briefly incarcerated in the Upper Bavaria mental home in southern Munich. All in all, Josepha was confined to this institution over a dozen times during the next 25 years, with stints lasting from one to six months. Her diagnosis progressed to "hysteria" by 1898 and then to "manic depression" in her final years (she died of pneumonia in 1910 while in the clinic). So when her son began depicting "female hysteria" on stage with his characters Salome, Herodias, Elektra, and Klytämnestra, he was recreating states of mind that leading doctors had diagnosed in his own mother. In doing so, perhaps he endeavored to find some kind of personal catharsis.

According to expert opinion in Munich at the time, Josepha's condition was potentially hereditary, leaving her offspring with a "reduced resistance"

---

[4] Strauss, "Reminiscences of My Father," 131.
[5] Sace Elder, "A Right to Beat a Child? Corporal Punishment and the Law in Wilhelmine Germany," *Central European History* 47, no. 1 (2014), 54–75.

to mental illness that could be triggered by "unfavorable influences."[6] Josepha is one of very few patients whose files went missing from the archives of her former clinic, and it seems likely they were judiciously "lost" during the Nazi period to protect Strauss and his family (had she been born 60 years later, the Nazis would have forcibly sterilized her, and in fact, her clinic became the first to participate in the Nazis' euthanasia of the mentally ill). While any objective assessment of Josepha's condition remains impossible, the chronology suggests that she was committed at certain times to save her son from embarrassment; for example, she was incarcerated exactly nine days before Richard's engagement to Pauline de Ahna and was let out again after the formalities had ended.

If one were afflicted with mental illness in the late nineteenth century, then Bavaria was the place to be, because the precarious mental state of the local royals had prompted much investment in the science of psychiatry. The head of Josepha's asylum during her first stay was Bernhard von Gudden, an enlightened man who died soon afterwards in mysterious circumstances at the Starnberg Lake along with his most famous patient, King Ludwig II. Von Gudden was succeeded as head by his son-in-law, Hubert von Grashey, though it seems to have been the theories of von Gudden's assistant, Emil Kraepelin, that had the biggest impact on psychiatry in Munich (Josepha's final diagnosis, "manic depression," was a term he standardized).

In light of his family background, Strauss's departure for Meiningen in 1885 has broad significance, offering a convenient demarcation line at the end of his childhood. The vehemence with which he abandoned his father's straitjacket aesthetic, siding instead with the New Germans, suggests less a desire to cut the paternal apron strings than to shred, burn, and bury them. He had hitherto composed mostly absolute music, but now expunged the traditional genres from his catalog – there would be no Third Symphony, no more piano sonatas, no more string quartets, but symphonic poems and music dramas instead. And he would seek out progressive father surrogates to replace his own conservative model, first Hans von Bülow and then Alexander Ritter (though he would in turn shred those apron strings too). Perhaps just as important, Strauss was able to put his unstable mother behind him; when perusing the dates of

---

[6] Emil Kraepelin, *Psychiatrie: Ein Lehrbuch für Studirende und Aerzte*, 6th ed. (Leipzig: Barth, 1899), 1:95, and 7th ed. (Leipzig: Barth, 1903), 1:120. Both editions were condensed, adapted, and translated by A. Ross Diefendorf as *Clinical Psychiatry: A Text-Book for Students and Physicians* (New York: Macmillan, 1902 and 1907).

Josepha's confinements, it becomes obvious that Strauss never rushed home when she was ill but continued with his career commitments.

Mahler's complaint that he was "thrice homeless" is often quoted: a Bohemian in Austria, an Austrian in Germany, and everywhere a Jew. While Strauss never had to cope with the insidious injustices of anti-Semitism, one could nevertheless construct for him a similar state of non-belonging: as an "Old Catholic" in a Roman Catholic city, as a Bavarian in Prussia, and everywhere the son of an irascible horn player and a hysteric. Unlike Mahler, who so often comes across as anguished and suffering, Strauss seemed to glide through life with Teflon ease, unmoved by whatever might hurt him. But this was surely an act of will. If all he had inherited from his mother was a "reduced resistance" to her condition, then he could at least endeavor to ensure that no "unfavorable influences" would impinge on him. He could immerse himself in the rigors of hard work, submit to a precise professional and domestic regimen, and keep to a strict diet with daily exercise. He could cultivate a cold, unmoving exterior to keep at bay any hint of inner turmoil, not least from himself. And most of all, he could earn money – lots of it – partly to serve as a cushion for his wife and son, should he ultimately share his mother's fate, but mostly because he will have learned from Uncle Pschorr that wealth brings a status that can wash away the societal sins of poverty, illegitimacy, and even mental illness. Perhaps the enigma of the cold and distant composer adept at depicting red-hot emotion in music can best be solved by pondering the little boy raised back in that bug-infested apartment with an impoverished and violent but ambitious father; a submissive, unstable mother; and a wealthy uncle.

CHAPTER 2

Formative Influences

David Larkin

No man is an island. The same is true of great artists, no matter how original or independent they may become. Strauss's formative years were rich with encounters that helped shape his future creativity. A significant contribution was made by Friedrich Wilhelm Meyer, his instructor in harmony and counterpoint between 1875 and 1880. Although Meyer is regularly glossed over as a conservative if conscientious teacher, he deserves greater recognition than he has hitherto received for having supplied Strauss with the solid technical skills that grounded his later innovations. Another figure who had a brief but important impact on the young Strauss was Johannes Brahms. Strauss experienced what he later described as a "Brahms-infatuation" in 1884–85, and the older composer was encouraging but not uncritical when he looked over Strauss's Symphony in F Minor (1884). Brahms advised Strauss to work on his melodic construction and to avoid pseudo-counterpoint (where the individual lines simply employ different notes of the same underlying chords). Strauss credited to this intervention his later willingness to utilize popular melodies and dissonant contrapuntal lines whenever they were poetically justified.

Rising above these are three figures who stand out for the extent and significance of their impact on the young composer: Richard's father, Franz Strauss, Hans von Bülow, and Alexander Ritter. The latter two were quondam professional colleagues of Strauss but, given the age differences, they were also in part father figures to him. All three of Strauss's mentors were acquainted with each other, but there were many points of professional disagreement between them, which complicated their personal relationships. Because their musical tastes were strongly distinctive, each provided Strauss with different ideas and experiences that helped mold his brand of creative and professional music-making. And while Strauss acknowledged learning an enormous amount from all three, he ultimately had to break free from their influence and assert his independence. The point of divergence in each case concerned Wagner's music and its interpretation.

From Franz to Hans

Having one of the greatest orchestral horn players of the age as a father gave Richard Strauss a huge head start in his early musical development. As a performer in the service of the Bavarian Court Orchestra, Franz Strauss was intimately involved in the musical life of Munich at a particularly exciting time in its history. The presence of Wagner in the city in 1864–65 as the favorite of King Ludwig II led to regular productions of his works over the decades that followed, including the premieres of *Tristan und Isolde* (1865), *Die Meistersinger von Nürnberg* (1868), *Das Rheingold* (1869), and *Die Walküre* (1870). In his capacity as first horn, Franz came into contact with Hans von Bülow, who conducted the orchestra from 1864 to early 1869. Relations between the two were never going to be easy. Strauss senior was of decidedly conservative tastes and vehemently disliked modern music, which included everything by Wagner after the 1845 *Tannhäuser*. Even *Lohengrin* was "too sweet" for his liking, as his son later recalled. Bülow at that point was an ardent proponent of progressive music in general, and Wagner in particular, and there were frequent clashes between the taciturn hornist and irascible conductor. In spite of this, there was a grudging professional respect between them, and they proved to be capable of laying aside their ideological differences in their dealings over Richard.

Through his father, Strauss had unparalleled access to concerts and opera performances, and more so than Meyer's lessons, it was his engagement with past masterpieces that provided the bedrock of his musical education. Strauss senior imparted to his son a lifelong worship of Mozart and Beethoven, and Strauss in his turn would later insist that budding composers ought to be thoroughly schooled in the classics, even if their inclinations were to write more adventurous fare. Franz was less successful in imprinting on his son his own dislike of Wagner's music. Although Strauss's letters from the period initially parrot his father's negative opinions, by the age of seventeen Richard had succumbed to *Tristan*'s intoxicating harmonies. This teenage rebellion against parental tastes laid the foundations for his full-blown Wagner worship that emerged in the later 1880s. Franz brought Richard along to Bayreuth for the premiere of *Parsifal* in 1882, a gesture implying that Strauss senior could appreciate the significance of the event, little though his own views had changed.

As he took his first steps in forging a musical career, Richard began to visit other cities outside Bavaria, and, on a trip to Berlin in the winter of 1883–84, he made the personal acquaintance of Bülow. Nearly two decades had passed since Bülow conducted the premiere of *Tristan*, and his circumstances and tastes had changed radically in the intervening period. His first wife, Cosima, daughter of Franz Liszt, had left him for Wagner, and the ensuing bitterness had left Bülow disenchanted with the progressive camp. Most noticeably, his attitude toward his former father-in-law deteriorated sharply. Bülow had studied piano with Liszt in the early 1850s and thereafter was one of his greatest supporters, performing and conducting the Hungarian's works frequently and defending in print the so-called "music of the future" of which Liszt was a standard-bearer. In this same decade he had composed an orchestral "mood picture" clearly in the vein of Liszt's symphonic poems entitled *Nirwana* (1854). Although there was no open breach between them during Liszt's lifetime, two years after his teacher's death Bülow confessed that "the works and even the name of the 'great master' whom I idolized for decades have today become the object of my unreserved and irrevocable abhorrence."[1] His new enthusiasm was the music of Brahms, then perceived as the polar opposite of Wagner and Liszt.

Despite his checkered history with Franz Strauss, Bülow took more than a casual interest in the talented teenager he met in Berlin. He included Strauss's Wind Serenade, Op. 7 in the touring repertoire of the Meiningen Court Orchestra and commissioned the Wind Suite, Op. 4 for the same group. On Bülow's insistence, Strauss made his conducting debut with the Suite in Munich on November 18, 1884; to make matters more daunting, there was no time for any rehearsal beforehand. In his "Reminiscences of Hans von Bülow," Strauss recalled that he conducted "in a state of slight coma" but avoided making mistakes. The experience was slightly soured when past grievances caused Bülow to harangue Franz Strauss backstage after the concert, but for once Strauss senior did not hold a grudge.[2] The following year, Bülow selected Richard to be his assistant in Meiningen, ahead of other talented applicants for the position, such as Mahler and Felix Weingartner.

---

[1] Letter from Bülow to Hans von Bronsart, July 30, 1888, in Hans von Bülow, *Briefe und Schriften*, ed. Marie von Bülow (Leipzig: Breitkopf & Härtel, 1908), 8: 203.
[2] Richard Strauss, "Reminiscences of Hans von Bülow," in *Recollections and Reflections*, ed. Willi Schuh, trans. L. J. Lawrence (London: Boosey & Hawkes, 1953), 119–20.

Although Strauss's father had conducted an amateur orchestra in Munich (the Wilde Gung'l), Bülow was on another level entirely as an orchestral director, and it was in this capacity that he most influenced the 20-year-old Strauss. After leaving Munich in 1869, Bülow toured extensively in the United States and elsewhere as a pianist during the 1870s and thereafter cemented his reputation as a conductor with stints in Hannover (1878–80) and subsequently Meiningen (1880–85). In less than six years, Bülow turned the provincial Meiningen Court Orchestra into one of the premiere ensembles in Germany, one that played its repertoire from memory with all the musicians standing. In rehearsals Bülow was a martinet, known for his cutting sarcasm and occasional outbursts of rage, but his musicianship was legendary. His interpretations were founded on close attention to the details of the score and ironed out through many lengthy rehearsals. During his Meiningen apprenticeship, Strauss watched Bülow work with the orchestra daily and was awed by the professionalism and artistry of his mentor:

> the way in which he brought out the poetic content of Beethoven's and Wagner's works [was] absolutely convincing. There was no trace anywhere of arbitrariness. Everything was of compelling necessity, born of the form and content of the work itself; [. . .] his loyalty to the spirit and the letter of the work of art (these two are more akin than is commonly believed) ensured that by dint of painstaking rehearsals these works were performed with a clarity which to this day constitutes for me the zenith of perfection in the performance of orchestral works.[3]

The apprenticeship was cut short after barely two months (October–November 1885), when Bülow resigned his position in dudgeon after Brahms repeatedly took over the conducting of his own Fourth Symphony during a Meiningen Court Orchestra tour. From afar Bülow continued to correspond with his former protégé even after Strauss moved to Munich in Autumn 1886 and later in 1889 to Weimar. The relationship transitioned smoothly from one of pupillage to one of collegiality. As well as receiving occasional career advice, Strauss was now in a position to provide assistance to his older colleague: for instance, Bülow asked for certain scores used at the Munich Court Opera, including altered versions of Mozart's *Die Zauberflöte* and *Idomeneo*, a reminder that neither Bülow nor Strauss fetishized score purity.

After Meiningen, Bülow relocated to Hamburg, where he quickly became involved in the concert and operatic life of the city.

---

[3] Ibid.

From 1887 to 1892, he also took charge of the Berlin Philharmonic, and it was his tenure that really established the orchestra's stellar reputation. Bülow's orchestral programs in this era were centered on the classics – his opening concert in Berlin consisted solely of symphonies by Haydn, Mozart, and Beethoven – and his admiration for Beethoven is further attested by the legendary series of piano recitals he gave throughout Germany, the United Kingdom, and the United States, in which he performed 25 major works by Beethoven over four long evenings. However, he also included plenty of contemporary music on his orchestral programs, not just that of Brahms (to whom he had been reconciled).

Bülow's actions towards Strauss provide ample evidence of his practical pluralism. By the end of the decade, Strauss had become an ardent proponent of program music and had confessed as much to Bülow in an 1888 letter. The latter was hardly going to welcome the news that Strauss was cultivating the symphonic poem, the very genre Liszt had invented. Some of Strauss's earlier compositions had already filled him with reservations. In the symphonic fantasy *Aus Italien* (1886), he felt that the composer "frequently overstepped the limits of what is possible (in the realms of sonic beauty)."[4] When Strauss played his first tone poem, *Macbeth* (1888 rev. 1891) on the piano for Bülow, the dissonances caused the older man to grind his teeth. He had a very similar reaction when Mahler played him the first movement of his Second Symphony, calling it incomprehensible. Still less appealing to him than the "harshness and the monstrosity" of *Macbeth* was the pictorialism of *Tod und Verklärung* (1889), Strauss's third tone poem.[5] Significantly, however, Bülow's private distaste for some aspects of Strauss's aesthetic program did not stop him from supporting his former protégé. His recommendation induced Eugen Spitzweg to publish *Aus Italien*, followed in due course by *Macbeth* and other important early works. At Bülow's invitation, Strauss conducted both *Tod und Verklärung* and the revised version of *Macbeth* in Berlin, and Bülow himself directed Strauss's second tone poem, *Don Juan*, in January 1890, although he took it much slower than when Strauss himself conducted it, increasing the performance time by a third. Despite positive reviews, Strauss regarded this performance as a failure, which he ascribed to Bülow's lack of interest in the poetic dimension.

---

[4] Letter from Bülow to Alexander Ritter, December 30, 1887; in Bülow, *Briefe und Schriften*, 8: 174.
[5] Letter from Bülow to Strauss, February 1, 1892; in *Correspondence of Hans von Bülow and Richard Strauss*, ed. Willi Schuh & Franz Trenner, trans. Anthony Gishford (London: Boosey & Hawkes, 1955), 95.

This fiasco seems to have contributed to a cooling off between the two, with no letters exchanged for the next two years. However, the breach was eventually healed, and Strauss visited the terminally ill Bülow in January 1894. Although they managed to work through their aesthetic differences, after Bülow's death these resurfaced one last time. Strauss was supposed to conduct a memorial concert for his former mentor in Hamburg, but his proposed program (a symphonic poem by Liszt, Bülow's *Nirwana*, Beethoven's *Eroica*, and the Preludes to Wagner's *Meistersinger* and *Tristan*) proved to be too radical for Bülow's conservative supporters. Ultimately, Mahler replaced him, conducting a program of works by Bach, Beethoven, and Brahms – the "B" triumvirate that Bülow himself had coined and promoted. In death as in life, Bülow was the midwife for the creativity of others: his funeral service three days later drew to Mahler's attention the poem by Klopstock that he would go on to set in the final movement of his "Resurrection" Symphony, an irony Bülow would certainly have enjoyed.

Ritter the Progressive

If Franz Strauss was a performer who occasionally conducted, and Bülow a performer-conductor who occasionally composed, then Alexander Ritter, the third of Strauss's mentors, spent much of his career performing and conducting but ultimately chose to devote himself to composition. Like Bülow, Ritter had been with Liszt in Weimar, and both were heavily involved in the artistic battles over progressive music in the 1850s and 1860s. But where Bülow had abandoned his partisan activities and his taste for much of this music, Ritter remained obdurately devoted to the New German cause and bitterly resented Bülow's backsliding. After hearing Bülow conduct Wagner's *Tannhäuser* Overture in the 1880s, Ritter praised him and added pointedly, "It reminded me vividly of the time when we both worshipped an ideal to which *I* have remained faithful."[6] But Ritter was not content to voice his displeasure privately. In 1891, he wrote a satirical journal article in which Bülow was not named but still was recognizable as the "big rogue" who performed Brahms's music (full of ingenious but meaningless patterns, in Ritter's eyes) by "faking all the imaginable nuances of an artistic performance."[7] Immoderate though Ritter's zealotry may seem, it had a big impact on Strauss, and the

---

[6] Strauss, "Reminiscences of Hans von Bülow," 122.
[7] Alexander Ritter, "Vom – Spanisch Schönen," *Allgemeine Musik-Zeitung* 18, no. 10 (1891): 129.

Figure 2.1   Strauss and Ritter at the piano (1890).
Painting by Leopold von Kalckreuth

friendship between Ritter and Strauss probably contributed to the tempo-
rary breach between the latter and Bülow.

Ritter's career before meeting Strauss in 1885 was less stellar than
Bülow's and less stable than Franz Strauss's. After Weimar, he was concertmaster and music director at Stettin, but quit in disillusionment after a
couple of years. He worked as a violinist (both in the theater and as a
chamber musician) in various cities around Germany and even ran a music
shop for a decade. Bülow invited him to Meiningen as concertmaster in
1882, where he encountered Strauss, and the two were together in Munich
from 1886 to 1889. During this period Ritter played in the orchestra and
devoted himself to composition, producing two one-act operas, *Der faule
Hans* (1885) and *Wem die Krone?* (1890), as well as several programmatic
orchestral works.

According to Strauss's own testimony, Ritter's passionate advocacy
brought the latent Wagnerian out in Strauss. For his part, Ritter saw
in Strauss the next great hope of German music, someone who would

"build upon Wagner's works in *his [Wagner's] way*."[8] As early as 1887, Strauss began work on his first opera, *Guntram*, for which he followed Wagnerian practice by writing his own libretto. Long before this was finished, he had also followed Liszt's example by composing three tone poems. It was through Ritter that Strauss first became properly acquainted with Liszt's orchestral music, a fact Strauss acknowledged by dedicating *Macbeth* to him. Ritter wrote a number of programmatic works, including *Sursum corda! Eine Sturm- und Drangphantasie* and *Olafs Hochzeitsreigen* (both published in 1896). Decades after his friend's death in 1896, Strauss noted that "Ritter's music-historical importance as a bold pioneer following on from Richard Wagner is still not recognized" and credited the example of Ritter's own compositions with teaching him "how to learn from Wagner, without imitating him."[9]

Ritter's brand of Wagnerism was strongly inflected with Schopenhauerian-Christian mysticism, and so it is no surprise that he should have been particularly involved in the most metaphysically oriented of Strauss's early tone poems, *Tod und Verklärung*. After the music was completed, Strauss asked Ritter to cast the programmatic ideas that inspired him into poetic form, and this was published as the preface to the score. Still more important in Ritter's eyes was *Guntram*, which he hoped would be the long-awaited successor to Wagner's 'Christian' final work, *Parsifal*. He read early versions of the libretto and was warmly encouraging of Strauss. It is hard to miss the resemblance between Ritter and the character Friedhold, the wise older counselor to the eponymous hero. Strauss later revised the third Act, which now saw Guntram defying his mentor and boldly asserting his determination to act according to his own conscience rather than submit to the discipline of his artistic-religious brotherhood. This rejection of artistic communality deeply wounded Ritter. Suspecting that his young friend had been reading atheistic philosophers like Nietzsche and Stirner, Ritter wrote a long and passionate letter, begging Strauss to undo the changes that had made the work "immoral." Strauss argued in response that his opera was now a truer reflection of Schopenhauer's ideas than before, but Ritter would not be persuaded. All he could see was that Strauss had lost all trace of Wagner's worldview (*Weltanschauung*). "What alone of Wagner's

---

[8] Letter from Ritter to Strauss, May 14, 1893; in Charles Youmans, ed., "Ten Letters from Alexander Ritter to Richard Strauss 1887–1894," *Richard-Strauss-Blätter* 35 (1996): 15.

[9] Richard Strauss, *Späte Aufzeichnungen*, ed. Marion Beyer, Jürgen May, and Walter Werbeck (Mainz: Schott, 2016), 328–29.

remains in you? Only the mechanics of his art," he complained.[10] Their friendship never recovered.

During these formative years, there were several others who had a significant impact on the young Strauss, notable among them Cosima Wagner, Bülow's former wife, but Franz Strauss, Bülow, and Ritter had the most far-reaching effects on him. All three of these mentors were strong, passionate, even irascible characters. The more phlegmatic Strauss clearly enjoyed such interactions. Upon reading through Bülow's published letters in the 1940s, Strauss even compared him to "my dear, temperamental wife."[11] But he eventually needed to put some distance between himself and his mentors in order to achieve his own independent artistic voice. Others he knew from his youth would remain friends for life (for instance, Friedrich Rösch), and he had influential collaborators aplenty in later years (including Hugo von Hofmannsthal, Ernst Schuch, and Max Reinhardt), but in all these interactions Strauss was never less than an equal partner.

[10] Letter from Ritter to Strauss, January 17, 1893; Youmans, "Ten Letters," 16.
[11] Strauss, *Späte Aufzeichnungen*, 34.

CHAPTER 3

Pauline de Ahna

Katharina Hottmann
(Translation by Matthew Werley)

The perception of Pauline Strauss-de Ahna – a singer who features in musicological research only because of her marriage to one of the most prominent and controversial composers of modernity – is shaped almost exclusively by various second-hand reports rather than by more objective, scholarly depictions derived from sources. By all accounts an unusually temperamental, mercurial, class-conscious, and ambitious woman, she supported her husband as equally as she pursued her own agendas, all the while provoking extreme reactions from outsiders. Telling, for example, are the frequently cited derogatory remarks by Alma Mahler-Werfel, not to mention the vivid statement by Felicitas von Reznicek (daughter of Strauss's colleague Emil von Reznicek), who claimed "she was a bitch, but an amusing bitch."[1] The autobiographical opera *Intermezzo*, a historically unique musical-theatrical portrait, seems to afford the most intimate and authentic insights into the couple's private affairs. No portrait from Pauline herself exists to counter the image that Richard Strauss tendered to the public. Countless letters to her husband, relatives, and acquaintances – which would otherwise enable research into her communication strategies, self-portrayal, and assertiveness – currently remain in possession of the Strauss family and thus inaccessible to most scholars. Opera and concert reviews from 1884 to 1908 attest to her singing career, but no audio recordings have survived. Due to the low number of available sources, this chapter can only offer a preliminary reconstruction of the life decisions of a female musician (who incidentally was also the wife of a famous composer) against the backdrop of contemporary gender norms.

---

[1] Chris Walton, "Mad Mothers, Fractious Fathers and Fractured Cowbells: Richard Strauss Reconsidered," *The Musical Times* 157, no. 1934 (2016): 28.

Biographical Sketch

When Pauline de Ahna followed the young Kapellmeister Richard Strauss to Weimar in 1889, the consequences of this decision for her later life could hardly have been foreseeable. Born in 1863 in Ingolstadt as the daughter of the Royal Bavarian Major General Adolf de Ahna and Marie Huber, she was raised by a family with deep musical affinities. According to a commemorative statement penned by Strauss for his wife in 1947, Pauline's father sang opera arias and Lieder at family gatherings with a "beautiful baritone voice." Indeed, two of his younger siblings were professional musicians: his brother Heinrich de Ahna was concertmaster and violin professor in Berlin as well as the long-serving second violinist of the famous Joseph Joachim Quartet. His sister Eleonore de Ahna was an opera singer at the Berlin Court Opera until her tragic death in 1865 prevented her from serving as a role model or mentor to her niece. Conditions for Pauline could easily have been quite different. While Eleonore de Ahna had to take up a career due to her family's financial problems, such monetary instabilities were foreign to Pauline, whose father supported her training not only as a matter of expertise but also financial obligation.

Pauline began her training as a singer during a time when the professional education of middle-class and aristocratic daughters became an increasingly important topic of public discourse. The relatively late age for women marrying (26 on average) led to a minimum ten-year developmental phase between childhood and marriage, one that had to be meaningfully filled in accordance with changes in both domestic advancements (e.g., the increasing possibility of purchasing "readymade" clothing and groceries instead of having to self-produce them) and women's growing educational ambitions. Once marriage prospects had faded, which would otherwise usually terminate any gainful employment, an independent life and occupational training for women could commence. For upper-class daughters, a musical qualification – particularly on piano or singing – was especially obvious, as such skills could be used in the private salon or in teaching (as was socially acceptable for women). A career on the stage was always treated with hesitation, which is why opera singers had to exercise careful behavior so as not to raise suspicion that moral boundaries and conventions had been overstepped.

Pauline de Ahna began her studies in 1883 in solo singing (not opera) at Munich's Königliche Musikschule. While the faculty counted only one female (the *Kammersängerin* Johanna Jachmann-Wagner), male–female ratios among students were equal (ninety-one of each). While male students applied themselves to a variety of instruments, their female counterparts registered for piano, solo singing, opera, and acting. Pauline's primary teacher was Adolf Schimon, who in 1883–84 supervised six male and nine female students.[2] On April 28, 1884, in Munich's Odeonsaal, Pauline sang one of Agathe's longer arias from *Der Freischütz*, which years later Strauss recalled as having been "belted out […] with the naive brazenness of a dilettante, much to the acclaim of her military admirers."[3] What appears to be her first public review in the *Münchner Allgemeine Zeitung*, on May 1, 1884, presented a mixed message: she was "proficiently trained" and had a "soft and agreeable voice." In the recitative, however, she clipped a longer phrase, which steered her off course, causing her to gloss the "necessary inner warmth of the recitation" – but none of this prevented a "lavish applause." According to Strauss, Pauline's father was displeased with the "manners" of the institution, which incidentally included Strauss's father as horn instructor, his childhood friend Ludwig Thuille as piano instructor, and Arthur Seidl as cello student. Thereafter she continued her studies privately with Max Steinitzer – one of Strauss's old school friends and subsequently his first biographer.

That she changed instructors to Strauss in 1887 was entirely in accordance with the ethos established by Adolf de Ahna, who quite rightly expected the young Kapellmeister at the Munich Court Opera to provide his daughter with the necessary experience and contacts in the theatrical establishment. She then studied voice with Emilie Herzog (also one of Schimon's students) and acting with Franziska Ritter. As Ritter was Wagner's niece and also the wife of Alexander Ritter – who in turn was friends with Liszt and Wagner and a mentor to the young Strauss – she was able to consolidate an aesthetic position that saw Strauss abandon the familiar musical conservatism in exchange for the New German School.

When Strauss took up his position as Kapellmeister at the Weimar Court in 1889, Pauline de Ahna followed. Alongside her part studies with Strauss, she finished her formal training under the supervision of Emilie Merian-Genast and Rosa von Milde. Her debut as Pamina in *Die Zauberflöte* took place on May 22, 1890. Although the reviewer for the *Weimarische Zeitung* found her performance agreeable, he was not

---

[2] *Zehnter Jahresbericht der K. Musikschule in München: Veröffentlicht am Schlusse des Schuljahres 1883/84* (Munich: Dr. C. Wolf & Sohn, 1884), 6.
[3] Richard Strauss, *Späte Aufzeichnungen*, ed. Marion Beyer, Jürgen May, and Walter Werbeck (Mainz: Schott, 2016), 318.

entirely uncritical. He lauded her "musical intelligence" and acting, but claimed her voice lacked balance.[4]

The first phase of Pauline's career was not only made possible by her father's finances, but also his advice and occasional interventions when conflicts arose. He and Strauss corresponded about upcoming decisions, and on one occasion (before her debut) he offered to pay for a string quartet so his daughter could focus attention on rehearsing on-stage movements in sync with the conductor, musicians, and fellow actors. She herself was ambitious and impulsive. In 1892, for example, a conflict arose between her and the soprano Agnes Stavenhagen, where, upon Strauss's council, she offered her resignation in the hope that the Grand Duke might intervene in the personal affairs of the intendant Hans von Bronsart. It soon became obvious that both had miscalculated. Pauline de Ahna offered an apology and requested to withdraw the decision, which she supported by quoting in detail from a letter from her father, who assured her that he favored the intendant, with whom he shared a military background.

Pauline de Ahna appeared in a total of twenty-four roles at the Weimar Court Theater, most frequently in the operas of Mozart and Wagner. She also sang in German Romantic operas, French repertoire, and new works such as Alexander Ritter's *Der faule Hans* and Engelbert Humperdinck's *Hänsel und Gretel*. The partially contradictory reactions published in newspaper reviews make it difficult to reconstruct a vivid picture of her singing career, though it is clear that her lively acting and sonorously warm middle register were convincing. The artistic highpoint for Strauss and his student was undoubtedly their participation at the 1891 Bayreuth Festival, where she appeared as a flower maiden in *Parsifal* and, more importantly, Elisabeth in *Tannhäuser*. Reviews were again mixed. Although the Leipzig-based *Musikalisches Wochenblatt* regarded her "voice as pretty in and of itself," though "cold" and "much too forced in its affect," the critic from the *Wiener Zeitung* claimed it lacked a certain greatness, but was nevertheless highly effective in delicate and tender passages.[5] To what extent politics between singers played a role can be left open to further scrutiny,

---

[4] Cited from Helga Schmidt-Neusatz, "Pauline Strauss-de Ahna: Weg und Wirkung als Sängerin," *Richard Strauss-Blätter* 44 (2000): 7.
[5] Pf. R. Pfau, "Bayreuther Bühnenfestspielberichte," *Musikalisches Wochenblatt*, August 20, 1891, 444; Dr. H. P. [Hans Paumgartner], "Die Bayreuther Festspiele des heurigen Jahres. II. Tannhäuser," *Wiener Abendpost*, No. 172, supplement to *Wiener Zeitung*, July 30, 1891, 2.

but Pauline de Ahna was clearly disappointed not to be asked back to Bayreuth the following year. Nevertheless, she reprised both roles in 1894.

It was in this year that their engagement and marriage took place. Pauline was thirty and Richard sixteen months younger, both comparatively late in age when measured against European marriage patterns. In March 1894, Strauss asked Pauline's parents for her hand, which they gladly gave. The decision triggered in her severe ambivalences, which Richard disclosed in various letters to his parents over the many weeks leading up to the couple's decision finally to announce their engagement on May 10.

Pauline was distressed by the question of how to negotiate her artistic career alongside her role as a wife. The numerous female singers in her professional and private spheres embodied a wide spectrum of spousal models. The singer Anna Regan, for example, continued to give concerts and teach after marrying Schimon (later Pauline's singing teacher) in 1872. Likewise, Emilie Herzog (Pauline's other teacher) remained an opera singer after she married music historian Heinrich Welti in 1890. On the other side of the spectrum, Pauline's teacher in Weimar, Emilie Merian-Genast, promptly relinquished her career when she married the director of a Swiss insurance company in 1863 only to resume it after becoming a widow. Rosa von Milde continued her opera career at the Weimar Court Theater until 1867 while married to singer Hans von Milde, and Pauline's rival Agnes Denninghof married pianist Bernhard Stavenhagen in 1890 and sang opera for another seven years. Soprano Jenny Alt, on the other hand, gave up her career on the Weimar stage after her marriage in 1891, while pianist Ingeborg Stark, who in 1861 had married Hans von Bronsart, gave up her performing career when her husband took over as intendant in Hannover, but nevertheless remained active as a composer. (Pauline likely saw the world premiere of her opera *Hiarne* in Weimar in 1891.) On top of all this, the dissolution of musical marriages had also become a matter of public discourse; the most notable example was Joseph and Amalie Joachim's divorce in 1884, which resulted from an suspicion of unfaithfulness (she had "sacrificed" her career as an opera singer for the sake of their marriage but then continued to work as a concert singer and teacher).

All in all, Pauline de Ahna had a variety of options to consider. That there was no default expectation to leave the stage after marriage is reflected in Bronsart's congratulations on her betrothal, which followed with a short request as to whether "Ms. de Ahna might soon cancel her engagements upon her approaching marriage. A reply of yes or no (leave or stay) would suffice."[6] Her father also saw no problem and wrote: "You can combine the two so easily" and urged her to stop fighting with her fiancé so that they could become "a very happy and contented musical couple."[7]

When they celebrated their marriage on September 10, 1894, Pauline took the name Strauss-de Ahna. The following month Strauss was under contract as Kapellmeister at the Munich Court Opera but failed to secure his wife a guest appointment that included forty guaranteed appearances. In Munich, she sang in individual performances and took to the operatic stage for the last time as Marzelline in *Fidelio* on August 11, 1896. Thereafter she mainly became an interpreter of her husband's Lieder. During her pregnancy, she sang in public, appearing in a concert with her husband in Paris in late November 1896, only months before the birth of their only son, Franz, on April 12, 1897. During this time, she sought to return to the operatic stage, just as Strauss was also seeking to improve his career prospects. A few months later, she made her final attempt to secure an appointment at the same opera house. As this proved too difficult, she wrote to her husband:

> As far as your question about a position is concerned, after careful consideration and self-reflection I ask you not to take account of my commitment ... If you would like to go to Hamburg, then go *without* pushing for my engagement. I'll then come along, and if I'm *sufficiently* satisfied that the atmosphere, circumstance, and *your* domestic amenities allow me to resume my artistic career, then there will always be time to think about me.

In the same letter, however, she confessed that she had cried all day in a "rather gloomy mood." With palpable relief, Richard thanked her emphatically for her "great, beautiful sacrifice," which marked her final farewell from the operatic stage.[8] This stemmed neither from social considerations nor family planning, but from the mutual decision to prioritize the family's financial security through giving the most advantageous position possible to her husband, at the time arguably Germany's most prominent composer.

[6] Letter to Richard Strauss of May 31, 1894, in *Lieber Collega!: Richard Strauss im Briefwechsel mit zeitgenössischen Komponisten und Dirigenten*, ed. Gabriele Strauss (Berlin: Henschel, 1996), 188.
[7] Willi Schuh, *Richard Strauss: A Chronicle of the Early Years 1864–1898*, trans. Mary Whittall (Cambridge: Cambridge University Press, 1982), 356–57.
[8] Letters to Richard Strauss of September 1, 1897, and Pauline Strauss of September 3, 1897, in *Der Strom der Töne trug mich fort: Die Welt um Richard Strauss in Briefen*, ed. Franz Grasberger (Tutzing: Hans Schneider, 1967), 106 and 108.

Figure 3.1   Pauline de Ahna, ca. 1900.
Photographer unknown

Having found improved working conditions in Munich, Richard remained there and, over the next few years, they gave numerous concerts together both at home and abroad (her mother looked after their child during her travels). In 1897, they concentrated their efforts in cities such as Amsterdam, Barcelona, Brussels, London, and Paris, and in the following year, Madrid, where she mostly sang in concerts featuring her husband's orchestral songs. The highpoint of her career was the 1904 North American tour, where she enjoyed enthusiastic reviews and sympathetic audiences. Thereafter her appearances gradually became less frequent, and on January 10, 1909, she gave what was likely her last concert, a matinee (directed by her husband) for the Munich Lehrer-Gesangverein.

Sources for the later decades are sparse. The couple split the majority of their time between Garmisch and Vienna, where they witnessed the marriage of their son and rearing of two grandchildren. Pauline certainly held "anti-democratic, nationalistic, and even antisemitic convictions," but it is difficult to ascertain to what extent her convictions related to the political development of National Socialism, which her husband had briefly served during its early years.[9] After the end of the war, they both resided in Switzerland and returned to Garmisch in 1949. There Pauline outlived her husband by just nine months, passing away on May 13, 1950.

Musical Sketches

While it is understandable that Strauss composed numerous songs for his wife, it is remarkable that he portrayed her musically on more than one occasion in his tone poems. In *Ein Heldenleben*, he portrayed Pauline's complex psychological profile in the movement titled "The Hero's Companion," and then again in *Symphonia domestica*, a shameless autobiography that sonically depicts scenes of parental bliss, marital strife, love, and reconciliation. Equally unique is the fact that Strauss made his marriage the subject of an opera. Hermann Bahr had originally intended to write the libretto to *Intermezzo* following Strauss's detailed instructions, but then declined after a few attempts and encouraged the composer to write it himself. Strauss finally plucked up the courage to set the material to words in an "almost memoir-like, natural [...] even strictly empirical manner."[10] The piece is based on a true story that had brought the couple into crisis in May 1902. As Strauss was on a concert tour in England, Pauline opened a card addressed to Strauss as "Dearest Love" from a certain Mieze Mücke, who asked to meet him in a bar. Confronted by his wife, both exchanged letters, of which only one from Strauss was preserved

---

[9] Walter Werbeck, "Strauss-Bilder," in *Richard Strauss Handbuch*, ed. Walter Werbeck (Stuttgart: Metzler, 2014), 6.

[10] Letter to Hermann Bahr of July 10, 1917, in *Der Strom der Töne trug mich fort: Die Welt um Richard Strauss in Briefen*, ed. Franz Grasberger (Tutzing: Hans Schneider, 1967), 224.

(the others from him, whether read or unread, were burned by Pauline). Although the matter finally turned out to be a mix-up, the conflict touched upon the foundations of bourgeois marriage and artistic life. She countered Richard's criticism (i.e., that she should have trusted him to provide a prompt explanation rather than withdraw money and prepare for a separation) by claiming that his Skat partners made her all too familiar with the habits of artistic types. Ernst Kraus, a tenor from the Court Opera whom Pauline had contacted to clarify the facts, was for example often under suspicion of infidelity by his wife for vulgarly "fishing for something fine" for himself at places like the Metropol, one of Berlin's entertainment theaters frequented by the upper bourgeoisie and nobility. Alongside fears about her husband's extramarital sexual adventures – fears which if hardly innocent were also hardly unfounded either – the accusation appears again and again in her letters that he is constantly complaining about domestic boredom or the fact that he can only amuse himself with Skat.

As problematic as it must seem to read a work of musical theater as an autobiographical source, the libretto of this "bourgeois comedy" reflects the real life of a court Kapellmeister not only in its constellation of characters and realistic ambience, but also in its carefully structured psychological and social dialogue, which reveals profound insights into the distribution of roles, emotional dispositions, values, life goals, and conflict structures of bourgeois marriage. The dispute over the recognition of female housework, which the protagonist Robert Storch dismisses as "no serious work" in comparison to his "mental work" seems downright modern. Another friction point in the drama touches on the question of social class, especially Christine's accusation that his family cannot be compared to the nobility of hers. (A wife's social status was determined by her husband's heritage, not by her family's.) Pauline de Ahna apparently struggled with not marrying into the nobility. As her alter ego in *Intermezzo* bemoaned, "and what am I and what was I as a 'composer's wife'? One hardly suitable for the court." The problem of social interaction in the artist's life, which was also negotiated in real marriage conflicts, is expressed in the same way by Christine, who does not fit into "the entire milieu" where the "public and whatnot intrudes on the artist." Conveying her regrets that her husband is "hardly a ladies man," Christine in fact quotes the heroine of Theodor Fontane's novel *Effi Briest*, which uses this very phrase to characterize the man with whom she would later have an affair. In *Intermezzo*, the marital threat appears in the form of the young Baron Lummer, who, until he asks for money, initially offers Christine a welcome diversion. Going behind her back, the Baron then meets a "sweet lass," thus practicing exactly the kind of liberal life she accuses her husband of after she receives the telegram from Mieze Meier (Mieze Mücke's operatic double).

Even after the error has been discovered, they continue to argue. Before the inevitable happy ending, she complains that he "never appreciated her, never understood her, always neglected her," and says: "I don't want to be your housekeeper anymore!" Indeed, as realistic as the piece is conceived in many details, it is striking that the operatic character Christine has no artistic past, thus reducing the real Pauline to her essential personality traits and qualifications. Even if Lotte Lehmann sang the lead female part beautifully, it was not easy for her to see herself on stage as moody, quarrelsome, and often unjust to her interlocutors. In the final analysis, of course, Pauline hardly had the means to retaliate publicly, at least in any socially accepted form.

CHAPTER 4

Close Friends

Walter Werbeck

The question of whether Richard Strauss had friends is not easily answered. It seems that he only engaged in close friendships, as equals, as a young man. Two people in particular play an important role in this context: Ludwig Thuille and Friedrich Rösch. Not only were they friends whom Strauss addressed with the more personal "Du" rather than the formal "Sie," but their relationships with him remained relatively stable throughout their lives. Both figures are discussed in detail here.

In addition to Thuille and Rösch, Strauss had other friends in his early years whom he addressed with "Du": the composers Engelbert Humperdinck and Max Schillings, the philosopher and writer on music Arthur Seidl, the conductor Felix Weingartner, and the publishers Eugen Spitzweg and Otto Fürstner. Most of these friendships ended, however, as Strauss became more famous. Thus, he enjoyed close friendships from the late 1880s until the World War I or so. After that, his only remaining close friend was Rösch. By the time Rösch passed away in 1925, Thuille, Spitzweg, and Humperdinck were already dead, and Seidl (d. 1928) and Schillings (d. 1933) followed a few years later.

After Rösch's death, Strauss mostly surrounded himself with and only confided in members of his own family. Strauss had always been a family man, and, as time progressed, he leaned more on his relatives both in private affairs and professional matters wherever possible. A year before losing Rösch, the family was extended when his son Franz married Alice von Grab-Hermannswörth. From then on, Strauss's new daughter-in-law worked as his private secretary, while her husband acted (or had to act) as the family's legal advisor. In this tight-knit family business, there was little room for friends, and their numbers continued to decrease as Strauss became more artistically secluded, suspiciously eyeing the tide of the times. Some remained close with Strauss in his later years, such as the conductors Karl Böhm and Clemens Krauss, and the latter's wife, the singer Viorica Ursuleac. In letters to Böhm and Krauss, Strauss usually addressed them as

"Lieber Freund" (Dear friend). His correspondents, however, replied with "Lieber Herr Doktor" (Dear Doctor) or "Hochverehrter Herr Doktor" (Esteemed Doctor). Perhaps their reverence for his artistic genius deterred an intimate closeness. It is no coincidence that Strauss never invited them to address him with the personal and informal "Du."

Ludwig Thuille (1861–1907)

Family ties existed with Ludwig Thuille from South Tyrol and his foster parents, the Nagillers. Strauss met Ludwig no later than 1877; that year marked the beginning of their correspondence, which, with some interruptions, lasted until Thuille's untimely death in 1907. Their letters testify to a mutual trust that withstood serious tensions between 1902 and 1906, when the correspondence stopped completely. In his later years, Strauss referred to Thuille as a "friend from his schooldays" who "probably had the biggest influence on my development."[1] Indeed, Thuille was the only friend whom Strauss accepted at least temporarily as a sort of composition teacher. There are many indications that Thuille, who had been a pupil of Joseph Rheinberger in Munich since 1879 (and was therefore in close proximity to Strauss), became a true mentor to his younger friend in the early 1880s, thereby succeeding Friedrich Wilhelm Meyer, with whom Strauss had studied composition and instrumentation in the years prior. Thuille most likely encouraged young Richard to compose mainly chamber music. Only a year after Thuille's first published work, his Violin Sonata in D Minor (1880), Strauss published some chamber music of his own: the String Quartet, Op. 2 and Five Piano Pieces, Op. 3. Furthermore, Strauss radically revised his Piano Sonata in B Minor, Op. 5 (1881) as a direct result of criticism by Thuille, who called the piece "ridiculous in every aspect."[2] This fate was shared by the Cello Sonata in F Major, Op. 6 (1883), which Strauss also likely modified in light of Thuille's critiques.

Ludwig may also have inspired or influenced Strauss's turn from chamber music to orchestral works. The Serenade for Wind Instruments, Op. 7 was possibly Thuille's idea, and the fact that Strauss completed the Violin Concerto, Op. 8 in spring 1882, shortly after a piano concerto by Thuille, is hardly a coincidence. And in the mid-1880s, both Thuille and Strauss

---

[1] Richard Strauss, *Späte Aufzeichnungen*, ed. Marion Beyer, Jürgen May, and Walter Werbeck (Mainz: Schott, 2016), 326.

[2] Walter Werbeck. "'Gährend Drachengift' versus 'Milch der frommen Denkungsart'? Richard Strauss und Ludwig Thuille," in *Facetten II: Kleine Studien; Edition und Interpretation bei Chopin; Die Münchner Schule und Max Reger*, ed. Claus Bockmaier (München: Allitera, 2016), 250.

Figure 4.1   Ludwig Thuille, ca. 1899.
Photographer unknown

went on to tackle symphonic works: Strauss completed his Second Symphony in F Minor, Op. 12 in January 1884, and Thuille's Symphony in F Major followed less than two years later, premiered by Strauss in Meiningen on February 23, 1886. While Strauss seemed to follow his mentor in this regard, he did not lose sight of his own style. Unlike Thuille, whose music recalls Mendelssohn and Schumann, with occasional flashes of Grieg, Strauss modeled his work on Beethoven or Brahms. Long passages of Thuille's symphony are serenade-like with pleasant themes, but they lack the intensive, dynamic processes employed by Strauss. Perhaps these musical differences can be linked to Thuille's studies with Rheinberger or to his position (since 1883) as a piano and theory teacher at the Königliche Musikschule (Royal Music School) in Munich.

Early in his work as a pedagogue, Thuille's musical thinking found a new impetus. In the summer of 1886, the fanatical Wagnerian Alexander Ritter moved with Strauss (who had met Ritter in Meiningen) to Munich. There, Ritter successfully convinced a circle of young musicians to adopt his convictions on music history and aesthetics. Members of "Ritters Tafelrunde" (Ritter's Round Table) included Thuille, Strauss, Rösch, and (at least for a short time) Arthur Seidl. They all saw Ritter as their leader – affectionately calling him "uncle" – and were won over by the music of the New German School, especially that of Liszt and Wagner. While Strauss immediately and without reservation pursued this new course, Thuille responded more hesitantly and composed a sextet for piano and wind instruments right at the peak of Ritter's influence (1886–88); chamber music was the domain of Brahms, whom Ritter criticized heavily. The sextet's first horn theme is highly evocative of the beginning of Brahms's Second Piano Concerto, and the influence of Brahms is also unmistakable elsewhere. While Strauss ridiculed his friend as "an eternal Schumannian and nocturne performer," Thuille's caution clearly aided in advancing his own career.[3] In 1890, he was appointed professor of piano and harmony, from 1899 he taught counterpoint and composition, and in 1901 he and two colleagues succeeded Rheinberger in the area of composition.[4]

It was not until the 1890s that Thuille himself turned to the Wagner-dominated music theater, although this did not prevent him from writing numerous Lieder and works for men's chorus. The libretto of his first opera, *Theuerdank*, after a comedy by Hermann von Schmid and with a late-medieval plot, was written by Ritter and includes allusions to Wagner. The central characters are Max, a prince, dressed up as a Minnesinger, and Editha, a young woman engaged to Hermann but adored by Max – a dramatic constellation that evokes *Tannhäuser* and especially *Die Meistersinger von Nürnberg*, with Sachs (Max), Eva (Editha), and Stolzing (Hermann). Thuille's score (1893–95), with its declamatory style and altered harmonies in addition to some associative leitmotifs, was clearly inspired by Wagner. But Strauss also left his footprint, both in the libretto – his *Guntram* was a Minnesinger – and in the music, especially the overture, which Thuille composed at Strauss's request after completing the opera. (It was then published separately as *Romantische Ouvertüre*, Op. 16.) The overture clearly echoes the rhythmic drive of Strauss's *Don Juan*, which Thuille knew intimately since he had prepared the four-hand piano reduction.

Theuerdank was canceled in Munich in the spring of 1897 after four performances, but Thuille's second opera, *Lobetanz*, composed in 1896 to a libretto by Otto Julius Bierbaum, had great success and was performed in Germany, Switzerland, Austria, and even the United States. The plot centers on a fiddler who redeems a melancholic princess and her court. The incorporation of spoken dialogue, melodrama, songs, through-composed scenes, and dance inspired Thuille to

[3] *Richard Strauss – Ludwig Thuille: Ein Briefwechsel*, ed. Franz Trenner (Tutzing: Hans Schneider, 1980), 117.
[4] Bernd Edelmann, "Königliche Musikschule und Akademie der Tonkunst in München 1874–1914," in *Geschichte der Hochschule für Musik und Theater München von den Anfängen bis 1945*, ed. Stephan Schmitt (Tutzing: Hans Schneider, 2005), 178.

write a work that combines features of opera and Singspiel and thus suggested a path beyond Wagner.

Unlike Strauss, who, despite a critical distance to the Bayreuth Wagner cult, shared Wagner's historical and aesthetic worldview, Thuille was neither an unconditional Wagnerian nor a fan of parodistic tone poems that broke every harmonic rule, even though his friend's compositional powers unquestionably impressed him. Above all, Thuille saw himself not only as a composer but also as a teacher, and, as such, he was interested in a synthesis of the New German musical language and the Classical/Romantic heritage. This strategy was successful, as demonstrated by his many pupils who became famous composers, such as Walter Braunfels, Clemens von Franckenstein, and Rudi Stephan. As a highly influential professor, Thuille founded a Munich school of composers, which held a prominent position in German musical life around the turn of the century. But it was his collaboration with the Munich writer and composer Rudolf Louis on *Harmonielehre* (first edition 1907) that kept Thuille in good memory for generations. The volume explores the development of tonality and harmony, illustrated through examples ranging from the seventeenth to the early twentieth century, thus balancing historical theoretical practices with the sonic experiments of modern composers such as Debussy and Strauss.

Although their careers had followed rather different tracks, Thuille and Strauss stayed in touch, particularly between 1894 and 1898 when Strauss again worked in Munich. They also continued to associate privately, and Thuille (with Rösch and Eugen Spitzweg) was among the attendees at Strauss's marriage to Pauline de Ahna on September 10, 1894. In spite of this, Strauss's close relationship with his native town was over. He never again called Munich home, and the exchange of ideas he had cultivated with Thuille in earlier years was not rekindled, since Strauss was no longer particularly interested in his friend's music nor in that of Thuille's students or colleagues. Conversely, Thuille, from the perspective of a teacher, increasingly viewed his friend's compositional career in a somewhat critical light. When Strauss moved to Berlin in 1898, the distance between them increased. Strauss continued to accept Thuille's advice unreservedly only as an expert on harmony and counterpoint. While working on what was to become the *Alpensinfonie*, for instance, he consulted with his old friend on the countersubject of a fugue, although neither the subject nor Thuille's countersubject made it into the final version of the piece.

Friedrich Rösch (1862–1925)

With regard to the biography of Rösch, likely Strauss's most important friend, we remain almost completely in the dark. What little we know is derived mostly from encyclopedias. A year younger than Thuille and a year and a half older than Strauss, Rösch, who hailed from Swabia in southern Germany, attended the Ludwigsgymnasium in Munich with Strauss. He was evidently a gifted student – a "star pupil" according to Strauss – and studied law (probably in Munich) while also pursuing a musical career at the Royal Music School.[5] He studied composition and conducting, first with Andreas Wohlmuth until 1884 and then from 1885 with Rheinberger. According to Max Steinitzer, Strauss and Rösch met around 1878, although the latter is not mentioned in Strauss's correspondence with Thuille at that time.

In addition to law and music, Rösch received an education in philosophy. Presumably, it was with him and Arthur Seidl that Strauss conversed about Schopenhauer's philosophy of the arts during his brief stint at the University of Munich in 1882–83. Rösch seems to have been a very engaged contributor to Ritter's round tables. In Strauss's recollections of the period, Rösch held a place of honor next to Ritter. Like Strauss and Thuille, Rösch emerged from these conversations as a committed follower of Liszt and Wagner, and in the years that followed, he made it his mission to promote their musical and aesthetic ideals – which, as with Thuille, also meant advocating for Strauss's tone poems.

Between 1889 and 1892, Rösch moved from Munich to Berlin, apparently for further study in conducting with Hans von Bülow. He also mentioned studies in opera in a letter to Strauss. In the spirit of Ritter, he made every effort to persuade Bülow to reject his infatuation with Brahms, return to his earlier New German ideals, and make an unconditional commitment to Strauss's music. Rösch only partly achieved these goals, however. On October 20, 1889, he wrote to Strauss: "I am now convinced that *Macbeth* no longer has a chance with Mr. v. B. [...] On the other hand, I am certain that your *Don Juan* has now definitely won him over, and that he may later also be a pushover for *Tod und Verklärung*."[6] In fact, it was Bülow who conducted the first Berlin performance of *Don Juan* at the end of January 1890 and organized the premiere of the third version of *Macbeth*, which Strauss conducted on February 29,

---

[5] Strauss, *Späte Aufzeichnungen*, 135 (footnote 1).
[6] This and the subsequent quotation are from letters held at the Richard-Strauss-Archiv.

1892 in Berlin. But Rösch ultimately failed in his broader goal of winning Bülow back to Liszt and Wagner, though at times he thought he was well on his way. In early 1892, for example, he believed he had completed his "mission" successfully, as he wrote to Strauss on January 28: "Mr. v. Bülow has broken all relations with Hermann Wolff and his entire Jewish entourage (including Joachim)." Bülow did not break with his concert promoter Hermann Wolff, however.

Rösch apparently did not hold a permanent position in Berlin, a situation that does not seem to have changed during the following years in Munich. He occasionally conducted musical events of the local Akademische Gesangverein (academic choral society), sometimes programming his own compositions. For instance, the society performed his *Antonius* after Wilhelm Busch for male chorus, soloists, and orchestra in 1887 (a work Strauss praised as a "witty parody of an oratorio"), and, later, the operettas *Melopomene oder der Gummimann* (1893) and *Marsyas* (1895).[7] Strauss was fascinated by Rösch's music with its allusions to Wagner, dry liturgical formulas, and polkas and waltzes, perhaps because it anticipated the parodistic elements later adopted by Strauss himself, such as in the second cycle of tone poems and *Feuersnot*.

Over time Rösch's relationship with Strauss became closer, not least through his relationship with Marie Ritter (a great-niece of Alexander Ritter), whom Rösch married in 1902. Marie possessed funds that enabled Rösch to break off an engagement as Kapellmeister in Prague in 1892 and take his time in searching for a suitable position. This allowed him ample opportunity to spend time with Strauss, who in return thanked him not only with recommendations for conducting appointments and scholarships but also sought his advice in artistic matters. In March 1892, while Strauss was finishing the first version of the *Guntram* text, Rösch likely accompanied Marie Ritter when she visited Strauss in Weimar, where they discussed the plan of a Don Juan opera inspired by Max Stirner. Conversations like this potentially spurred Strauss to rework the third act of *Guntram* during his trip to Egypt. He emancipated Guntram to an autonomous person free of any influence, even of the religious brotherhood to which he had belonged. However, with Guntram, it was his creator Strauss who emancipated himself from Ritter's aesthetic with its Christian foundation and from the prevailing (Romantic) view of music as religious experience. It is no wonder that Ritter was deeply disappointed. At this critical moment in Strauss's development, Rösch again became a

---

[7] Strauss, *Späte Aufzeichnungen*, 328.

key point of contact. He wrote comprehensive discourses to his friend on the philosophies of Schopenhauer and Nietzsche, encouraging Strauss to reject Wagnerian redemption.

During Strauss's second engagement in Munich, Rösch was Kapellmeister in St. Petersburg (1896–98), the birthplace of his future wife, while also pursuing journalistic activities in which he demonstrated a combative character. In 1897, he published *Musik-ästhetische Streitfragen* (*Music-Aesthetic Controversies*), in which he interpreted Bülow as a true disciple of Wagner and Liszt (contrary to the image of Bülow spread by his widow) and proposed an apology for the New German (and in particular Liszt's) aesthetics of musical progress.[8] Rösch praises Strauss but is relentless in his admonitions against excessive musical realism, probably in light of *Till Eulenspiegel*. In the same year, he argued in print with Max Schillings and Richard Batka, the latter a writer on music from Prague, about melodrama, which Rösch (with reference to Wagner) roundly rejected. While Strauss was aware of the feud, he seems to have withheld his judgments, presumably in part because he had composed his own melodrama, *Enoch Arden*, Op. 38 in early 1897. However, Strauss did not distance himself from Rösch, and if there was occasional friction, it was either of a private nature or resulted from Rösch's self-confidence, which made him vigorously oppose any apparent degradation as a "subordinate or student" of his famous friend.[9] Furthermore, Rösch remained an important advisor both in career-related and compositional matters. For example, Strauss willingly implemented his suggestions to rework the ending of *Ein Heldenleben*, and, in 1899, Rösch also wrote a commentary on the piece similar to the one he had published on *Don Juan* three years earlier. He was probably also involved in the formulation of the six internal headings in the score ("The Hero," "The Hero's Adversary," etc.).

Until the end of his time in St. Petersburg, Rösch appears to have remained active in the field of music. This changed, however, from the beginning of 1897 with the efforts to reform copyright law and publishing rights and to improve the social situation of composers in Germany through the creation of a royalty institution. Rösch and Strauss actively joined the project in 1898. Strauss championed the initiative with his prominent name, while Rösch provided legal support and kept things moving forward. Working with great expertise, he also proved to be a

---

[8] Friedrich Rösch, *Musik-ästhetische Streitfragen. Streiflichter und Schlagschatten zu den Ausgewählten Schriften von Hans von Bülow. Ein kritischer Waffengang* (Leipzig: Hofmeister, 1897).
[9] Letter to Richard Strauss of July 4, 1898, Richard-Strauss-Archiv.

clever tactician, outmatching his friend. All of the vital documents written by Strauss on this matter – perhaps as early as his open letter to German composers in July 1898 – had most likely been edited by Rösch. Strauss expressed his gratitude for Rösch's commitment by dedicating his second opera *Feuersnot* to him in 1902 (having previously done so with *Tod und Verklärung*). Later, the University of Jena bestowed an honorary doctorate in law on Rösch in 1913, and by 1916 at the latest, he received the honorary title of *Bayerischer Hofrat*.

Not only was Rösch indispensable in his capacity as a lawyer for the Genossenschaft Deutscher Tonsetzer (Association of German Composers) and the Anstalt für musikalisches Aufführungsrecht (Institute for Musical Performing Rights), but Strauss also consulted him repeatedly on private legal issues. In 1899, for example, Rösch joined negotiations with the publishers Leuckart and Bock concerning the three choruses for male voices, Op. 45. In 1903, he mediated in the Strausses' marital crisis following the composer's apparent affair with Mieze Mücke, and in September 1910, he helped to ensure that the negotiations with Dresden regarding the premiere of *Der Rosenkavalier* reached a satisfactory conclusion. Later, in the spring of 1918, he successfully advised Strauss in his dispute with his publisher Hugo Bock about the Op. 66 Lieder that were later published as *Krämerspiegel*. Strauss also dedicated this work to his friend.

A year later, Rösch took on the post of chair for the Allgemeine Deutsche Musikverein (General German Music Society) on top of all his other functions. Few details have survived concerning his activities in this capacity, but we do know that he pursued a more liberal programming policy, since he was convinced that – as his successor Siegmund von Hausegger put it in a letter to Strauss – it would be "completely wrong [. . .] to exclude the atonal heroes and thus turn them into martyrs."[10] For Strauss, Rösch remained an authority until his death. As a lawyer, Strauss's son Franz was able to replace him, but a friend like Rösch, who kept his independence until the end and whom Strauss cherished for just this very reason, Strauss never had again.

---

[10] Letter to Richard Strauss of May 10, 1928, Richard-Strauss-Archiv.

CHAPTER 5

Hofmannsthal

Ingeborg Haase and Dirk Hoffmann

... we were born for one another and are certain to do fine things together ...

The above quotation, taken from a 1906 letter from Richard Strauss to Hugo von Hofmannsthal, marks the beginning of an enduring, albeit unlikely partnership. It was enduring because it lasted for 23 years until Hofmannsthal's sudden death in 1929. It was unlikely, at least on the surface, because they seemed such different personalities; Hofmannsthal lamented often in letters to friends that Strauss had a tendency toward the trivial, kitschy, and vulgar while complaining that he wished for a more artistically refined composer. In spite of these comments, Strauss and Hofmannsthal remained partners, as the poet realized that they complemented each other. As early as the 1890s, Hofmannsthal had contemplated combining text and music as demonstrated by two unpublished manuscripts; among his literary remains are fragments of musical comedies (*Singspiele*), the first titled *Prinzessin auf dem verzauberten Berg* (*Princess on the Enchanted Mountain*) and the second *Die Gräfin* (*The Countess*, based on Goethe's *Wilhelm Meisters Lehrjahre* and *Wanderjahre*). Music, as Hofmannsthal pointed out in 1919 to the German writer and philosopher Rudolf Pannwitz, can elevate language, referencing remarks by the character Jarno in *Wilhelm Meister* "about the magic of the sung dialogue in contrast to the spoken one."[1]

Hugo Laurenz August Hofmann, Edler von Hofmannsthal was born in Vienna on February 1, 1874. The title "Edler von Hofmannsthal" dated back to his great-grandfather Isaak Löw Hofmann, a Jewish merchant

---

[1] *Hugo von Hofmannsthal – Rudolf Pannwitz: Briefwechsel,* ed. Gerhard Schuster (Frankfurt: Fischer, 1993), 458.

ennobled in 1835 by Austrian emperor Ferdinand I. His grandfather was heir to the family business but distanced himself from his roots, marrying an Italian woman and converting to Catholicism. His father, Hugo August Peter von Hofmannsthal was a lawyer and bank director. He married Anna Maria Josefa, née Fohleutner, daughter of a judge and royal solicitor. Hugo junior was their only child. Homeschooled by private tutors until he entered the Wiener Akademische Gymnasium at the age of ten, his primary pastime in early childhood was reading. Goethe, Schiller, Kleist, and Grillparzer formed part of his curriculum, as well as the works of Homer, Dante, Voltaire, Shakespeare, Byron, and Browning in their original languages. His education was rounded off by regular visits to the theater and opera. These experiences led Hofmannsthal to see himself already at the age of 15 as the future dramatist of the Burgtheater, the main theater in Vienna. It is no wonder he began to write poems and short lyrical dramas (*lyrische Dramen*) in his teens on topics as grandiose as the soul, life, dreams, and death.

After the publication of these first attention-grabbing works and reviews under the pseudonyms Loris Melikow and Theophil Morren, young intellectuals and writers in Vienna (many of whom later formed a group known as Jung-Wien) wondered about the identity of this new poet. In the fall of 1890, Hofmannsthal was introduced to this group; different legends exist regarding who actually brought him along. One thing is clear: he soon became a regular guest. The writer and critic Hermann Bahr, one of the doyens of Jung-Wien and whose play *Die Mutter* had been reviewed by "Loris," believed him to be an established middle-aged writer before learning that Hofmannsthal was a teenager. Hofmannsthal's fame as a literary prodigy was established quickly and became a source of woe during his life. Even decades later, when he was among a pool of candidates for the Nobel Prize in literature, his early oeuvre often overshadowed his later accomplishments. Among these youthful works is *Der Tor und der Tod* (*Death and the Fool*, 1893), situated between poetry and drama, which fascinated many of his generation at the turn of the century because it captured a mood only too familiar to them: the feeling of nausea and ennui caused by an intellectual dissolution of existing values.

His early literary experiments, which included many genres besides poetry, for example, narratives, essays about art, and short dramas, often dissolved traditional boundaries. Their common characteristic was a highly exquisite and esoteric choice of words and imagery. The poem *Lebenslied* (1896) became an oft-cited example (here is its first stanza):

Lebenslied	Song of Life
Den Erben lass verschwenden	On eagle, lamb, and peacock
An Adler, Lamm und Pfau	The heir may freely spend
Das Salböl aus den Händen	The precious cruse of ointment
Der toten alten Frau!	From the dead old woman's hand!
Die Toten, die entgleiten,	The dead that glide away,
Die Wipfel in dem Weiten –	Far treetops where they sway,
Ihm sind sie wie das Schreiten	He counts as light as they
Der Tänzerinnen wert!	Were steps the dancers weave.[2]

Such verses established his reputation as a model decadent aesthete, an artist who valued artifice over a naive view of nature. The leading figure of this movement in the English-speaking world was Oscar Wilde, with whose work Hofmannsthal was utterly familiar. Even at an early age, Hofmannsthal was the incarnation of a mediator between cultures. And Wilde's *Salomé* (1891), of course, became one of the important works for Strauss.

It was no surprise when Stefan George, the infamous symbolist poet who tried to establish an elite circle of literati, approached the young Hofmannsthal in 1891 because he saw him as one of "the chosen few." Although many facets drew Hofmannsthal to George and his world, in one respect their dreams and ideas stood in opposition. While Hofmannsthal was fascinated with the theater and even with individual actors (the person who embodied this world of the stage for Hofmannsthal in his youth was the Italian actress Eleonora Duse), George abhorred both.

The following year, in 1892, Hofmannsthal graduated from high school with honors. His parents rewarded his success with a traditional bourgeois educational journey (*Bildungsreise*) to France. After his return, he began – encouraged by his parents – to study law to ensure a profitable future career. He enrolled at the university in Vienna and passed the state exam in 1894, but law was not his passion. While taking a break from the university, he enlisted voluntarily for a year of military service (as mandated by his social status). It was a world far removed from his life up to this time. Returning to Vienna and the university, he switched his major to Romance Literature and completed a dissertation on language usage by the

---

[2] Hugo von Hofmannsthal, "Lebenslied," trans. Arthur Davidson, in *Poems and Verse Plays*, ed. Michael Hamburger (New York: Pantheon Books, 1961), 17.

French poets *La Pléiade* (1899). Subsequently, plans for attaining a professorship led him to pursue research on Victor Hugo. Yet, he was unsure if a teaching and research job would really suit him. Similarly, he felt uneasy about the idea of engaging with culture on an administrative level as a director of a museum or theater, although these desires continued to play a role in his later life and surfaced repeatedly in various forms. Unsure of his future, Hofmannsthal experienced a sustained bout of depression.

An extended trip to Paris in 1900 showed the way to recovery, as there Hofmannsthal met many kindred spirits: Stéphane Mallarmé, Édouard Manet, Anatole France, Auguste Rodin, and Maurice Maeterlinck. These encounters helped to clear his mind and, after returning to Vienna in 1901, he withdrew the submission of his dissertation on Victor Hugo before the university reached a decision. Especially important for his future was his marriage in the same year to Gertrude (Gerty) Schlesinger, daughter of a banker and sister of a good friend. Hofmannsthal was finally able to move out of his parents' apartment to a small villa in Rodaun, near Vienna, where he would live until the end of his life. The countryside guaranteed the peace and quiet that Hofmannsthal craved. His wife protected him from unwelcome visitors as well as from himself, that is, from mood swings caused by the weather and his hypersensitivity. Gerty thus enabled his dream of becoming a freelance writer, editor, and lecturer.

Recognition in intellectual, literary, and artistic circles did not translate to popular success – especially not on stage. Audiences and critics were rather disparaging about his early dramas. But these experiences helped him to clarify his language skepticism: the awareness of the seductive power of words. The resulting reflections on language – inspired by scientists (Ernst Mach), linguists (Fritz Mauthner), and philosophers (Friedrich Nietzsche, Franz Brentano) – were expressed in the fictional *Ein Brief* (*Letter of Lord Chandos*, 1902), which became a seminal work of modern literature and one of Hofmannsthal's best known writings. In it, he ponders the isolation of the individual and the inability of language to express coherently one's innermost thoughts and feelings and thereby to establish social and intellectual bonds. Foremost among the many echoes in literature and philosophy was Ludwig Wittgenstein's *Tractatus* (1921), viewed as the culmination of the Viennese philosopher's investigation of language.

The result of Hofmannsthal's language crisis was not silence but, on the contrary, a renewed effort to overcome aestheticism as well as to fulfill the demands of the theater while addressing a wider public. He was on his way "from the temple to the street," as the German literary scholar Richard

Alewyn stated in 1949, quoting Hofmannsthal's own words.[3] Three people were especially important in achieving this goal: Strauss, theater director Max Reinhardt (both master communicators without words of their own), and diplomat, writer, cultural reformer, art collector, and patron of modern art, Harry Graf Kessler.

Reinhardt's and Hofmannsthal's most transformative meeting occurred in the spring of 1903, when the Kleine Theater, based in Berlin, gave a performance in Vienna of Reinhardt's extremely popular production of Maxim Gorki's *The Lower Depths*. Hermann Bahr, the tireless spokesman for all cultural innovations, arranged a get-together for the ensemble with his friends. Besides Reinhardt, the actress Gertrud Eysoldt was the star at this occasion. The previous year, she had made a name for herself in the title role of Wilde's *Salomé* and had motivated Strauss to set the play to music after seeing her on stage. The discussions at Bahr's social event must also have been very inspirational for Hofmannsthal. A few months later, he finally completed (with Reinhardt's encouragement) the drama *Elektra*, a work he had been pondering since 1901 as part of his efforts to rejuvenate classical theater. Reinhardt premiered *Elektra* to great acclaim in October 1903, and it proved to be a milestone in the history of modern theater: a rewriting of a classical play that incorporated the latest psychological research, combining text and expressive dance, and was performed most effectively by Eysoldt.

The play was not only the beginning of a close working relationship with Reinhardt but also with Strauss. Hofmannsthal had met the composer briefly in Berlin in 1899 and again in Paris in 1900. It was Strauss's attendance at a performance of *Elektra* in 1905 that led to a renewed and decisive contact between the two – the beginning of their long-lasting collaboration. Strauss saw in Hofmannsthal's drama a perfect text for an opera. The only hesitation Strauss had, and eventually overcame, was the perceived similarity between his earlier opera *Salome* and the drama *Elektra*.

The third person important for Hofmannsthal in his dramatic endeavors, Harry Graf Kessler, he had known since 1898. For years, Kessler was a major source of cultural information for Hofmannsthal, widening his circle of artistic friends and helping him with structural suggestions for streamlining his ideas for plays. Kessler's most important contribution to Hofmannsthal's development was his co-authorship of *Der*

---

[3] Richard Alewyn, *Über Hugo von Hofmannsthal*, 4th ed. (Göttingen: Vandenhoeck & Ruprecht, 1967), 186.

Rosenkavalier (premiered in Dresden in January 1911) that led to one of Hofmannsthal's greatest successes and fulfilled his wish to create a world that mirrored the full range of social life. Kessler shared in vivid detail an obscure operetta he had seen in Paris in 1908, which inspired Hofmannsthal to quickly draft jointly with Kessler a detailed scenario of a new libretto, one with all the vicissitudes and moments of intimacy alternating with tumultuous mass scenes that make a play effective. The driving force was no sublime idea but the requirements of the stage. Now, Hofmannsthal could focus almost exclusively on the right tone for the characters – one of his absolute strengths.[4] As a result, Hofmannsthal's erudition was put to use so subtly that it enhanced the playfulness of the plot and added just a touch of intellectual spice and philosophical reflection, such as in the Marschallin's ponderings about the passing of time.

For Hofmannsthal, librettos had the same literary value as his other work. Throughout the collaboration with Strauss, his attitude was determined by a "totally idealistic conception of opera as an art form in which words and music are of equal importance."[5] That Strauss had the dramatic instinct to temper his librettist's poetic flights made them ideal partners.

In December 1911, Hofmannsthal had a second major success: *Jedermann*, a modern adaptation of the medieval morality play *Everyman* about the life and death of a wealthy man that grotesquely depicts a materialistic and ruthless world. Steeped in guilt, Everyman is saved from eternal damnation by his few good deeds and the mercy of God. The plan had been on Hofmannsthal's mind since 1903, and staging this universal theme, with its archetypal patterns of human relationships, was already discussed with Reinhardt before the premiere of *Der Rosenkavalier*. The plan for this "fairy tale in Christian clothes" (as he called it) was realized in a relatively short time.[6] Reinhardt, known for his ability to work on a large scale, was able to find an appropriate setting for the premiere: a circus arena in Berlin. After World War I, Reinhardt discovered an even more suitable venue, the Domplatz in Salzburg, where it has been performed annually as part of the Salzburg Festival, only interrupted by World War II.

---

[4] See Michael Reynolds, *Creating "Der Rosenkavalier": From Chevalier to Cavalier* (London: Boydell Press, 2016); and Dirk O. Hoffmann, *Hugo von Hofmannsthal/Richard Strauss: Der Rosenkavalier – Textfassungen und Zeilenkommentar* (Vienna: Hollitzer, 2016).

[5] Steven Paul Scher, "Hofmannsthal as Librettist to Richard Strauss: Some Aspects of their Collaboration," *Journal of the International Arthur Schnitzler Research Association* 5, no. 2 (1966): 30.

[6] Hugo von Hofmannsthal, "Das Spiel vor der Menge," *Pan* 2, no. 6 (1911): 176–79.

Figure 5.1   Hugo von Hofmannsthal, ca. 1910.
Photograph by Nicola Perscheid

This reductive process – returning to fairy tales, mythology, and classical plays – became Hofmannsthal's usual approach to writing and had both positive and negative consequences. Some critics saw it as overly dependent on literary models, others more positively as a dialogue with tradition. In an oft-cited article, the literary scholar Martin Stern regarded it as a means for Hofmannsthal to hide his personal confessions in a discrete way, describing the process as "revealing through concealing."[7] Unquestionably, this way of writing produced a fascinating oeuvre, including prose narratives (many praised as literary masterpieces) and dramas. One example is *Der Turm*, based on Pedro Calderón's *La vida es sueño*, which is a meditation on such fundamental questions as the conflict between spirituality and power and the legitimacy of government – a work seen by later critics as a prophecy of the emerging fascism. No less impressive were the librettos *Ariadne auf Naxos*, *Die ägyptische Helena*, and *Die Frau ohne Schatten* that inspired Strauss's extraordinary compositions.

Owing to Strauss's music, the librettos outrank Hofmannsthal's other works for the theater in terms of popular success. The list of most often performed works by Hofmannsthal is headed by *Der Rosenkavalier*, followed by *Ariadne*, *Elektra*, and *Arabella*. Next are the plays *Jedermann* and *Das Salzburger Große Welttheater*. The erudition displayed in these as well as the other less popular works helped not only to establish him as one of the towering figures of German literature in the first decades of the twentieth century and of classical modernism, but also gave support to his early fame as a *Bildungspoet* (elitist poet). Therefore, it is not surprising that books by Hofmannsthal are not on the bestseller lists, although his oeuvre is part of the canon of German literature, and contemporary Hofmannsthal scholarship is extensive, encouraged by a very active Hofmannsthal Society (Hugo von Hofmannsthal-Gesellschaft, founded 1968). Even a multi-volume critical edition has been published – an honor not accorded to many writers.

Hofmannsthal's perspective on the tumultuous era in which he lived added to this multi-faceted image. His views were characterized by a return to the past to solve contemporary problems. At first, he welcomed the outbreak of World War I as a possible stimulus for a renewal of the "Austrian Idea," that is, the revival of a union that transcended nationalities – an idea that was, in his view, once embodied in the Holy Roman Empire of which Austria had been the successor. Hofmannsthal believed

---

[7] Martin Stern, "Hofmannsthals verbergendes Enthüllen: Seine Schaffensweise in den vier Fassungen der Florindo/Cristina-Komödie," *Deutsche Vierteljahresschrift für Literaturwissenschaft und Geistesgeschichte* 30, no. 1 (1959): 38–62.

Figure 5.2   Cover page of the satirical magazine *Die Muskete* (February 16, 1911).[8]

---

[8] *Der Rosenkavalier* was and still is their biggest success. The opera caused a real stir: special trains ran to Dresden, and even a mild cigarette called "Rosenkavalier" was sold. This magazine cover offers further evidence of the opera's popularity; the caption reads: "Welcome, dear Rosenkavalier! But next time have one of our people fabricate the libretto for you."

very much in a common European culture comprised of various traditions transmitted by its different languages, but he had little political sensitivity for the feelings of suppression that minor cultures experienced in the real world. Thus, many of his cultural activities that were intended to further the European cause came across as nationalistic, among them the book series *Österreichische Bibliothek* (*Austrian Library*, 26 volumes) and lectures such as *Österreich im Spiegel seiner Dichtung* (*Austria in the Mirror of Its Literature*). By 1917, after experiencing in a very personal way the Czech efforts for independence in Prague (Czech authors whom he had wanted to attract as participants in his publication efforts rejected the invitation because of the injustices their culture had endured in the past), and after learning about the cruelties and horrors of war, his euphoria vanished. Yet, his conservative attitude remained more or less the same, and he regretted the religious as well as political divisions in Europe. He believed that a search for the old national identity and common roots of a united Europe would help overcome the negative reality of nationalistic hubris, an idea formulated in his speech *Das Schrifttum als geistiger Raum der Nation* (*The Written Word as the Spiritual Space of the Nation*, 1927). His most important post-war success in working toward a cultural restoration was the creation of the Salzburg Festival (1920), together with Reinhardt, Strauss, and others.

In the post-war years, Hofmannsthal returned to comedies. He explained his action using a quote from the German Romantic poet Novalis: "After an unsuccessful war, comedies must be written." Hofmannsthal continued: "The essence of comedy is irony, and nothing is better suited to make clear to us the irony that rules over all the things of the earth than a war that ends unhappily."[9] With *Der Schwierige* (*The Difficult Gentleman*, 1921), judged by many as his best comedy, and *Der Unbestechliche* (*The Incorruptible Servant*, 1923), he established himself as one of the great writers of comedies in the German language although not the most frequently performed. In a way, the two plays can be seen as companion pieces. The first, reviving the topic of the *Letter of Lord Chandos*, questions the adequacy of language as a tool for communication, while the second shows the manipulative power of language. *Der Schwierige* especially hit a nerve because of its existential theme: endangered human relationships in uncertain times.

---

[9] Hugo von Hofmannsthal, "Three Small Observations," in *Hugo von Hofmannsthal and the Austrian Idea: Selected Essays and Addresses, 1906–1927*, ed. and trans. David S. Luft (West Lafayette, IN: Purdue University Press), 111.

Hofmannsthal's last collaborative work with Strauss was the lyrical comedy *Arabella*. While Hofmannsthal tried to revive the spirit of *Der Rosenkavalier* (although quite different in tone), Strauss feared that the subject matter was too conventional. But in the extremely collaborative fashion that can be seen throughout their partnership, Hofmannsthal extensively reworked the first act in response to Strauss's critique. Unfortunately, he never read the positive reply by Strauss confirming that their working relationship was still as good as ever: "First act excellent. Many thanks and congratulations. Sincerely Richard Strauss."[10] The same day the telegram arrived, July 15, 1929, Hofmannsthal suffered a stroke and died while preparing for the funeral of his son, Franz, who had committed suicide two days before. As a reminiscence and homage to his longtime librettist, Strauss completed *Arabella* based on Hofmannsthal's last version. The successful premiere of the opera was in Dresden on July 1, 1933 – an appropriate ending to an impressive partnership.

---

[10] *The Correspondence between Richard Strauss and Hugo von Hofmannsthal*, trans. Hans Hammelmann and Ewald Osers (Cambridge: Cambridge University Press, 1980), 536.

CHAPTER 6

The Other Librettists

Kenneth Birkin

Hugo von Hofmannsthal's death in 1929 left Strauss in a quandary. The will to compose was undiminished, and a replacement of similar caliber was difficult to find. Over the ensuing 20 years, Strauss enlisted the services of three further librettists. First was the celebrated Jewish writer Stefan Zweig, who based *Die schweigsame Frau* on Ben Jonson's comedy *The Silent Woman*. After Zweig exiled himself from his Austrian homeland in 1936, the distraught composer turned to the Viennese theater historian Joseph Gregor as collaborator on *Friedenstag, Daphne,* and *Die Liebe der Danae*, which premiered under Clemens Krauss after Strauss's death. It was Krauss who at Strauss's request had been monitoring Gregor's work; a consummate theater man, Krauss was ultimately entrusted with the libretto of *Capriccio*, Strauss's last opera, whose premiere he conducted in 1942. Many decades earlier, Strauss himself wrote the text for his first music drama, *Guntram*, but it was "song-and-dance-man" Ernst von Wolzogen, the librettist of *Feuersnot*, whose racy libretto served to loosen the Wagnerian chains that had bound the composer in *Guntram* and pointed Strauss in a direction that would lead to the Hofmannsthalian masterpieces of the next three decades.

Ernst Freiherr von Wolzogen (1855–1934)

Wolzogen's father, Karl August Alfred, was a Breslau government official with literary pretensions. His first wife, Elisabeth, daughter of Berlin architect Karl Schinkel, died in 1854. Alfred promptly remarried, and his second son Ernst was born in 1855. In 1867, Alfred became Intendant of the Schwerin Court Theater, and both Ernst and his elder brother, Hans Paul, grew up with literary and musical ambitions. Hans became a close associate of Wagner and editor of the *Bayreuther Blätter*; Ernst, a keen amateur violinist, studied art, music, and literature in Strasbourg and then philosophy in Leipzig before settling in Weimar in 1879. There, he worked for Grand Duke Carl Alexander, migrating to Berlin in 1882 where he undertook editorial work for the publisher Auerbach. In Berlin, Wolzogen wrote 17 novels, 11 stage works, and numerous short stories, the latter exploring a satirical vein of folk literature. It was the novel *Der Kraft Mayr* (1897), however, that placed him securely on the literary map. Set in neoclassical Weimar, the story unfolds against a backdrop dominated by the patriarchal figure of Franz Liszt. Mayr, a personification of the author and an outcast, ultimately triumphs over opposition. Wolzogen brought to this tale a degree of personal authenticity, having fleetingly circulated on the periphery of the Liszt circle in the late 1870s.

Wolzogen moved to Munich in 1893, one year before Strauss commenced his second term at the Court Opera. They had met in Leipzig in 1892 (courtesy of Cosima Wagner) and, in Munich, both moved in a social circle that included Otto Julius Bierbaum and Ferdinand von Sporck. Deliberations over a prospective collaboration did not take place until the fall of 1898, prior to Strauss's transfer to Berlin.

Wolzogen's Munich activities initially centered on the so-called theatrical "fringe" under the banner of the Akademisch-dramatischer Verein (academic drama society). Ibsen, Strindberg, and Hauptmann figured prominently in his repertoire, but undertaken with "scratch" players, his efforts were poorly received. Undeterred, in July 1897 he cofounded the Freie Literarische Gesellschaft, staging performances of Tolstoi's *The Power of Darkness* at the Theater am Gärtnerplatz. Works by Otto Hartleben, Karl Piper, and Ernst Rosmer followed, but the project closest to his heart, an expensive performance of Shakespeare's *Troilus and Cressida* (with an all-male cast), proved his downfall. The Gesellschaft claimed Wolzogen had defamed the name of Shakespeare and damaged the Society's reputation; to his chagrin, he was hounded out of the very organization he had founded. The press closed ranks against him, and future projects were roughly treated. Thoroughly disillusioned, he made common cause with Strauss in his battle against Munich obtusity. A grudge jointly held against provincial cultural dilettantism linked writer and musician in an artistically fruitful and popularly conceived "unholy" alliance. Set in Munich, their opera *Feuersnot* (1901) pairs Wolzogen's witty, salacious text with Strauss in *Till Eulenspiegel* mode.

The move to Berlin came in 1900. Wolzogen's *Überbrettl* cabaret opened at the Alexanderstrasse theater on January 18, 1901, and saw his fortunes at a brief zenith. His scheme to introduce a form of light-hearted theatrical entertainment (with literary overtones) to Germany had been formulated in 1899, consolidated by forays into Montmartre nightlife at the Paris World Exhibition (1900). The *Überbrettl* concept aimed to elevate French cabaret, with its satirical song-and-dance comedy, to the German stage. Despite a range of talented literary and musical associates – Wedekind, Dehmel, Bierbaum, Hans Heinz Ewers, Ludwig Thoma, Victor Hollaender, Oscar Straus, Leo Fall and, fleetingly, even the 27-year-old Arnold Schoenberg – initial success was not sustained. The ensemble moved to a larger venue in November 1901, but the project soon ran out of steam. To Wolzogen's annoyance, his concept was subsequently taken up, debased and popularized, in other Berlin nightlife venues. "When I hit on the title 'Überbrettl'," he ruefully observed, "I signed my own death warrant."[1] The "Überbrettl Baron" was left to peddle his wares in Scandinavia and the German provinces. Later, in a desperate effort to revive his flagging fortunes, he founded a short-lived opera company and unsuccessfully tempted Strauss with a new libretto. The composer had attended an *Überbrettl* performance on April 8, 1901; kinship of Wolzogen's cabaret settings with *Feuersnot*'s provocative Munich ditties would hardly have escaped his notice. Indeed, both *Feuersnot* and *Überbrettl* reflected a forward-looking theatrical trend in turn-of-the-century Berlin, proposing a new realism and objectivity that mocked ingrained conservatism and challenged establishment prudery. Analogous to Viennese *Jugendstil*, its pre–World War I cultural impact was considerable, setting the tone for later music-dramatic manifestations from the likes of Weill, Orff, and Hindemith.

Wolzogen was an eccentric, flamboyant of character and of ready talent. His ventures, however, fueled by an enormous ego, were undertaken with doubtful financial backing. Unable to accept responsibility for failure, he inevitably blamed others. The *Überbrettl* venture drove him, neither for the first nor the last time, into bankruptcy. Lecture tours in England, Russia, and the United States followed in an attempt to settle his debts and service double claims of alimony. After a stint in the military, he continued his dramatic (*Weibchen*, 1915) and literary (*Die verdammte Liebe*, 1917) activities. A serious bladder operation in 1920 failed to curtail his creativity, but by the 1930s, he had outlived his reputation. He died in Wolfratshausen in 1934.

Stefan Zweig (1881–1942)

After Hofmannsthal's death, on Anton Kippenberg's recommendation, Strauss turned to the fêted writer and dramatist Zweig, arguably the most

---

[1] Ernst von Wolzogen, *Verse zu meinem Leben* (Berlin: F. Fontane, 1907), 132.

widely read and translated literary figure of his time. The second son of a Christian-convert Jewish family, he was raised in Vienna in affluent circumstances. The family textile business dominated the Czech and Balkan markets, and with brother Alfred groomed to succeed their millionaire father, Stefan was free to cultivate his own interests. He found the fin-de-siècle Viennese cultural milieu entrancing: Brahms still walked the streets, literary "greats" forgathered in the cafés, and renowned actors and singers performed at the Burgtheater and Court Opera where Mahler officiated. Zweig's passion for literature awakened the poetic muse; *Silberne Saiten* appeared in 1901, and on April 11, 1902, to the envy of his peers, the *Neue Freie Presse* published his novella *Die Wanderung*. His reputation was soon augmented by translation projects, notably of the Belgian poet Émile Verhaeren – a "missionary" activity that introduced Verhaeren to the German-speaking public as an optimist with a forward-looking European vision. A developing friendship with the poet inspired a two-volume study of the man and his work (1908), preceded by a monograph on Verlaine (1905) and his own verse drama *Tersites* (1907). Zweig's concept of a culturally united Europe, sharpened by subsequent worldwide travel, was crystallized by contact with like-minded spirits such as Romain Rolland and Walter Rathenau. By this time, Zweig had established himself in Vienna's Kochgasse, a haven for his rapidly expanding autograph collection and a much-needed fixed address for a burgeoning literary correspondence.

Zweig's world was shattered by the outbreak of hostilities in 1914. Service in the Austrian war ministry and a visit to the Balkan front destroyed his illusions of a united Europe. Nevertheless, the post-war period witnessed further literary achievements as short stories, plays, and translations poured from his pen together with two further poetry volumes and the pacifist drama *Jeremias* (1917). Two years later, with his future wife Frederike, he abandoned Vienna for a more tranquil environment on the Kapuzinerberg overlooking Salzburg. A series of monographs (e.g., on Dickens, Balzac, and Dostoevsky, later augmented by thumbnail studies of Casanova, Stendhal, and Tolstoy) preceded biographies of Rolland and Frans Masereel. But it was *Joseph Fouché* (1929), *Marie Antoinette* (1933), and *Maria Stuart* (1935) that sealed his popularity and reputation as a well-researched historical novelist. The politically slanted *Fouché* was succeeded by two autobiographical studies of prophetic significance: *Erasmus* (1934) and *Castellio gegen Calvin* (1936). They reflect Zweig's personal and political dilemma of the mid- to late 1930s, and the *Die schweigsame Frau* libretto (1933–35) was written in this context. The burning of the books (1933) shocked Zweig to the core, but, while his colleagues urged him to speak out, he remained silent. The emigrant lobby, unable to attract him to its cause, spitefully dubbed his silence "regime friendly." Beset on all sides, he chose the middle way; Erasmus-like, he pronounced for none. Increasing despair led to self-exile, first to England, then the United States where he completed his autobiography *Die Welt von Gestern* (*The World of Yesterday*). In Brazil, together with his second wife, Lotte, he committed suicide in 1942.

Our understanding of Zweig's inner life, hopes, and fears, stems from his voluminous correspondences with contemporary artists, musicians, and writers. His pacifism and endeavor to promote friendship and understanding between men and nations drew many world-renowned figures into his orbit.[2] His intimates included the Austrian poet Felix Braun and the writers Josef Roth, Richard Friedenthal, Erwin Rieger, and Joseph Gregor. The latter's first collection of short stories and novel *Isabella von Orta* (1920) immediately caught Zweig's attention.

Many have testified to Zweig's ready dispensation of advice, encouragement, and even monetary assistance to struggling young writers. Reminiscing on Zweig's generosity of spirit, Gregor wrote:

> at supper in the Münchnerhof restaurant, a certain well-known gentleman, who I only knew by sight, suddenly jumped up and without any introduction crossed over to my table: "I read your novel this afternoon! What an unparalleled stroke of luck to meet you on the same day!" We shook hands like old friends and conversed together until midnight as if we had known each other for months, or, indeed, for years.[3]

That meeting took place in 1921.

Joseph Gregor (1888–1960)

Son of a Sudetenland architect, Gregor was born in 1888 in Czernowitz, the capital of Bukovina. His high school education included modern European languages, while private study of Latin and Greek stimulated a life-long passion for antiquity. From childhood, he expressed a keen interest in theater, and in 1907, like many of his contemporaries

---

[2] His cosmopolitanism is aptly summarized in the title of Donald Prater's 1982 Zweig biography *A European of Yesterday*. Donald A. Prater, *European of Yesterday: A Biography of Stefan Zweig* (Oxford: Clarendon Press, 1972).

[3] Letter of June 6, 1929; *Stefan Zweig – Joseph Gregor: Correspondence 1921–1938*, ed. Kenneth Birkin (Dunedin: University of Otago, 1991), 72.

(including his cousin, the painter Oskar Laske), he gravitated to Vienna, where he studied philology under Jakob Minor and philosophy under Friedrich Jodl at the university. He soon published on music-related subjects, and as a fledgling pianist, he supplemented his studies with private lessons from composer Robert Fuchs and musicologist Guido Adler. In 1910, he joined Felix Weingartner's drama production class at the Court Opera, where he met artists who had served under Mahler. Gregor soon came to the attention of Max Reinhardt, who invited him to assist in the production of Goethe's *Faust II* at the Deutsches Theater in Berlin where he met Alfred Roller and Edward Gordon Craig. In 1911, Gregor successfully submitted his doctoral dissertation entitled *The Development of Musical Expression* in Vienna and then taught musicology at the university in Czernowitz until 1914. He served as a volunteer during World War I, working, after demobilization, on his first volume of poetry (1921). His marriage to Sophie Eulenthal (1915) was dissolved in 1922, and he married Felizitas (Lizzy) Huber the following year.

Gregor succeeded Alexander von Weilen at the Österreichische Nationalbibliothek (Austrian National Library, ÖNB) in Vienna in November 1918. From 1918 to 1922 he was active in organizing the *Theatersammlung*, cataloguing material previously housed in the ÖNB Manuscript Collection (the complete Burgtheater archive) and initiating new acquisitions that saved many priceless documents from appropriation as "spoils of war." In 1922, he acquired the archives of the Theater an der Wien, Carltheater, Theater in der Josefstadt, and Deutsches Volkstheater, while former contacts such as Hugo Thimig, Edward Gordon Craig, Hugo Held, Hermann Bahr, and Anna Bahr-Mildenburg were persuaded to contribute to what was rapidly becoming a unique record of Austrian theater history.[4]

Styled "the great director" by Josef Mayerhöfer, one of his successors, Gregor was not only eminent as *Bibliothekar* but also active as a creative writer. His dramatic work focuses on Baroque theater, on the revival and reconstruction of important works of the past and thus the preservation of a living historical tradition. *Der Ackermann aus Böhmen*, based on material by Hofmannsthal (a tribute to the poet), was produced at the Schlosstheater Schönbrunn in 1929, while subsequent adaptations of Bidermann, Calderón, and Hafner were mounted at the Burgtheater in 1933, 1936, and 1947.

---

[4] In the words of Agnes Bleier Brody, the collection "allows 'theatre' to evolve out of the sum of the materialistic and spiritual ideals of its time"; see "Joseph Gregor: Zwanzig Jahre nach seinen Tode," *Richard Strauss-Blätter* 3 (1980): 9.

Gregor's reputation rests primarily upon his scholarly oeuvre. If not in the first rank as a creative writer, he nonetheless emerged as a powerful interpreter of the European theater history and tradition. As such, he attracted the attention of Strauss, not only through his numerous ÖNB exhibitions but also his encyclopedic *Weltgeschichte des Theaters* (1933), which the composer read and re-read with delight. He also contributed innumerable articles to magazines, journals, and newspapers on a wide range of theater- and music-related subjects. In 1924, the first volume of his 12-volume *Denkmäler des Theaters* (*Monuments of Theater*) appeared, a work that offered a comprehensive historical record of stage decoration and costume design from Baroque to modern times. *Weltgeschichte des Theaters* was succeeded by a long list of scholarly books from *Shakespeare* (1935) to *Alexander der Große* (1941); his Strauss biography *Der Meister der Oper* appeared in 1939. Emerging relatively unscathed from Nazi occupation (avoiding Party membership), his output continued with biographies of Hauptmann (1952) and Krauss (1953).

Gregor's ÖNB post lent authenticity to his work, and he was recognized as an outstanding authority in his field. Like Zweig and Hofmannsthal, he believed art had a unifying role to play in Europe, transcending linguistic and political boundaries. Thus, in 1932, he took his Goethe Exhibition to Paris – the first stage in a goodwill initiative that would not survive the electoral crisis in Germany, the fall of the Weimar Republic, and the rise of National Socialism. Gregor retired from the ÖNB in 1954. He had been on staff at the Reinhardt Seminary at Schönbrunn since 1929 and lectured at the University of Vienna since 1947. He lived his final years heaped with honors. Professor and *Wirklicher Hofrat*, he held Vienna's Medal of Honor and was awarded the Vienna Philharmonic's Nikolai medal in 1958. He died on October 12, 1960 at the age of 72.

Gregor's collaboration with Strauss was not the happiest. His scholarly, somewhat pedantic approach and Strauss's intransigence threatened at one stage to destroy the relationship altogether. Nonetheless, Gregor's contributions should not be underestimated; if *Die Liebe der Danae* is diffuse and symbolically problematic, *Friedenstag* and especially *Daphne* are, respectively, works of considerable power and beauty. Some important aspects of *Daphne* owe a debt to the conductor Krauss, Strauss's friend and favored interpreter: the composer sought his advice on Gregor's scripts, asking him to monitor progress and submit ideas. Krauss inspired the orchestral "transformation" at the expense of Gregor's choral concept at the conclusion of *Daphne*. Impressed, Strauss began to rely increasingly on Krauss's advice and later entrusted him with the libretto for *Capriccio* (1942).

Clemens Krauss (1893–1954)

Born of "theater stock," Krauss was raised in Vienna during the Mahler era. His great aunt Gabrielle had been a noted prima donna, while his mother Clementine (a ballet dancer) still graced the Court Opera stage. His musical education, which began in the Vienna Boys' Choir, was completed at the Akademie für Musik und darstellende Kunst (Imperial Academy of Music and Performing Arts). In 1912, he was engaged as assistant Répétiteur at the Brünn Stadttheater where in 1913 he conducted his first opera, Lortzing's *Zar und Zimmermann*. Appointments at sundry provincial houses followed, culminating in the post of first Kapellmeister in Vienna from 1922 to 1924 during the Strauss–Schalk regime. By this time, he had directed major works including *Der Rosenkavalier, Salome, Ariadne auf Naxos,* and *Elektra* – performances that considerably impressed the composer. This appointment constituted a milestone in Krauss's career; as a Strauss protégé, he adopted precepts learned from the master himself.

After Vienna, Krauss served from 1924 to 1929 as Intendant in Frankfurt with full control over a major opera house. Here, with a resident company contracted on a yearly basis, he confirmed allegiance to the "ensemble tradition" whereby assembled artists comprising the company remained together over a period of time. These years were marked by exemplary performances of repertoire classics, supported by the formidable Wallerstein/Sievert production/design team. Krauss exemplified the belief that an opera house chief, while keeping abreast of new developments, should not neglect the works of older masters. Nonetheless, within the context of a traditional format, he championed rarities such as Busoni's *Doktor Faust* in 1927, gave the world premiere of Hindemith's *Cardillac* (1928), and in 1930 mounted performances of Berg's *Wozzeck* in Vienna, which the composer himself regarded as definitive.

It is his association with Strauss, not least as co-librettist of *Capriccio,* that keeps his name alive. A developing relationship through the Frankfurt years led to the directorship of the Vienna State Opera (1929–34). In 1933, Krauss was entrusted with his first Strauss premiere, *Arabella,* in Dresden. This was followed by *Friedenstag* (of which he was dedicatee), *Capriccio* (Munich, 1938 and 1942, respectively), and *Die Liebe der Danae* (Salzburg dress rehearsal, 1944), together with its posthumous Salzburg premiere in 1952. By nature innovative, his sanctioning of rehearsal recordings at the Vienna State Opera was epoch-making. His advocacy of the "ensemble tradition" as opposed to the "star performer trend," however, fueled in-house political intrigue, and his steadfast refusal to sully music with internal politics drove him from Vienna, first to Berlin from 1935 to 1936, and then to Munich in 1937.

After the annulment in 1930 of his first marriage to Margarete Otmar, Krauss married the soprano Viorica Ursuleac in 1945. The Nazi Hermann Göring's patronage of Ursuleac leaves an open question: was Krauss's career after 1933 advanced by contact with members of the National Socialist hierarchy? Racially uninfluenced, especially where music was concerned, and never a Party member, he regularly intervened on behalf of embattled Jewish colleagues. While it is difficult to view an appointment so directly in Hitler's gift dispassionately, Krauss accepted the Munich post primarily on musical grounds. There, under wartime conditions over eight years, he initiated 48 new productions, gathering a team that included Sievert and Hartmann as well as the singers Hotter, von Milankovic, and Ursuleac. Added to his Munich responsibilities in 1939 was directorship of the Salzburg Mozarteum, where Ernst Märzendorfer, Otmar Suitner, Silvio Varviso, and Karl Münchinger benefited from his tutelage. A tireless orchestral trainer, he was exacting in rehearsal and, as surviving recordings testify, delivered un-idiosyncratic and authoritative performances that demonstrated outstanding musicianship. A thoroughgoing theater man, widely read, and culturally aware, his collaboration with Strauss was testimony to their common aesthetic and historical interests.

Krauss's ultimate goal was reinstatement as Staatsoperndirektor in Vienna. In April 1945, he drew up re-organizational plans for the State Opera, including a series of morale-boosting concerts with the Philharmonic, which he directed in virtually impossible conditions. His indictment by the allies in September 1945 ended such activity. Rehabilitated in April 1947, he returned to participate in the city's musical life, but political intrigue once again deprived him of the opportunity to lead it. He died during a concert tour in Mexico City on May 16, 1954, spared the 1955 inauguration of the rebuilt State Opera under Karl Böhm's directorship.

It was Zweig, Gregor, and Krauss who rescued Strauss from his post-Hofmannsthal depression, facilitating his operatic work into old age. Their efforts are particularly commendable since they presaged (e.g., in *Daphne*) the Indian Summer works of his later years. At the other end of the scale, Wolzogen's ribaldry, wit, and cabaret humor set the composer on a new post-Wagnerian path. *Feuersnot*, indeed, is the first of three single-act operas that ended with the first Hofmannsthal collaboration (*Elektra*).

CHAPTER 7

Stage Collaborators

Ryan M. Prendergast

I serve the eternal laws of the theater.

—La Roche, *Capriccio*

As a composer and conductor, Richard Strauss keenly understood that the success of a theatrical work depended on its dramatic presentation as much as its musical execution. He put this view bluntly to Hugo von Hofmannsthal following the premiere of *Die Frau ohne Schatten* in 1919: "The music simply cannot achieve everything by itself – and magic least of all – unless one were to write an oratorio and give up on the stage altogether! Yet the 'semistage' does not go far enough because without that which fully satisfies the eye the fantasy of the audience is impeded."[1] The varied demands of Strauss's stage works, fantastic or otherwise, meant that expert and trustworthy collaborators were essential for their realization. Detailed stage directions and staging manuals (*Regiebücher*) only went so far. Quality hinged on the human element, the alchemic component that makes the theater what it is.

Strauss actively stewarded his stage progeny throughout his life and in the process forged important theatrical relationships across a range of geographical and institutional networks. Most of his works premiered in either Germany or Austria at a subsidized court opera (*Hofoper*) or, after the collapse of the monarchies in 1918, a state opera (*Staatsoper*).[2] Hierarchy at the court and state operas often varied between principalities and cities. The structural framework, however, usually included an Intendant, the equivalent of a modern general manager; one or more stage

---

[1] Letter from Strauss to Hofmannsthal, March 8, 1920; in *A Working Friendship: The Correspondence Between Richard Strauss and Hugo von Hofmannsthal*, trans. Hanns Hammelmann and Ewald Osers (New York: Vienna House, 1974), 335. All translations are my own.

[2] Other labels included court theater (*Hoftheater*), state theater (*Staatstheater*), and opera theater (*Operntheater*). The occasional designation of national theater (*Nationaltheater*) was more a nominal gesture than an indicator of a truly "national" institution. The actual venues for these productions, furthermore, often had distinct names of their own.

directors (*Regisseure*); a principal stage director (*Oberregisseur*); various heads (*Vorstände*) of departments for technical direction, scenery, costumes, lighting, properties, and stage effects; stage managers (*Inspizienten*); and stagehands (*Bühnenarbeiter*).

Amid these networks, a key group of celebrated and frequent stage collaborators emerged. These included directors such as Max Reinhardt and Rudolf Hartmann, choreographers such as Heinrich Kröller and the duo of Pino and Pia Mlakar, and designers such as Alfred Roller and Ludwig Sievert. Several of these associations solidified in the cities Strauss favored for his premieres, namely Dresden and later Munich. Several would be reinforced under the auspices of the Salzburg Festival. There was also a shared historical dimension to these collaborations. Most of these artists, including Strauss, honed their crafts under the leading theatrical figures of the late nineteenth century.

Beginnings

The theatrical associations of Strauss's early professional life were auspicious. During his stint in Meiningen between 1885 and 1886, he observed the celebrated work of the court's theater ensemble, known as *Die Meininger*. The troupe was led by the famed "theater duke" Georg II of Saxe-Meiningen in conjunction with his wife Ellen Franz and Ludwig Chronegk, both actors of great experience. The revolutionary stage aesthetic of *Die Meininger* emphasized a well-trained and unified acting ensemble, the strict coordination and historical accuracy of design elements, and the creation of dynamic and painterly stage pictures. Equally influential for Strauss and many of his later collaborators were summers spent working at the Bayreuth Festival under the leadership of Wagner's second wife and widow Cosima. Key to her conservative aesthetic was stringent attention to productions that Wagner himself supervised, literal interpretations of stage directions, historicist décor, a highly schematized approach to stage movement, and a marked subordination of the music to the dramatic thrust of the work. These tenets came to the fore in her 1891 production of *Tannhäuser*, which made a strong impression on Strauss. Despite their eventual estrangement, he later ranked Cosima amongst the foremost directors of the age.[3]

---

[3] Letter from Strauss to Joseph Gregor, January 8, 1935; in *Richard Strauss und Joseph Gregor: Briefwechsel, 1935–1949*, ed. Roland Tenschert (Salzburg: Otto Müller, 1955), 16.

Cosima's example served Strauss well for his tenure in Weimar (1889–94), a famed theater court thanks to the legacies of Goethe, Schiller, and Liszt. There, Strauss maintained an engaging partnership with *Oberregisseur* Fritz Brandt. Part of the venerable dynasty of theater technicians and architects, Brandt assisted his father, the famous Darmstadt machinist Carl Brandt, with the technical direction of the first Bayreuth Festival and later realized the world premiere production of *Parsifal* in 1882, which Strauss attended. Cosima described Fritz Brandt as "a difficult character, but a capable man and a true talent."[4] Useful to Strauss was Brandt's "superhuman energy," an indispensable asset given the Weimar Court Theater's occasional financial and technical shortcomings. In addition to collaborating on the premiere of Humperdinck's *Hänsel und Gretel* in 1893, Brandt oversaw the stage direction and design for Strauss's first ventures as a Wagner conductor.

Leaving Weimar in 1894 for a second appointment in Munich (his first lasted from 1886 to 1889), Strauss renewed contact with one of the luminaries of the German-speaking stage, the actor and director Ernst von Possart. Possart arrived in the city in 1864, and by the 1890s, he had risen to the position of *Generalintendant* of Munich's court theaters where he staged both plays and operas. These included the famed private performances for King Ludwig II, a monarch with notoriously perspicacious demands of historical accuracy on the stage. In a bid against Bayreuth, Possart later spearheaded the construction of Munich's Prinzregententheater with a design that deliberately imitated Wagner's own theater. Though their institutional relationship was frosty from the beginning, Strauss and Possart collaborated fruitfully on the so-called Mozart "renaissance" productions at the Cuvilliés Theater in Munich's Residenz palace, which involved the technologically-advanced revolving stage of Carl Lautenschläger.

Directors

Despite his acute dramatic sensibility, Strauss notably did not aspire to be a director of his own works to the same extent as Wagner before him. The significance and definition of this position began to crystallize in the late nineteenth century, and Strauss experienced much of this firsthand in Meiningen. The training of directors, however, was not yet a separate sphere. Most rose to their positions from the ranks of actors and singers

---

[4] Letter from Cosima Wagner to Strauss, October 4, 1890; in *Cosima Wagner–Richard Strauss: Ein Briefwechsel*, ed. Franz Trenner (Tutzing: Hans Schneider, 1978), 64.

within ensembles. Such was the case with Ferdinand Wiedey, who staged the premiere of *Guntram* (1894) in Weimar while simultaneously portraying the role of Friedhold. Maximilian Moris, director of the premiere of *Feuersnot* in 1901, worked as a performer and director before he joined the Dresden ensemble in 1900. Willi Wirk, *Regisseur* for opera in Munich and a former buffo-tenor, staged the premiere of *Salome* (1905) as a guest in Dresden.

Of all of Strauss's directing collaborators, Georg Toller has attracted the most notoriety. At the start of his career, Toller worked as an actor and bass-baritone before joining the Dresden Court Theater in 1906. He also spent time in Bayreuth, serving as a stage manager for the 1904 revival of *Der Ring des Nibelungen*. While Toller competently staged the premiere of Strauss's *Elektra* (1909), the composer felt he was unsuited for the more complicated demands of *Der Rosenkavalier* (1911). In Strauss's view, to be merely satisfactory was a risky compromise for a momentous production: "The better is once more the enemy of the good."[5]

Strauss's partnership with Hofmannsthal marked a more critical approach to stage collaborators. Infamously exacting, Hofmannsthal took an active role in arranging and superintending production details with artists he too could trust. Thus, Max Reinhardt was engaged to assist with the premiere of *Der Rosenkavalier*. At the time, Reinhardt stood as the vanguard of the German stage. Following his apprentice years as an actor and director, Reinhardt assumed the leadership of the Deutsches Theater in Berlin in 1905. This quickly became the hub of a vast theatrical empire later branching to Munich, Vienna, and Salzburg. Reinhardt's work as a director embraced experiment and variety in both content and scale. Eschewing naturalism, he favored a heightened sense of fantasy and atmosphere, particularly in the virtuosic performances of his actors and his treatment of spectacle. His productions of Oscar Wilde's *Salomé* (1902/1903) and Hofmannsthal's *Elektra* (1903) were influential experiences for Strauss. Despite Reinhardt's celebrity, or perhaps because of it, the officials of the court operas considered him an interloper from the commercial theater. He was denied directing credit in Dresden for *Der Rosenkavalier* in favor of Toller and the premiere of the original *Ariadne auf Naxos* (1912) in Stuttgart was hampered by institutional protocols. His next collaboration with Strauss and Hofmannsthal, *Der Bürger als Edelmann* (1918), took place amid the more supportive environment of

---

[5] Letter from Strauss to Schuch, December 2, 1910; in *Richard Strauss–Ernst von Schuch: Ein Briefwechsel*, ed. Gabriella Hanke Knaus (Berlin: Henschel, 1999), 169.

the Deutsches Theater. While Reinhardt privately considered himself unmusical, his successful stagings of the works of Jacques Offenbach and Johann Strauss II evinced a genuine musical talent.

Venue influenced the choice of collaborators for the revised *Ariadne* (1916) in Vienna. The task of staging this premiere fell to Wilhelm von Wymetal, an actor who became *Oberregisseur* for the Vienna Court Opera after Mahler's departure in 1907. A determined critic of Mahler and Alfred Roller's artistic reforms, Wymetal proved to be, in Hofmannsthal's words, a "principally hellish troublemaker."[6] Following these difficulties, *Regisseur* Hans Breuer, a former tenor in the ensemble, worked closely with the librettist to stage *Die Frau ohne Schatten* in Vienna three years later. When Strauss resumed his association with the rechristened Saxon State Opera in Dresden in the 1920s, a rotating roster of directors helmed his remaining premieres: Alois Mora for *Intermezzo* (1924); Otto Erhardt for *Die ägyptische Helena* (1928); Josef Gielen for *Arabella* (1933) and *Die schweigsame Frau* (1935); and Max Hofmüller for *Daphne* (1938).

In this same period, Strauss developed a fruitful association with Lothar Wallerstein. Trained as a physician, Wallerstein began his career as a musical coach in Dresden before moving to directing. Following a productive period in Frankfurt in the 1920s with conductor Clemens Krauss and designer Ludwig Sievert, Wallerstein joined the staff of the Vienna State Opera where his Strauss stagings became a house specialty. He was a pivotal force for opera at the Salzburg Festival before the *Anschluss* in 1938 forced him and his wife to flee to the Netherlands and finally the United States. His last completed production was a double bill of *Salome* and Stravinsky's *Petrushka*.

When Munich became Strauss's artistic center in the final decade of his life, Rudolf Hartmann became his last great directing collaborator – the "Stanislavsky and Reinhardt of opera."[7] Under the triumvirate of Hartmann, Krauss, and Sievert, the Bavarian State Opera produced a series of model productions (*Musteraufführungen*) of the composer's works from 1937 to 1943. Strauss later claimed to his friend and biographer Willi Schuh that this atmosphere achieved what Hofmannsthal intended for Salzburg in terms of quality. This series included the premieres of *Friedenstag* (1938) and *Capriccio* (1942). While Hartmann's premiere

---

[6] Letter from Hofmannsthal to Strauss, early August 1916; in *A Working Friendship*, 261.
[7] Letter from Strauss to Hartmann, June 17, 1948; in *Richard Strauss – Rudolf Hartmann: Ein Briefwechsel mit Aufsätzen und Regiearbeiten*, ed. Roswitha Schlötterer (Tutzing: Hans Schneider, 1984), 80. The emphases are the composer's.

production of *Die Liebe der Danae* (1944) at the Salzburg Festival was reduced to a single dress rehearsal, he later staged the official public premiere there in 1952. Through Hartmann's later productions and writings, especially the essential volume *Richard Strauss: The Staging of His Operas and Ballets*, Strauss's theatrical imprimatur persisted into the second half of the twentieth century.

Choreographers

The centrality of dance to Strauss's stage works made his choreographic collaborators no less important than his stage directors. Many of these were singular interactions, such as that of August Berger, the Dresden ballet master who choreographed the first "Dance of the Seven Veils" for the *Salome* premiere, and Michel Fokine, who choreographed *Josephslegende* (1914) for the Ballets Russes. For a hybrid work like the first version of *Ariadne auf Naxos*, Hofmannsthal engaged famed dancer Grete Wiesenthal to choreograph and perform the roles of the Tailor's Journeyman and the Kitchen Boy for the Stuttgart premiere.

More sustained was Strauss's relationship with choreographer Heinrich Kröller, whom Strauss brought to Vienna to develop the ballet company at the State Opera. Kröller choreographed the world premieres of Strauss's *Ballettsoirée* (1923) and *Schlagobers* (1924) as well as a new production of *Josephslegende*. The duo of Pino and Pia Mlakar became integral to Strauss's later years in Munich. Students of famed choreographer and movement theorist Rudolf Laban, they first caught the composer's attention when they prepared an evening of Strauss ballets in Zurich in 1936. Brought to Munich by Krauss, they choreographed Beethoven's *Die Geschöpfe von Prometheus* as a curtain raiser for the premiere of *Friedenstag*, in addition to Strauss's last balletic work, *Verklungene Feste* (1941).

Designers

At the start of Strauss's career, the task of design at the court theaters was carried out by one or more of the heads of the production departments rather than independent designers. Scenery and costumes were constructed either in-house or by independent ateliers, but scarce resources frequently meant that materials were borrowed or cannibalized from other productions. This was the case with the Weimar premiere of *Guntram*. Strauss lamented to Hofmannsthal early in their partnership about the cheap level of décor afforded his stage works, yet this situation changed as they flourished in the repertoire. In Dresden, the scenery and costumes of most of Strauss's premieres were executed between Emil Rieck, Leonhard Fanto, and Adolf Mahnke. For the original *Ariadne* and *Der Bürger als Edelmann*, Ernst Stern was engaged from Max Reinhardt's company in Berlin.

As with Reinhardt, the engagement of Alfred Roller for the premieres of *Der Rosenkavalier* and *Die Frau ohne Schatten* signaled a conscious shift in Strauss's approach to design. An active member of the Vienna Secession and the director of the city's Kunstgewerbeschule (School for Applied Arts), Roller famously imbued his work for the stage with the sensitivies of contemporary visual art. Befitting the motto emblazoned on the Secession Building – "To the age its art, to art its freedom" – Roller and his contemporaries did not adhere to a strict style apart from rejecting the historicism espoused by the art academies. He became something of a legend through his aesthetic reforms as Director of Production (*Vorstand des Ausstattungswesens*) at the Court Opera under Mahler. Here, Roller expurgated the fripperies of the nineteenth-century illusionistic stage in favor of designs more critical in their use of line, color, space, light, and, above all, atmosphere. His duties for *Der Rosenkavalier* involved the design of scenery and costumes as well as the preparation of a detailed staging manual that would guide subsequent productions. Despite certain reservations over the premiere of *Die Frau ohne Schatten*, Strauss held the designer's work in high regard, especially the productions during their years in Vienna. Their final collaboration would be unveiled after Roller's death: a new "model" *Rosenkavalier* for Munich.

Designs for the remaining model productions in Munich alternated between Rochus Gliese and Ludwig Sievert, both long-time associates of Clemens Krauss. Gliese was a veteran of expressionist cinema in the interwar period, but his Strauss specialty in Munich was historical fancy, particularly with the premieres of *Verklungene Feste* and *Capriccio*. Sievert began his career as a set painter before moving on to design and direction. His expressionistic productions of Wagner and Hindemith in Frankfurt gained him significant attention, though his later efforts for Strauss in Munich showed more conservative restraint.

Salzburg – The Ultimate Collaboration?

As an institution, the Salzburg Festival remains Strauss's most expansive and impactful collaboration. Though his involvement in the early seasons was somewhat ambivalent, his stage works became and remain a core part of the Festival repertoire. Now spanning late July to late August every year, the Festival presents a diverse program of opera, theater, ballet, and concert offerings that reflect a truly catholic range of influences.

Attempts at the end of the nineteenth century to establish a sustainable festival in Mozart's birth city briefly flowered only to eventually wither. The effort gained a new impetus with the cultural and political collapse of the Austro-Hungarian Empire at the close of World War I. At the time of his death, Strauss was the last surviving member of the artistic advisory council of the Salzburg Festival Theater Society (Salzburger Festspielhaus-Gemeinde) which included Reinhardt, Roller, conductor Franz Schalk, and Hofmannsthal, who took up the ideological mission of the Festival with zeal. Of these five, Reinhardt had the strongest ties to the city. He had his first legitimate engagement as an actor in Salzburg in 1893 and later purchased the local palace of Leopoldskron as a residence. In a letter to the Austrian court theater administration in 1918, Reinhardt singled out the rich diversity of the empire's cultural heritage as clear grounds for establishing a festival in the city. Unlike the limited works presented at the Wagner festivals in Bayreuth, the repertoire in Salzburg would reflect a continuum of cultures and creators. In his own essays, Hofmannsthal similarly highlighted the uniqueness of the city (and Austria by extension) as a geographic and spiritual center for a fragmented Europe.

The early years of the Festival were precarious given the dire financial and political straits of the fledgling Austrian Republic coupled with the Festival's amorphous artistic vision as part restorative, part progressive. Fittingly, the only offering of the first Festival in 1920 was Hofmannsthal's *Jedermann*, newly staged by Reinhardt in front of Salzburg Cathedral. The year 1921 marked the first year of concerts at the Salzburg Mozarteum, and Strauss helped introduce opera to the program in 1922 with a Mozart series. While most of Reinhardt's theatrical productions (including works of Molière, Goethe, and Goldoni) were original to Salzburg, the early opera productions were transplants from Vienna designed by Roller and restaged by Breuer and Wallerstein. The first Strauss opera to appear at the Festival was the revised *Ariadne* in 1926. Apart from Hofmannsthal's Mozart-Molière pastiche *Die grüne Flöte*, Reinhardt staged no opera in Salzburg. A planned production of *Die Fledermaus* under his direction never came to fruition after he emigrated to the United States.

Despite friction with the Third Reich before and after the *Anschluss* in March 1938, the Festival continued nearly without interruption through the end of World War II. In the postwar period, Herbert von Karajan became the dominant force of the summer Festivals and the later satellite Whitsun and Easter Festivals. Born in the city, Karajan made his Festival debut in 1933, conducting the incidental music for Reinhardt's mammoth production of *Faust, Part I.* In his own time, Karajan pointedly shaped the scope and repertoire of the Festival as an artistic director in addition to conducting and staging his own productions. In 1960, the Great Festival Theater (Grosses Festspielhaus) designed by Clemens Holzmeister opened with a sumptuous new production of *Der Rosenkavalier* directed by Hartmann and conducted by Karajan. In this and other Festival venues like the Riding School (Felsenreitschule) and the Haus für Mozart, directors such as Götz Friedrich, Harry Kupfer, Christof Loy, Luc Bondy, and Romeo Castellucci have all staged works by Strauss.

The importance of Salzburg for Strauss's theatrical legacy is best illustrated by his insistence that *Die Liebe der Danae* should have its true public premiere at the Festival. Though this would be a posthumous event, the details preoccupied him in his final weeks when Hartmann paid a final visit to Garmisch-Partenkirchen. Even at the end, Strauss remained resolute. His animated discussion of *Danae* and other theatrical plans lightened the most somber of moments. After reflecting on the state of the German theaters, Strauss wistfully recalled the plea of Wagner's Isolde: "Greet the world for me" ("Grüss mir die Welt").[8] For all its ostensible resignation, Strauss's statement carried a clear invocation for the future. His work with his stage collaborators laid solid foundations for future generations of theater artists. Through them, Strauss's stage works continue to greet the world and its audiences as vibrantly as ever.

[8] Rudolf Hartmann, "The Last Visit with Richard Strauss," trans. Susan Gillespie, in *Richard Strauss and His World*, ed. Bryan Gilliam (Princeton: Princeton University Press, 1992), 300.

CHAPTER 8

Champions

Bryan Gilliam

No contemporary of Richard Strauss composed music of such quantity, breadth, and depth. As we look back on his long, prodigious career, it might all seem to be the inevitable product of superlative technique and talent – so much so, that we might overlook the family and friends who helped him as a child prodigy on the verge of notoriety. Strauss grew up, thanks to his mother's family (the Pschorrs), in economic comfort and an environment where active domestic music making was taken for granted. Especially influential were his uncles, Carl Hörberger and Anton Knötzinger, both serious amateur musicians for whom Strauss wrote several works, including the Romanze and Sonata for Cello and Piano. His aunt, Johanna, was a singer, and most of Strauss's earliest Lieder were written for her. The Pschorr family hosted regular musicales on Saturday nights and Sunday afternoons and sponsored the publications of numerous early works. Strauss's most famous opera, *Der Rosenkavalier*, was dedicated to the Pschorrs in thanks for all they did for him as a young composer who had now emerged as one of the greatest composers of tone poems, Lieder, and opera in Germany.

His father, Franz Strauss, was a great horn player, gifted conductor, talented composer, and his son's first mentor and champion – a domineering individual very much in the mold of Leopold Mozart. The family grew up in Munich, a metropolis of some 150,000 people, and father Strauss, first hornist of the Court Orchestra, knew most of the influential musicians and benefactors of the city who could be useful to his son, both as teachers and later as colleagues. Richard was a remarkable prodigy, playing the piano by age three and taking lessons a year later. Franz, much like Abraham Mendelssohn, wanted his son to have a liberal arts education, emphasizing literature, history, Greek, and Latin. The conservatory was out of the question; all music education was done on the side. August Tombo, first harpist in the orchestra, taught him piano when he was four; Benno Walter, concertmaster of the orchestra, taught him violin at age eight; and Friedrich Wilhelm Meyer offered composition lessons to Richard when he was 11.

Hans von Bülow was Strauss's first major champion beyond his father. As one of Germany's leading conductors and pianists, he served in several prestigious posts, but, for Strauss, his most important appointment was as Generalmusikdirektor of the Meiningen Court Orchestra (1880–85) where Strauss assisted him in his final year. Strauss's duties were to conduct the female choir and to serve as von Bülow's personal musical assistant, which included attending all of his orchestral rehearsals. His strict and exacting approach to rehearsing and his elasticity in tempi made a huge impression on Strauss. Their published correspondence (1883–93) is rich in information concerning Strauss's evolving opinions on musical form and aesthetics. In a letter dated August 24, 1888, young Strauss declared that it was a "legitimate artistic method to create a correspondingly new form for every new subject" and that "formalistic, Hanslickian music-making will no longer be possible."[1]

The relationship with Bülow might never have come about were it not for another important champion, Eugen Spitzweg, who headed the Munich-based publishing company Joseph Aibl. Spitzweg was a friend of Bülow and, seeing great promise in the young composer, sent him Strauss's Op. 3, Five Piano Pieces, which Bülow rejected as evidence of talent but not brilliance; yet the loyal, farsighted Spitzweg published them anyway. He later sent Bülow the score to Strauss's Op. 7 Serenade (1881), but this time the conductor was quite impressed: he not only immediately programmed it but also commissioned Strauss for another woodwind piece (the Op. 13 Suite for Winds of 1884). Spitzweg published nearly all of his early works as well as the tone poems through *Don Quixote* (1897).

The Serenade premiered in Dresden under the baton of Franz Wüllner, another early Strauss champion. A noted conductor and composer, he was also the father of Ludwig Wüllner, a baritone who sang under Strauss's baton numerous times. Franz Wüllner came to Munich in 1865 and conducted the Royal Chapel Choir (Königliche Vokalkapelle). Against the wishes of Wagner, Ludwig II of Bavaria wanted a Munich premiere for *Das Rheingold* (1869) and *Die Walküre* (1870). As Bülow had already left Munich and other conductors refused to deny Wagner's wishes, it fell on young Wüllner to conduct the premieres. It was a great success, and Wüllner was named First Kapellmeister and Director of the Academy

[1] *Hans von Bülow–Richard Strauss: Correspondence*, ed. Willi Schuh and Franz Trenner, trans. Anthony Gishford (London: Boosey and Hawkes, 1953), 82–83.

Concerts with the Bavarian Court Orchestra. There, he developed a friendship with Franz Strauss and his son.

Both Wüllner and Bülow maintained friendships with Brahms and Wagner, which was unusual for the time, and this had a lasting effect on Strauss in the 1880s. In 1884, Wüllner established the Gürzenich concerts in Cologne, which Strauss often attended, and he was on hand for the premiere of the choral work *Wandrers Sturmlied*, which Strauss conducted in Cologne and dedicated to Wüllner in 1887. The Cologne Gürzenich concerts saw the premieres of all Strauss tone poems save those few conducted by the composer himself. Wüllner also conducted the first German performance of the Second Symphony in F Minor in 1885 and premiered the Violin Concerto in 1890.

What Wüllner had done for Strauss in the realm of instrumental and symphonic music could be said for Ernst von Schuch with the operatic stage. Born in 1846 in Graz, Schuch did youthful stints in Basel, Graz, Prague, and Würzburg, among others, before coming at age twenty-six to Dresden, where he remained until his death in 1914. In 1889, he was appointed Generalmusikdirektor, which put him in full charge of the Dresden Court Opera. Schuch loyally directed the house through its rebuilding in 1878 and brought the opera to international fame, in no small part through his association with Strauss. The two probably met in 1882, when Schuch spent his first year in Dresden with Wüllner, also at the helm, conducting Strauss's Op. 7 Wind Serenade. By the turn of the century, the court orchestra had become one of the great pit orchestras in Germany. Certainly under the recent leadership of the late Giuseppe Sinopoli and Christian Thielemann, it remains so today.

When Strauss later served as music director in Berlin, censorship difficulties in that city led him to entrust the premiere of *Feuersnot* (1901) to Schuch. The opera proved difficult to perform and stage, but Strauss was so pleased with the result that he entrusted Schuch with the premieres of each subsequent opera through *Der Rosenkavalier* (1911). He recognized in Schuch precisely what he saw in Bülow: strict attention to detail and a marvelous sense of tempo elasticity. By the turn of the century, Strauss was determined to become Germany's leading opera composer, and the faith he put in Schuch helped him achieve his ambition. In six years, with the Dresden premieres of *Salome*, *Elektra*, and *Der Rosenkavalier*, Strauss emerged not only as Germany's major composer but also as a leading figure in opera houses across Europe and the United States. In a eulogy following Schuch's death in 1914, Strauss referred to him as his soulmate, praising his "courage, loyalty, and musical expertise" and then conducted his own *Tod und Verklärung.*[2]

Another important early twentieth-century champion was Gustav Mahler. Their relationship was unique in many ways; both were great composer-conductors, Wagnerians, Mozartians, husbands of musical wives, Vienna opera directors, and made successful visits to the United States. Both were also obsessed with Bülow's conducting (his spontaneous approach to tempi). Mahler stood up for Strauss and his *Guntram* (1893) during a time when others doubted the initial operatic endeavor, and he even tried to get a Hamburg premiere of it despite local anti-Straussian politics. Mahler later delighted in programming *Guntram* excerpts in Vienna and New York.

If *Tristan* is about redemption through love, *Feuersnot* is about redemption through sex, and Berlin and Vienna at first would not have it. But Mahler attended the Dresden premiere (1901) and fought a protracted and successful battle with the Vienna Court Opera so that by January 27, 1902, he conducted its premiere. Strauss was terribly moved and sent his "heartfelt thanks for the incomparably beautiful rendition you gave of my work," and, despite the derisive critics, Mahler mounted a new production in 1905, and he frequently conducted *Feuersnot* excerpts as he did with *Guntram.*[3]

Rising anti-Semitism, especially an ugly campaign in the press, forced Mahler to resign his Vienna position, and he was replaced by Strauss's nemesis, the conductor-composer Felix Weingartner from 1908 to 1911, and then the arts administrator Hans Gregor from 1911 to 1918. In 1918, an organized campaign to lure Strauss from Berlin (where his contract had not been renewed) was underway. There was significant opposition in parts of the press egged on by Gregor and others; they suggested that the opera would become merely a venue for Strauss's own works. Strauss hesitated until 1919, when Viennese champions posted an open telegram entreating the composer to come to the State Opera. Among the signees were such luminaries as Hugo von Hofmannsthal, Stefan Zweig, Alma Mahler-Gropius, Adolf Loos, Alfred Schnitzler, and Alfred Roller.

In Vienna, Strauss had some of the world's finest singers at his disposal, most of whom were ardent Strauss advocates: Maria Jeritza, Lotte Lehman,

[2] Friedrich von Schuch, *Richard Strauss, Ernst von Schuch und Dresdens Oper* (Leipzig: Breitkopf und Härtel, 1953), 121.
[3] *Gustav Mahler–Richard Strauss: Correspondence 1888–1911*, ed., Herta Blaukopf, trans. Edmund Jephcott (Chicago: University of Chicago Press, 1984), 66.

Richard Mayr, Anna Bahr-Mildenburg, Marie Gutheil-Schoder, and Elisabeth Schumann, among others. Jeritza joined the Court Opera in 1912 and remained a favorite during Strauss's tenure as codirector of the Vienna State Opera (with Franz Schalk) from 1919 to 1924. As the predominant singing actress of her day, she particularly impressed Strauss and Hofmannsthal as Elektra and the Marschallin, and she premiered both Ariadnes in the first performances of the two versions of the opera (Stuttgart, 1912, and Vienna, 1916). Her premiere as the Empress in *Die Frau ohne Schatten* (Vienna, 1919) was hailed by the press. The title role in *Die ägyptische Helena* (1928) was written with her in mind, but Dresden would not pay her high fee; she later sang the role at the Metropolitan Opera premiere in November 1928, five months after Dresden. Strauss composed what is technically his last song for her ("Malven" or "Mallows"): "To the beloved Maria, here this last rose."

Lotte Lehmann, another star associated with the Vienna opera, also participated in the Vienna premiere of *Die Frau ohne Schatten* of 1919, as the Dyer's wife. Indeed, Strauss had her in mind when he composed the role, having been most impressed with her as the Composer in the Vienna premiere of the second version of *Ariadne auf Naxos* (1916). She sang to great acclaim, and Strauss was excited enough to have her premiere the central role of Christine (alias Pauline Strauss) for his next opera, *Intermezzo* (1924), his autobiographical "opera domestica." Lehmann would become best known for her highly-nuanced interpretations of the Marschallin and, in retirement, even directed a production of *Der Rosen-kavalier* in 1962 for the Metropolitan Opera.

Elisabeth Schumann, the third star soprano at the Vienna opera from 1919 to 1938, accompanied Strauss during his second tour of North America; the first tour had featured the composer's wife in 1904, when she was near the end of her career. Next to his wife, Strauss saw Schumann as one of the finest interpreters of his Lieder, and she considered the tour one of the great artistic experiences of her life.[4] Another great singer-actor of Strauss was Richard Mayr, whom Strauss and Hofmannsthal hoped would premiere the role of Baron Ochs for the Dresden premiere of *Der Rosenkavalier* in January 1911. Prohibited by his contract with Vienna, however, Mayr was unavailable, but he did sing the Baron that April in Vienna. The role launched his career to world fame after performing Ochs in London and New York. He also participated in the Vienna premiere of *Die Frau ohne Schatten* in the role of Barak.

---

[4] Schumann wrote a lengthy memoir of the trip, available in typescript at the Richard-Strauss-Archiv.

Though their relationship ended in animosity, Franz Schalk, Strauss's codirector in Vienna from 1919 to 1924, was a champion of Strauss, having conducted the Vienna *Rosenkavalier* premiere, as well as the world premiere of the revised *Ariadne auf Naxos* in October 1916. Born in 1863 and a student of Anton Bruckner, Schalk welcomed Strauss to Vienna with genuine friendship, but the artistic–administrative relationship was doomed to fail, for Strauss had little interest in the daily administrative matters and spent more than half the year away from Vienna, though he wanted authority over all final artistic decisions. In an age where most long-distance negotiating was done by mail, Schalk resented undertaking daily administrative work in Vienna while Strauss basked in the international spotlight, often from afar. It became increasingly difficult for Schalk to conduct business in Vienna with the composer in Garmisch or on tour. Strauss ultimately resigned his post in 1924.

That year was the composer's 60th birthday, and it saw the completion of a villa in Vienna, along the eastern edge of the Belvedere. The mansion itself was built at his own expense with funds from his American tour and the financial support of his daughter-in-law's (Alice's) father, Emanuel Grab, an affluent Viennese banker originally from Prague, and a mutual friend, the conductor Leo Blech, who conducted Strauss operas (to the composer's great satisfaction) at the Berlin State Opera Unter den Linden from 1906 to 1936. Because of his close friendship with Strauss, he was – as a Jew – able to stay in Nazi Germany for an unusual amount of time, finally emigrating to Riga in 1941.

This "second Viennese period" produced a number of new, remarkable Strauss productions with the help of another champion, Lothar Wallerstein, who served as State Opera Regisseur and unofficial advisor on dramaturgical issues in the libretti after Hofmannsthal's death (1929); he also collaborated on a revised version of Mozart's *Idomeneo* in 1931, the 150th anniversary of the opera's premiere. Wallerstein provided the German translated text and Strauss recomposed the recitatives, adding some new orchestral music as well. After the *Anschluss* of Austria in 1938, Wallerstein, a Jew, emigrated with a lengthy affidavit by Strauss in hand.[5]

By the 1930s, the issue was less championship among conductors but rather a competition for his favor, and that spirit of competitiveness was especially pronounced among Hans Knappertsbusch, Karl Böhm, and Clemens Krauss. Knappertsbusch, well known as the leading Wagnerian

---

[5] This document is in private hands in Winston-Salem, NC. I am grateful to the party who shared it with me.

conductor of his day, having worked with Siegfried Wagner and Hans
Richter in Bayreuth, was also a renowned Straussian and had become
director of the Munich opera in 1922. It was during this time that he
developed a friendship with Strauss, though he never premiered any stage
works by the composer. During this period, Fritz Busch, as music director
of the Dresden Staatskapelle, premiered two operas: *Intermezzo* (1924) and
Die ägyptische Helena (1928). Though the two were not close friends,
Strauss greatly admired Busch's work and codedicated to him his next
opera, *Arabella* (1933). Busch was scheduled to conduct the premiere in
1933 but was dismissed from Dresden because of his aversion to the new
National Socialist regime; he emigrated in protest in 1934, and Karl Böhm
replaced him. After Busch left, Knappertsbusch (who was to conduct the
Munich *Arabella* premiere) expected that he would take over the Dresden
first performance, but Strauss gave the baton to Krauss. Böhm, who was to
premiere a double bill of *Friedenstag* and *Daphne* in Dresden (October 15,
1938) learned, to his disappointment, that Krauss had talked Strauss into
allowing *Friedenstag* to be premiered separately on July 24, 1938, as part of
the annual Munich Opera Festival.[6]

Knappertsbusch never forgot the slight. While their friendship suffered,
the younger Böhm, who got to conduct two premieres (*Die schweigsame
Frau* and *Daphne*), remained an enthusiastic Strauss advocate until his
death in 1981. Indeed, the extensive 80th birthday festival (June 1944) in
Vienna featured Böhm as its music director. His landmark recording
(1956) of *Die Frau ohne Schatten* and its first performance in New York
for the opening of the Metropolitan Opera in Lincoln Center (1966)
secured the opera as a work of international stature after World War II.

In 1937, Krauss became music director of the Munich State Opera, a
move that pleased Strauss immensely, for there, not far from his home in
Garmisch, Krauss and his team of Ludwig Sievert (stage designer) and
Rudolf Hartmann (stage director) worked tirelessly in conjunction with
the composer to stage what Strauss deemed *Musteraufführungen* or "model
productions." Beyond the highly acclaimed newly-staged productions such
as *Arabella* and *Die Frau ohne Schatten* (for Strauss's 75th birthday), Krauss
conducted three opera premieres: *Friedenstag*, *Capriccio*, and *Die Liebe der
Danae*.[7]

---

[6] It was paired with Strauss and Hofmannsthal's version of Beethoven's *Creatures of Prometheus*.
[7] The *Danae* performance at the Salzburg Festival was not the premiere but a dress rehearsal for a
production that never took place. The Nazis had closed all theaters with Goebbels's declaration of
total war following the July 1944 assassination attempt on Hitler. The world premiere, conducted by
Krauss, did not occur until the 1952 Salzburg Festival.

This "team" was extended to singers as well, namely Viorica Ursuleac, Krauss's wife and Strauss's "most faithful of the faithful" sopranos. She not only premiered Arabella in Dresden but also the leading soprano roles for the three other premieres just mentioned. Beyond being a member of the Straussian team in Munich, Krauss stood out as the composer's most trusted companion from the mid-1930s to the end of Strauss's life. During moments of impasse between Strauss and Joseph Gregor, who was not a librettist at the level of his predecessors Hofmannsthal and Zweig, the composer sought advice from Krauss with great success. Gregor's efforts to write the libretto for *Capriccio* disappointed Strauss. In this instance, Krauss became more than an advisor: the composer took Gregor off the project and took on Krauss as his collaborator in this co-authored libretto.

This chapter would not be complete without mention of an important and lifelong non-German champion, namely Sir Thomas Beecham. Two years before Strauss's death in 1949, the composer made a final concert tour to London, arranged in part by Beecham. Strauss conducted a total of three concerts at the Albert Hall, including some tone poems and the *Burleske* for piano and orchestra. The highlight, however, was two broadcast performances of *Elektra* under Beecham at the BBC Maida Vale studio, with Strauss in attendance for the first. It was not the first time that Strauss attended a Beecham *Elektra*. On March 12, 1910, the composer visited London for the city's premiere of the opera under Beecham, who also conducted the English premieres of *Feuersnot* (July 9, 1910), *Salome* (December 8, 1910), *Der Rosenkavalier* (January 29, 1913), and the original version of *Ariadne auf Naxos* (June 27, 1913).

After his death, Strauss was no longer in need of champions as a tone poet and the composer of *Salome, Elektra, Der Rosenkavalier, Ariadne auf Naxos*, the *Metamorphosen*, and numerous Lieder including the so-called *Vier letzte Lieder* (*Four Last Songs*).[8] But the later operas, especially outside Germany, needed their advocates, and one of the most important such promoters was John Crosby, founder and music director (until 2000) of the Santa Fe Opera Festival. Excluding the hiatus from 1969 to 1977, Crosby conducted Strauss operas annually from Santa Fe's founding in 1957, when he spearheaded the first professional American performance of *Capriccio*. Subsequent productions included *Intermezzo, Die ägyptische Helena, Arabella, Die schweigsame Frau, Friedenstag, Daphne*, and *Die Liebe*

---

[8] This title was assigned by his publisher, Boosey and Hawkes.

der Danae.[9] Indeed, Crosby conducted 171 performances of Strauss's operas while at Santa Fe, encompassing all of the operas except *Guntram* and *Die Frau ohne Schatten.*

In the studio, Rudolf Kempe recorded the entire catalog of orchestral works with the Dresden Staatskapelle in the late 1960s and 1970s, as did Georg Solti over the same period with his stunning *Salome, Elektra,* and *Der Rosenkavalier.*[10] Another project, tinged with tragedy, was a plan by Strauss's last great champion, Giuseppe Sinopoli, to record the entire cycle of Strauss operas. This was to feature the Dresden Staatskapelle and the State Opera under the musical direction of Sinopoli, who died while conducting *Aïda* in Berlin in 2001. His recordings of *Elektra, Ariadne auf Naxos, Die Frau ohne Schatten,* and *Friedenstag* were released a year after his death in 2001.

[9] Crosby conducted the second American performance of the early *Feuersnot* in 1985 at the Manhattan School of Music, with a subsequent performance in Santa Fe in 1988.
[10] Solti had already recorded a studio *Arabella* for Decca in 1957.

PART II

Career Stations

CHAPTER 9

Munich and Garmisch

Sebastian Bolz

The cities of Munich and Garmisch frame Richard Strauss's life as the places of his birth and death. Located in southeast Germany, the two are linked not only through their association with Strauss but also share a history of social and cultural intersections. This chapter explores these two cities vis-à-vis Strauss, focusing on the decades during which the composer worked and resided in their cultural milieus.

Munich

Richard Strauss's birth in 1864 coincided with a colorful phase in Munich's history. King Ludwig II ascended the Bavarian throne that year, and his initial ambitions bred growing resentment between the crown, constitutional powers, and public opinion. During this period, the quarrels that surrounded Wagner's residence in 1864–65 and the world premieres of both *Tristan* and *Meistersinger* are perhaps the topics that have been covered in greatest detail by music historians. Wagner's impact on the city's musical culture was deep; while plans for an opera house would not develop into the Prinzregententheater until 1901, the conservatory saw a restructuring fueled by Wagner's 1865 essay *Bericht an Seine Majestät den König Ludwig II. von Bayern über eine in München zu errichtende deutsche Musikschule* (*Report to His Majesty King Ludwig II of Bavaria on a German Music School to be Established in Munich*) initially emphasizing vocal education and opera. By the time Franz Strauss was appointed professor in 1870, Wagner's influence had already declined due to the departure of Hans von Bülow. However, ties between the conservatory and the Court Opera remained strong as Karl von Perfall presided over both.[1]

---

[1] For an overview, see Sebastian Bolz and Hartmut Schick, eds., *Richard Wagner in München* (Munich: Allitera, 2015); and Stephan Schmitt, ed., *Geschichte der Hochschule für Musik und Theater München von den Anfängen bis 1945* (Tutzing: Schneider, 2005).

Apart from professional musical practice, Munich's bustling scene of amateur orchestras and music groups provided the Strauss family with an environment in which they carried out various musical roles. Franz Strauss served as conductor for the Harbni Orchestra and the Wilde Gung'l, for which his son played violin. The father's ensembles premiered young Richard's early compositions from time to time, while more adolescent works entered the professional sphere under the baton of Hermann Levi. Strauss and Levi were later colleagues when the former became third Kapellmeister at the Court Theater in 1886, the year of Ludwig II's death and the beginning of the "Prinzregentenzeit" (the period of Prince Regent Luitpold).

With a population that swelled from 100,000 inhabitants in the early 1850s to half a million by 1900, Munich was one of the largest cities in the German Reich – surpassed by Berlin (at about four times the size) as well as Hamburg and Breslau. The Strausses resided modestly and were probably subsidized by Josephine Strauss's family, the wealthy Pschorr dynasty. By the time Richard was born, and again some years later, they lived in the Altstadt (the historic district) in an area shaped by juxtapositions and a heterogeneous social structure. Not far from the Residenz complex with the opera and next to the Alte Akademie, home of the Bavarian Academy of Arts and Sciences, the Strauss apartment also neighbored a cluster of breweries and beer-halls that saw a profound remodeling in the latter decades of the nineteenth century. Thus, not only vital cultural venues, such as the Court Opera and other performance spaces, but also cafés and beer cellars were close by and well-frequented.[2]

In contrast to this lively cultural scene, the city owed its enduring reputation as a "rural metropolis" to a traditional economic profile. In Munich, the fin-de-siècle tendencies remained in tension with conservatism, sometimes parochialism and urbanity, which meant a coexistence of elitism and subculture. It is precisely this environment of megalomaniac coziness that *Feuersnot* so stridently mocks. The opera testifies not only to the composer's involvement with the mindset of his hometown but also his occupation with a cultural landscape to which *Salome* and *Elektra* later contributed.

Despite the clichés of traditionalism, one distinctive aspect of Munich around 1900 was its scope of cultural institutions. Strauss was mostly connected to official establishments; by the time of his second term as conductor at the Court Opera in the 1890s, the house was a prestigious

---

[2] Friederike Kaiser, ed., *Wirtshäuser in München um 1900* (Munich: Buchendorfer, 1997).

venue under the batons of Hermann Levi and Felix Mottl, two of the era's most distinguished conductors. Admittedly, most of the works that premiered during the years of Strauss's enculturation as an opera conductor did not leave permanent marks: Zemlinsky's *Sarema* failed to achieve lasting success as did the first version of Humperdinck's *Königskinder* and the comic operas of Wolf-Ferrari. Likewise, many of the pieces that had dominated the repertoire soon disappeared from the stages, such as the works of Ignaz Brüll or Wilhelm Kienzl. Strauss himself was occupied with Italian and French repertoire, which made up a considerable portion of the schedule. With the opening of the Prinzregententheater, Munich eventually confirmed its authoritative standing as a major venue for the performance of Wagner's works. But while the Court Theater strengthened its position as a site of theatrical modernity with the installation of electrical lights in 1885, its organizational background demonstrated a certain provincial belligerence in the continuing quarrels over the resignation of its director Karl von Perfall in 1894, the year Strauss returned to the city.

Apart from the opera (and partially connected to it), fin-de-siècle Munich maintained prestigious concert venues such as the Odeon, home to the Akademiekonzerte over which Strauss temporarily presided, and the Kaimsaal. Founded in 1893, the Kaim Orchestra soon attained international fame under Felix Weingartner and, from 1901 to 1911, premiered three of Mahler's symphonies. Alongside these institutions that presented both canonic and the latest repertoire, a concert-goer in 1890s Munich witnessed a Mozart "renaissance" (in which Strauss and more so Levi played a crucial part), the rise of an early music movement, and also a lively coffee house culture with music at its core. The local *Elf Scharfrichter* cabaret, the first of its kind in Germany, soon shared common ground with the Berlin *Überbrettl*, the latter founded by *Feuersnot* librettist Ernst von Wolzogen. Equally vibrant was the theatrical scene; the new Künstlertheater went from Georg Fuchs's community drama to Reinhardt's mass stagings (another connection with Berlin) to Kandinsky's experimentalism. Simultaneously, scandals surrounded Frank Wedekind, the playwright-poet who celebrated the turn of the century in prison thanks to a local censorship that would also object to *Feuersnot*.[3]

Munich's cultural milieu attracted a diverse community of artists, writers, and bohemians. It seems characteristic of this setting that so many

---

[3] Tobias Grill, *Die Rezeption der Alten Musik in München zwischen ca. 1880 und 1930* (University of Munich, 2007); Judith Kemp, "*Ein winzig Bild vom großen Leben*" (Munich: Allitera, 2017).

of its (self-)descriptions tumble ironically between the ecstatic, the abyss, and the beery: The pseudo-apocalyptic fantasies in the "heat lightning" of Thomas Mann's *Gladius Dei* and the labels of "Wahnmoching" (Franziska zu Reventlow) and "Schwabylon," a portmanteau built from the quartier of Schwabing and the infamous Babylon, carry these overtones, just as the satirical journal *Simplicissimus* both expressed and ridiculed an ambiguity with modernism. The "age of nervousness" that has become almost synonymous with the period around 1900 might not appear as prominent in Munich as it was in metropolises of modernity such as Berlin and Vienna – albeit complaints about a city's impositions were not lacking, as demonstrated by Theodor Lessing's 1908 "polemic against the sounds of our life" *Der Lärm*. Munich was also home to Wilhelm Diefenbach's Lebensreform colony, Michael Georg Conrad's Modern Life Society (and his influential journal *Die Gesellschaft*), Anita Augspurg's and Ika Freudenberg's Society for the Promotion of Women's Intellectual Interests, and ideologically complex groups such as the Kosmiker and the George Circle. It also hosted the salons of Elsa and Max Bernstein and Elsa and Hugo Bruckmann (that would later welcome guests like Houston Stewart Chamberlain and Adolf Hitler), which were manifestations of a bourgeois culture.

This milieu enabled *l'art pour l'art* artists such as Stefan George and fostered the early career of Thomas Mann, who began his writing in Munich while working a day job as an insurance employee. Central Munich entertained a dense literary scene in Schwabing's cafés and pubs, where writers and theater artists of the most varied backgrounds, generations, and aspirations met, including the multifaceted Otto Julius Bierbaum (editor of several influential journals), the novelist Carry Brachvogel (who contributed to women artists' rights), the writer Lion Feuchtwanger (who later located the story of his *Erfolg* in Munich), and the satirist Oscar Panizza. Schwabing was the birthplace of the famous comic duo Karl Valentin and Liesl Karlstadt as well as the venue for the regional writers Ludwig Thoma and Ludwig Ganghofer. The latter befriended the young poet Rainer Maria Rilke, who had come to Munich as a student. Here Rilke made the acquaintance of Lou Andreas-Salomé, the intellectual who had published literary works and a study of her friend Friedrich Nietzsche. The infamous bohemian Franziska zu Reventlow later memorialized this ambience in her novel *Herrn Dames Aufzeichnung*, as did Max Halbe and Georg Fuchs. Strauss repeatedly turned to literary Munich in choosing texts for his songs, setting to music verses not only by contemporaries like Bierbaum and Morgenstern, but also by slightly older poets who had belonged to the Munich sphere, like Adolf Friedrich Schack and Detlev von Liliencron.[4]

Similar contrasts evolved in a musical culture with such different composers as Max von Schillings and Josef Rheinberger, observed by a confrontational lineup of erudite critics. Rudolf Louis, who coauthored a *Harmonielehre* with Strauss's friend Ludwig Thuille, and Alexander Dillmann, lead opera critic of the *Münchner Neueste Nachrichten*, tended to champion the "New Germans," while the *Allgemeine Zeitung* was more critical of them. Other reviewers included Arthur Seidl, Alfred Einstein, Theodor Kroyer, Edgar Istel, and Eugen Schmitz – all academically trained. The intellectual climate proved conducive to the institutionalization of musicology: Adolf Sandberger became the first "professor" at the university in 1900.

Journals like *Der Kunstwart* and *Die Jugend*, the latter a leading proponent of Jugendstil that also published some of Strauss's songs, backed a community of influential artists. Within the Secession (to whose 1897 exposition Strauss contributed a symphonic choral piece), the Künstlergenossenschaft, and the Dachau-based Künstlerkolonie, the city's art scene brought together painters like Münter, Kandinsky, Marc, Kubin (all involved with the Blaue Reiter), Hölzel, and Stuck. Some of the artists of fin-de-siècle Munich were involved with Strauss during their respective careers. The composer had already made the acquaintance of Franz von Lenbach during his stay in Italy in 1886, for instance. Lovis Corinth illustrated the first edition of the *Elektra* vocal score in 1908, and Max Liebermann famously portrayed Strauss a decade later. This rich artistic sphere soon scattered to Berlin and other cities. In architecture, the era witnessed landmark buildings that still shape the city today: Gabriel von Seidl's Lenbachhaus, the Villa Stuck, the Bayerisches Nationalmuseum, the Prinzregententheater, the Seidlvilla, and the Hofbräuhaus in its current form.

While Munich established a week dedicated to Strauss's works in 1910 (as did Stuttgart and Dresden around the same time), the composer treated his hometown mostly as a stopover on his way to Garmisch after the World War I. He rented a small apartment near the Englischer Garten between 1917 and 1919, but mostly stayed at the prestigious Vier Jahreszeiten hotel after 1914. In doing so, he missed the city becoming a

---

[4] See Waldemar Fromm, Manfred Knedlik, and Marcel Schellong, eds., *Literaturgeschichte Münchens* (Regensburg: Pustet, 2019); and Ingvild Richardsen, ed., *Evas Töchter. Münchner Schriftstellerinnen und die moderne Frauenbewegung 1894–1933* (Munich: Volk, 2018).

center of National Socialist politics. As a consequence of Munich's prominent role, allied airstrikes in 1943 and 1944 destroyed 90 percent of the
city's historic district and thus most of the buildings that had been
perceived as central to its identity. The Nationaltheater (home of the State
Opera), the Odeon (the former prime concert venue and location of the
Akademie der Tonkunst), the Konzerthalle (the former Kaimsaal), and
the Residenz were demolished, as were the homes of around 300,000
people. As these institutions loomed large in Strauss's musical past, his
1938–39 composition *München: ein Gelegenheitswalzer* has been regarded
as a document of grief.[5] With its references to *Feuersnot* and its subtitle
reformulated in the 1945 revision to *Ein Gedächtniswalzer*, the work
contained an additional "In Memoriam" section and serves as a reflection
on Munich's prime around 1900 and its later extinction.

　　Following Strauss's funeral at Munich's Ostfriedhof, the city continued
to dedicate central aspects of its musical life to Richard Strauss. After its
rebuilding, the Bavarian State Opera re-opened in 1963 with *Die Frau
ohne Schatten* (whose 1919 premiere had been moved from Munich to
Vienna) in a private performance, while the public opening presented
Meistersinger. At the same time, the city's second professional music school
was renamed Richard-Strauss-Konservatorium until its integration into
the Hochschule für Musik und Theater in 2008. And while Strauss
was often viewed skeptically as an object of musicological study, the
German-speaking music(ological) community also promoted Strauss
research: in 1976, Franz Trenner, Alfons Ott, and Wolfgang Sawallisch
founded the Richard-Strauss-Gesellschaft, for instance. A year later, the
society began to publish Straussiana and established a Strauss-Institut (later
re-opened in Garmisch-Partenkirchen). Around this time, Reinhold
Schlötterer initiated a Strauss-Arbeitsgruppe at the Ludwig-Maximilians-
Universität. More recently, beginning in 2011, LMU's Forschungsstelle
Richard-Strauss-Ausgabe, a long-term project funded by the Bavarian
Academy of Sciences and Humanities, has been preparing the first critical
edition of Strauss's works.

Garmisch

The town of Garmisch draws its historical significance in relation to
Strauss from the mansion the family built in the early 1900s, inhabited

---

[5] For *Metamorphosen*, a more complicated argument has been made; see Neil Gregor, "Music,
Memory, Emotion: Richard Strauss and the Legacies of War," *Music & Letters* 96, no. 1 (2015):
55–76.

for over four decades, and still takes care of today. In what was a village of around 2,300 inhabitants (then officially independent from the adjacent Partenkirchen, about the same size), Strauss bought a parcel in 1906, notably from the revenues of his *Salome* success. He might have sought what visitors described as a "rural Tusculum" to which he withdrew to "contemplate, create, and rest." The composer himself continued to praise the area as the most beautiful place in all of Bavaria and Austria.[6]

However, when the family moved into the villa, designed by renowned architect Emanuel von Seidl, in 1908, Garmisch was not as isolated as the postcard image of rural Bavaria might suggest. The picturesque location in the German–Austrian border region close to the Zugspitze, Germany's tallest mountain, inspired scientists like Eva Kriner-Fischer in her 1930 study of the region to use language akin to an Eichendorffian nature poem. Around the turn of the century, owing to the rise of mass tourism and glorification of the Alpine, Garmisch began to attract a stream of visitors. The impoverished region, once wealthy due to its strategic location on an early modern trade route but one of Bavaria's poorest districts throughout the nineteenth century, experienced an economic revival. The number of overnight guests quadrupled between 1890 and 1910 following its connection to the railroad in 1889. In 1900, Garmisch was accessible from Munich in about three hours. This caused the region's employment structure to shift from mostly agriculture to tourism.[7] Regarding the potent rural cliché, most Trachtenvereine who treasured traditional costumes were founded only in the 1880s, probably with tourism in mind in one way or another.

The Werdenfelser Land, an area named for the medieval castle Werdenfels, attracted audiences from far and wide. Georg Hirth strengthened the ties with Munich's fashionable society. As early as 1876, he had founded a hotel near Garmisch. Later he co-owned and published the *Münchner Neueste Nachrichten* and also founded the journal *Die Jugend*. Later came artists such as Franz von Lenbach and Paul Heyse. Some members of Strauss's urban environment had even pre-empted the move to Garmisch as a permanent residence. Hermann Levi, inhabitant of Partenkirchen since 1896 and its *Ehrenbürger* (honorary citizen) since 1898, built a mansion in Garmisch's neighboring village in the

[6] Alfred Holzbock, "Richard Strauss und seine 'Elektra'," *Berliner Lokal-Anzeiger*, September 20, 1908, 2; Richard Strauss to Pauline Strauss, October 31, 1930, in *Der Strom der Töne trug mich fort*, ed. Franz Grasberger (Tutzing: Schneider, 1967), 335.

[7] Josef Ostler, *Garmisch und Partenkirchen 1870–1935* (Garmisch-Partenkirchen: Verein für Geschichte, Kunst- und Kulturgeschichte, 2000).

mid-1890s, where he died only a few years later and was buried in a mausoleum.

Some traveled from farther away, such as the philosopher Ernst Bloch, who formed a somewhat improbable friendship with Pauline Strauss-de Ahna during his visits in 1911. With his 1930 novel *Erfolg*, a fictionalized account of the rise and fall of Nazism in the region, Lion Feuchtwanger set an ambiguous monument to 1920s Munich and its Garmisch-affiliate society, mocking the village's worldwide recognition. Certainly, the region enjoyed an international reputation: Edward Elgar's song set *Scenes from the Bavarian Highlands* (1895) exudes an Alpine charm that the composer had witnessed during his vacations.

Unlike Levi, who took part in the local life (e.g., by cofunding water infrastructure projects, for example), Strauss was more reluctant to establish personal connections with Garmisch. He seems to have maintained no relations with the local musical scene, largely consisting of brass and wind orchestras that shaped the village's soundscape with performances on secular and religious occasions such as parish fairs, carnival processions, beer tents, and spa orchestra concerts. Strauss's reservation towards his surroundings turned into resentment in situations that involved his role as a resident and taxpayer. They illustrate the fault lines between the area's concurrent claims of rusticity and modernization. Correspondence kept at Garmisch's Marktarchiv gives evidence of a conflict in 1918 that evolved from the village's plan to create a sports arena close to Strauss's property. Fearing for their quiet and exclusivity, the composer and some of his neighbors (like the conductor-friend Fritz Cortolezis) successfully intervened at the municipality. A position of reserve became evident once more during preparations for the 1936 Winter Olympics, a process during which Garmisch and Partenkirchen were officially merged on order of the state secretary. Once again, Strauss, who generally despised sports as plebeian, feared a public waste of money. In a letter to the local council from January 1933 (held at the German Bundesarchiv), he denounced the "new citizen tax for the coverage of the sports nuisance" and pointed to his existing burdens of "federal taxes for the support of idlers, social welfare, and the house begging that were particularly rampant in Garmisch."

Plans to re-host the Olympics in 1940 were canceled due to the war. However, some of the Olympic venues played a peculiar role after the war when the allies used them as camps for war prisoners, among them the young Martin Walser. The town had already been the aim of the so-called Kinderlandverschickung, the evacuation of children from places endangered by war, and its population escalated in the early 1940s with the arrival of bombing victims from the cities. Strauss notably prevented his property from being occupied with the help of high-level state officials in 1943 and again in early 1945. During the last days of the war, Strauss successfully refused to quarter American soldiers before the family left for a Swiss exile until 1949. While still in the villa, he faced autograph hunters, journalists (among them Thomas Mann's son Klaus, who preferred to go unrecognized), a film team, and military delegations (one of which included the oboist John de Lancie, whose question about an oboe concerto is said to have triggered Strauss's sole contribution to the genre).

The villa survives as Richard and Pauline Strauss left it at their deaths in 1949 and 1950. Today, Garmisch-Partenkirchen displays its bonds with the composer through public sites like the Strauss-Brunnen and maintains a major location of Strauss research. Still procured by the Strauss family today, the composer's daughter-in-law Alice Strauss had already set up the Richard-Strauss-Archiv of manuscripts, study scores, and a considerable amount of the composer's papers in the villa during his lifetime. Since 1989, an annual festival has provided a combination of concerts, master-classes, and Strauss-related events and, in 1999, the Richard-Strauss-Institut re-opened in the Villa Christina. The institute maintains a specialized library that houses important archival documents, and it co-organizes the renowned Richard-Strauss-Wettbewerb (competition) for young singers and pianists.

The cities of Munich and Garmisch were central to Strauss's personal and professional life. Both call him *Ehrenbürger*, with Munich awarding honorary citizenship in 1924 and Garmisch-Partenkirchen (as it was officially called since 1935) following in 1949. Ties between these cities extend well beyond the Strauss legacy, however, and provide an example of how socio-cultural exchange complicates popular notions of center and periphery. A glance at today's economic conditions in Munich and Garmisch reveals the interpenetration of urban and rural areas. Garmisch-Partenkirchen now has several major business partners: the market town's official website (www.gapa.de) displays the logos of the Munich car manufacturer BMW and Coca Cola, but also the brewery König Ludwig Weißbier, thus covering both global corporations and local companies. It may be possible to trace this glocalization trend back to the time when Strauss first settled there.

CHAPTER 10

Meiningen and Weimar

Michael Saffle

Germany's musical heritage is remarkably rich. Johann Sebastian Bach, Ludwig van Beethoven (born in Bonn, although he spent most of his life in Austria), and Richard Wagner are among its finest composers. But much of German music history has involved other individuals, not all of it associated with Berlin and other large cities. During the mid-nineteenth century, for instance, composers such as Peter Cornelius, Engelbert Humperdinck, Carl Reinecke, Louis Spohr, and Friedrich Robert Volkmann contributed greatly to the nation's musical life, and several of them worked with Liszt and visited the still charming, still somewhat old-fashioned towns of Meiningen and Weimar. Both towns continue to attract tourists, and both possess important musical archives. The Max-Reger-Archiv (Meiningen), the Anna-Amalia-Bibliothek (Weimar), and the Goethe- und Schiller-Archiv (Weimar) are but three examples. More to the point: Richard Strauss worked in Meiningen and Weimar near the beginning of his professional life, and the years he spent in both communities – 1885–86 in Meiningen, 1889–94 initially in Weimar – help us better understand pre–World War I Germany's cultural life as well as Strauss's own development as composer, conductor, and pianist.

Both Meiningen and Weimar belong to Thuringia, a *Land* (or principal political division; the plural is *Länder*) of twenty-first-century Germany. Thuringia once consisted of a host of smaller fiefdoms, including the Duchy of Saxe-Coburg and Gotha. Albert, Queen Victoria's Prince Consort who lived in England from 1839 until his death in 1861, belonged to the House of Wetten that ruled Coburg after it became part of Bavaria in 1861. Even after the second German empire (*zweites Deutsches Reich*) was established in 1871, both towns remained aristocratic strongholds. As long ago as 1680, for example, Meiningen became the capital of the Duchy of Saxe-Meiningen, while Weimar served for decades as the capital of the Grand Duchy of Saxe-Weimar-Eisenach.

Only after World War I was Germany reorganized politically. Emperor Wilhelm II abdicated in 1918, and during the short civil war of 1918–19, Wilhelm Ernst, the last Duke to reign in Weimar, also abdicated. From 1919 until Hitler's rise to power in 1933, Weimar flourished as the capital of the short-lived Weimar Republic. Subsequently, and until 1948, it served as the capital of Thuringia. Then, in 1949, all of eastern Germany was annexed by Communist insurgents and became part of East Germany (DDR or Deutsche Demokratische Republik).[1] Only in 1990 did the Federal Republic of Germany (BRD or Bundesrepublik Deutschland) absorb the former DDR, and both towns became part of today's reunified German nation.

Meiningen and Weimar both have lengthy and prestigious musical histories. For several decades, especially during the later nineteenth century, Meiningen's most celebrated cultural organization was the Court Theater (*Hoftheater*), which toured widely in Europe and earned an international reputation that persists in professional circles to the present day. Georg II – known as the "Theater Duke" for his sponsorship of the town's forward-looking dramatic activities – oversaw certain productions (including Shakespeare's *Julius Caesar* and Schiller's *Wilhelm Tell*), insisted upon historical accuracy and authenticity, supervised the scheduling of long, carefully planned rehearsals, and eschewed traditional stage scenery (painted flats, heavy furniture, etc.) in favor of presenting actors in neutral settings. All these activities brought Meiningen productions closer to twentieth-century practices and in fact influenced them. Perhaps to concentrate his efforts on theatrical undertakings, the Duke closed the Meiningen Opera: a move that helped the town's orchestra, the Meiningen Court Orchestra (*Meininger Hofkapelle*), and added eight musicians to its roster. Founded in 1690 by Duke Bernhard I, the orchestra also boasts an illustrious history. As early as 1706, Johann Ludwig Bach, a cousin of Johann Sebastian, became the duchy's Kapellmeister. In 1867, under conductor Emil Blücher, the Meiningen orchestra and town hosted a gathering of the General German Music Society (Allgemeiner Deutscher Musikverein; ADMV). In 1861, in order to support the cause of "New German" music, Liszt and Franz Brendel founded the ADMV, which sponsored concerts in a great many German cities, including Weimar and Cologne, until it was disbanded in 1937 by Nazi leader

---

[1] Although DDR officials did not prohibit researchers from working in many of Weimar's archives, they did close the local Staatsarchiv (national archive) to visitors. The Max-Reger-Archiv in Meiningen was closed altogether for decades.

Joseph Goebbels on account of its purportedly offensive artistic "elitism."
The Meiningen ADMV festival promoted contemporary compositions by
Eduard Lassen, Felix Draeseke, and Volkmann (all associates of Liszt) as
well as Leopold Damrosch. In 1887 Strauss also joined the ADMV, and
from 1901 to 1909 he served as the organization's president. In 1876,
Wagner invited the orchestra to perform at the first Bayreuth Festival,
which introduced Germany and other Western nations to several of that
composer's later music dramas. In 1895, the first Saxe-Meiningen music
festival took place, with a choir of more than 300 and an orchestra of 100.
Directed by Fritz Steinbach, these ensembles presented works by Bach,
Beethoven, and Brahms.

In October 1880, Hans von Bülow, another associate of Liszt, became
Meiningen's Kapellmeister and raised the ensemble's performing standards, using what he called his "Meiningen principles." In an interview
published in the *Weimarer Zeitung*, that town's newspaper, Bülow
explained that his principles involved separate rehearsals for winds and
strings as well as sectional rehearsals for each string section (first violins,
second violins, and so on) – all unusual at the time and all similar in spirit
with Georg II's theatrical innovations. "In Art there are no trivial things,"
Bülow proclaimed.[2] However, Bülow worked at that time within a system
of aristocratic privilege as well as support. Even an artist of his caliber,
often rude and dismissive in his personal relationships, and as a musician
insistent that every artistic decision be his alone, Bülow was nevertheless
expected to give piano lessons to Princess Marie, the Duke's daughter, and
he was given to understand that everything he did depended upon Georg
II's approval. Strauss too was later expected in Meiningen to fulfill similar
duties, including piano lessons for Princess Marie; he also appeared in
performances of chamber music, and he directed one of several local choral
societies.

To understand Bülow's accomplishments in Meiningen, in light of
musical life in Europe and the United States during the 1880s, consider
contemporaneous claims about the character of German and American
orchestras. In 1881, the *Boston Musical Herald*, boasting of its own city's
ensemble, the Boston Symphony, declared that "[an] orchestra pure and
simple does not exist in all Europe."[3] In one sense this was correct, because

---

[2] Quoted in Alan Walker, *Hans von Bülow: A Life and Times* (New York: Oxford University Press, 2010), 281.
[3] Quoted in Robert Philip, *Performing Music in the Age of Recording* (New Haven, CT: Yale University Press, 2004), 9.

professional German orchestras were and still are largely or even entirely dependent upon patronage rather than ticket sales. Aristocrats, not boards of directors, were final authorities. Membership further separated later nineteenth-century German and American ensembles. At its height Meiningen's orchestra boasted some 50 musicians (only 36 when Bülow arrived in 1880). In 1842, when the New York Philharmonic gave its first performance, some 63 musicians participated. By 1867, the Philharmonic had grown to 100 members, although it remained a part-time organization in terms of scheduling and salaries until Mahler briefly became its music director in 1909. Nevertheless, Meiningen's orchestra helped bridge the gap between the salaried court establishments of eighteenth-century Europe and today's financially autonomous, professional ensembles.

Bülow brought several important composers to Meiningen, including Brahms. In a letter to Georg II and referring indirectly to Bülow's "Meiningen principles," Brahms praised Bülow's strict rehearsals and high standards, while Liszt wrote during the 1880s that "the little Meiningen phalanx, thanks to its present conductor, is in advance of the largest battalions."[4] Brahms's Fourth Symphony received its premiere in Meiningen, and it was for Richard Mühlfeld, the orchestra's principal clarinetist, that Brahms composed his Quintet for Clarinet and Strings, Op. 115, and his two Sonatas for Clarinet and Piano, Op. 120. In 1885, however, Bülow abruptly left Meiningen due to a quarrel with Brahms over who would conduct that composer's Third Symphony: Brahms or Bülow. From October 1885 to April 1886, Richard Strauss took over most of Bülow's responsibilities and served briefly as town and court Kapellmeister.

Throughout the early 1880s, Bülow followed Strauss's youthful musical progress. In 1881, Bülow conducted the premiere of Strauss's Serenade for Thirteen Wind Instruments in Berlin, and he allowed Strauss to conduct the same work, again in Berlin, although at that time Strauss had never before held a baton in his hands! Gaining confidence through experience, Strauss soon after conducted performances of his own Symphony in F Minor and *Macbeth*, one of his earliest tone poems. In 1884, Bülow commissioned Strauss to write something new for Meiningen's ensemble, and the 20-year-old composer produced a Suite in B-flat Major, again scored for 13 winds. In 1885, when Franz Mannstädt, then Meiningen's

---

[4] Translated from *Franz Liszts Briefe*, ed., "La Mara" [Marie Lipsius] (Leipzig: Breitkopf & Härtel, 1893–1905), 2: 257. Bülow frequently performed Liszt's music, devoting entire evenings as a pianist to his keyboard works. See Walker, *Hans von Bülow*, 292–93.

assistant conductor, left for Berlin, a host of musicians, including Mahler, applied for the position. But Bülow chose Strauss.

With the approval of Georg II, Strauss took up his position in Meiningen on October 1, 1885, and he consolidated that position in a debut 18 days later. Sharing the podium with Bülow, he led the ensemble in his own Symphony in F Minor and played the solo part in a performance of Mozart's Concerto for Piano and Orchestra in C Minor, K. 491.[5] Strauss even wrote his own cadenza for the concerto's first movement. Brahms, who attended the concert, was not entirely convinced of the young composer's abilities, but Bülow praised his protégé in a letter to Hermann Wolff, calling Strauss's Symphony "very important ... original, mature in form ... and [he is] a born conductor."[6] "In this triple capacity of conductor, pianist, and composer, the twenty-one-year-old [Strauss] achieved a notable triumph."[7]

As it happened, however, that triumph was short-lived. A week later, and immediately after his quarrel with Brahms, Bülow spent weeks as guest conductor with the St. Petersburg Russian Musical Society. Only after his return to Meiningen in January 1886 did he resign his Kapellmeister position. Strauss left three months later, choosing instead to spend the years 1886–89 with the Munich Court Opera. Before his departure from Meiningen, however, Strauss successfully conducted other works such as Mozart's Requiem, and he led the orchestra in Schubert's "Unfinished" Symphony at an 1885 Christmas concert.

If his Meiningen and intervening Munich positions together served as Strauss's conducting apprenticeship, his work in Weimar during 1889–94 consolidated his growing reputation as a masterful orchestral leader and a successful, increasingly controversial composer of "new music." Weimar's musical history is exceptional. From 1708 to 1717 Sebastian Bach worked there, and during the later eighteenth and early nineteenth centuries, Weimar's cultural leaders included Johann Wolfgang von Goethe and Friedrich Schiller, two of Germany's greatest authors, as well as the pianist and composer Johann Nepomuk Hummel. This "Age of Goethe" (*Goethezeit*), also known as Weimar's "Golden" or "Classical" age (1758–1832), was followed by a "Silver" age (1832–1918), during which, and at the invitation of Grand Duke Karl Alexander, Liszt lived in that city from

---

[5] A facsimile of the concert program in question is reproduced in Walker, *Hans von Bülow*, 323.
[6] Quoted in Raymond Holden, *Richard Strauss: A Musical Life* (Yale University Press, 2011), 20; emphases in the original.
[7] Walker, *Hans von Bülow*, 322.

1848–61 and held the position of Kapellmeister for most of that time. (Liszt also lived part of each year in Weimar from the mid-1860s until his death in 1886.) Weimar's orchestra during Liszt's tenure as Kapellmeister boasted only 35 regular musicians, but additional performers were summoned for certain performances. In 1860 the Grand-Ducal Saxon Art School – the predecessor of the celebrated Bauhaus, a twentieth-century center of modernist architecture, industrial design, and painting – was established by Karl Alexander, and the orchestral school founded in 1872 flourishes today as the Hochschule für Musik Franz Liszt.

Under Liszt's leadership, Weimar's orchestra gave important performances of many Romantic works, including operas and music dramas by Berlioz and Wagner. From 1889 to 1894 Strauss held the position of second conductor of Weimar's Staatskapelle (state or national musical ensemble), an ensemble founded in 1491 as the Ducal Ensemble (*Herzogliche Hofkapelle*). Later renamed the Staatskapelle, this was the organization that employed Bach, Hummel, and Liszt. With the approval of Grand Duke Karl August, Hans von Bronsart invited the relatively inexperienced musician to settle in Weimar and conduct both concerts and operatic performances as well as teach classes at the Musikhochschule, all of which Strauss began to do in September 1889. Strauss had sought the position of First Kapellmeister, held at the time by Eduard Lassen, but accepted the subordinate second position with the town's operatic troupe after dickering with Bronsart over salary and responsibilities.

Even during the later nineteenth century, and after its "Golden" and "Silver" eras, Weimar – also known as the "Athens of the North" – had already become a popular tourist destination and a goal for many music students. Although small by the standards of Berlin and Munich, with a population of some 12,000 individuals, Weimar was and to some extent still is filled with narrow cobbled streets and gabled houses. The town boasted a surprising number and variety of monuments. The Altenburg, a palatial house, was Liszt's residence during his official Weimar tenure. Two ducal country palaces lie a short distance from the central market, and the Russischer Hof, a prominent hostelry, was closed during DDR days but has since been reopened and restored with considerable success.

No wonder Strauss was thrilled to be working in Weimar and wrote to his father, "I feel wonderful . . . The orchestra is enchanted with me," and so on.[8] Almost immediately, he set about demonstrating his unusual

---

[8] Translated from Kenneth Birkin, "Richard Strauss in Weimar. Part 1: The Concert Hall," *Richard Strauss-Blätter* no. 33 (1995): 4.

musical abilities. During his first year performing with Weimar's Court Orchestra (a separate organization from the town's Court Opera), Strauss conducted works by composers as different from one another as Luigi Cherubini, Franz Joseph Haydn, August Ritter, Robert Schumann, and Bedřich Smetana. Most of these choices reflected local tastes, although Smetana's music seemed a bit experimental to many listeners prior to World War I. Several years earlier, Strauss had been influenced by Brahms, and he remained a lifelong devotee of eighteenth-century music, especially Mozart's. In Weimar, however, he turned more pointedly to "Music of the Future" (*Zukunftsmusik*) in general, and more specifically to Liszt's tone poems for inspiration. The program of Strauss's January 12, 1891, Weimar concert included both the "Prelude and Liebestod" (or Love-Death) from Wagner's *Tristan und Isolde* and Liszt's challenging *Ce qu'on entend sur la montagne*. Nevertheless, 11 of Strauss's 16 Court Orchestra evenings included symphonies, overtures, and concertos by Beethoven. Nor did he neglect the music of Brahms.

As second conductor of the Court Opera, Strauss mostly chose works that were already familiar at that time to operagoers. Operas by Heinrich Marschner, Mozart, and Carl Maria von Weber were repeatedly presented in 1889–90 along with Wagner's earlier *Tannhäuser* and *Lohengrin*. During the 1890–91 season, Strauss added Wagner's *Rienzi* to his repertory. In spite of some conservative opposition to newer works, all this reflected the city's association with both the "advanced political and social ideas" that culminated in both the international celebrity accorded the Bauhaus and the ideas that found expression in the Weimar Republic of the 1920s and early 1930s.

Guntram, the first of Strauss's many operatic compositions, was not too successful with Weimar's music-lovers, and later the composer recycled portions of its music in his tone poem *Ein Heldenleben*. Other important earlier works were more explicitly Lisztian, including *Don Juan*. On August 24, 1888, shortly before accepting an appointment in Weimar, Strauss wrote to Bülow to explain that the only possible way for him "to create a work of art that is unified in its mood and consistent in its structure ... is [through the inspiration of] a poetical idea," and that he considered it "a legitimate artistic method to create a correspondingly new form for every subject."[9] All this came down to drawing upon extra-musical sources for musical creativity: a prominent principle behind the innovations of such advocates of the New German School

[9] Quoted in Holden, *Richard Strauss*, 31.

(*Neudeutsche Schule*) of composition as Berlioz and Wagner as well as Liszt. At that time, Liszt was still considered a radical innovator in many European musical circles, even by some of Weimar's concertgoers, and the prominent Viennese music critic Eduard Hanslick repeatedly dismissed him as a programmatic composer, instead supporting the cause of musical "absolutism," with form and content held to be independent of any extra-musical influences. Richard Pohl, on the other hand, who lived in Weimar from 1854 to 1863, defended Liszt under the pseudonym "Hoplit" (or foot soldier) in the pages of the *Neue Zeitschrift für Musik*, and later in other journals. Franz Brendel, who had edited the *Neue Zeitschrift* before Pohl, as well as Cornelius and Joachim Raff, also stood by Liszt and in certain of their compositions incorporated some of his musical gestures. All these issues continued to draw attention to Weimar throughout the later nineteenth century.

Don Juan proved an extraordinarily ambitious work, striking in content and extremely difficult to perform (at least at first). Nevertheless, and after some griping, the members of Weimar's Court Orchestra mastered its challenges, and it remained central to Strauss's later conducting career. During the last decade of the nineteenth century, *Don Juan* was widely accepted as an avant-garde experiment, exemplary of musical modernism, and in spite of its novelty it proved enormously successful. During the next few decades Strauss went on to write works even more shocking – at least in the opinions of critics such as New York City's Henry Krehbiel, who called the composer's opera *Salome* "disgusting." Others all but worshipped Strauss's compositions, especially his numerous symphonic poems. By the time he turned 40, a year before *Salome* received its premiere in Dresden, Strauss had become one of the world's most talked-about, lauded, and criticized musicians of his age.

Unfortunately, Strauss suffered from several illnesses during his Weimar appointment. In 1891 he came down with pneumonia and took a leave of absence from his responsibilities; in June 1892 he suffered an attack of pleurisy. Then, in 1893, in spite of momentary doubts raised as to his physical fitness, Strauss was offered a position with the Munich Court Opera. Having already proven himself in Munich during the later 1880s, he seemed a natural choice. On October 1, 1894, Strauss arrived in Bavaria's capital to begin the next phase of his career.

CHAPTER 11

Bayreuth

Ulrich Konrad

From the last quarter of the nineteenth century on, Bayreuth has stood for the realization of a new kind of musical theater developed by Richard Wagner, which has since been recognized as a major contribution to the world's cultural heritage. For young composers such as Richard Strauss, both Wagner and Bayreuth were profoundly influential, a circumstance they had to confront in shaping their own artistic identities.

In the Wagner house in Tribschen, the composer and his future wife Cosima spent the evening of March 5, 1870, together discussing all kinds of current and artistic developments. Cosima's diary provides a detail of the conversation: "When we subsequently talk of the production of these works, I tell R. he should look up the article on *Baireuth* in the encyclopedia; R. had mentioned this place as the one he would choose. To our delight we read in the list of buildings of a splendid old opera house!"[1] This is the first known mention of Wagner's idea of realizing his lofty theatrical plans in this town where a margrave once resided between the mountain ranges Fichtelgebirge and Fränkische Schweiz.

One can imagine how strange the plan must have seemed to contemporaries when one examines Bayreuth's historical situation. The small town, with around 18,000 inhabitants in 1870, was able to look back on a cultural blossoming in the eighteenth century. But after the end of the margravate in 1791, short periods as a Prussian possession (until 1806) and occupation by Napoleon's French troops (until 1810) had followed before it was incorporated into the kingdom of Bavaria as a local administrative center. From then on it belonged to the Franconian province of Main, where it was in some respects bypassed by the developments of the time, particularly in the economic sense. Wagner's decision to implement his idea for a theatrical festival in the periphery rather than a major urban

---

[1] *Cosima Wagner's Diaries: Volume I, 1869–1877*, ed. Martin Gregor-Dellin and Dietrich Mack, trans. Geoffrey Skelton (New York: Harcourt Brace Jovanovich, 1978), 196.

center was linked to his experiences in Munich and with the young Bavarian king. It was at Wagner's suggestion in 1865, and on the orders of Ludwig II, that the architect Gottfried Semper had drawn up plans for a monumental festival theater in Munich, the royal seat on the Isar. By 1870, however, the composer rejected such demonstrative splendor set amidst the trappings of state power in favor of a remote "place of pilgrimage" focused entirely on art. It was on the periphery that he wished his audience to come together to immerse itself entirely in the "artwork of the future" during short festival seasons exclusively presenting his theatrical creations. The tension between periphery and center resulting from Wagner's decision to elevate Bayreuth to the location for his festivals would determine the fate of the town from that time onwards. For ten months of the year, tranquility dominated (and still dominates) the life of the Upper Franconian provincial town. For two months in summer, however, Bayreuth is transformed into a cosmopolitan center of music theater, converged on by droves of leading figures from politics, industry and society, artists of the highest rank, and lovers of Wagner's art from all over the world. From the last quarter of the nineteenth century to the present, the weeks of the Bayreuth Festival have reflected, in a unique and curious way, the changing artistic, ideological, and social movements of the day – from the German Empire, the Weimar Republic, and the National Socialist dictatorship to the democratic Federal Republic of today.

Such developments, of course, were unforeseeable in 1870. The first point in favor of Bayreuth, a town yet unknown to Wagner, was information found in the encyclopedia about its "splendid old opera house." When Wagner saw it for the first time on April 19, 1871, it had been closed for more than a century: "But the theater will not do for us at all; so we must build – and all the better. Now to find a house [. . .], nothing is quite suitable, so we must build for ourselves, too."[2] In these lapidary diary entries by Cosima, the two building projects of the coming years are announced: the spectacular Festival Hall and the stately Wahnfried, the Wagners' family domicile. The composer certainly did not shy away from decisions. By May 22, 1872, the foundation for the Festival Hall had already been laid, on April 28, 1874, the Wagners moved into Wahnfried, and on August 13, 1876, the first Bayreuth Festival began. The event drew the political, social, and artistic elite from near and far; attendees included Emperor Wilhelm I, the philosopher Nietzsche, and composers such as Liszt, Bruckner, Saint-Saëns, Tchaikovsky, and Grieg.

[2] Ibid., 356–57.

On this occasion a member of the Bavarian Court Orchestra, Franz Strauss, could have taken part as first horn: after all, this virtuoso had played in all previous (first) performances of Wagner's works in Munich. Although Franz Strauss had dutifully played the challenging parts with artistic perfection and to the admiration of all, he otherwise persisted in a stubborn opposition to Wagner and did not volunteer for service in Bayreuth. Not until Ludwig II sent his Court Orchestra there for the first performance of *Parsifal* in 1882 did Franz enter the Festival Hall. His son Richard, who had just turned 18 and recently left school with solid university entrance qualifications, was allowed to go with him for a short time. The young man had already acquired substantial knowledge of Wagner's stage works. Nothing is known of his impressions of the first production of *Parsifal* – it seems Strauss's first visit to Bayreuth was not a deep experience that left its mark on the rest of his life. He did see Wagner, but was too shy to introduce himself. Six months later, the "Master" was dead.

After Wagner's death, his widow took over the directorship of the festival as the legally recognized heiress. She did this comprehensively, as guardian of the works and ideas of her husband and also as absolute ruler in all artistic and organizational matters on the "Green Hill." The canonization of the oeuvre brought with it an ideologization of the Wagnerian artistic and worldview in the form cultivated by the circle around Cosima. Hans von Wolzogen, Heinrich von Stein, Karl Friedrich Glasenapp, Ludwig Schemann, Henry Thode, and later Houston Stewart Chamberlain formed the core of this circle. Those who distanced themselves spoke of a "congregation that believes in its Messiah and listens intently to his revelations with the devotion of the believer. The veneration for his person and his works is reaching the level of a cult; his books are published as confessions, as symbolic books of the new aesthetic belief."[3] As the home of Wagnerian orthodoxy, Bayreuth stood on the one hand for the authentic cultivation of the works in the sacrosanct spirit of the "Master" and on the other hand for the unconditional implementation of a worldview centered on the composer's ideas for cultural reform; "regeneration" was the key term. Wagner's broad and utopian idea for a festival gradually metamorphosed over the decades of Cosima's autocratic and high-priestly rule into a "Wahnfried ideology" with an ethnic and anti-Semitic stamp. Its resonance may have been very broad, but the sound was polarized: on one side was the consonance of unconditional

---

[3] Wilhelm Heinrich Riehl, *Kulturgeschichtliche Charakterköpfe* (Stuttgart: Cotta, 1891), 475.

discipleship, personified in "Wagnerian" or "Bayreuthian," and on the other side the dissonance of blunt rejection or vehement opposition. The point of contention was never purely music, theater, or art, but always the larger question of politics and society. Whatever position they finally adopted on Bayreuth, only a few persons of rank abstained from Wagner and the pilgrimage to his shrine. And the debate over the pros and cons of the Bayreuth Festival under Wagner's successors is evidence of the ambivalent fascination with this paradoxical place.

It was more or less inevitable that Strauss, too, would be drawn into the Bayreuth milieu. Despite the authoritative influence of his father and notwithstanding the aesthetic orientation of his early years towards the ideals of the Classical period and the music of Brahms, growing insight into all that was new in Wagner's scores and his practical experience with them sowed the seeds for a re-orientation of his own artistic worldview. The person most closely connected with this change was Alexander Ritter, a fanatical supporter of Wagner and the "New German" movement in art. (As the husband of Wagner's niece, Franziska, he was also linked to his idol on a family level.) Ritter was over 50 when Strauss first met him in October 1885 in Meiningen. Hans von Bülow was instrumental in bringing the composer there, where Ritter worked as second concertmaster in the ducal court orchestra. Strauss found in him an intellectual mentor of a kind he had never encountered, so much so that he later admitted that Ritter marked a turning point in his life. Strauss was happy to be introduced to Wagner's view of art by Ritter and declare his allegiance to it, meanwhile reading Wagner's theoretical treatises under Ritter's guidance and forming his picture of the course of musical development, which he saw in the lineage of Beethoven, Berlioz, Liszt, and Wagner. For his part, Ritter was deeply impressed by Strauss's receptiveness and considered his protégé a legitimate heir of Wagner and his generative concept of culture. He furthermore expected that the young Strauss's future works would become evidence of this.

Strauss was among the audience of the 1886 Festival, attending two performances of *Tristan und Isolde* (its Bayreuth premiere) as well as *Parsifal*. From then on, annual journeys became almost the rule. In 1887 he was among the guests at the soirée in Wahnfried, 1888 was probably the year of his first personal meeting with Cosima, and by 1889 Strauss found himself among the eight conductors invited to Bayreuth to assist with rehearsals. He had been recommended by his immediate superior in Munich, Hermann Levi, court music director and conductor of the first-ever performance of *Parsifal*. In his letter thanking

Cosima, Strauss added an assurance that he would consider "it at all times one of my greatest and finest duties to serve the cause of Bayreuth faithfully with all the strength that I can offer."[4] Proof that this was more than mere lip service came during his time as Grand Ducal Music Director in Weimar. Despite the limited means at his disposal, he strove to produce model performances of Wagner's works, adhering unconditionally to Bayreuth performance ideals, such as the interdiction of cuts. Before the end of 1889, *Lohengrin* had its premiere, *Tannhäuser* came in spring 1890, *Rienzi* at the end of the same year, and *Tristan* in 1892. A lively exchange of letters between Weimar and Bayreuth arose concerning these productions, and Strauss sought closeness to Cosima as authoritative verification of his Wagner interpretations. Strauss's support for a Richard Wagner Association in Weimar played no small role in authenticating Strauss as a Bayreuth disciple. His place in the creative heritage of the "Master" was achieved, incidentally, in 1890 with his new arrangement of Gluck's *Iphigenie en Tauride* (Wagner had performed his version of Gluck's *Iphigenie auf Aulis* in Dresden in 1847), a project that earned Strauss the greatest praise from Bayreuth. And finally, with *Guntram*, he wished to prove himself as a poet-composer of the Wagner ilk.

What would be Strauss's last visit for some time took place in 1896; prior to that, he had been in Bayreuth in 1890, 1891, and 1894. The latter year saw his conducting debut in the Festival Hall. He was originally due to receive this honor in 1892 when Cosima initially offered him *Tristan* or *Tannhäuser*. She retracted that invitation, however, due to claims by other conductors, so that in the end, only rehearsal assistance for *Meistersinger* remained for Strauss. He felt self-confident enough to turn down this offer and did so with a measure of indignation. A detectable shadow fell over their once-untroubled relationship into which the "Mistress" had been gradually mixing discreet hopes of marriage with her daughter Eva. Strauss's severe illness in the spring of 1892 saved the relationship from a final test. The 30-year-old conducted some repertoire performances of *Tannhäuser* two years later (with his fiancée Pauline de Ahna as Elisabeth), but after that, what had been an intense attachment to Bayreuth lost its importance for Strauss. Even more significantly, he explicitly cut his inner ties with the ideologized artistic world of Cosima – now also the world of hers and Richard's son Siegfried, who was growing into his role as heir and

---

[4] *Cosima Wagner – Richard Strauss: Ein Briefwechsel*, ed. Franz Trenner (Tutzing: Hans Schneider, 1978), 3.

Figure 11.1   Postcard of the Bayreuth Festspielhaus, 1895.

had long been using the familiar "Du" with Strauss. On January 11, 1896, Strauss wrote in his diary: "Notable conversation with Siegfried Wagner. Although unspoken, separation from Wahnfried-Bayreuth is complete. Only indirectly my fault."[5] No light has yet been cast on the subject of that conversation, but it may well be that Strauss, with his optimistic view of future developments in art, could no longer see a place for himself in the increasingly narrow ideology in Bayreuth. Perhaps there is an oblique reference to this in the article "Is there an Avant-Garde in music?" that Strauss wrote for a newspaper in 1907:

> I therefore leave such [programmatic] proclamations now and in the future to those who have no desire to lead a life devoid of slogans, or who are deluded enough to believe that they are capable of halting the natural course of progress with dogmatic prohibitions, such as the opponents of futurist music or such Wagnerians as, sinning against the spirit of their

[5] Franz Trenner, *Richard Strauss: Chronik zu Leben und Werk*, ed. Florian Trenner (Mainz: Schott, 2003), 131.

master, have become no less petrified than the Mozartians around Franz
Lachner, the Mendelssohnians around Carl Reinecke, or the Lisztians
behind Draeseke.[6]

In August 1896, during his last visit to the Festival, he wrote to his wife
Pauline: "O Bayreuth, pigsty to beat all pigsties."[7]

Bayreuth – the fossil pit of the Wagner preservationists for Strauss? Over
a period of 37 years, Strauss avoided this cultic center where Siegfried
Wagner had taken power in 1908 until his widow, Winifred, assumed the
directorship in 1930. Although the challenges of a creative mediation
between tradition and renewal were still present, they were not always
met adequately, for a wide variety of reasons. Wagner's son lacked a vision
for the future of the Festival idea. Above all, he would or could not offer
any resistance to the politicization of Bayreuth advanced principally by
Chamberlain. On August 2, 1914, the Festival had to be broken off
abruptly because of the outbreak of the World War I. The ensuing
fatalities and consequences were not only major factors in plunging the
enterprise into a deep financial crisis, but also provided the final impulse in
welding together the Wahnfried ideology and National Socialism. The first
meeting between Hitler and the Wagner family took place as early as
September 1923. Their mutual sympathy found indicative expression in
Siegfried's offering Hitler the friendly "Du" form of address. When the
curtain went up again on the Green Hill in 1924, visitors could read about
the new spirit of the undertaking in the "Official Bayreuth Festival Guide."
As Karl Holl summarized in the *Frankfurter Zeitung* on August 3, 1924:
"Here, artistic and civic Byzantinism, nationalism, and anti-Semitism
come together in a splendid unity." As it ended, the performance of
Meistersinger turned into a political demonstration. At Hans Sachs's final
words, with his appeal to honor the "German masters," the audience rose
to its feet and, after the first salvo of applause, sang all three stanzas of the
Deutschlandlied. Bayreuth was on course to becoming "Hitler's Royal
Theater."[8]

The 120th anniversary of Wagner's birth and the 50th anniversary of
his death were marked in 1933. At the beginning of that celebratory
year, Berlin saw Hitler seize power, while in Bayreuth, the NSDAP

---

[6] Richard Strauss, *Recollections and Reflections*, ed. Willi Schuh, trans. L. J. Lawrence (London: Boosey
& Hawkes, 1953), 12–13.
[7] Willi Schuh, *Richard Strauss: A Chronicle of the Early Years 1864–1898*, trans. Mary Whittall
(Cambridge: Cambridge University Press, 1982), 416.
[8] *Im Schatten Wagners: Thomas Mann über Richard Wagner, Texte und Zeugnisse 1895–1955*, ed. Hans
Rudolf Vaget (Frankfurt am Main: Fischer Taschenbuch Verlag, 2005), 211.

(Nationalsozialistische Deutsche Arbeiterpartei: National Socialist German Worker's Party) emerged from the recent election as the strongest party. The largest swastika flag in town was hoisted at the Festival Hall on the orders of Winifred Wagner. Periphery and center were well aware of their inner agreement. During the tumultuous beginning of Hitler's rule, in which the dictatorial structures had to be formed and established on all levels, the Festival directorship and organization were subjected to a number of turbulent events. One was unleashed on May 30, 1933, by the conductor Toscanini, greatly admired in Bayreuth and also wooed by Hitler, when he refused to conduct *Die Meistersinger* and *Parsifal* under the prevailing political circumstances. In this precarious situation, Winifred traveled to Garmisch, where she hoped to win Strauss for the task. The request could not have come at a less opportune moment. He was working on Act II of *Die schweigsame Frau*, the first performance of *Arabella* was due to take place soon in Dresden, and he had obligations at the Salzburg Festival. He nevertheless agreed to conduct at least five performances of *Parsifal* (but not the *Meistersinger* performance programmed as the spectacular opening of the Festival), and a performance of Beethoven's Ninth on the anniversary of Siegfried Wagner's death – all expressly without honorarium. The reason for accepting *Parsifal* may have been that he had so far conducted the work only four times, all in Berlin in 1917. Despite relatively few rehearsals, a widely praised and musically transparent production was created, 20 minutes tauter than Toscanini's interpretation. Alfred Einstein wrote in the *Berliner Tageblatt* on July 26, 1933, that, from the Kundry scene to the end of the second act, Strauss had achieved "something most elevated and sublime, a seduction in sound and spirit," adding that "as conductor, Strauss has surely never produced anything greater, more unified, and more comprehensive." Pauline Strauss noted that "to Richard he [Hitler] said 'I thank you'."[9]

For the next year, Winifred, supported by Hitler and facing substantial resistance from strict Wagnerians, succeeded in programming a new staging of *Parsifal*, the consecratory work of the Festival. Strauss agreed to conduct this production, and on July 22, 1934, 40 years to the day after his Bayreuth debut, he stood on the podium in the Festival Hall. Hitler once again warmly shook his hand, but there was tension in the air because of conflicts over permission to perform his new opera *Die schweigsame Frau* – for which Strauss had asked Stefan Zweig, a Jew, to provide the libretto – and the threat of being barred from performing at the Salzburg

---

[9] Trenner, *Chronik*, 540.

Festival. With the third performance of *Parsifal* on August 3, 1934, Strauss's activities in Bayreuth came to a definitive end. At the wish of the "Führer" he was omitted from the invitations to the next Festival in 1936. *Parsifal* was taken over by Wilhelm Furtwängler.

For Strauss, Bayreuth was a place of contradictions, both biographically and artistically. In his early years, he could see in it the fulfilment of his aesthetic ideals and accordingly sought closeness to the milieu of the idolized "Master." With increasing maturity, it became clear to him that, although Wagner was always one of the fixed stars in his musical and dramatic thinking, the "Wahnfried ideology" would remain foreign to his nature. As early as Weimar, Hans Bronsart had voiced the opinion that the "cult of Wagner," as something "alien," had been "forced upon Strauss."[10] In this regard, Strauss overcame Bayreuth. For him, the study and performance of Wagner's works – above all *Meistersinger* and *Tristan* – soon ceased to require the aura of the Festival Hall, especially since he rightly considered its much-praised acoustics to be far short of perfect. In juxtaposition to the Bayreuth episode in Strauss's early years, with its important contribution to his development, the two engagements of 1933–34, when the composer had attained wide fame, take on the dubious appearance of a moral lapse. It is true that he had not thrust himself forward, but unlike Toscanini and Fritz Busch, he offered no resistance due to apparently selfish concerns for his own well-being and creative work. He lacked the strength to gain the insight that guided Busch: "a supposed stain on one's honor means *nothing* compared to the real stain of serving evil."[11] That applies not only to Strauss, but also to Germany's fall from grace in the twentieth century.

[10] Schuh, *Chronicle*, 201.
[11] Fritz Busch, *Aus dem Leben eines Musikers* (Frankfurt: Fischer, 2001), 212.

CHAPTER 12

Berlin

Dietmar Schenk

For two decades, from 1898 until the abolishment of the German monarchy in 1918, Richard Strauss was engaged at the Königliche Hofoper
(Royal Court Opera) in Berlin. He served first as a Kapellmeister and was
elevated to the rank of Generalmusikdirektor in 1908. Although he
reduced his obligations in Berlin at several stages and eventually spent no
more than two months per year in the city, he remained in his position at
the Prussian capital until Emperor Wilhelm II abdicated during the
German revolution of November 1918. In the months that followed, amid
the revolutionary turmoil, Strauss became the interim chief of Berlin's
former court opera before moving to Vienna. Thus, Strauss held significant positions in Berlin for many years. He retained contact with the city
during the 1920s and 1930s, visiting it as the capital of the Weimar
Republic (1918–33) and the Third Reich (1933–45) many times, for
instance, to serve as a guest conductor at the State Opera.

For some music aficionados today, Strauss may seem an unlikely figure
to be so extensively associated with Berlin. One might not think of him
first when asked to name composers and musicians who maintained close
ties with Berlin. In the context of the *Jahrhundertwende* (the turn of the
twentieth century), one might instead mention Paul Lincke, a composer of
operettas, or the actress and singer Fritzi Massary, who also focused on
light music. As precursors of the "golden" twenties, figures such as Lincke
and Massary might seem better suited to one's present image of Berlin
than Strauss, who was undoubtedly a much more important figure. Hail-
ing from Bavaria, Strauss did not represent Prussian art and culture or the
regional features of cultural life in Berlin. Furthermore, the mixture of
modernist radicalism, mass culture, and a highly politicized art scene
during the Weimar Republic overshadowed earlier, equally modernist
(though quite different) trends to which Strauss belonged.

Considering Strauss's long and spectacular career, however, the years he
spent in Berlin were truly crucial. His success may be attributed in no

small part to the cultural environment of the German capital, where the local artistic life provided ideas, contacts, and opportunities that enabled him to develop professionally in the way he did. Although Strauss premiered his operas *Feuersnot* (1901), *Salome* (1905), *Elektra* (1909), and *Der Rosenkavalier* (1911) at Dresden's Semperoper, influential music critics from Berlin were in attendance thanks to the railway link between Dresden and Berlin; Dresden, the residence city of the kingdom of Saxony, was little more than a hundred miles away. These critics' glowing reviews contributed significantly to Strauss's rising fame.

This chapter explores the rise of Berlin during the nineteenth century as a key urban center while documenting the city's cultural panorama. It discusses Berlin's most important musical institutions and summarizes some characteristic aspects of its musical life, examining Strauss's role in the broader art scene through his personal links and institutional affiliations. The final section considers the contemporary voice of Adolf Weissmann, who argued that Berlin experienced a "Richard Strauss period" in the years before the World War I.

The Rise of Berlin

A generation before Strauss arrived, Berlin, the city where the Electors of Brandenburg and the Prussian Kings had long resided, was proclaimed the German capital. Strauss moved to the city nearly 30 years after the victory of the Prussian troops and their allies in the Franco-Prussian War of 1870–71, which precipitated German unification. From that point forward, Berlin was the capital of a nation-state that endeavored to be recognized as a *Weltstadt* (metropolis). The Berlin of the 1870s differed vastly from that of 1914: fields and meadows were replaced by crossroads with heavy traffic, the "old" Berlin reminiscent of the Biedermeier era had disappeared, and the buildings of Karl Friedrich Schinkel's school were replaced by new architecture in a pompous style preferred under the reign of Emperor Wilhelm II (1888–1918). During this period, Berlin's population grew from less than a million to approximately four million inhabitants. These were the figures for the agglomeration of *Groß-Berlin* (Greater Berlin), which included several towns not incorporated until after the war. Strauss lived in various places in Charlottenburg, an affluent town just west of Berlin where he was employed; at that time, the two cities were in the process of merging. The German capital developed rapidly, not only as a result of having become a political center, but also due to the rapid processes of industrialization and urbanization that peaked around 1900.

Figure 12.1   Postcard of Charlottenburg, ca. 1904.

Urban planning proceeded with the expectation that population would swell further to about six million – a forecast that was never met. In the wake of the catastrophes of the twentieth century, not least the World War II with its bombings and the division of the city by the Berlin Wall, the population today is still less than that of 1914.

During the Wilhelmine era, Germany, in general, and Berlin in particular, experienced a strong economy that followed the *Große Depression* (Great Depression) that stretched from 1873 to the early 1890s. With the outbreak of war in the summer of 1914, more than four decades of peace and prosperity ended abruptly. Over this timespan, the poor working class increased in number and gained in socio-political importance, and the emerging middle class, among them a significant Jewish population, was pivotal to a cultural boom.

Musical Institutions and Musical Life

The nineteenth century was a fascinating period in the history of musical life in Berlin. Even in the early 1800s, the court no longer completely shaped the cultural life of the upper classes. A bourgeois musical life was organized, for instance, by the city's choral enthusiasts, the best example being the Sing-Akademie, an amateur choir founded in 1791.

Such organizations relied upon ongoing subsidies from the Prussian state, however. A hundred years later, at the cusp of the twentieth century, Berlin's most turbulent social transformation had reached its climax. Well-to-do Berliners no longer required support from the court or state to pursue their cultural activities; the flourishing musical life at the time is largely attributable to the wealth of a new middle class. New organizations were established in all branches of the arts, especially in literature, theater, fine art, and music. Since the 1880s, the most notable were independent from both the Hohenzollern court and the Prussian government. Owing to this independence, the politically powerless but wealthy middle class gained self-assurance in terms of its cultural expression.

Yet modernist trends influenced the city's musical life as well. Among the emerging institutions that succeeded in counterbalancing the "official" culture was the Berlin Philharmonic Orchestra (founded in 1882), whose 2,000-seat hall in the Bernburger Strasse had formerly served as a skating rink. The concert agency of Hermann Wolff that managed the orchestra had a global mindset and represented a wide array of notable musicians around the world, including Hans von Bülow and Arthur Nikisch who held the principal conductorship of this orchestra in 1887–93 and 1895–1922, respectively.

In the realm of music theater, however, the Royal Court Opera was largely able to maintain its monopoly. Located not far from the Stadt-schloss (Royal City Palace) on the boulevard Unter den Linden, the Court Opera was founded in 1743 during the reign of Frederick the Great. By the end of the nineteenth century, given the projections for the city's continued population growth, the venue seemed far too small to accommodate an ever-expanding audience. A new spacious building was planned for a location outside the Brandenburg Gate, but the outbreak of the World War I prevented its construction.

In the years prior to the War, Berlin's other theaters could not challenge the prestige and success of the Court Opera, and most found it difficult to survive. It was quite expensive even under the prosperous circumstances of the Wilhelmine era to produce operas through private entrepreneurship. The privately operated [Alte] Komische Oper of Hans Gregor, located at the Weidendammer Brücke near the Friedrichstrasse railway station, was distinct from the Court Opera in that it increasingly specialized in light genres. The venerable Deutsches Opernhaus (now Deutsche Oper) in Charlottenburg, a venue with close ties to Wagner's operas, did not open until 1912. Thus, for much of Strauss's time in Berlin, his Court Opera faced little competition.

Over time, musical life in Berlin developed a more international dimension. Music students came from Scandinavia, Eastern Europe, North America, and Japan to complete their professional training or pursue a musical career in Berlin. A guide titled "What a Music Student needs to know about Berlin" was published between 1909 and 1914 to help foreign students settle in the rapidly growing metropolis.[1] The guide listed hundreds of music teachers for every imaginable instrument and gave valuable tips on questions such as how to purchase a piano, rent an apartment, find concert tickets, or even buy a hat. Along these lines, the Stern'sches Konservatorium der Musik, a renowned private conservatory founded in 1850, offered instruction on music theory in English and Russian in addition to German.

Despite the fractures caused by two world wars and the Nazi tyranny, the Sing-Akademie, the two opera houses, and the Philharmonic still play a leading role in Berlin's musical life today. The conservatory, however, suffered a different fate: its Jewish owners were expropriated by the Nazis, and the institution no longer exists.

Modernism and Its Conflicts

There were strong tensions in pre–World War I Berlin between the "official culture" of the Hohenzollern court and the Prussian government institutions on the one hand and modernist trends on the other. From today's perspective, the modern movements of the era do not seem radical, but they were highly controversial at the time. Close connections between different arts were cultivated, and disputes about "new art" eventually spread to cultural life in general. All aspects of urban life and its atmosphere became artistic topics. Writers such as Robert Walser from Switzerland and Alfred Kerr, the renowned theatrical critic who grew up in Silesia, published feature articles on Berlin that are still consulted today. In many respects, the modernist attitude of the time was a bourgeois invention, as one German historian has aptly expressed.[2] The term *Berliner Moderne* (Berlin Modernism), which originated from contemporary discourses comparing Berlin to Vienna, came to capture the spirit of the age.

Naturalism and the Berlin Secession exemplify this modernism. In 1893, the Naturalist poet Gerhart Hauptmann caused a sensation with

---

[1] Richard Stern, ed., *Was muss der Musikstudierende von Berlin wissen?* (Berlin: Stern Musikverlag, 1909–14).

[2] Thomas Nipperdey, *Wie das Bürgertum die Moderne fand* (Berlin: Siedler Verlag, 1988).

his drama *Die Weber*, on the subject of an uprising in 1844, a few years before the *Märzrevolution* (the March Revolution of 1848). Other key writers of Hauptmann's time lived in Friedrichshagen, where they formed a famous poetry circle named after this small town, now a suburb. About a decade later, Max Reinhardt took over the Deutsches Theater in Berlin, a venue initially established by adherents of Naturalism, and he gradually became an internationally renowned stage director.

An art censorship scandal in 1892 stemming from the premature closure of an exhibition of paintings by Norwegian painter Edvard Munch sparked the Berlin Secession, an association of painters and sculptors that included Max Liebermann, Max Slevogt, and Walter Leistikow at the forefront. Founded in 1898, the year Strauss moved to the capital, the Secession opposed the academic approach to fine art and the old-fashioned taste championed by Emperor Wilhelm II. The secessionists, among them important representatives of German Impressionism, exhibited their works separately from the annual exhibition of the Königliche Akademie der Künste (Royal Academy of Arts).

Some, however, held an ambivalent attitude toward these modern times. Many innovative artists and their advocates were skeptical of the profound changes – economic, social, and political – taking place in Berlin and did not share the widespread pride and optimism. Even among those who favored modernist trends, change was not necessarily indicative of progress. The art critic Karl Scheffler, for instance, promoted the impressionists but articulated a sense of unease in stating that Berlin was a city "condemned forever to becoming and never being."[3] His words became famous as a characterization of the city's unique urban development.

Strauss's Personal Links and Institutional Affiliations

Strauss witnessed profound changes in society and the broader cultural world that were particular to Berlin. How this influenced his dramatic works beginning with *Feuersnot* can be closely examined by looking at his status in the local art scene. Strauss was 34 years old when he started his job as Kapellmeister in 1898, and he immediately became immersed in the vivid cultural life of the German capital. For Strauss, as a conductor at the court opera and a budding operatic composer, the genre obviously took on special significance. In addition to his own creative activities, Strauss had

---

[3] Karl Scheffler concluded thus in his *Berlin, ein Stadtschicksal* (Berlin: Suhrkamp Verlag, 2015) [1st ed. 1910].

to fulfill various institutional duties. When he arrived in Berlin, the Generalintendant of the Court Opera was Graf Bolko von Hochberg. After Hochberg's withdrawal, partially caused by Strauss and the conflicts around his racy opera *Feuersnot*, Georg von Hülsen-Haeseler followed in that role. The main task for both him and Strauss was to satisfy the demands of the Emperor, who claimed to shape culture in Germany and especially in "his" capital. In his narrow-minded understanding of "true art," Wilhelm II rejected artistic manifestations "descending in the gutter" as he put it in a notorious speech in 1901.[4]

Although in courtly circles artistic taste was strictly traditional, and the wishes of the royal family were carried out faithfully, the quality of productions under conductors like Felix von Weingartner (1891–98), Karl Muck (1892–1912), and Leo Blech (from 1906) was excellent. Singers such as Emmy Destinn, who performed the role of Salome in the staging of Strauss's opera at the Court Opera, Lola Artôt de Padilla, and Paul Knüpfer were equally impressive. Though reluctant, the Court Opera performed the operas by its conductor, such as *Salome* in 1906 and *Der Rosenkavalier* in 1911. Some considered the story of *Salome* blasphemous, while others felt that the racy libretto of *Der Rosenkavalier* was much too permissive. The Generalintendant himself revised the text in order to render it more acceptable. In short, the court disliked eroticism and the burlesque.

Strauss's engagements were not limited to opera. He first conducted the Berlin Philharmonic in 1888 (a decade before his appointment as court conductor) and headed the orchestra between the death of Bülow in 1894 and appointment of Nikisch in 1895. As court conductor, Strauss directed the prestigious symphony concerts of the Court Orchestra for many years. He even exercised a certain influence on the opera repertoire in spite of the court's strictly traditional orientation. He championed contemporary artists such as Siegfried Wagner and Eugen d'Albert while also promoting Peter Cornelius.

Strauss was in touch with several Berlin writers. He set to music poems by John Henry Mackay and Richard Dehmel and collaborated with Ernst von Wolzogen on the libretto of *Feuersnot* (1901). Wolzogen had just established the first cabaret in the German capital following the successes of similar shows in Paris. Its name *Überbrettl* (superstage) alluded to

---

[4] Johannes Penzler, ed., *Die Reden Kaiser Wilhelms II. in den Jahren 1901 – Ende 1905*. 3. Teil (Lepzig: Reclam, [1907]), 573.

Nietzsche's *Übermensch* (superhuman). In the few years it existed, Schoenberg was among the artists Wolzogen engaged.

Of particular importance to Strauss's career in Berlin was his acquaintance with Reinhardt, the illustrious theater owner and director who founded the cabaret *Schall und Rauch* (*Sound and Smoke*) in 1901. The following year, Reinhardt staged Oscar Wilde's play *Salomé* in his Kleines Theater (Little Theatre, as he had renamed the cabaret theater), and Strauss was among the audience members. Thus, while the premiere of Strauss's *Salome* took place in Dresden in 1905, its creation and conceptualization were inspired by his links to Berlin. Strauss met many other artists associated with Reinhardt and collaborated with some of them. For instance, Strauss engaged Reinhardt's stage painter, Ernst Stern, for the premiere of *Ariadne auf Naxos* in Stuttgart in 1912. Earlier, the owner and director of the Stern'sches Konservatorium, Gustav Hollaender, a brother of Reinhardt's dramaturge Felix Hollaender, invited Strauss to head a composition master class shortly after he was appointed court conductor by the Emperor. Strauss did not accept but stayed in touch with Hollaender. In 1902, Strauss successfully recommended Arnold Schoenberg for the post.

Fortunately, the earlier controversies in which Strauss was involved did not harm his reputation. In the years immediately preceding the outbreak of the World War I, Strauss was finally appreciated and recognized as the leading representative of modern music in Germany. In a contemporary illustrated book featuring portraits of numerous composers and performers, Strauss was placed first despite the other musicians appearing in alphabetical order.[5] His high standing was further reflected by the number of distinguished portraits produced of him, including a sculpture by Hugo Lederer (1903), an etching by Emil Orlik (1917), and, best known, a painting by Liebermann (1918).

At the start of the twentieth century, Berlin was home to dozens of newspapers and other periodicals, and, in contrast to his situation in Munich, Strauss received mostly positive responses to his new compositions in the press. Many felt that the development of "modern music" culminated in the musical works of Richard Strauss. Indeed, he counted several influential writers and critics among his friends. He had the opportunity to acquaint himself with influential promoters such as Leopold Schmidt from the *Berliner Tageblatt* and Wilhelm Klatte from the *Berliner Lokal-Anzeiger*. Oscar Bie, a gifted writer and critic for the *Berliner*

---

[5] Wilhelm Spemann, ed., *Spemanns goldenes Buch der Musik* (Berlin: W. Spemann, 1900).

Börsen-Courier who specialized in opera, dance, and fine art, was a particularly ardent admirer of Strauss.[6] Herwarth Walden, later the founder of the famous expressionist Sturm Gallery, edited an introduction to Strauss's compositional oeuvre.[7]

Berlin's "Richard Strauss Period"

Even from the viewpoint of contemporaries, Berlin experienced a "Richard Strauss period." This phrase was used by the nearly forgotten writer and journalist Adolf Weissmann in the preface of his book *Berlin als Musikstadt* (*Berlin as a City of Music*). Then a major figure in music criticism, Weissmann surveys the history of opera and concert performances in Berlin up to 1911. He regarded Strauss as the main successor to Wagner, whose operas required a great deal of time before they were accepted by audiences in Berlin. For Weissmann, the "newest development" was the rise of Strauss, which presupposed Wagner's inevitable and overwhelming success.

In Weissmann's portrayal of Berlin as a dynamic and vibrant "city of music," he notes that "the musical life of the Imperial capital [was] an enormous organism where multi-faceted tendencies [overlapped]."[8] Modernist tendencies conflicted with traditional ideals, and the "official" art favored by Wilhelm II was often criticized, even in an ironic and sarcastic manner. This criticism could be observed in the leading liberal newspapers – not just in the radical utterances of a few artists and outsiders. Although the Emperor impeded the development of modern art, cultural life was nonetheless far from monolithic. During his tenure in Berlin, Strauss had to reconcile these conflicting views. He was a servant of the court but also a modernist – and he clearly succeeded in that difficult role.

When the German monarchy ended in 1918, Strauss was recognized alongside Hauptmann, Liebermann, and Reinhardt as one of the most well-known exponents of German culture. The public regarded these artists as major cultural figures and great characters. As such, they formed a counterweight to the Emperor in a society that, despite not being autocratic, still longed for authority.

---

[6] Oscar Bie, *Die moderne Musik und Richard Strauß* (Berlin: Marquardt, 1906).

[7] Herwarth Walden, ed., *Richard Strauss: Symphonien und Tondichtungen* (Berlin: Schlesinger, [1908]).

[8] Adolf Weissmann, *Berlin als Musikstadt: Geschichte der Oper und des Konzerts von 1740 bis 1911* (Berlin & Leipzig: Schuster & Loeffler, 1911), 8.

CHAPTER 13

Vienna

Joseph E. Jones

The year 1882 was pivotal for Strauss. After turning 18 in June, he traveled with his father that August to the Bayreuth Festival to witness the inaugural production of Wagner's *Parsifal*. He then enrolled at the Ludwig-Maximilians-Universität in Munich but dropped out after one term to fully pursue a career in music. On December 1, he made his first journey to Vienna for the premiere of his Violin Concerto in the Bösendorfersaal of the Palais Liechtenstein (demolished 1913). More than 12 years passed before Strauss returned to the Austro-Hungarian capital, in April 1895, when he appeared as guest conductor with the Berlin Philharmonic in a performance of Beethoven's Seventh and the *Meistersinger* prelude. These were Strauss's only trips to Vienna before his 35th birthday, despite the city's rich musical heritage.

After assuming the directorship of the Berlin Court Opera in 1898, Strauss continued to spend the bulk of his time in Germany. He visited Vienna periodically between 1901 and 1906 to conduct his own works, particularly *Feuersnot* and the tone poems, meeting occasionally with Mahler. It was not until 1907 that Strauss began traveling regularly to Vienna, spending at least some time in the city most years through the end of the First Austrian Republic in 1933. He was on an extended stay in Italy when the Nazis annexed Austria in March 1938, and he returned that October to conduct his *Festliches Präludium* and Beethoven 9 at a concert celebrating the 25th anniversary of the Konzerthaus. A couple of season-long engagements drew him back in the early 1940s, and 80th-birthday celebrations in June 1944 prompted what would be his final visit to Vienna. He departed for Garmisch on June 19, three days after American planes bombed oil refineries on the outskirts of the city.

Strauss's contacts with Vienna thus spanned more than six decades, from the time of his brief stint as a university student in 1882 through the Allied air campaigns of 1944. This chapter centers on Vienna during the period of his tenure as codirector of the State Opera from 1919 to 1924, years defined by the founding of the Republic and policies instituted by the Municipal Council in response to ongoing economic turmoil. While the situation was less dire than in Berlin, Vienna was a city in crisis when Strauss arrived in early December 1919. Examination of "Red Vienna," named for initiatives of the ruling Social Democratic Party, serves as context for the cultural life in which he participated as a highly-respected and well-paid musical celebrity. Attention then shifts to Strauss's life and work in Vienna with a focus on the institutions and figures that comprised his private and professional orbit.

Red Vienna

The Armistice of Villa Giusti, signed November 3, 1918, marked the final days of the Austria-Hungary dual monarchy and six and half centuries of Habsburg rule. Nine days later, officials from the former Imperial Council declared themselves the provisional National Assembly of the Republic of German-Austria. The newly-formed country, which claimed territories in northern Italy, Bohemia, Moravia, and Silesia, was short lived. The Treaty of Saint-Germain-en-Laye, ratified by Emperor Karl I and the Allied Powers on September 10, 1919, officially dissolved the empire while establishing the independence of German-speaking territories beyond Austria's borders. The name Republic of Austria (or First Austrian Republic) replaced "German-Austria," for the treaty prohibited any union with Germany.

The conservative Christian Social Party ("blacks") were favored in the outer Austrian states, while the Social Democratic Party ("reds") held a majority in the capital. Social Democrat Karl Renner was named provisional chancellor, while city elections in May 1919 elevated fellow Social Democrat Jakob Reumann to the position of Vienna's mayor. The two political parties initially formed a coalition and treated one another with consideration. In the early days of the Republic, they developed an unemployment benefits program, established a worker's union, and instituted an eight-hour workday. This relatively harmonious period came to an end when the Christian Social Party won the National Council elections of October 1920 and subsequently formed a new government with the antisemitic nationalist Greater German People's Party. Vienna officially split from Lower Austria on January 1, 1922, to become an independent federal province and, while the Social Democrats had little hope of securing a majority in rural areas where Christian Socials were favored, they retained power in the capital for the next decade.

For many, the immediate post-war period in Vienna was one of untold misery. The economy suffered from hyperinflation, middle-class savings were wiped out from worthless war bonds, thousands succumbed to an influenza epidemic, and the city faced a severe housing shortage. Hofmannsthal wrote in April 1919, "The poverty here is truly awful ... We have nothing to eat; now even the horse meat, on which we have subsisted for the past year and a half, is no longer affordable and no longer available."[1] Various remedies were proposed to alleviate the deplorable conditions, among them the sale of imperial treasures to foreign collectors in order to procure the wherewithal for food. Families often sold their personal possessions in order to pay the exorbitant prices that shops charged for the necessities of life.

The Social Democratic administration pursued policies aimed at the elimination of poverty and want. To the position of Finance Councilor, Reumann appointed bank director Hugo Breitner, who levied new taxes aimed at squeezing the well-to-do in order to finance the municipality's social schemes. These taxes funded a range of projects without the need to borrow. The city could afford to offer a range of medical services without cost and supported families with children by providing infant clothing (paid for with proceeds from horse race betting), free school lunches, and additional options for childcare. Otto Glöckel, who served as Education Minister from 1919 to 1920 and later as Vienna City School Council president, oversaw the construction of new Kindergartens and curriculum revision that made religious instruction optional. Access to common education was extended through age 14. Julius Tandler, university professor and director of the Public Health Office, was instrumental in implementing progressive policies. His chief concern was the prevention of tuberculosis, a disease that had assumed epidemic proportions and to which large numbers of young people had fallen victim. Tandler expanded social services in several areas, for instance, by opening facilities that encouraged participation in leisure and exercise activities.

The Municipal Council also sought to address the housing shortage while raising the standards of accommodations. Wartime regulations protecting tenants against eviction and excessive rent hikes remained, for any increase would have led to a corresponding rise in wages, which in turn would have driven up production costs making it harder to sell Austrian goods in foreign markets. Breitner continued as Finance Councilor under

---

[1] Marie-Therese Miller-Degenfeld, ed., *The Poet and the Countess: Hugo von Hofmannsthal's Correspondence with Countess Ottonie Degenfeld* (Rochester: Camden House, 2000), 331.

Karl Seitz, who succeeded Reumann in November 1923 and remained in the mayor's office until the Republic's collapse in 1934. In addition to taxes on hotel rooms, alcohol, horses, automobiles, and other luxury goods, Breitner's construction tax funded a vast public housing initiative. The city erected around 64,000 units in new municipality buildings, or *Gemeindebauten*, through 1934, with rents fixed at 4 percent of household income. Nearly a third of Viennese residents today live in such buildings, many still bearing signage that reads "Constructed by means of the Viennese housing tax" (*Errichtet aus Mitteln der Wiener Wohnbausteuer*).

While the Christian Social Party decried Vienna as a welfare state, similar reforms were enacted at the national level. Nonetheless, ever-present tensions both within and between political parties led to radicalization that spurred protests and violence. The Social Democrats formed a paramilitary wing in 1923 called the Republican Protection League, and the Christian Social Party and Communist Party of Austria maintained their own auxiliary military forces: the Home Guard and Red Guard, respectively. Tensions boiled over in the July Revolt of 1927, which left more than 90 dead and 600 injured. The global financial crash of 1929 exacerbated matters as Vienna suffered once again from hyperinflation and high unemployment. These extraordinary economic circumstances and political polarization culminated in the Austria Civil War of February 1934, which enabled the rise of Austrofascism.

The collapse of the pre-1914 social order had widespread repercussions. No longer the hub of a large empire, Vienna became the somewhat forlorn capital of a minor state, a circumstance that further impoverished it by stemming the influx of intellectuals from neighboring countries. Still, for a decade or so, the initiatives of Vienna's predominantly Social Democratic Municipal Council cemented its reputation as a progressive city. As health and education standards improved, and housing and employment initiatives were deemed successful, much of Europe viewed Vienna as a model for recovery. Yet when Strauss arrived in December 1919 to assume codirectorship of the opera, three months after the Treaty of Saint-Germain-en-Laye, Vienna was still, in many ways, a city in crisis.

Musical Life and Culture

In July 1918, during the waning months of the war, Emperor Charles I appointed Leopold Andrian general intendant of imperial court theaters. Andrian soon began work to lure Strauss from Berlin, spearheading the arrangement of a double directorship with Franz Schalk. Reception to the plan was mixed. A vocal opposition bristled at paying a "foreigner" a massive salary for four to five months of work per year, preferring to hire someone local who knew the musicians and institutions more personally and would spend more time in Vienna. Some believed Strauss would use the position to promote his own works while other popular repertoire languished. Noteworthy dissenters included the music critic Julius Korngold, who succeeded Eduard Hanslick at the *Neue Freie Presse*, and the conductor-composer Felix Weingartner, who knew Strauss from Berlin and previously held the podium following Mahler's resignation. Passed over for reappointment after the war, Weingartner accepted a similar role at the rival Volksoper. Others voiced encouragement, however, and Schalk himself endorsed Andrian's plan. Taking the reins from Hans Gregor (1911–18), Schalk agreed to work as interim director until the following winter.

When the Court Opera resolved to engage Strauss on April 10, 1919, the institution was in a weak financial state and a period of transition, like Austria at large. April was the same month Hofmannsthal wrote of the desperate conditions experienced by many Viennese, who could scarcely afford the luxury of attending concerts. The loss of imperial patronage and subsequent implementation of socialist policies greatly diminished the support for music. The illustrious opera house on the Ringstrasse was no exception. The Hofburgtheater and Court Opera were brought into state ownership as Vienna transitioned from capital of the empire to that of the short-lived Republic of German-Austria. This meant name changes for some former imperial venues, including the Court Opera, which became the State Opera. With the contract settled, Strauss returned to Vienna in May 1919 to participate in celebrations marking the 50th anniversary of the State Opera building. Over 12 days, he conducted Mozart and Wagner as well as his own *Ariadne auf Naxos*, and he met at least once with Schalk, presumably to discuss plans for the upcoming season. Strauss's contract officially began on December 1, 1919, and his inaugural performance, one week later, was Beethoven's *Fidelio*.

Their first days in Vienna, the Strauss's lodged with friends at Löwel-strasse 8, part of the Palais Figdor built in 1875 by the architect Victor Rumpelmayer. Situated behind the Volksgarten and adjacent to the Stadt-palais Liechtenstein, it was a prestigious address in the city center that today houses the Embassy of Liechtenstein. Richard and Pauline were guests of the Mautner family, whom the Strausses had known for several years. The Mautners regularly hosted artists in their lavish residence, including Hofmannsthal, the writer and critic Felix Salten (author of

Bambi), Arthur Schnitzler, and Max Reinhardt. Actors from the nearby Burgtheater often stopped by after performances. Isidor Mautner owned a textile factory, and his wife, Jenny (Eugenie), was an amateur musician and patron. Strauss dedicated his Fünf kleine Lieder Op. 69, No. 4 "Waldesfahrt" to Frau Mautner.

On December 6, the Strausses moved to Mozartgasse 4, where their neighbors included a retired Lieutenant Field Marshal Schmid and a businessman named Rosenthal.[2] The neoclassical building, number four, was a recent reconstruction by Max Kaiser for the industrialist Oscar Mayer von Gunthof. The Mozart Fountain (1905) at the center of the square provided a further modern touch; designed by Otto Schönthal with sculptures by Carl Wolleck, it exemplifies Vienna's leading role in the broader Jugendstil (Art Nouveau) movement. A 15-minute walk from his work at the State Opera, Musikverein, and Konzerthaus, the Mozartgasse location proved convenient for Strauss.

Beyond these venues, the city was home to dozens of institutions that contributed to a rich and diverse musical culture. The main complement and competitor to the State Opera was the Volksoper (People's Opera), which transformed in 1903–04 from a spoken-language theater to one that staged music in various forms, including operetta and Singspiel. Operetta had a long history in Vienna by the 1920s and, despite the tumult of the interwar period, around 150 new productions appeared on stages such as the Volksoper, Raimundtheater, Johann Strauss-Theater, and Neues Wiener Stadttheater. Perhaps most closely associated with the golden age of operetta was the Theater an der Wien, founded in 1801 by Emanuel Schikaneder. While operetta was fading in popularity in the mid-1920s, the Theater an der Wien was crucial to its sustained relevance.

By 1919, the Musikverein (Music Association), operated by the Gesellschaft der Musikfreunde (Society of Friends of Music), was well established as guardian of Vienna's classical music tradition. Like the State Opera, the building (1870) was constructed as part of a massive urban redevelopment project centered along the Ringstrasse that encircles the first district. Since then, it has been home to the Vienna Philharmonic. Weingartner led the orchestra from 1908 through 1927 and was succeeded by Wilhelm Furtwängler, who held the post until 1930. Strauss appeared frequently as guest conductor both in Vienna and on tours, and to help fundraise through challenging economic times, traveled with the orchestra

[2] Allan S. Janik and Hans Veigl, *Wittgenstein in Vienna: A Biographical Excursion through the City and Its History* (Vienna: Springer-Verlag, 1998), 155.

on voyages to South America (September–November 1920 and June–August 1923) and the United States (October 1921–January 1922). Programming heavily favored canonical German composers, for example, a week-long festival commemorating the 125th anniversary of Schubert's birth, while Strauss's own works dominated the contemporary repertoire that also included works by Gustav Holst, Maurice Ravel, and Igor Stravinsky.

Programming at the State Opera was somewhat more diverse. Between December 1919 and October 1924, the period of the Schalk–Strauss codirectorship, the State Opera staged 51 different operas.[3] Austro-Germans composed roughly 60 percent of this total, although three of the five most popular operas by performances were Puccini's *Tosca* (54), Bizet's *Carmen* (46), and Verdi's *Aïda* (41). Surely confirming some of his critics' misgivings, the most represented composer was Strauss himself (146), trailed by Verdi (121), Wagner (105), Puccini (80), and Mozart (72). While the bulk of the repertoire dates from the eighteenth and nineteenth centuries, living and active composers accounted for nearly 30 percent of performances at the State Opera. (Strauss, again, skews this number.) Popular works that receive less attention today include d'Albert's *Tiefland* (1903), Pfitzner's *Palestrina* (1915), and most notably, Korngold's *Die tote Stadt* (1920), staged 34 times in three years. Strauss conducted Mozart, Wagner, and his own operas almost exclusively.

He also performed often at the Konzerthaus, a short walk from the Musikverein and a comparably-sized venue. The art nouveau building was inaugurated less than a year before the outbreak of World War I and serves as home of the Wiener Symphoniker (Vienna Symphony), then called the Wiener Sinfonie-Orchester. To build their audience during the hard economic times, the ensemble routinely programmed what the Philharmonic did not: popular works and more modern compositions; works by Debussy, Mahler, Bartók, and Sibelius were presented during this era.[4] Ferdinand Löwe founded the ensemble in 1900 and served as its chief conductor until Furtwängler, while concurrently directing the Musikverein, held the post from 1927 to 1930. Its affiliated society, the Konzerthausgesellschaft, had a significant and progressive influence on musical life in Vienna during the interwar period.

[3] The State Opera publishes historical data on works, composers, artists, and roles dating back to 1869. See https://archiv.wiener-staatsoper.at.

[4] A broader summary of the various orchestras' repertoire appears in Theophil Antonicek, Derek Beales, Leon Botstein, Rudolf Klein, and Harald Goertz, "Vienna," *Grove Music Online*, accessed July 18, 2019, www.oxfordmusiconline.com.

A modernist force in the city was the Verein für Musikalische Privataufführungen (Society for Private Musical Performances), established by Arnold Schoenberg in 1918. Pursuing an idealistic vision of the concert setting, the society presented new music exclusively for a private membership. Journalists were not admitted and audiences refrained from demonstrations of approval or disapproval. From 1919 until it disbanded in 1921, the society organized more than 350 performances, principally chamber music including transcriptions of large-scale works. Alban Berg was one of its directors along with Rudolf Kolisch (of the Kolisch Quartet), Edwin Stein, and Eduard Steuermann – all pupils of Schoenberg. Another prominent student, Anton Webern, led the Arbeiter-Sinfoniekonzerte (Workers' Symphony Concerts) from 1922 to 1924 and the Arbeitersingverein (Workers' Singing Society) from 1923, both having ties to the socialist workers' movement. Schoenberg announced his 12-tone method to friends in February 1923 and left Vienna for a professorship in Berlin in January 1926.

Even a cursory account of the dozens of artists, intellectuals, and politicians who impacted Viennese society and culture from 1919 to 1924 would exceed the scope of this chapter. A list of influential figures active in Vienna after Strauss's arrival would include Alfred Adler, Sigmund Freud, Karl Krauss, Adolf Loos, Hofmannsthal, Karl Polanyi, Schnitzler, Ludwig Wittgenstein, and Stefan Zweig. Along with Korngold, prominent music critics and historians of the era were Elsa Bienefeld, Max Graf, Heinrich von Kralik, and Paul Stefan.

Returning to Strauss's life and work in Vienna, the circumstances that ended his partnership with Schalk are well documented. Their contracts did not fully specify job duties, and Strauss, the international musical celebrity, spent much of the year away. He assumed the native Schalk would handle the administrative tasks, as Schalk had been active in the city for nearly two decades and knew the personnel. Their relationship was often tense, and open conflict was not uncommon. Strauss attempted to negotiate a new contract in April 1924, predicated on Schalk's retirement, but Schalk outmaneuvered him and convinced the leadership to appoint him sole director through 1929. Accepting that he would effectively resign, Strauss conducted two concerts in May at the Musikverein honoring his 60th year (he spent his birthday proper in Karlsruhe) and went on to lead his final performance as codirector on October 1. Whereas he held the podium in Berlin for 20 years, the Vienna contract fell just short of five. Nonetheless, this period at the State Opera was an artistic success, featuring new productions of canonical repertoire and several premieres by living composers.

Figure 13.1   The Strauss Villa at Jacquingasse 8–10.
Photograph by the author

Despite ongoing tensions at work, Strauss forged ahead with plans to build a house (Figure 13.1). In 1922, city officials suggested two possible locations near Schönbrunn Palace, but Strauss rejected them due to their distance from the city center.[5] They eventually agreed upon a section of the eastern grounds of the Belvedere complex. The larger Upper Belvedere had served as the private residence of the heir to the throne, Archduke Franz Ferdinand, whose assassination precipitated World War I. The Lower Belvedere had been a state-owned museum since 1903 and the Upper was incorporated after the war. Strauss and the city entered into a 60-year lease after which the property would return to the government. Strauss consented to pay all architectural and building costs, and also to donate valuable manuscripts including the autograph scores of *Der Rosenkavalier* and *Schlagobers*. Strauss further agreed to conduct 100 performances over five years without compensation. Published details

[5] Georg Markus, *Adressen mit Geschichte: Wo berühmte Menschen lebten* (Wien: Amalthea Verlag, 2005).

concerning the villa's completion are often contradictory; for instance, several sources list the construction dates as 1922–24, and some note that the family took possession in 1924. In fact, Strauss was still engaged in preliminary discussions with the architect, Michael Rosenauer, in May 1923, and the lease for the site at Jacquingasse 8–10 was not finalized until August 1924. More than a year passed before the Strausses began furnishing the house. According to Strauss's travel log, he returned from a trip to Turin on December 10, 1925, and received the keys the following day.[6]

The State Opera contract was Strauss's last regular conducting engagement. With their beautiful residence in the Jacquingasse completed, the family spent considerable time in Vienna through the end of the Republic. From publishing royalties and fees earned as a guest conductor, he could afford to travel while maintaining both the Jacquingasse property and his villa in Garmisch. Strauss deeply appreciated Vienna's commitment to its musical culture, and with the economic and political situation in Germany often comparably worse, the Austrian capital offered an attractive alternative.

---

[6] Today, the "Strauss-Schlössel" (Villa Strauss) serves as the residence for the Embassy of the Netherlands.

PART III

Cultural Engagement and Musical Life

CHAPTER 14

Strauss as Reader

Matthew Werley

When will I receive the Chinese heist novel?
Strauss to Anton Kippenberg[1]

In the libretto to Alfred Kerr's opera *Der Chronoplan* (1933), a surreal plot in which Einstein invents a time machine and abducts Lord Byron from the year 1801, teleporting him into the late Weimar Republic, Richard Strauss appears as a character on stage alongside the painter Max Liebermann, dramatist Gerhart Hauptmann, and playwright George Bernard Shaw. As Einstein invites each of his illustrious contemporaries to test out his theory of relativity by traveling into the past with him (a literal *Zeitoper*), Strauss blithely tenders the excuse that he would prefer to read about Salome from the comfort of his armchair than ever encounter his operatic subject in person. In the end, Germany's most famous living composer remains ensconced in his *gemütlich* Garmisch study, Byron is appalled by what he witnesses of late-Weimar culture and begs to be returned home, and the opera itself was never staged.

Although a fantastically pithy scenario, Kerr's theatrical depiction of his former collaborator distills his real-life subject's fundamental belief that literature, rather than first-hand experience, has the ability to convey the deeper essence of historical "truth." For Europeans born and educated before the World War I, this assumption was surprisingly widespread. In what could have substituted for Strauss's reply to Kerr, Ravel once assimilated Proust's position that, "there is no need to travel in order to discover [the past] again; we must dig down inwardly to discover it." Likewise, the most widely read author of historical novels at the time, Stefan Zweig, reasoned in his 1931 essay *History as Poetess*, "there is perhaps no actual history in itself, in a general sense, but it is only through the art of writing,

---

[1] Strauss to Kippenberg, January 18, 1935; in "Richard Strauss und Anton Kippenberg – Briefwechsel," in *Richard Strauss Jahrbuch 1959/60*, ed. Willi Schuh (Bonn: Boosey & Hawkes, 1959–60), 125.

the vision of the narrator, [that] the very factual date of history is *willed*."[2] The implications of such a hermeneutic disposition were surprisingly far-reaching for the ways in which modern composers, especially Strauss, positioned their careers in relation to literature.

Composers have long engaged with texts, but the extent to which they have consciously constructed a literary cosmos around their musical works and private lives has radically changed over the last two centuries. To trace the quantitative leaps taken since Beethoven reverently gestured to the superiority of Handel's scores sitting in his personal library, to Wagner's revelatory "discovery" of the Greek classics in 1847, Liszt's upping the stakes of the interpretative game between listeners and literature in the symphonic poem, and the emergence of *Literaturoper* around 1900, would be to outline how the successive enfranchisement of the post-Enlightenment reader gradually reconfigured the dynamics in which listener–composer relations are negotiated. For modern composers, it has been increasingly common to read not merely to enrich intellectual horizons or scour for musically settable material, but as a means to tap into an increasingly available reservoir of texts through which the reception of their works can add a layer of cultural legitimation – one that can, in turn, potentially vouchsafe present-day success or curate any future grafting into the repertoire.

Viewed against this wider context, the extensive library that Strauss collected, read, and selectively presented to audiences in various musical formats symbolizes neither the physical legacy of a lifelong bibliophile (Brahms) nor the quiet spiritual refuge of a well-heeled bourgeois (Elgar). Rather, it constitutes the material footprint of an intellectual disposition toward the world that stems from a deeper-held set of beliefs about the cultural mission of literature in Western European history, one spanning from the ancient Greeks to the modern German nation-state.

As a methodological starting point, it can hardly suffice to state the obvious, as Norman Del Mar and others have done, that literature "was grist to his mill as he sat quietly day after day at his desk systematically filling the pages of score-paper with his thin immaculate manuscript."[3] No doubt it was, but Strauss's life-long habit of composing with one eye turned to literature was a praxis that emerged against the backdrop of a

---

[2] Proust, quoted from Michael Puri, *Ravel the Decadent: Memory, Sublimation, and Desire* (Oxford: Oxford University Press, 2011), 21; Zweig, from *Messages from a Lost World: Europe on the Brink*, trans. Will Stone (London: Pushkin Press, 2016), 78.

[3] Norman Del Mar, "Some Centenary Reflections," *Tempo* no. 69 (1964): 2.

particular socio-cultural moment in Germany's history – one whose privileged conditions were hardly available to previous generations. When at the age of six the Bavarian composer became a citizen of the Empire under Bismarck, he could take it for granted that domestic audiences enjoyed comparatively higher literacy rates – not to mention material comforts, industrial standards, and military prowess – than those of any other European nation. Strauss's ability to capitalize on the literate masses, by framing his music against widely-circulated cultural reference points, provided his *oeuvre* with unprecedented access to global markets – despite the often daunting technical and aesthetic challenges his works presented. Indeed, that the most successful, ambitious, and cosmopolitan composer of the post-Wagnerian generation cut such a remarkable profile across music history by repeatedly staking out his career along the pillars of first-rate literature, from Elizabethan drama to contemporary Swiss poetry, had consequences for music's contribution to cultural history. That is, the highly international array of literary figures that stand as a metonym for his unbroken chain of musical successes – Shakespeare (English), Lenau (Austrian), Nietzsche (German), Cervantes (Spanish), Dehmel (German), Wilde (Irish), Hofmannsthal (Austrian), Molière (French), Zweig/Jonson (Austrian/English), and Hesse (Swiss) – sublimates the transnational border-crossing ideals of Goethe's World Literature into the sphere of art music in ways no previous composer had ever imagined.

Considering his personal life, the scale and depth of his literary proclivities were singular. While his forebears such as Brahms and Wagner cultivated friendships with aristocrats, artists, and other musicians, Strauss associated almost exclusively with authors of international standing. He counted two Nobel-Prize laureates for literature, Gerhart Hauptmann and Romain Rolland, among his lifelong friends. His introduction to Hugo von Hofmannsthal came about through his friend Harry Graf Kessler, founder of the Cranach-Presse, just as his collaboration with Zweig was brokered through Anton Kippenberg, the twentieth century's most important collector of Goethe manuscripts and director of Germany's distinguished publishing house, Insel Verlag. Such figures as Hermann Bahr, Arthur Schnitzler, and Franz Werfel (Austrian); and Otto Julius Bierbaum, Richard Dehmel, Karl Henckell, and Alfred Kerr (German), were all his confidantes. No composer cultivated friendships with such an illustrious coterie of novelists, dramatists, poets, and theater critics.

Strauss's knowledge of literature was certainly equal to the company he kept. To a Kapellmeister such as Karl Böhm, his erudition even appeared intimidating. "Sometimes it was completely impossible to follow Strauss in every topic of conversation," Böhm once confessed. In order to do so, "one had to be just as well informed in the field of music as in literature. He was at home with German literature like no other musician. [...] 'Faust' he knew by heart. He knew Russian literature just as well." According to Clemens Krauss, Strauss possessed a formidable intellect that commanded foreign literature and European history in equal measure: "He knew pieces by Lope de Vegas, Goldoni or the French just as well as the novels by Dickens; he could quote the letters of Maria Theresa with the same familiarity as the conversations of Goethe or the Viennese folk comedies of the Vormärz."[4]

Blind spots in his literary horizon were seemingly few and far between. By no means was he culturally disadvantaged against Hofmannsthal, who had read all of the English, French, Italian, Spanish, and Russian classics, as well as literary "greats" of antiquity by the age of 18. If little of either's literary knowledge comes to the foreground in their correspondence, it only contrasts with the densely erudite exchanges about literary and theater history with Zweig, Joseph Gregor, and Krauss. Judged by this yardstick, the dilettantism of the *Realschule*-educated Schoenberg, and even Mahler, who once hailed the now all-but-forgotten provincial Styrian poet Peter Rosegger as the greatest literary figure of his day, serves only to delineate Strauss as an exceptionally prolific and sophisticated reader with broad-ranging tastes and penetrating lateral insights.

Bibliotheca Domestica

The roots of Strauss's voracious literary appetite can be partially traced back to his privileged upbringing in Munich. The library his working-class father furnished for his family held a standard assortment of poets that inspired his young son to set verses by Ludwig Uhland, Hoffmann von Fallersleben, and Goethe. It also contained Breitkopf & Härtel's first Mozart edition, which appeared during his impressionable teenage years. Both poetic and musical texts decisively shaped Strauss's early artistic sensibilities, but only inasmuch as they represented pre-existent "givens" in his intellectual landscape. What books he acquired during his early formal studies is more difficult to reconstruct.

The cornerstone of Strauss's early library was undoubtedly Wagner's prose writings. Before leaving for Weimar in 1889, his friend Ludwig

---

[4] Karl Böhm, *Ich erinnere mich ganz genau: Autobiographie* (Vienna: Kremayr & Scheriau, 1968), 101; Krauss quoted in Herbert Zeman, "Aspekte des Opernschaffens von Richard Strauss: Literarische Bildung und musikalisches Leben," *Österreichische Musikzeitschrift* 54, nos. 7–8 (1999): 11.

Thuille presented him with the missing volumes in his collection. Close study of Wagner's potent ideas about opera, aesthetics, and German nationalism allowed Strauss to engage intellectually with much older and distinguished figures such as Alexander Ritter, Cosima Wagner, and members of the so-called Bayreuth Circle. If this heady intellectual brew muffled his individual voice, his readings of Schopenhauer and Nietzsche during his Mediterranean convalescence of 1892–93 spurred a radical rethinking of his position in the post-Wagnerian musical landscape. Yet even as Schopenhauer receded in importance, Wagner's writings continued to hold pride of place.

It cannot be underestimated to what extent Strauss's years in Weimar, Germany's literary capital, helped refine his understanding of literature's relationship to music, theater, philosophy, and politics. Not only did he lay the foundation for his engagement with 80 different authors (with Goethe, Dehmel, Rückert, Uhland, and Kerr ranking at the top), but his intense absorption of art, history, and philosophy resulted in an intellectual maturity and aesthetic *volte-face* that delineates the first and second tone-poem cycles.

While Strauss's absorption of lofty philosophical texts had far-reaching consequences for his modernist aesthetic, the interface between reading and composing was often shockingly *ad hoc* and mundane in practice. On May 4, 1895, for example, Strauss stood waiting in the entranceway of his Munich apartment on the Hildegardstrasse, while Pauline, his wife of eight months, dressed for their afternoon stroll. With his coat already donned, he became impatient and quickly grabbed a slender volume of poetry (Bierbaum's *Nemt, Frouwe, disen Kranz: Ausgewählte Gedichte* of 1894), read the two-stanza poem on page 35, and set it to music before Pauline, bemused, appeared for their walk. The composer often relished the opportunity to recount the almost banal domestic circumstances that attended the genesis of *Traum durch die Dämmerung*, his most popular Lied at the turn of the century; but the episode was hardly atypical of the fluid dynamic that existed between Strauss's literary appetite and ability to draw musical inspiration from his immediate surroundings. The genesis of the postwar Hesse/Eichendorff settings (*Vier letzte Lieder*) was not qualitatively different, nor was the moment of ennui in late 1932 that likely led Strauss to pick up a copy of *Alpenrosen: Ein Schweizer-Almanach auf das Jahr 1814* in a Swiss hotel, where he probably read and earmarked Charlotte Otth's poem *Das Bächlein*. Sparks of inspiration ignited during conversations, travels, and museum visits, but they flew most spectacularly when the printed word lay close to hand.

Figure 14.1   The Garmisch Library in 1909.
Photograph by Frank Eugene[5]

It was therefore paramount that Strauss maintained a private library in all of his residences from Weimar onward. The prospect of being able to amass a significant literary collection of his own came in 1906, when the architect Emanuel von Seidl presented the composer with a total-design project for a villa in Garmisch. Seidl set about with ruthless pragmatism and poetic imagination when designing a structure that facilitated the interaction between music and literature. His solution was to integrate a compositional workshop and library within a single space. On the eastern wall of his study, essentially the backbone of the house, rest five integrated cherrywood bookshelves, which Seidl flanked with artwork to generate a museum-like aura around their contents. He also oriented the room westward so the late-afternoon sun would illuminate the red-gold undertones of the encasements. Nowhere had the materiality of reading as the catalyst of musical inspiration found fuller expression than in this sublime juxtaposition of Alpine landscape and resplendent empire décor (Figure 14.1). When the Viennese musicologist Max Graf interviewed

[5] Printed in Wilhelm Michel, "Emanuel von Seidl – München," *Innen-Dekoration* no. 21 (1910): 14.

Strauss at home in December 1931, he hailed the composer in his surroundings as an organic harmony: "Every artist is a piece of nature, mysteriously connected to Nature and dependent upon air and atmosphere. Imagination is tied to the creative life of Nature." When Zweig visited just over a year later, he confessed his shock at Strauss's library: "What surprises me [...] is that he does not read scores at all, that there are hardly any in his library (by contrast with the great musicians), that he hardly knows of new publications and that he actually does not want to know."[6] What then captured Strauss's interest as a reader?

Forgotten Constellations: Leopold von Ranke, Oswald Spengler, and Egon Friedell

The Weimar Classicists, Wieland, Herder, Schiller, and Goethe, constituted the core of Strauss's intellectual world, augmented by Homer, the Greek Classics, Nietzsche's writings, and various monographs on art and theater history. Musicological texts typically drew sharp criticism, as he much preferred the sweeping cultural assessments by the likes of Jacob Burckhardt, Thomas Carlyle, and Joseph Gregor, whose *A World History of the Theater* (*Weltgeschichte des Theaters*, 1933) he lavished with praise. Above all, however, Strauss gravitated to historical non-fiction. To appreciate his intellectual disposition as a reader, one must understand three towering figures in his intellectual horizon.

During the decades surrounding 1900, Strauss read numerous historical monographs when mining for potential operatic material. But the narrow window of early 1911 that framed the world premiere of *Der Rosenkavalier*'s imaginary eighteenth century and the untimely death of Mahler presaged a sobering encounter with the works of the nineteenth-century German historian Leopold von Ranke. Ranke had become a pioneer in the field by advocating for rigorous examination of archival sources, most of which had long been guarded by state and ecclesiastical gatekeepers. For Strauss and his generation raised on historical novels, Ranke's scholarship represented a new standard of research that reported to explain things "as they really were." Reading the non-romanticized depiction of the German nations during the bloody Protestant Reformation in Ranke's six-volume *German History in the Age of the Reformation* (*Deutsche*

---

[6] Max Graf, "Besuch bei Dr. Richard Strauss in Garmisch," *Die Bühne: Zeitschrift für Theater und Gesellschaft* no. 321 (1932): 29; Zweig's unpublished diary for February 1, 1933 (Literaturarchiv Salzburg).

Geschichte im Zeitalter der Reformation, 1839–47) was a revelation to the 46-year-old composer. Not only did this account complement his prior absorption of Nietzsche's critique of church and state, it also equipped him with an empirically based rationale that emboldened his pre-1914 political conviction that maintained that true and lasting cultural renewal in Germany could occur only once the nation had shed its Christian heritage. Aiming to express this cocktail of Rankean historical prognosis, Nietzschean philosophy, and nationalist fervor, Strauss hatched the idea for a hyper-naturalistic, neo-pagan symphony titled "the Antichrist," his sobriquet for *Eine Alpensinfonie* (1911–15).

Yet if the colossal war of modern nation states preemptively undermined the atheistic ideology of *Eine Alpensinfonie* before its 1915 premiere, by the time Germany was facing a humiliating defeat at the hands of the Allies three years later, Strauss's interest in Ranke (and the chauvinistic nationalism it once helped him voice), had been thrown into crisis. When Schnitzler and Clemens von Franckenstein visited Garmisch during late August 1918, they found him aimlessly thumbing through Ranke's works without any new musical projects on the horizon. Whatever comfort the historian provided at this dark hour of Germany's history remains a matter of speculation, but Strauss consistently returned to Ranke whenever sobering historical perspective was required: most poignantly in October 1944, when he read the seven-volume *History of England* (*Englische Geschichte*, 1859–69) just after Goebbels's Total-War campaign had forced closure of German-speaking theaters.

The August 1918 publication of Oswald Spengler's *The Decline of the West* (*Untergang des Abendlandes*) was nothing short of meteoric for the defeated German nation. An author whose worldview reflected the intellectual concerns and scientific debates of modern times, Spengler interpreted Europe's interweaving social, political, and cultural histories through the organic life-cycle metaphors of growth, flourishment, and death. Strauss likely read Spengler no later than 1920, and its influence on his thinking during the early interwar years cannot be overestimated. The despondent mentality that informed his familiar "last-of-the-mountain-range" statements regarding his place in music history stemmed from this encounter during the chaotic aftermath of the Great War. For other pessimists from Schoenberg to Furtwängler, Spengler's analysis influenced the mental outlook of a generation desperate to come to terms with the collapse of Western European cultural and political structures.

Yet the book that provided the most decisive intellectual catalyst for the composer – a majestic analysis of cultural history that echoed the kind of irreverent poetic imaginaries he found attractive in the writings of the Weimar Classicists and Nietzsche – was Egon Friedell's three-volume *A Cultural History of the Modern Age* (*Kulturgeschichte der Neuzeit*, 1927–31). When Strauss first read Friedell in 1928, he discovered a seductive historical narrative though which he could not only triangulate his own artistic legacy in relation to major historical events, but also mentally collate the extensive repository of experiences accumulated across a 60-plus-year career as world traveler, composer, performer, and cultural icon.

Largely forgotten outside Austria, Friedell was the true polymath among the *fin-de-siècle* Viennese Modernists. Having written a doctorate on Novalis's philosophy, he became Max Reinhardt's protégé before rocketing to fame for his stage portrayal of Goethe at Vienna's Kabarett Fledermaus. Contemporaries christened him "the laughing philosopher" for his literary verve and intellectual breadth as a Kabarett artist, but his true talent lay as a stage actor, where embodying various historical personalities made him the ideal candidate to reflect with nuanced sensitivity on the history of *mentalités*. Spanning the Middle Ages to the World War I, his *Cultural History* offers a Montaigne-like meditation on what it means to be a modern subject entangled in a web of competing historical narratives. Avoiding the kind of systematic categories found in academic monographs, Friedell's account runs fast with facts, making his narrative more performance than treatise. He contends, for example, that the deeper meaning of history lies beyond empirical details, and condones the placement of strategically spun fictions in order to animate history like a ventriloquist. Friedell also queries whether plagiarism and intellectual property are themselves tenuous constructs open to questioning by the principal agents of historical change.

This elegantly witty, paradoxical presentation of cultural development – where history and myth collide to transcend into a higher, mutually complementary narrative – appealed enormously to Strauss's penchant for deploying eclectically stylistic anachronisms to revitalize older music for present-day purposes. Friedell's selective genealogy of European events, mixed with half-poisoned half-truths, emerged as the brightest star in Strauss's intellectual horizon during his final two decades. Many of his statements on music history, the sharp pronouncements about cultural decline, and obtuse assessments of his own artistic contribution to European culture, first appeared as provocative marginalia in his heavily used copy. In short, no other text influenced the fundamental tone of Strauss's late-period aesthetic and writings more than Friedell's.

An Open Book

Reconstructing Strauss's libraries to the extent available in Hofmannsthal and Zweig research would prove enormously valuable to future studies, even if the challenges remain formidable. Countless items from the privately maintained Garmisch library have been dispersed over the years, and the library of his Viennese residence was partially lost during the 1945 Soviet occupation. More problematically, defining the relationships among reading habits, musical life, and cultural tastes presents methodological quandaries long overlooked by musicologists and cultural historians. Mapping out the ways in which Strauss's prolific activities as conductor and cultural administrator informed his literary interests, thus potentially prejudicing his selection of material to present to the public as composer or theater director, remains an elusively complex interdisciplinary problem. Whether any broader patterns can be detected remains open to scrutiny, but when in 1935 Strauss proscribed to the Reichstheaterkammer's Bruno von Niessen what repertoire theaters should be offering, he suggested an ideal ratio of 3:1, German to foreign works. The same year an American academic surveying German reading habits (as reflected in book club titles) identified virtually the same trend: 73 to 27.[7] Certainly for Strauss the reader, musical life was always already enmeshed within larger cultural contexts.

---

[7] Guy R. Vowles, "What Do the Germans Read?," *The German Quarterly* 8, no. 3 (1935): 106–9.

CHAPTER 15

Antiquity

Jason Geary

Richard Strauss's fascination with the Greeks spanned the entirety of his long artistic career, beginning with a setting in 1881 of a chorus from Sophocles' *Elektra* completed as a 17-year-old student for a performance at the Ludwigsgymnasium in Munich. This youthful effort points to the importance of classical antiquity within the curricula of such schools and also reflects the nineteenth-century German trend of setting Greek tragedy to music that originated with Mendelssohn's 1841 score for a production of Sophocles' *Antigone* staged at the Prussian royal court. Strauss the Hellenist would later find a kindred spirit in the Austrian playwright and poet Hugo von Hofmannsthal, with whom he collaborated on three operas drawn from Greek mythology: *Elektra* (1908), *Ariadne auf Naxos* (1912, rev. 1916), and *Die ägyptische Helena* (1927). To this body of work he added two operas with librettos by Joseph Gregor, *Daphne* (1937) and *Die Liebe der Danae* (1940), along with a handful of less known stage works on Greek themes. Strictly speaking, of course, works such as *Salome* and *Also sprach Zarathustra* also reveal a connection to antiquity, but it is only Strauss's Greek-inspired compositions that form a connective thread throughout his oeuvre. What follows offers insight into the cultural, intellectual, and sociopolitical context surrounding these five operas. This chapter traces the development of a long and rich history of German engagement with classical Greece from the eighteenth century to the Third Reich and explores some of the ways in which the changing nature of this relationship informs an understanding of Strauss's operas based on Greek myth.

The Emergence of German Hellenism

Strauss's obsession with the Greeks mirrors a broader German one dating back to the eighteenth century and the pioneering art historian Johann Joachim Winckelmann. Rejecting the prevailing tradition of a French

137

humanism centered on Rome, Winckelmann pointed to ancient Greece as the ultimate cultural and artistic model. In his seminal work, *Reflections on the Imitation of Greek Works in Painting and Sculpture* (1755), he boldly proclaimed that "the only way for us to become great ... is by imitating the ancients," maintaining that Greek art revealed an ideal beauty characterized by "noble simplicity and tranquil grandeur."[1] Winckelmann's idealized notions of Greek antiquity profoundly shaped the views of his contemporaries as well as a subsequent generation of intellectuals including Lessing, Herder, Goethe, and Schiller, for whom the beauty and harmony of Greece offered a stark contrast to the modern world.

In large part because it rejected French humanism, German Hellenism contributed to an emerging national identity that, at least until the establishment of a unified German nation in 1871, was defined by a shared cultural heritage of which the ancient Greek legacy was a key element. Perhaps nowhere is this connection more evident than in the Weimar classicism of Goethe and Schiller, which drew inspiration from Greek literary models while giving expression to a belief in Germany's ability to become for the modern world what Greece had been for the ancient one. The philosopher and diplomat Wilhelm von Humboldt attested to this unique affinity when he wrote in his 1807 essay on the "Geschichte des Verfalls und Untergangs der griechischen Freistaaten" ("History of the Decline and Fall of the Greek City-States") that the Germans maintained a stronger and tighter-knit bond with the Greeks than any other nation on earth. Even amid the emergence of a nineteenth-century Romanticism that shifted emphasis away from antiquity toward a Christian, medieval past, Greece remained a powerful symbol of cultural and artistic renewal, as evidenced by the works of such influential figures as Hegel, Wagner, and Nietzsche. Wagner, for example, saw in Greek tragedy the seeds of a modern-day *Gesamtkunstwerk* that embodied a harmonious union of all the arts and that would mark the advent of a monumental operatic reform, itself occasioned by the destruction of existing social and political structures along with a return to the unity of the individual and society that had defined classical Greece in its prime. Nietzsche, as we shall see, espoused a vision of Greece that challenged conventional notions of antiquity while still embracing aspects of Wagner's music and philosophy. The views of both were well known to Strauss and would come to exert a significant influence on his understanding of Greek

---

[1] Quoted in *German Aesthetic and Literary Criticism*, ed. H. B. Nisbet (Cambridge: Cambridge University Press, 1985), 33.

antiquity, while the overall importance of Greece within German culture as a whole would extend well into the twentieth century.

Elektra and the Tragic Dionysian

Strauss's engagement with the Greeks began in earnest with his decision in 1905 to write an opera based on Hofmannsthal's "free" adaptation of Sophocles' *Elektra* (1903). Hofmannsthal had undertaken this work at a time of literary crisis, defined by a rejection of lyric poetry in favor of drama and a loss of faith in the ability of language alone to adequately reflect human experience – a sentiment famously expressed in his so-called "Chandos" letter of 1902. Seeking to harness the power of non-verbal expression latent in drama, he turned increasingly to Greek myth, which, in keeping with long-held German perceptions of ancient Greece, he viewed as a source of cultural renewal for the modern German-speaking world.

The reigning aesthetic of Hofmannsthal's work, however, reflects a late nineteenth-century phase in German Hellenism marked by a challenge to the sunny, cheerful view of the Greeks first espoused by Winckelmann. Emblematic of this trend is Nietzsche's influential *Birth of Tragedy* (1872), which offered a bold reinterpretation of ancient Greece in hopes of revitalizing modern culture through a genuine rebirth of tragic myth. Nietzsche identified Greek tragedy as the expression of a unique balance between two opposing forces: the Apollonian, associated with a work's poetic element and defined by moderation and restraint, and the Dionysian, associated with the musical component of ancient tragedy and characterized by excess and transgression. Nietzsche claimed that tragedy's demise had resulted from a gradual purging of its Dionysian impulse, and that the prevailing image of Greece as centered on notions of beauty and harmony was a distillation of only its Apollonian qualities. His aim was to dismantle the elaborate façade of Apollonian culture and to reawaken the Dionysian impulse, a process that he believed had already been initiated through Wagnerian music drama.

Nietzsche's essay was an affront not only to Winckelmann's idealized view of the Greeks but also to established academicians, who saw it as a perversion of classical scholarship. Renowned classicist Ulrich von Wilamowitz-Möllendorff responded immediately with an essay derisively titled *Zukunftsphilologie!* (*Philology of the Future!*), in which he dismissed Nietzsche as a mere acolyte of Wagner and maligned his "philosophical" approach to philology. Describing a "joyful and exuberant" Homeric world in opposition to Nietzsche's dark portrait of Homer and arguing that the study of antiquity should be rational and objective, he effectively took an Apollonian stance against Nietzsche's Dionysian reading of the Greeks. Such opposing viewpoints came to define late nineteenth- and early twentieth-century debates in Germany concerning the legacy of ancient Greece and its role in forging a German modernist aesthetic.

Both Hofmannsthal's *Elektra* and Strauss's 1908 rendering of it reveal a self-consciously Dionysian reading of Sophocles' tragedy. Hofmannsthal once described his objective as creating a work opposed in spirit to Goethe's "devilishly humane" *Iphigenie auf Tauris* (1779). Shedding the mantle of classical restraint, Hofmannsthal highlights the psychopathology of characters consumed by their obsessions. Klytämnestra, former wife and murderer of Agamemnon, is plagued by strange dreams and superstitions rooted in a fear of retribution carried out by her long-absent son, Orest, and Elektra, her daughter, is so consumed by a desire for revenge that, in a striking departure from Sophocles' original, she dies in the throes of an ecstatic dance celebrating the murders of Klytämnestra and her lover, Aegisth, at the hands of Orest. Elektra's animalistic portrayal, intensified by Strauss's music, resonates with turn-of-the-century depictions of the *femme fatale* amid women's changing societal roles and evokes a hysteria and neurosis that calls to mind the work of Sigmund Freud, with which Hofmannsthal was familiar.

Strauss's intensely expressionist music depicts the dark, psychological world inhabited by these characters and captures the Dionysian frenzy of Elektra's "death dance" using a rich orchestral palette. Similar to Hofmannsthal, Strauss articulated a desire to draw a contrast between the "possessed, exalted Greece of the sixth century" inherent in the Elektra myth and "Winckelmann's Roman copies and Goethe's humanism."[2] Strauss's complex, highly chromatic musical language continued down a path established by *Salome* and led many contemporary observers to regard *Elektra* as being at the vanguard of modern German opera. Reaction to *Elektra* was decidedly mixed, however, with critics of the opera generally dismayed by what they perceived as a modernist assault on Sophocles' play and the classical aesthetic it represented. These negative views were rooted in a belief that Hofmannsthal and Strauss had failed to reflect traditional German views of the Greeks, underscoring the degree to which Strauss's

[2] Richard Strauss, "Reminiscences of the First Performance of My Operas (1942)," in *Recollections and Reflections*, ed. Willi Schuh, trans. L. J. Lawrence (London: Boosey & Hawkes, 1953), 155.

Elektra is bound up with competing attitudes toward ancient Greece in late-nineteenth and early-twentieth century Germany.

An Apollonian Retreat

Although Strauss returned to Greek mythology several times throughout his career, never again would he pursue the tragic Dionysian with the same intensity and focus as shown in *Elektra*. Indeed, his next two operas on Greek themes can be seen as a wholesale retreat, evoking aspects of the serene classical ideal against which *Elektra* was directed. In *Ariadne auf Naxos* (1912, rev. 1916), the Greek myth upon which the opera is based is used primarily as a means of exploring complex human relationships while nonetheless playing on the idea of contrast in ways that question the fundamental relationship between the present and the past. The opera is ultimately a pastiche that references a variety of historical styles and even specific works from an established European canon. It also functions on some level as a parody, not least in the way that the seriousness of tragic myth is undermined by comic elements drawn from the *commedia dell'arte* tradition.

Strauss and Hofmannsthal's next mythological opera, *Die ägyptische Helena* (1927), took an even more decisive turn away from the tragic Dionysian. As Strauss himself would later recall, drawing a contrast with *Elektra*, the style of *Die ägyptische Helena* approached "the resounding ideal beauty of the Goethe/Winckelmann Hellenism."[3] Its music and libretto avoid any blatant reference to the dark, irrational side of the Greeks, steering clear of the Nietzschean cultural framework that defined *Elektra*. As in *Ariadne auf Naxos*, Greek myth is used more objectively as a vehicle for portraying the depth and nuance of human interaction. In both operas, the reference to the past is more broadly historical than it is specifically Greek. Hofmannsthal himself hinted at this perspective when he explained in a letter to Strauss that he had envisioned *Ariadne* "not as a slavish imitation, but as a spirited paraphrase of the old heroic style."[4]

The sunnier brand of Hellenism found in these two operas recalls the legacy of Winckelmann and the Weimar classicism that defined the age of Goethe. The image of antiquity reflected in these works seems far removed

[3] Cited in Michael P. Steinberg, "Richard Strauss and the Question," in *Richard Strauss and His World*, ed. Bryan Gilliam (Princeton, NJ: Princeton University Press, 1992), 180.
[4] Letter of Hofmannsthal to Strauss, May 19, 1911; in *The Correspondence between Richard Strauss and Hugo von Hofmannsthal*, trans. Hanns Hammelmann and Ewald Osers (London: Collins, 1961), 80.

from the heated debates over whether to view the Greeks through a fundamentally Apollonian or Dionysian lens. Classical antiquity emerges rather as a cultural trope, albeit one with a deeply powerful historical resonance. This more neutral stance toward antiquity can be seen as emblematic of an increasingly pervasive and institutionalized view that Germans held of themselves as the foremost representatives of Western culture, along with its Hellenic roots. It is perhaps for this reason that contemporary reviews of both operas, in contrast to those of *Elektra*, dwell less on the Greek subject matter and the nature of its rendering and more on details of plot and musical style.

Strauss began work on *Ariadne* in the years leading up to the World War I and completed a revised version of the opera in 1916, at which time Germany's view of itself as a nation of poets and thinkers was under strain from characterizations of Germany as barbaric by Allied countries. In this context, ongoing engagement with familiar Hellenic themes would have served to ease such anxieties by affirming the long-established spiritual connection between ancient Greece and modern-day Germany. Strauss and Hofmannsthal began work on *Die ägyptische Helena* in the early 1920s, though the score would not be completed until 1927, nearly a decade after the Treaty of Versailles. The sheer brutality and destruction of the Great War, fueled by modern technological innovation, had profoundly shaken society's faith in the redemptive promise of classical humanism, and partly in response Hofmannsthal embraced as a goal in *Die ägyptische Helena* the blurring of traditional lines between tragedy and comedy, a stance that helps explain his characterization of the work as "mythological operetta."

Antiquity in the Era of National Socialism

Strauss adopted the same stance in his final two Greek operas, *Daphne* (1937) and *Die Liebe der Danae* (1940), employing classical myth primarily as a historical frame within which to explore human relationships that would seem familiar to his audiences. The difference, however, is that these works were completed during the National Socialist regime at a time when classical antiquity had come to assume an important role within the formation of a German identity tied increasingly to notions of race and ethnicity as well as to claims of inherent biological superiority.

Strauss composed both operas between 1936 and 1940, though in the case of *Danae*, the libretto was fashioned by Joseph Gregor based on a sketch by Hofmannsthal that dated back to 1920. This period from the mid-to-late 1930s followed on the heels of Strauss's fall from grace within the National Socialist regime, a fall that had resulted from the discovery of a letter critical of the Nazis that the composer had written to his Jewish collaborator Stefan Zweig. This time frame also included the German annexation of Austria in 1938, which was one of several factors that contributed to the start of the World War II. While on the surface these two operas may appear utterly indifferent to the anxious mood of the time, their ostensibly objective use of Greek myth takes on a somewhat darker dimension when one considers the uses to which classical antiquity, and in particular ancient Greece, were put in Nazi Germany.

Even as humanism came to be viewed with increasing skepticism from some quarters, many scholars and political theorists were at pains to show that National Socialist ideology, including its vicious politics of racial supremacy, was rooted in a classical heritage unique to Germany and an Indo-Germanic lineage that traced back to the ancient Greeks. Influential voices within the Nazi party embraced such ideas as the foundation of what they saw as an inherently political German citizenry modeled on the totality of the ancient Greek individual and thus defined by strength of both mind and body. As Alfred Rosenberg, one of the chief architects of National Socialist ideology, pointed out in a speech of 1934 with reference to ancient Greece: "The renaissance of antiquity that we see at work in the soul of today's new Germany is also in essence a renaissance of the free Germanic man, and the only true task of the National Socialist movement is to reinforce these values of our character."[5] But whereas the Weimar classicism of the late Enlightenment was a universalizing, apolitical brand of humanism that emphasized the intellectual development of the mind, this updated version equally stressed the importance of the body and specifically of a masculine paradigm that was on full display at the Olympic Games staged in Berlin in 1936, just one year before Strauss would complete *Daphne*.

This duality of mind and body that was being held up as one of the defining elements of a new German identity in some ways recalls the duality of the Dionysian and the Apollonian – categories that were clearly on Strauss's mind as he composed *Daphne*. To begin with, one of the opera's main characters is the god Apollo who appears disguised in human form at the feast of Dionysus. It is here that he first sees Daphne, with whom he instantly falls in love. Strauss himself characterized these

[5] Cited in Johann Chapoutot, *Greeks, Romans, Germans: How the Nazis Usurped Europe's Classical Past*, trans. Richard R. Nybakken (Oakland: University of California Press, 2016), 114.

amorous intentions toward the young, chaste Daphne as Dionysian, claiming that they represented a betrayal of Apollo's divine nature. He further explained the need for Apollo to undergo a "purification" that entailed a purging of the Dionysian element from within himself. According to Strauss, the symbol of this purification is Daphne's own transformation into a laurel tree at the conclusion of the opera.[6] Strauss's music throughout the opera reflects a similar opposition between the Apollonian and the Dionysian, alternating between moments of pastoral calm that are often inflected by distinctive woodwind sonorities and those of heightened tension that at times echo the complex textures, pungent dissonances, and angular gestures found in *Elektra*.

Reflecting back near the end of his life on his lasting engagement with antiquity, Strauss made clear that he saw himself as part of a long line of German artists and intellectuals who had looked to the ancient Greeks for inspiration. He described himself in two separate instances as a "German Greek" (*germanischer Grieche*) and a "Greek German" (*griechischer Germane*), and he pointed to his operas on mythological themes as proof of his sustained commitment to celebrating the genius of the Greeks through music.[7] Referring to Wagner's use of myth, he also identified an important distinction between his own relationship to antiquity and that of his older colleague. Whereas Wagner had brought about the long-awaited fulfillment of a "Germanic-Christian" myth in works like *Tristan und Isolde*, the *Ring*, and *Parsifal*, his own aim was to achieve a similar fulfillment of Greek myth, combining it with a non-religious impulse that would ensure the continuing relevance of ancient Greece for a modern, secular world.[8] The limited impact of Strauss's Greek operas as a whole would seem to indicate that his goals were overly ambitious, but this body of work nonetheless provides ample testament to the composer's lifelong fascination with antiquity and to the pervasive influence of classical Greece within German culture of the late nineteenth century and the first half of the twentieth century.

[6] Letter of March 9, 1936, to Joseph Gregor; in "Selections from the Strauss-Gregor Correspondence: The Genesis of Daphne," trans. Susan Gillespie, in *Richard Strauss and His World*, 254.

[7] Richard Strauss, "Letter on the 'Humanistische Gymnasium' (1945)," in *Recollections and Reflections*, ed. Willi Schuh, trans. L. J. Lawrence (London: Boosey & Hawkes, 1953), 89; and "Letzte Aufzeichnung" (1949), *Betrachtungen und Erinnerungen*, 2nd ed., ed. Willi Schuh (Zurich: Atlantis, 1957), 182.

[8] See Walter Werbeck, "Der 'griechische Germane': Griechische Antike und Mythologie im Werk von Richard Strauss – eine vorläufige Bilanz," in *Richard Strauss: Der griechische Germane*, ed. Ulrich Tadday (Munich: Edition Text + Kritik, 2005): 5–24.

CHAPTER 16

Philosophy and Religion

Charles Youmans

In the southern nation of Strauss's birth – Bavaria, not Germany, for unification would take another seven years – Catholicism held sway among Christian denominations. Yet the *alt-katholisch* (Old Catholic) faith practiced by his parents was anything but conservative. Founded by the church historian and priest Johann Joseph Ignaz von Döllinger shortly after the First Vatican Council (1869–70), this breakaway movement emerged from a veritable schism and promoted liberal doctrines including the rejection of papal infallibility, liturgical use of the vernacular, and, in 1874, the ending of the requirement of celibacy for priests. Von Döllinger would eventually be excommunicated, earning thereby a reputation as a minor modern-day Luther.

Thus it was that Strauss "became a freethinker early in his life," according to Johanna Strauss von Rauchenberger, his sister and the only witness to leave commentary on his childhood worldview.[1] The parents abandoned the Roman Catholic faith, and the son abandoned faith altogether, thanks to a socio-religious context that allowed such things. Johanna told also of a friend's proposal that he compose a mass, which he rejected as "rather impossible for me." Franz Strauss would have been pleased, on both musical and religious grounds. And yet: a teenager already emotionally secure in his atheism would soon prove just as comfortable freeing himself from musical dogma, to the chagrin of a father still worshipping at the altar of Haydn, Mozart, and Beethoven.

In what context, then, did Strauss feel something like religious or philosophical passion? First of all, with his explicit embrace of Wagnerism, which began in the fall of 1885 and focused particularly on the role of Schopenhauer in the Master's creative life. The proximate cause of this development was the violinist and composer Alexander Ritter, whom

---

[1] Robert Breuer, "'My Brother, Richard Strauss': An Interview with Johanna von Rauchenberger-Strauss," *The Saturday Review* (New York), December 27, 1958, 33.

Strauss met in the fall of 1885 while Bülow's apprentice at Meiningen. Strauss would call this friendship "the decisive factor in my future development"; Bülow oriented him in the profession, but Ritter illuminated the philosophical counterpart that motivated his change of creative direction. The relationship collapsed eight years later, and the erstwhile mentor's lament clarifies his contribution:

> Words fail to capture the profound joy I felt when I saw your understanding of Wagner's *creative output* becoming ever deeper, as more and more you penetrated and adopted Wagner's worldview, which rests entirely on Schopenhauer's epistemology and ideal-Christian *religiosity*.[2]

Strauss's published comments confirm that this outlook comprised a set of interrelationships among the musical, the intellectual, and the spiritual: the role of a "poetic idea" in creating a musical structure; the capacity of music for "expression" (in the sense of Friedrich von Hausegger); and most important the central place of Schopenhauer's *Willensverneinung* (denial of the Will).

The broad outlines of Schopenhauer's philosophy are easy enough to discern in the arrangement of his magnum opus, *The World as Will and Representation* (1818). Organized in four books, the work lays out a theory of idealism that builds on Platonic roots while introducing an idiosyncratic definition of metaphysical reality, with important implications for artists, particularly musicians. The first two books explain that behind the everyday world of representations, that is, appearances, lies a force – the will – that manifests itself in all phenomena, living and inanimate, and constitutes the universe's ultimate metaphysical reality. The fundamental human problem, addressed in the third and fourth books, is how to bring a halt to the endless striving – which is to say suffering – that characterizes all existence.

For Schopenhauer art offered a respite, by imitating phenomena in such a way as to make the will perceptible, in fleeting moments of "will-less knowing." Music, moreover, accomplished this mission more effectively than other arts, by engaging directly with the will rather than with the phenomena by which the will manifested itself. But while music thereby leapt to the top of the hierarchy of the arts, in the end neither music nor any other art constituted a lasting solution. In a vitally important finding, and one consistently ignored by nineteenth-century composers,

---

[2] Ritter to Strauss, January 17, 1893. Charles Youmans, ed., "Ten Letters from Alexander Ritter to Richard Strauss, 1887–1894," *Richard Strauss-Blätter* no. 35 (1996): 15–16.

Schopenhauer closed book three of *The World as Will* by claiming that art could do no more than point toward the true manner of delivery from the will, asceticism. His fourth book, then, explored true redemption, defining it in terms of withdrawal, an entry into nothingness, to be achieved not through art but by imitating the "lives of the saints."

Ritter was by no means unique among musicians in drawing selectively on Schopenhauer to preserve the enhanced prestige outlined in book three. When Carl Dahlhaus called Schopenhauer's philosophy "the reigning theory of art" in the late nineteenth century, he acknowledged above all this irresistible appeal.[3] Mahler, for example, would always be a stalwart Schopenhauerian – not only in the Third Symphony (1896), where the philosopher's survey of the natural order became the model for Mahler's sequence of movements, but more profoundly in his repeated attempts to reach a metaphysical essence through music, in the last movement of the Third and likewise in the finales of the Second, Fourth, Eighth, and Ninth, to name only the most obvious. And in this tendency Mahler of course was following the model of Wagner, whose 1854 encounter with Schopenhauer led him to value music over words as the primary avenue to truth – upending the central argument of *Oper und Drama* – and to adopt a view of redemption as a desire for nothingness, which Nietzsche would mock as the "will to death."

After the initial encounter with Ritter, Strauss turned to the philosopher's own works for an intensive autodidactic engagement that has no documented equivalent among his contemporaries. The typical avenue for lay people interested in Schopenhauer was the one-volume distillation *Aphorisms on the Wisdom of Life*, said to have a place on the bookshelf of every middle-class German home. Strauss tackled *The World as Will* as a whole, in an edition given to him by his parents as a Christmas gift in 1889, and he left private notes on this reading, including annotations in the text that become especially numerous at the end of the third book. These, along with thoughts sent to philosophically inclined friends (Friedrich Rösch, Ludwig Thuille, Cosima Wagner), demonstrate a recognition that for Schopenhauer art did not provide a lasting experience of *Willensverneinung*. After underlining the relevant passage – "[art] does not become for him a quieter of the will, as we shall see in the following book in the case of the saint who has attained resignation; it does not deliver him from life forever, but only for a few moments" – Strauss reported to Ritter

---

[3] Carl Dahlhaus, *The Idea of Absolute Music*, trans. Roger Lustig (Chicago: The University of Chicago Press, 1989), 10.

that deploying art for metaphysical ends was "a Utopia (our friend Schopenhauer also takes this view in volume 3 of *The World as Will and Representation*)."[4] Music and metaphysics, Strauss concluded, must go their separate ways.

Philosophically astute listeners of Strauss's first opera, *Guntram* (premiered 1894), might have recognized this outwardly epigonic Wagnerian tragedy as a composing-out of *The World as Will*. Set in the Middle Ages and dealing with a brotherhood of minstrels who use music to spread spiritual truth, the work ends when the title character renounces that mission, destroys his lyre, and retires to a life of sylvan hermitry. Ritter was aghast, despite Strauss's reassurance that "*I* am not giving up art, and I am not Guntram either." And Strauss himself faced a dilemma: the need to develop a philosophical justification for remaining a musician. Private notes from this period (early 1893) show him developing an explicitly anti-Schopenhauerian theory of the "affirmation of the body," embodied in the "condition of the receiving woman" – a notion the outrageousness of which was not its least appealing feature to a confident creator in full lather. It is no surprise, then, that his philosophical interests soon turned toward a like-minded iconoclast: Friedrich Nietzsche.

Nietzsche's embrace and subsequent abandonment of Wagnerian musical idealism had followed a course remarkably similar to Strauss's, albeit with direct personal involvement. At the philosopher's first meeting with Wagner, in 1868, Schopenhauer had been at the heart of the attraction on both sides. With *The Birth of Tragedy* (1872) Nietzsche would become an advocate unsurpassed for his skill and passion, arguing that the third act of *Tristan*, if experienced "symphonically" (without words and scenery) would surely be fatal through its metaphysical immediacy. This youthful, not fully independent Nietzsche, who had his own bedroom at the Wagner home in Tribschen, would remain the definitive one for many of Strauss's contemporaries, for example the Pernerstorfer circle in Vienna, which included Mahler and remained influential into the twentieth century.

Nietzsche's private doubts, however, appeared in his notebooks already in 1874, and *Human, All Too Human* (1878) brought them fully into the open. Here the philosopher broke decisively with Wagner, Schopenhauer, Plato, and indeed all forms of idealism, musical or otherwise. Attacks on

---

[4] Strauss to Ritter, February 3, 1893. Willi Schuh, *Richard Strauss: A Chronicle of the Early Years 1864–1898*, trans. Mary Whittall (Cambridge: Cambridge University Press, 1982), 285 (translation slightly emended).

these "enemies" would henceforth be the central mission of his work, whether he was targeting conventional ethics, as in *On the Genealogy of Morals* (1887), where he defined art as anti-ascetic, a "noble morality"; or Plato's "good in itself," with its attendant "religious neurosis," explored in *Beyond Good and Evil* (1886); or Wagner directly, an "actor" who, consumed by pessimism and his own music's narcotic effects, "collapsed before the Christian cross."

On a medically mandated trip to Greece and Egypt in 1892–93, Strauss brought along a copy of *Beyond Good and Evil*, tuning in with remarkable speed to the Nietzsche craze set off by Georg Brandes's 1888 lectures in Copenhagen, published in 1890 in *Freie Bühne für modernes Leben* (later *Die neue Rundschau*). What the later Nietzsche provided him – intellectual justification for a break with Wagner – was only too clear to Ritter. The critic Arthur Seidl likewise could see that Strauss had understood Nietzsche's shift and used it as a model for his own; in fact he would make the intriguing claim that Strauss's tone poem on *Also sprach Zarathustra* took *Human, All Too Human* as its true programmatic subject. Strauss had embarked, in his idiosyncratic way, on a project akin to Georg Simmel's: to follow Nietzsche in obliterating the remnants of idealism (particularly as they related to aesthetic products), and to find a new grounding for culture.[5] But this emerging Nietzschean worldview, consonant with the work of progressive colleagues in other disciplines, would play out for the laconic Strauss not in words but in the music of the last six tone poems (from *Till Eulenspiegel* [1895] through *Eine Alpensinfonie* [1899–1916]).[6] Those works answered the demands of a market thirsty for anything remotely Nietzschean, even as they addressed a private need of the composer.

For better or worse, Strauss's Nietzschean anti-Wagnerism would remain largely unnoticed, partly because it was entirely anomalous for its time. The substance and chronology of Nietzsche's Wagner critique has been at best imperfectly grasped by non-specialists, particularly musicians, who in Strauss's time found other sources of interest when they engaged with the philosopher. Mahler's poignant setting of the "Midnight Song" from *Zarathustra* in the fourth movement of the Third Symphony, with its warm chiming of the word "eternity" and its urgent pleas to humankind,

---

[5] Helmut Loiskandl, Deena Weinstein and Michael Weinstein, "Introduction," in *Schopenhauer and Nietzsche*, ed. Georg Simmel, trans. Helmut Loiskandl, Deena Weinstein and Michael Weinstein (Amherst: University of Massachusetts Press, 1986), xi–xii.

[6] See Charles Youmans, *Richard Strauss's Orchestral Music and the German Intellectual Tradition* (Bloomington: Indiana University Press, 2005), 83–113, 180–213.

ignores the poem's central point: the joyful, eternal abandonment of metaphysical hope, a perspective that Mahler's music obstinately resists. To follow that movement with a cherubic *musica coelestis* and then an adagio instrumental redemptive vision – "sentimental slush," in the words of Donal Henahan – is to ignore the mature Nietzsche's ideas, if not to flout them openly. And such was the norm; Frederick Delius's setting of *Zarathustra* in *A Mass of Life* likewise underlines evocative poetic elements, which, hazy and lovely, are also sharply disengaged from the blunt details of Nietzsche's critique of idealism.

The core of Strauss's interest in Nietzsche, conversely, would be precisely the attack on metaphysics. This we can infer not only from the works he is known to have read in the 1890s (in fact Seidl claimed that by 1894 Strauss knew "all the main works") but from comments on that reading. In correspondence with Rösch he praised Nietzsche's critique of the enemies of physicality and his redirection of philosophy toward objectivity, which for Strauss made him the "first pathbreaker" of modern thought. To Cosima he confessed finding the antidemocratic tendency of *Beyond Good and Evil* "highly sympathetic," specifically in the identification of democracy as a manifestation of the Schopenhauerian "herd" whose members sought refuge from real life in an imagined noumenal realm.[7] Platonic philosophy, Christian spirituality, democracy, and Wagnerian musical idealism blended into one target for Nietzsche, and for Strauss. It became the basis of a "philosophy of the future," the composer wrote, and that philosophy would be a red thread running through his mature tone poems.

Strauss did think philosophically, then: he read important thinkers, he reacted critically to them, and he brought their ideas into his creative process. With the growth of scholarly interest since the mid-1980s, that personal reality has been brought to light, revealing him as not just a skilled craftsman and shrewd businessman but a well-read, sensitive intellect.

In that respect, he followed the example of his lifelong intellectual role model, Goethe, who stands as the defining context of Strauss's personal and creative existence. Surveying the composer's long career, one finds him consistently drawn to that endlessly curious, encyclopedically knowledgeable, nonchalantly profound, emotionally aloof poet-scientist. For Strauss, Goethe was more than a source of texts and dramatic subjects; he was a

[7] Letter of April 10, 1893. *Cosima Wagner – Richard Strauss: Ein Briefwechsel*, ed. Franz Trenner (Tutzing: Hans Schneider, 1978), 155.

human ideal, to be studied daily and emulated constantly. Thus when the distraught Strauss determined in the fall of 1944 to reread all of Goethe – "I will be young again with Goethe and then once again old with him" – he set out to revisit the major way-stations of his creative life.[8] Goethe was the only poet whom Strauss set in every decade of his life from the 1870s on. Remarks about the novels, plays, essays, and conversations pepper his correspondence and personal notes. If no Goethe-inspired work can be counted among his major contributions, it is nonetheless true that at each of the four major transition points in his career he turned to a creative project involving Goethe. And to him Strauss would turn at the end, to make sense of the debacle in which he lived his final years.

The works he chose at those moments of change reflect a broad awareness of the pillars of Goethe's personality: his connection to classical culture, his break with Romanticism, his links to the east, and his introspective lyricism. The first creative engagement came in May 1885 with *Wandrers Sturmlied*, the Brahmsian Pindaric ode in which the emergent adult composer found his "Brahmsschwärmerei" (Brahms-enthusiasm) unconsciously invaded by Wagnerian influence. Rightly sensing an imminent upheaval in his musical world, Strauss drew encouragement from Goethe's claim that the Artist-Genius, "göttergleich" (like a god) could withstand any tempest. Ten years later, as he disengaged from Wagnerian partisanship, the singspiel *Lila* (unfinished, 1895) allowed him to juxtapose (as he told Cosima Wagner) "music as the expression of the psyche" and "music as the play of notes." Although *Also sprach Zarathustra* (1896) would divert him from this incipient neoclassicism, a foundation had been laid for *Der Rosenkavalier* (1910) and *Ariadne auf Naxos* (1912; rev. 1916). After *Die Frau ohne Schatten* (1917), his "epitaph to post-Romanticism," Strauss again looked to Goethe for a viable path into the twentieth century; three poems from the *West-östlicher Divan* helped him defuse conflicts between the individual and the collective, by means of eastern resignation, withdrawal, and acceptance. That Mahlerian tendency would intensify in the last and greatest Goethean work, *Metamorphosen* (1945), which draws on an abandoned setting of the short poem "Niemand wird sich selber kennen" ("No one can know himself"). Here the dangers of decentered subjectivity came home to him; wearing masks had earned him notoriety in youth, but, in old age, it hinted at philosophical responsibility for national disintegration.

[8] Walter Thomas, *Bis der Vorhang fiel: berichtet nach Aufzeichnungen aus den Jahren 1940 bis 1945* (Dortmund: Schwalvenberg, 1947), 226–27.

More than any of his contemporaries, Strauss regarded himself as a Goethean composer, and this was a clear-eyed assessment. Even Adorno saw the resemblance, noting that Strauss "amassed a wide range of knowledge and information outside his field, collected assiduously," and remained creatively active to the end.[9] Both lived long lives through massive political changes. Both embraced and rejected romanticism. Both hid behind public personae, even as they explored artistic autobiography. Both lurched from one artistic style to another, sometimes in adjacent works. Both rejected the noumenal as a belief but explored it as a metaphor (as did Mahler, who nonetheless, in his musical realization of "eternal femininity" in the Eighth, explicitly maintained faith with "that which on earth we could only desire or strive for").[10] And both treated art not as a means to religion, but as a replacement for religion. "Music is a product of culture," Strauss would say, and, in the end, culture would fill the gap left by outdated philosophies.

---

[9] Theodor Adorno, "Richard Strauss. Born June 11, 1864," trans. Samuel and Shierry Weber, *Perspectives of New Music* 4, no. 1 (1965): 25.

[10] Mahler to Alma Mahler, June 22, 1909. Henry-Louis de La Grange and Günther Weiss, eds., *Gustav Mahler: Letters to His Wife*, in collab. with Knud Martner, trans. Antony Beaumont (Ithaca: Cornell University Press, 2004), 327.

CHAPTER 17

The Allgemeine Deutsche Musikverein

James Deaville

Richard Strauss assumed leadership over the Allgemeine Deutsche Musikverein (ADMV; General German Music Society) following a period of considerable uncertainty and instability within the organization. Upon the deaths of Wagner (1883) and Liszt (1886), the ADMV experienced an identity crisis – with the passing of its leading figures, the Society found itself unclear regarding its mission. The late 1880s and the 1890s brought performances of music by members of the conservative opposition (e.g. Brahms), by non-German composers (among others, Rachmaninoff and Verdi), and by historical figures (Bach, Handel, and even Alessandro Scarlatti). There is little doubt that had nothing occurred to shake the organization out of its leadership malaise and increasing distance from its founding principles, the ADMV would have dwindled in importance and possibly even ceased to exist after the turn of the century. In taking the society's helm at the Heidelberg festival of 1901, Strauss re-affirmed its founding mission "to cultivate musical art and support artists" by promoting the work of leading contemporaries like Mahler, Reger, and even Schoenberg. German music and musical life benefited from the 75-year activity of the ADMV – a fitting legacy for its far-sighted founders, Liszt and Brendel.

The ADMV before Strauss

The ADMV was founded in 1861 under the auspices of Franz Liszt, Franz Brendel, and their like-minded New-German associates, primarily from Weimar and Leipzig. In 1845, Brendel had taken over the editorship of the *Neue Zeitschrift für Musik* from its founder, Robert Schumann, and over the course of the next decade transformed it into the publication vehicle for the progressive musical movement of Liszt, Wagner, and Berlioz. As an advocate of Hegelian thought, Brendel was a firm believer in musical progress as it unfolded in stages according to historical and social developments.

Brendel coined the designation New German School in 1859 at a festival in Leipzig that served multiple purposes: it celebrated the 25th anniversary of Schumann's journal while also advocating for progress in music. It was at the 1861 festival in Weimar that the Society was constituted to embrace the ideals of its organizers, which included the gathering of German musicians, the promotion of musical progress, and the education of the public. While the ADMV participated in the festive culture of mid-nineteenth-century Germany, such lofty goals were without parallel at the time. They were to be realized through annual festivals occurring at alternating locations throughout German-speaking Europe, where composers, performers, pedagogues, and scholars would meet to hear (and discuss) the latest musical creations. At the same time, they could attend the occasional lecture about musical topics of interest, participate in organized social activities, and enjoy the sights of the host city and region. Brendel may have served as *Vorsitzender* (Chair) from 1861 to his death in 1868, but the guiding figure behind the ADMV was Liszt, who received the title of Honorary President in 1873. It was his music and aesthetic ideals that dominated the organization in its early years and provided the inspiration for a younger generation of composers (despite their repeated presence on programs, neither Berlioz nor Wagner took an active role in the society).

The leadership of Brendel and Liszt notwithstanding, the operation of the ADMV relied upon the work of its members, especially the local arrangements committee and the program committee, both of which continued functioning until the Society's dissolution in 1937. Because of the changing sites for festivals, the ADMV relied heavily upon local forces, including the city's musical institutions and artists (conductors, orchestral members, singers), the municipal authorities, and even restauranteurs and hoteliers. The program committee was particularly important because it determined which compositional voices would be heard – its rotating membership was responsible for maintaining the organization's vision for musical progress while satisfying the desires of local audiences to hear works by composers from their midst and from the past.

The typical ADMV festival lasted four days, with a mix of sacred, chamber, and orchestral concerts. The sacred performances characteristically featured older compositions for chorus and orchestra, above all by Bach and Beethoven, while the orchestral ones predominantly included works of the recent past, and not just Liszt, Wagner, and Berlioz: names like Raff, Draeseke, Cornelius, Eduard Lassen, Friedrich Kiel, and Robert Volkmann figured on programs from the 1860s and

1870s. It stands to reason that cities where Liszt and his circle were best known – primarily those in Thuringia, Anhalt, and Saxony – would host the first festivals, including Weimar, Leipzig, and Dessau (Berlin was not a festival site until 1891, and Hamburg hosted first in 1935). The strategy behind site selection extended to considerations of audience size, press response, and local membership, the last factor quite important for the hosting of a successful event. From press reports, we know for example that over 700 people attended the 1861 festival in Weimar, which is a considerable number for a relatively small court city, but we must keep in mind that the audiences – most of them pedagogues, vocalists and instrumentalists, and conductors – traveled from far and wide to hear the latest musical creations professionally selected and well performed.

Certain historical developments – Liszt's departure from Weimar in 1861, Brendel's untimely death in 1868, the passing of Berlioz in 1869, and the rise of Wagner in Bayreuth after 1870 – conspired to shape the activities of the ADMV in the decades after its founding. Liszt continued to serve as *spiritus rector* of the Society, his music annually presented at the festivals, but as time passed and under less visionary leaders after Brendel, the ADMV seems to have lost some of its forward-looking momentum. One-time New-German foe Brahms appeared on the programs as did some of his conservative associates like Heinrich von Herzogenberg, Max Bruch, and Albert Dietrich. Moreover, the Society no longer exclusively promoted new German compositions, but also programmed works from France (Saint-Saëns, Franck), Russia (Anton Rubinstein, Rimsky-Korsakov, Tchaikovsky), and Scandinavia (Grieg) as well as music of earlier eras (Gluck's *Iphigenia in Tauris*, Giuseppe Tartini's violin works, and a host of compositions by J. S. Bach). One could argue that, by the time of Strauss's affiliation with the ADMV, it had lost sight of its founding mission.

Strauss' Early Involvement

When Strauss arrived in Meiningen in 1885, he carried on regular discussions there with Liszt's associate Alexander Ritter, who not only exposed the young musician to the music and aesthetics of the New German School but undoubtedly familiarized Strauss with the ADMV as well. Thus, in 1886, he submitted his Second Symphony for performance at the next festival (Cologne), but it was not accepted because he was not a member – he subsequently joined the Society in March 1887 after he had taken up his post as third conductor in Munich.[1] Two years later, upon Strauss's growing reputation as conductor and composer, President Hans Bronsart engaged the 25 year old Strauss as conductor for the 1889 *Tonkünstlerversammlung* (Musicians Assembly) in Wiesbaden. At the same time, he was accepted onto the *Vorstand* (Board of Managing Directors) of the ADMV, a position Strauss held until 1898.

In 1890, Strauss received an appointment to the powerful program committee through which he was able to advance the music of his "progressive" colleagues. Thus in the 1890 program for Eisenach, we find the young talent of Ludwig Thuille next to the "veteran" New Germans Draeseke and Ritter, in 1891, Hans Sommer and Eugen d'Albert were well represented, and in 1893, Robert Kahn appeared as one of the promising new voices in German composition. However, at the same time, festival audiences heard more conservative figures like Brahms, Herzogenberg, and Robert Fuchs, non-Germans like Smetana, Tchaikovsky, and Edward Macdowell, and earlier music by Bach and Handel. The ADMV seemed to have lost its vision for advocating German musical progress.

It did present the fruits of Strauss's muse. At the 1890 festival in Eisenach, premiere performances of the tone poem *Tod und Verklärung* and the *Burleske* for piano and orchestra received general praise. He continued to use the festivals as vehicles for his compositions: 1896 in Leipzig for *Don Juan*, 1897 in Mannheim for *Also sprach Zarathustra* and Lieder, 1899 in Dortmund for Lieder, and 1900 in Bremen for *Ein Heldenleben*.

A major opportunity for collaboration with the Society arose in 1894 when Strauss conducted *Guntram* at the Weimar festival. Strauss also helped with the preparations for the performance of Mahler's First Symphony, which he had recommended for the festival over the objections of certain board members.[2] Indeed, the work was not well received by either the public or the press, even though the audience in large part consisted of musicians dedicated to musical progress. This experience drew Strauss and Mahler together and spurred more active correspondence between them. Despite the negative reviews of Mahler's symphony, the overall favorable impression from the 1894 festival brought Strauss recognition within the inner circles of the Society.

---

[1] Irina Lucke-Kaminiarz, "Strauss und der Allgemeine Deutsche Musikverein," in *Richard Strauss-Handbuch*, ed. Walter Werbeck (Stuttgart: Metzler-Verlag, 2014), 35.

[2] Charles Youmans, *Mahler and Strauss: In Dialogue* (Bloomington, IN: Indiana University Press, 2016), 2.

The controversy surrounding Mahler illustrated how the Society was ever more challenged to function in the spirit of musical progress as inherited from Liszt. Festival audiences heard Strauss's music during the later 1890s; but other than Strauss and (with reservations) Mahler, the German figures who would carry musical art into the age of Modernism, such as Reger and Busoni, were absent from the programs. Instead, music by would-be organization *coryphaei* like Humperdinck and Emil von Reznicek among others filled the ADMV programs, individuals for whom musical progress did not serve as an imperative.

Several organizational issues came to a head for the ADMV at the end of the 1890s. While the underlying conflict among the Society's leading members concerned the representation of Modernism at the annual *Tonkünstlerversammlungen*, it was over the matter of copyright reform that a breach between older and younger generations occurred, in a dispute that pitted board member Oskar von Hase (owner of publishing firm Breitkopf & Härtel) and ADMV Chair Fritz Steinbach against Strauss and his composer friends, Sommer and Friedrich Rösch. The board's recommendation to support the establishment of an Anstalt für musikalisches Aufführungsrecht (Institution for Musical Performing Rights) with statutes that favored industry caused Strauss not to stand for re-election to the Society's program committee and Board of Managing Directors. Despite this discord, Strauss had his music performed at the festivals of 1899 and 1900.

The ADMV under Strauss (1901–09)

Strauss's advocacy for the new direction in music endeared him to the Society's faction of young composers, who helped him to the position of Chair at the 1901 festival in Heidelberg. The so-called "Heidelberg Revolution" at the business meeting not only elevated Strauss to the top leadership position, but also led some of the old-guard board members (e.g. Steinbach and von Hase) not to seek re-election. They were replaced over the course of time by more progressive-minded associates such as Rösch and Max von Schillings. At the end of the festival, the partially reconstituted board made a series of appointments to the Society's five committees, with Schillings (Strauss's friend from Munich) at the head of the important program committee. This consolidation of high-level backing represented the beginning of Strauss's efforts to re-direct the ADMV back to its founding tenets of promoting musical progress and supporting musicians.

One means to realize these goals was to schedule works by younger members who cultivated new directions in music. The Heidelberg program had not been drafted under Strauss's aegis, yet the repertoire nonetheless tilted toward the progressive: besides Strauss, the concerts featured works by members of his generation like Reger, Schillings, Thuille, and Siegmund von Hausegger, all composers associated to one extent or another with the so-called Munich School at the turn of the century. This group of rather conservative composers carried on the "music as expression" traditions of the New German School as manifested in the descriptive symphonic style of Strauss, counting among their further associates Friedrich Klose, Walter Braunfels, and Walter Courvoisier. The result of this was a late-Romantic epigonism that stood on ADMV programs side-by-side with more modern works by Mahler, Reger, Wolf, Delius, and Schoenberg as well as major compositions by the patron saints of German composition: Bach, Beethoven, and Liszt.

The program for the Krefeld festival (1902), the first under Strauss's leadership, reflects his purposeful selection and scheduling of works to achieve desired outcomes.[3] Even a cursory survey of the event's ambitious plan reveals the scope of the Chair's vision for the organization: four major orchestral/choral concerts over four days, with a Lieder matinee and a chamber-music concert earlier on the respective first and last days. Other than offering festival participants a mix of orchestral and chamber concerts, with the occasional opera or sacred concert, the Society had no set roster or sequence of musical events. Rather, the Society's program committee and the local committee had to come to an agreement on the performances in light of the available performing forces and venues as well as the successful program submissions.

The six performances at the Krefeld festival were given a quasi-symmetrical structure, with stand-alone performances of major orchestral-choral works by Liszt and Mahler, respectively, on the second and third days. At the festival's core, the oratorio *Christus* and the Symphony No. 3 form a pairing that suggest Strauss's attempt to bring the leading figures from the progressive movement of past and present into dialogue. The two compositions bear little resemblance, and yet both represent major works in which the composer endeavors to come to terms with key theological/philosophical systems of the day, on the one hand (Catholic) Christianity, on the other Nietzschean thought. Moreover, by

---

[3] See the author's ADMV website for a complete listing of festivals and their programs, at www3.carleton.ca/admv/index.html.

juxtaposing Society-founder Liszt with Mahler, Strauss could be regarded as giving "official" approval to his colleague in the same way Liszt had applied "Genie oblige!" towards his gifted associates.

Indeed, soon after his election, Strauss took steps to make clear his dedication to securing Liszt's legacy. Besides programming Liszt's music, the new Chair moved on two aspects of his predecessor's heritage: the Liszt Foundation of the ADMV and the collected edition of his musical works. The two projects were intertwined since the edition was to appear under the aegis of the Foundation, yet the parties could not come to agreement until 1907. In his capacity as leader of the ADMV, Strauss worked behind the scenes to secure the legacy of his eminent predecessor, and as a result, Breitkopf & Härtel produced 33 volumes of the edition between 1907 and 1936.

Throughout his tenure at the head of the Society, Strauss would reveal himself to the public as well as to the board as an advocate for the music of Mahler, programming the Second Symphony in Basel (1903), 13 orchestral songs in Graz (1905), and the premiere of the Sixth Symphony in Essen (1906). The program from Graz is particularly interesting, for there again the triumvirate Liszt–Strauss–Mahler is represented, with Liszt's oratorio *Die Legende von der heiligen Elisabeth* and Strauss's opera *Feuersnot* as two of the three major featured works (Austrian composer Wilhelm Kienzl's opera *Don Quixote* was the third). Mahler's orchestral songs were also on a program, sandwiched between a symphony by Austrian conservative Guido Peters and a symphonic poem by Liszt pupil and epigone Paul Ertel. Strauss's promotion of Mahler at the ADMV festivals was not lost on the professional critical community; contemporary Paul Stefan wrote in 1912 that "through the influence of Richard Strauss and Prof. Kretzschmar the First Symphony was set on the programme of the Tonkünstler Festival at Weimar in June 1894. The Allgemeine Deutsche Musikverein founded by Liszt, which arranges the Tonkünstler Festivals, was thereby of the greatest assistance to Mahler. Later, too, it has entered the lists in his behalf . . ."[4]

The Society's leader did not have absolute power over programming decisions, and yet the works of certain leading living composers did not have to undergo the program committee's assessment. Not only did this apply to Mahler (after 1901), but also Reger, for example, whom Strauss likewise promoted as a worthy figure for musical progress. It stands to

---

[4] Paul Stefan, *Gustav Mahler: A Study of His Personality and Work* (New York: G. Schirmer, 1913), 40–41.

reason that Strauss and Vice-Chair Schillings would not need to submit their works for approval to be featured on festival programs, Strauss presenting his own music every year during his term as Chair except in 1906, with the European premiere of the *Symphonia domestica* occurring in Frankfurt in 1904. Under his aegis the ADMV also mounted performances of works by such notable contemporaries as Sibelius (1901), Pfitzner (1902, 1904, 1905), Wolf (1902, 1903, 1905), Delius (1903, 1906, 1908), and Bloch (1903).

Undoubtedly, the most controversial new composition at a festival of the ADMV during the Strauss era was Schoenberg's String Quartet No. 1, performed in Dresden in 1907. Schoenberg had joined the Society in 1902; at that time, Strauss actively took up his cause by writing a reference for a teaching position and recommending to Schillings that Schoenberg receive an annual scholarship of 1,000 Marks from Society resources, which he did in 1903 and 1904. For the quartet performance, we know that Strauss authorized the late submission of orchestral songs and the quartet "under special agreement."[5] Performed by the Rosé Quartet, the work received a scandalous reception in the concert hall and was negatively reviewed by the press. Strauss himself weathered the storm, and Schoenberg, interestingly, remained a member even after Strauss's departure from leadership.

Whether by virtue of Strauss's *renommée*, the return of the ADMV to its original mission, or the quality of its festival programming, Strauss presided over a growing and thriving Society whose membership expanded from 700 before his election to over 1,000 at the time of his exit in 1909.[6] At the same time, composers had come to recognize the Society's renewed role in promoting their creations; for the Dresden festival, over 400 works were submitted for just 27 spots on the program. Under Strauss, the ADMV moreover took further steps in supporting musicians through recommendations for improving the economic conditions of performers and enhancing the quality of music education.

Strauss and his board colleagues were up for (re-)election at the business meeting of the 1909 festival in Stuttgart, but despite the assembly's affirmation, he stated that he could not accept the result because of his heavy workload and need for rest. Not to be deterred, the members in

---

[5] James Deaville, "Schoenberg's String Quartet No.1 in Dresden (1907): Programming the Unprogrammable, Performing the Unperformable," in *"I Feel the Air of Another Planet": Schoenberg's Chamber Music, Schoenberg's World*, ed. Alan Gillmor and James Wright (Hillsdale, NY: Pendragon, 2009), 13.

[6] Lucke-Kaminiarz, "Strauss und der Allgemeine Deutsche Musikverein," 38.

attendance unanimously declared him Honorary Chair in recognition of his service to the Society – it was a distinction Strauss would share with Liszt. The office did not confer any responsibilities to its bearer and, indeed, Strauss resisted any temptation to involve himself in its operations after his departure from leadership.

The ADMV after Strauss

The programs from the 1920s reveal the Society coming to terms with the "new music," so that the first festival featured Schoenberg's Five Pieces for Orchestra and the Berg-inspired First Symphony of Eduard Erdmann, albeit alongside the more conservative, late-Romantic figures Joseph Haas and Jean-Louis Nicodé. The 1924 festival in Frankfurt offered the most radical program of the post-war years, a panoramic overview of modern central European compositional styles: an opera by Krenek, a concert of quarter-tone music by Alois Hába, a ballet by the young Hindemith, selections from Stravinsky's *L'histoire du soldat*, and a selection from Berg's *Wozzeck*. As the years approached the political catastrophe of Germany's Nazification, more moderate if not outright conservative voices like Julius Weismann and Ernst Pepping prevailed, especially under the leadership of von Hausegger. ADMV members such as Paul Graener and Hermann Grabner continued their compositional activities into the 1940s, after the Society's disbandment. Still, the challenging, avant-garde music of Schoenberg, Hindemith, and Heinz Tiessen occasionally featured on programs of the late 1920s; in fact, Hindemith had served on the program committee in the early 1920s.

However, as the Society entered the 1930s, the music by Jewish composers eventually disappeared from the festival offerings, as did music by non-German composers. Strauss did not directly participate in the administration of the ADMV during this period of the Society's politicization, even though he served as President of the Reichsmusikkammer (Reich Music Chamber) from 1933 until his dismissal in 1935. Strauss's successor at the head of the Chamber was Peter Raabe, who both held that position (through the end of the Third Reich) and functioned as Chair of the ADMV. Ironically, the last festival was the largest, encompassing the cities Weimar, Eisenach, and Jena over the seven days from June 12 to 18, 1936. The consolidation of German musical life under Raabe led to the dissolution of the ADMV, its festivals replaced by the *Reichsmusiktage*.

CHAPTER 18

The Genossenschaft Deutscher Tonsetzer

Manuela Schmidt

The Genossenschaft Deutscher Tonsetzer (GDT; Association of German Composers) was founded on January 14, 1903, and became the first successful collective management organization in Germany. The first two sections of this chapter describe unsuccessful attempts to establish an institution for musical performing rights, which sets the stage for discussion of the founding of the GDT in the third section. Richard Strauss's role in this history is documented throughout.[1]

The First Attempt: The Leipziger Anstalt

Founded in France in 1851 and still active today, the first collective management organization in Europe was the Société des Auteurs, Compositeurs et Éditeurs de Musique (SACEM; Society of Authors, Composers and Publishers of Music). Discussions about collective rights management at two congresses of the Association Littéraire et Artistique Internationale (ALAI; an association of authors, artists, composers, lawyers, and publishers) in 1895 and 1896 spurred the German government to pursue the formation of a similar organization.[2] As a result, the Anstalt für musikalisches Aufführungsrecht (Institution for Musical Performing Rights) was founded in 1898 by the Verein der Deutschen Musikalienhändler zu Leipzig (Association of German Music Dealers in Leipzig) and its partner, the Allgemeine Deutsche Musikverein (ADMV; General German Music Society). Since it was based in Leipzig, it was also called

---

[1] This essay is dedicated to my dearest mother.

[2] For more information on the complexities of royalty development and legal aspects at this time, see Manuela Schmidt, *Die Anfänge der musikalischen Tantiemenbewegung in Deutschland: Eine Studie über den langen Weg bis zur Errichtung der Genossenschaft Deutscher Tonsetzer (GDT) im Jahre 1903 und zum Wirken des Komponisten Richard Strauss (1864–1949) für Verbesserungen des Urheberrechts* (Berlin: Duncker & Humblot, 2005), which draws on literature and original documents found in several archives.

the Leipziger Anstalt (Leipzig Institute).[3] It was dominated by music dealers; Oskar von Hase, president of the Verein der Deutschen Musikalienhändler, was elected to head the Anstalt. The music dealers who served on the managing board attended to day-to-day business, while the ADMV members served in a supervisory capacity. The distribution of revenue also reflected the primacy of music dealers: it was split evenly between them and composers, but the latter had to share with their lyricists.

The Leipziger Anstalt faced massive resistance even before it began charging royalties on October 1, 1898. Music users did not want to pay royalties (1 percent of gross income), arguing that performance fees were already built in to the price of sheet music. There was also resistance from some booksellers and music dealers, who, in spite of being overseers on behalf of the institute, refused to enforce the payments by music users, since the latter were also their customers – a situation that caused a clear conflict of interest. This was a difficult blow for the institution because it had tasked booksellers and music dealers with collecting royalties and ensuring that performers made use of legitimately purchased music as opposed to copies of unsanctioned reprints.

The Leipziger Anstalt also faced stiff resistance from composers. After its founding, the lawyer and composer Friedrich Rösch proposed to Strauss, his friend of some two decades, that they establish a professional association to protest against the institution. Rösch, Strauss, and the composer Hans Sommer planned to submit a petition for the introduction of perpetual copyright. Such a change would have marked a radical departure from the rules in place at the time; in 1898, performance rights were only protected during the author's lifetime plus 30 years, according to Article 52 (section 1) and Article 8 of the German law regarding copyright for written works, images, musical compositions, and dramatic works established on June 11, 1870 (henceforth: 1870 Copyright Act). When this term expired, the work entered the public domain and anyone could use it without

---

[3] The right of performance concerns public performances. The German Copyright Act (then and today) protects the work ("Werk") and its author ("Urheber"). The protection starts when the work is created; a copyright reservation is not a condition for the protection. The author has the original and exclusive right to authorize or forbid the use of the work. Depending on the category (e.g. musical, dramatic, literary, etc.), there are also different exploitation rights, such as reproduction, distribution, exhibition, recitation, and performance. The author may transfer one or more of these rights to a collective management organization or manage them independently. A collective management organization for performing rights (also called a collecting society) manages rights for protected musical works by composers, songwriters, music publishers, and their respective legal successors. It grants the rights of musical performance to users in exchange for license royalties and then distributes the revenue.

authorization or payment. The petition was Strauss's idea in response to a publication by Sommer, who in the spring of 1898 called for the introduction of perpetual copyright in an essay titled "Die Wertschätzung der Musik" ("The Appreciation of Music").[4] Sommer lamented the low appreciation of contemporary music that forced even highly talented composers to work as conductors to make a living. He found it unfortunate that publishers might spend little on an initial publication but then later make a substantial profit by selling print editions, even after the work in the meantime had entered the public domain. Composers and their heirs, on the other hand, could not benefit from such delayed success due to the 30-year copyright term *post mortem auctoris*. For Sommer, the solution was eternal copyright – a highly ambitious goal that was never achieved. The revenue generated by such a policy change could be used to promote contemporary music and support highly talented musicians through conservatory studies. His essay garnered widespread approval and inspired many composers to develop a new self-awareness, an important condition for the founding of the Genossenschaft Deutscher Komponisten.

In July 1898, Strauss penned and circulated a well-known letter to 160 composers in which he criticized the 30-year copyright duration as too short and petitioned them to support the introduction of perpetual copyright; without it, the Leipziger Anstalt would be of no use to them. He also criticized the fact that music publishers wielded more influence on the Anstalt than composers. Strauss thus urged his colleagues to form a unified front and to engage actively in the fight over copyright reform that was about to begin. With 119 approvals, his appeal was an unequivocal success. Two months later, in a second circular letter, Strauss proposed founding a professional association of composers. On September 16, he invited this group to an assembly in Leipzig at the end of that month. On September 21, Strauss notified the Reichsjustizamt (Imperial Justice Office) of the petition and asked it to grant the composers a representative to serve on the board of experts for the upcoming discussions on copyright reform. After a second inquiry from Rösch, the Office finally agreed.

As a result, the Genossenschaft Deutscher Komponisten was officially founded as a professional association on September 30, 1898. The date and location (Leipzig) of this meeting were chosen strategically: the Leipziger Anstalt began operating there the following day. Berlin, the

---

[4] Hans Sommer, "Die Wertschätzung der Musik," *Der Kunstwart* 11, no. 13–15 (1898): 10–14, 44–49, 82–87.

capital, was chosen as the home of the Genossenschaft, and Rösch was elected to represent the composers on the board of experts of the Reichjustizamt. The composers demanded perpetual copyright and rejected the Leipziger Anstalt as unacceptable. To them, founding a collective management organization without establishing perpetual copyright was both inappropriate and detrimental. The composers previously elected to the Leipziger Anstalt were asked to resign; Eugen d'Albert, Sommer, Engelbert Humperdinck, Carl Reinecke, and Hans Sitt complied with this request.

In the ensuing months, the new association enjoyed a tremendous level of support. On December 1, 1898, there were 233 approvals and seven approvals with reservations to the Genossenschaft Deutscher Komponisten (two of the latter seven soon approved, and three others approved but reserved the right to withdraw). The founding was an important milestone for German composers, who for the first time had their own professional association. At the second meeting of the Genossenschaft on February 20, 1899, Strauss was elected chairman, Rösch general secretary, Philipp Rüfer to the executive board, and Sommer chairman of the joint board. D'Albert, Humperdinck, Salomon Jadassohn, Joseph Joachim, Theodor Müller-Reuter, Jean Louis Nicodé, Reinecke, Joseph Rheinberger, Bernhard Scholz, Philipp Wolfrum, and Franz Wüllner also became members of the joint board.

The fight against the Leipziger Anstalt culminated in a public appeal for a boycott. Given the fierce resistance of composers, music publishers, and users, the Leipziger Anstalt stopped collecting fees on January 21, 1899, and refunded fees already collected. The Genossenschaft Deutscher Komponisten demanded that composers reserve the right of performance for themselves in the future. According to Article 50 (section 1) of the 1870 Copyright Act, a composer had the exclusive performance right of dramatic, musical, and music-dramatic works. But the subsequent section added a condition: for the protection of the performance right of a dramatic or music-dramatic work, it was irrelevant whether or not the work was published in a print edition. Published musical works could be performed in public without permission if the composer had not reserved that right on either the cover or the first page. As few composers had ever done so in the past, most of the performing rights were irrecoverably lost and could not be administered by a collective management organization. Following this new requirement, Strauss reserved the performance right of *Ein Heldenleben*, for example. He explained the new bearing to his publisher, Eugen Spitzweg, in an often-quoted letter: "Verlagsrechte dem Verleger. Urheberrechte dem Urheber. Anderen Modus gibt's künftig nicht" ("Publishing rights to the publisher, copyright to the author. There's no other way going forward").[5]

In this context, it is worth noting that the Leipziger Anstalt did not accept the necessity of reservation. It administered not only protected musical works and public performances of protected dramatic-musical works, but also the performing rights on musical works published without this reservation. Thus, it anticipated the repeal of Article 50 (section 2) of the 1870 Copyright Act, which would be enacted in the upcoming copyright reform. Since only the German legislature had the power to repeal the rule, this practice was not legal. The Anstalt also collected royalties with or without permission from the rights holder; it was apparently unaware that the law required permission and that unauthorized collection was therefore illegal.

The Second Attempt

After the failure of the Leipziger Anstalt, the Genossenschaft Deutscher Komponisten and the Verein der Deutschen Musikalienhändler explored other avenues for establishing a collective management organization. At the beginning of 1899, the executive board of the Genossenschaft Deutscher Komponisten, which included Strauss, Rösch, and Rüfer, finally ended its rebellious stance and assumed a more active role in the royalty movement. This was before the introduction of perpetual copyright; nonetheless, they preferred to found it after the new copyright act went into effect, which would later pass in 1901. This second attempt quickly collapsed, however. On May 5, 1899, the executive board ceased negotiations with the Verein der Deutschen Musikalienhändler after its general secretary, Oskar von Hase, failed to raise support for a new arrangement that would have the two institutions jointly support the Leipziger Anstalt, replacing the ADMV in that role. A week later, the ADMV withdrew from the Anstalt at its general meeting and did not engage further in the royalty movement.

The Third Attempt: The Genossenschaft Deutscher Tonsetzer

The Reichjustizamt had previously declared that perpetual copyright could not be introduced in the pending reform and that implementing an

---

[5] Letter of November 22, 1898, in *Der Strom der Töne trug mich fort: Die Welt um Richard Strauss in Briefen*, ed. Franz Grasberger with Franz and Alice Strauss (Tutzing: Hans Schneider, 1967), 119. Publishing rights included both reproduction and distribution.

extension of the performing rights protection from 30 to 50 years after the death of the author would require concerted action by composers and music publishers. The Genossenschaft Deutscher Komponisten wished to continue pursuing the extension, but when the Reichjustizamt was informed of the failure of the joint petition with the Verein der Deutschen Musikalienhändler, it removed the extension from the bill.

As a result, some Berlin music publishers (Hugo Bock, Willibald Challier, Hermann Erler, Adolph Fürstner, Robert Heinrich Lienau, and Johann Baptist [Hans] Simrock) offered their support to a new petition, which they submitted to the Reichsjustizamt on June 9, 1899. The petition demanded the extension of the performing rights protection from 30 to 50 years after the author's death and the retroactive repeal of the performing rights exceptions in Article 50 (section 2) of the 1870 Copyright Act in order to restore the lost performing rights. After an appeal from the aforementioned Berlin music publishers, many other publishers joined the petition. The Genossenschaft Deutscher Komponisten and Berlin publishers also decided that they would establish a collective management organization after the implementation of the new copyright law. The Genossenschaft drew up detailed plans that were soon accepted by the new partners.

The new law regarding copyright of literary and musical works (henceforth: the 1901 Copyright Act) passed on June 19, 1901, and went into effect on January 1, 1902. The copyright term for performing rights was not extended, however, and Article 27 contained some significant exemption clauses: musical performances at folk festivals, in associations, and at charity events were permitted without licensing through the author. Due to these exemptions, the Genossenschaft Deutscher Komponisten feared that the planned collective management organization would not be able to cover its costs since it could not collect fees for so many performances. Moreover, it would have a smaller repertoire than collective management organizations in other countries with copyright terms longer than 30 years after the author's death.[6] The 1901 Copyright Act was such a huge disappointment that, in March 1901, the alliance of the Genossenschaft Deutscher Komponisten and Berlin music publishers completely abandoned its plan to establish a collective management organization. The royalty movement came to a screeching halt.

---

[6] The fifty-year copyright duration was not implemented until 1934, at which time Strauss once again advocated for it.

In November 1902, the Austrian Gesellschaft der Autoren, Komponisten und Musikverleger (AKM; Society of Authors, Composers, and Music Publishers; founded in 1897 and still active today) announced its expansion to Germany, since no collective management organization had been founded there. In response, the Genossenschaft Deutscher Komponisten and their partners resolved in meetings on December 8 and 13–14, 1902, to pursue the formation of a collective management organization after all, and at its general meeting on January 14, 1903, the Genossenschaft decided to establish the Anstalt für musikalisches Aufführungsrecht (AFMA; Institute for Musical Performing Rights). It shared a home with the Genossenschaft in Berlin. At the same time, the Genossenschaft Deutscher Komponisten was renamed Genossenschaft Deutscher Tonsetzer (GDT).[7] Structured as a "wirtschaftlicher Verein" (economic association or club) according to Article 22 of the German Bürgerliches Gesetzbuch (civil code) of August 18, 1896 (enacted since January 1, 1900), the AFMA became the economic arm of the GDT and had no legal capacity of its own. Use of the title "Genossenschaft Deutscher Tonsetzer (Anstalt für musikalisches Aufführungsrecht)" reflects the GDT's status as the formal, legal entity. Strauss was elected president and, together with Rösch, Rüfer, Humperdinck, and Georg Schumann, served on the executive board. Members of the supervisory board included the composers d'Albert, Felix Draeseke, Friedrich Hegar, Joachim, Mahler, Felix Mottl, Müller-Reuter, Nicodé, Robert Radecke, Max von Schillings, Scholz, Sommer, Ludwig Thuille, Wolfrum, and Heinrich Zöllner. Members of the AFMA board of representatives were the composers Rudolf Buck, Richard Eilenberg, Friedrich Gernsheim, Wilhelm Klatte, Leopold Schmidt, and Ernst Eduard Taubert; the music publishers Bock, Challier, Fürstner, Lienau, Simrock, and Ludwig Strecker; and the lyricists Karl Friedrich Henckell, John Henry Mackay, and Christian Morgenstern.

The GDT (AFMA) administered only the performance rights of purely musical works, not those for the stage or other music-dramatic works. As the legal basis for its activity was the new 1901 Copyright Act, it did not manage works in the public domain or collect royalties for public performances at folk festivals, in associations, and at charity events because, as mentioned, these public performances did not require the author's permission due to the exemption clauses of Article 27. Composers and other rights holders transferred their rights to the GDT through contracts, and

[7] "Tonsetzer" is an antiquated German word for composer.

music users were granted single or blanket licenses. After deducting operating costs and transferring 10 percent to a relief fund, the remaining revenue was distributed to the beneficiaries: 50 percent to the composer, 25 percent to the publisher, and 25 percent to the lyricist. For works without text, the composer received 75 percent of the revenue and the publisher 25 percent. On the basis of reciprocal agreements, the GDT (AFMA) was also able to license the use of works managed by foreign collective management organizations. The AFMA began its activity in July 1903 and met with opposition. The Leipzig Gewandhaus issued a boycott appeal, for example, and the Verein der Deutschen Musikalienhändler published the names of the music publishers who rejected the new institution. The GDT succeeded in overcoming this resistance, however.

Conclusion

Establishing a collective management organization in Germany was a long and difficult process, but the third attempt of 1903 finally succeeded due to the collaborative efforts of the Genossenschaft Deutscher Komponisten and Berlin music publishers, who closely followed related reforms to the copyright act.

The founding of the GDT (AFMA) was a landmark moment for German music. At the beginning of the royalty movement, most performing rights had been irrecoverably lost, which led composers to begin reserving them for themselves. Now, for the first time, a formal institution helped manage performing rights. For composers and other rights holders, it became easier to transfer their rights to the GDT than to manage them on their own, since they would have to negotiate with each individual music user. Likewise, it was easier for the user to obtain a license from the new institution than to contact individual rights holders. Thus, the GDT provided fair compensation for the use of musical works and defended copyright by taking action against infringements, such as unlicensed public performances.

Establishing a collective management organization before the hoped-for introduction of eternal copyright was a wise decision. The GDT continued to operate and evolve for many years. In 1907, it established another institution, the Mechanische Abteilung (Mechanical Department), to manage mechanical reproduction rights via media such as records. In 1930, the GDT joined with competing organizations, the Genossenschaft zur Verwertung musikalischer Aufführungsrechte (Old GEMA; Society for the Utilization of Musical Performing Rights; founded in 1915) and the

Austrian AKM (which had expanded to include Germany) to found the
Musikschutzverband (Association for the Protection of Music) for the
purpose of collaboration. The fusion reduced administrative costs and
allowed users to purchase licenses from one organization rather than many
competing ones.

During the Third Reich, the Staatlich genehmigte Gesellschaft zur
Verwertung musikalischer Urheberrechte (STAGMA; State-Authorized
Society for the Utilization of Musical Copyright; established in 1933)
had a monopoly on rights management in music. Since the end of World
War II, it has continued its activity as the Gesellschaft für musikalische
Aufführungs- und mechanische Vervielfältigungsrechte (GEMA; Society
for Musical Performance and Mechanical Reproduction Rights). To this
day, collective management organizations operate successfully in many
countries, although there is still no eternal copyright. In the European
Union and Switzerland, for example, the copyright term now ends 70 years
after the author's death (as has been the case in the United States
since 1998).

Richard Strauss played an important role in the royalty movement. His
two circular letters were – along with Sommer's essay "Die Wertschätzung
der Musik" – critical in stimulating the founding of the Genossenschaft
Deutscher Komponisten. During the following years, he was actively
involved as chairman of the executive board of the Genossenschaft
Deutscher Komponisten and later served as president of the GDT. While
the support of the Berlin music publishers was necessary for the founding
of AFMA, Strauss nevertheless later harshly criticized Bock and Strecker in
his 1918 song cycle *Krämerspiegel*. But this critique resulted from their
involvement in founding the Anstalt für mechanisch-musikalische Rechte
GmbH (AMMRE; Institute for Mechanical-Musical Rights) in 1909 and
the so-called Old GEMA in 1915, two competing collective management
organizations.

We also must acknowledge the extraordinary contributions of Friedrich
Rösch. As both a composer and lawyer, he was the ideal leading figure.
Rösch was responsible for the correspondence and publications of
the Genossenschaft Deutscher Komponisten as well as the structuring
of the planned collective management organization while also representing
the Genossenschaft Deutscher Komponisten on the expert board
during the copyright reform.

PART IV

Professional and Musical Contexts

CHAPTER 19

The Composer

Jeremy R. Zima

The level of international fame and financial success achieved by Richard Strauss was highly unusual for German composers of his generation. Indeed, the composer and the profession of composition occupied a precarious position in German society during Strauss's lifetime. In the German cultural imagination, the composer was symbolic of the nation's intellectual and artistic superiority. This ideologically exalted status rarely translated to lived experience, however. In almost all cases, German composers had a difficult time gaining financial security from their art, to the extent that for most of Strauss's life it would be more accurate to think of composition as a vocation rather than as a viable profession in the strict sense. Limited performance opportunities, unfavorable publishing and copyright terms, disappearing avenues of patronage, and a lack of standardized credentialing processes or conservatory curricula for composers all contributed to this rather bleak state of affairs.[1] Although these problems were already evident to Strauss and many of his contemporaries by the turn of the century, the unstable political, cultural, and economic climate of the Weimar Republic made artists, audiences, and critics aware of the struggles faced by the vast majority of German composers. Strauss stood at the center of calls for reform to improve the economic situation of composers, especially in the areas of publishing and royalty collection. His extensive study of Nietzsche led him to reject the Romantic notion of the composer as genius. Instead, he conceived of the composer as an artisan, a consummate craftsman for whom financial success was confirmation of mastery. Strauss was not the only person of his generation engaging in a critical re-evaluation of the composer's duties. Gustav Mahler, Hans Pfitzner, and Franz Schreker also wrestled with the

---

[1] Alan E. Steinweis, *Art, Ideology, and Economics in Nazi Germany: The Reich Chambers of Music, Theater, and the Visual Arts* (Chapel Hill: University of North Carolina Press, 1993), esp. 10–12 and 14–15.

increasingly complex interplay of art and commerce in the twentieth century, often using their compositions as places to work through their professional anxieties. Novelists like Herman Hesse, Thomas Mann, and Franz Werfel obsessed over the relationship between composer, audience, and society in their writings of the period. The next generation of composers, born around 1900, especially Ernst Krenek and Paul Hindemith, were deeply influenced by Strauss's pragmatic approach to the economics of composition and attempted to emulate his example.

The idea that the composer needed to be free from the distractions of daily life in order to focus on creating masterworks was novel to nineteenth-century Romanticism. In 1809, Beethoven made a legal agreement with three Viennese noble families guaranteeing him 4,000 florins per year for life, allowing the composer to be "as free from care as possible," able to "devote himself to a single department of activity and create works of magnitude which are exalted" in order that "the necessaries of life shall not cause him embarrassment or clog his powerful genius."[2] Although later generations of composers and critics would view Beethoven's arrangement as a prescriptive ideal, his situation was fairly unique even in his day, and the ability to compose freely with the support of wealthy patrons was simply not an attainable reality for most composers at the turn of the twentieth century. The era of aristocratic patronage, already on the decline throughout the nineteenth century, ended suddenly and completely after the World War I. Additionally, publishing practices and copyright laws in Austria and Germany made it nearly impossible for composers to make a living from performances of their work, regardless of pedigree or reputation. This forced composers to seek other forms of employment. In best-case scenarios, this meant conducting or conservatory teaching – largely seasonal professions that allowed for several months to be spent on composition. These positions were relatively few in number, however, and tended to be given to established composers, leaving young composers to take jobs that allowed them little time for composing. This chapter discusses some of the challenges faced by German composers in the early twentieth century while also describing the opportunities for career advancement available to Strauss and his colleagues. What emerges is a picture of a profession in transition, simultaneously attempting to redefine its economic relationship with the public and its legal standing.

Underlying the many problems and economic insecurities facing composers during Strauss's life was the issue of professional classification.

---

[2] Elliot Forbes, ed., *Thayer's Life of Beethoven* (Princeton: Princeton University Press, 1967), 1: 457.

Under the 1870 German *Gewerbeordnung* or Industrial Code (and later the Weimar constitution), composers were classified as members of the *freie Berufe*, or "free professions." Free professions were largely unencumbered by government regulations, leaving artists (in theory) to pursue their creative impulses without state interference. This freedom was costly, however; although composers could create without the threat of political interference, they lacked any official standing in the state and were ineligible for government protections, including unemployment and health insurance. Trade unions like the Allgemeine Deutsche Musikverein (General German Music Society; ADMV) and the Genossenschaft Deutscher Tonsetzer (Association of German Composers; GDT) sought to reposition the standing of the various music professions, including composition, in the eyes of the state. This meant showing that artistic production, like musical composition, could be regulated like other skilled trades, and that mastery of craft and dedication to the discipline were more important than individual inspiration.

Increasingly over the course of the twentieth century, a rigorous conservatory education became the primary path for composers and other musicians to acquire professional credentials while demonstrating mastery of craft in a competitive and meritocratic environment. Strauss was an exception in this case; instead of attending conservatory, he received private instruction in counterpoint and harmony, in no small part so that the elder Strauss could closely monitor his son's development. Nearly all of Strauss's contemporaries, however, received at least some conservatory training where tutelage in composition entailed a detailed study of counterpoint, form, and orchestration. Free composition, however, was thought to necessitate an innate and unteachable talent that could not be judged objectively. The figure of the severe, pedantic, and out-of-step composition teacher was common in novels of the period, usually contrasted with the mentally unstable and emotionally troubled young composer. In Hermann Hesse's *Gertrude* (1910), the composer Kuhn shares an early composition with his teacher, who agrees to evaluate it. When the teacher returns the work, he faults it for a lack of technical correctness but is unable to provide a verdict on the non-formal aspects of the piece:

> There is something in it, without any doubt, and you may yet achieve something. [...] I expected something quieter and more pleasing, something more technically correct which could have been judged technically. But your work is not good technically, so I can say little about that. It is an audacious attempt, the merit of which I am unable to judge, but as your teacher I cannot praise it. I am too much of a schoolmaster to overlook

stylistic mistakes, and whether you will outweigh them with originality, I should not like to say.[3]

Experiences similar to the one described in Hesse's novel were common among Strauss's colleagues. Hans Pfitzner's experience at the Hoch Conservatory in Frankfurt was almost identical to the fictional account above. His teacher, Iwan Knorr, taught strict counterpoint and offered guidance only on a formal level, marking technical errors while leaving aside any subjective evaluation of Pfitzner's early works. At the Vienna Conservatory, Gustav Mahler studied harmony with Robert Fuchs and composition with Franz Krenn, whose dry approach did little to further Mahler's development. Although Mahler would win the Conservatory's composition prize for the first movement of a piano quintet, he worked on the project outside his formal studies. Fuchs later related to Mahler's wife Alma that he "always played truant and yet there was nothing that he couldn't do."[4] When Franz Schreker (also a pupil of Fuchs) was appointed Director of the Berlin Hochschule für Musik in 1920, he inherited a composition faculty who collectively viewed the nearly 60-year-old score of *Tristan und Isolde* as a bridge too far harmonically. Composers like Pfitzner, Mahler, and Schreker became successful largely in spite of their conservatory experiences. Schreker, the leading composition teacher of his generation, was particularly aware that the nineteenth-century conservatory model was not preparing students effectively for the musical landscape of the twentieth century and set about implementing reforms in his classes, first in Vienna, and after 1920 at the Berlin Hochschule für Musik. Schreker went beyond traditional form and counterpoint, guiding his students through the most up-to-date techniques in composition while encouraging them to find their own voices. This gained him a loyal following of students, several of whom (most notably Krenek) went on to have successful careers as composers. Schreker's emphasis on craft over inspiration and the notion that composition could be taught in a systematic way was another step toward redefining the composer as artisan and professionalizing the discipline.

One of the greatest challenges to the economic security of German composers was the powerful lobby of the music publishers, who used their influence to ensure favorable terms for themselves at the expense of composers. Most of the time composers, even established ones, sold their

[3] Herman Hesse, *Gertrude*, trans. Hilda Rosner (New York: The Noonday Press, 1969), 38.
[4] Alma Mahler, *Gustav Mahler: Memories and Letters*, 3rd ed., ed. Donald Mitchell and Knud Martner, trans. Basil Creighton (Seattle: University of Washington Press, 1975), 8.

works to a publisher for a one-time fee and relinquished any financial claims on future performances. Composers were sometimes granted a percentage of the sales of a composition, but only after the publisher's costs were met and usually only if the work went into a second printing. For internationally-known composers like Strauss, these fees were exceptionally high: he was paid 60,000 marks by Fürstner in 1905 for the rights to publish *Salome*, a sum that afforded him the ability to build a villa in Garmisch. For less-established composers, however, the terms were less favorable. In 1919, Hindemith was initially offered a mere 100 marks by Schott for a group of his early compositions. Hindemith countered that the fee would not even cover the cost of the ink and paper to produce the work. After some negotiation, Schott upped their offer to 1,000 marks for four chamber works, a number that by 1922 would only cover half the cost of copying the parts and score for the cello sonata and string quartet he was composing at the time – a cost that Hindemith bore out-of-pocket.[5] Nor was Hindemith's situation unique: Krenek's first contract with Universal Edition (a firm that specialized in new music) was similar. Although his fee rose to about 2,500 marks per composition in 1921–22, Hindemith was still obligated to work several jobs to make ends meet. Hindemith was a rapidly-rising star in Germany, and because of this, he was able to secure terms with Schott in late 1922 that allowed him to quit his job as concertmaster at the Frankfurt Opera, but only after tense and openly combative negotiations. A columnist lamented in 1927 that no other profession, save authors, worked "so cheaply or hopelessly" as composers, forced to take day jobs to make ends meet, sapping their creative energy and slowing their progress. Publishers preyed on young composers, taking nearly all the money generated by the performance of a new work in order to recoup their investments. Only the most famous composers (like Strauss), the columnist contended, ever profited from performances of their own work. Worst of all, he wrote, audiences were unsympathetic to the economic plight of composers, taking the view that these works of art were a kind of national property. Publishers were quick to embrace that claim, arguing that if composers' fees or copyright protections were increased, German cultural life itself would suffer at the hands of greedy composers.[6]

---

[5] Geoffrey Skelton, ed. and trans., *Selected Letters of Paul Hindemith* (New Haven: Yale University Press, 1995), 24–25.

[6] Fritz Müller-Rehrmann, "50 Jahre Autorenschutz," *Allgemeine Musikzeitung* 54 (1927): 445.

Looking at Strauss himself, a casual observer could be forgiven for assuming that composers made more than enough money. In 1927, the year in which the aforementioned article was written, Strauss owned both his Garmisch villa and a residence in the very exclusive heart of Vienna. In a wider context, 1927 was also the year of Ernst Krenek's smash hit *Jonny spielt auf*, an opera that spawned hundreds of performances in more than 50 cities over a two-year period, becoming a pop culture juggernaut and netting the composer a small fortune. But these were rare exceptions that proved the rule: for every *Jonny* there were ten operas like Schreker's *Der singende Teufel* (1929), a massively expensive work that closed after a handful of performances. Schreker, who could boast to Paul Bekker at the start of the decade that his composition royalties would soon allow him to quit teaching, saw his fortune largely erased by inflation. By the end of the decade, he relied almost entirely on his salary at the Hochschule and had to threaten to sue Universal Edition to secure the publication of *Der singende Teufel*, which the publisher correctly judged would be a commercial disaster. He and his family experienced real financial hardship when he was pensioned off in 1932.

For every failed orchestral or operatic work by an already established composer like Schreker, hundreds more could not gain a public hearing. As noted, young composers needed to hire and rehearse their own ensembles and pay out of pocket for the copying of parts. Such was the context for the premiere of Krenek's Symphony No. 1, Op. 7. Despite his relationship with the publisher, Universal Edition, Krenek had to rely on a generous gift from a private patron to cover the cost of copying the parts, while the conductor and editor of the journal *Melos*, Hermann Scherchen, needed to raise over 6,000 marks to pay the orchestra he had hired to premiere Krenek's symphony. Such a financial burden was simply beyond the means of the average aspiring composer. Writing in 1927, Strauss attempted to set the record straight about the relationship between publishers and the majority of composers in Germany:

> The German public has to know that among the 1,000–2,000 German composers very few – scarcely a single one if one takes serious music into consideration – are able to earn a livelihood from the income generated by their creative work, while hundreds of publishers, including their numerous staff, through the exploitation of these artistic creations, are able to have a secure existence.[7]

---

[7] Richard Strauss, "Zur Frage der Schutzfrist," *Allgemeine Musikzeitung* 54 (1927): 77.

Indeed, Strauss was the only composer of "serious" music in Germany who survived with any degree of comfort solely on the proceeds from his compositions, even as he maintained a busy and demanding career as a conductor throughout much of his adult life. Within the German context, no composers could, like Verdi, retire from professional life and rely on royalties as a secure means of income. Instead, most turned to conducting or teaching as their primary source of income. A high-profile conducting appointment such as those enjoyed by Strauss, Mahler, and Pfitzner was beneficial to a composer's career for many reasons. Conductors of publicly funded orchestras were classified as civil servants, and their compensation included vacation time, health and unemployment insurance, and a stable pension – none of which were available to freelance composers. Composer-conductors also benefited from increased name recognition and market-ability and had the opportunity to program their own works and those of composers they admired. Strauss was a powerful (and somewhat rare) early champion of Mahler's works, and Mahler programmed Strauss in Vienna and elsewhere as often as he was able. Although conducting was largely seasonal work, the time commitment was significant and could impact the compositional process. Strauss worked the task of sketching, composing, and orchestrating into his daily schedule even during the conducting season, and this regimented approach to composition allowed him to be creatively productive throughout the year, whereas Mahler accomplished almost no composing during the conducting season, spending his summers working feverishly in a secluded cabin.

Teaching positions at prestigious conservatories – like conducting posts – were often another form of recognition for successful composers. Conservatory teaching was also a form of civil service and therefore offered a secure salary and excellent benefits. One of the most prominent (and exclusive) teaching positions available to composers was the composition masterclass at the Preussische Akademie der Künste in Berlin. The post was essentially honorary until the 1920s and came with few mandated teaching duties. Strauss, Pfitzner, Busoni, and Schoenberg led classes at various times during the late Imperial and Weimar periods. Schoenberg's years teaching the masterclass were easily the best of his professional life; after years spent scraping together a living from private teaching and very occasional performances, he finally secured a state-sponsored post that required him to work only six months of the year at his discretion and gave him complete control over curricular decisions.

Most teaching posts were more demanding than the Berlin masterclass, though accomplished composers could negotiate leave time and other benefits into their contracts. When Schreker was appointed director of the Berlin Hochschule, he was given three months of leave per year and an administrative assistant to oversee the daily operations of the conservatory. Hans Pfitzner's 1908 appointment as director of the Conservatoire de Strasbourg gave him time to pursue his interest in opera composition and conducting; he revived a number of German romantic operas while composing his own most famous work, *Palestrina* (1917). Yet, despite the guarantees of creative leave and other benefits, the strain of classroom teaching and administration took a creative toll on teachers like Schreker. All of his greatest operatic successes took place before he came to Berlin. During the 1920s, he struggled to complete large projects, and the operas that he did manage to finish were not well received by his publisher, audiences, or critics. Schreker displayed his frustration with his teaching duties in his opera *Christophorus*, allegorizing himself in the opera as a composition teacher, Meister Johann, who has devoted his life to his students but has received very little back from them. After his wife left him for failing to create a musical masterpiece, Meister Johann turned to teaching. Years spent in the classroom leads him to lament: "Now as schoolmaster I trudge through my days, teaching young men the craft ... they suck me dry and feed on me as my wife once did, greedily taking the last piece that was left of me – and they too will go" (Act I, scene 6).

Conducting and conservatory positions were few in number, however. Instead, most aspiring composers taught privately or took jobs outside of music. Private teaching was a difficult and unpredictable way to make a living, and competition from amateurs was considerable. The problem of unlicensed and unregulated private music teachers was fiercely debated, especially during the Weimar Republic. Many composers lobbied for increased regulation and a licensing process for private music teachers. Composers who took jobs outside of music often found themselves too exhausted by the mental and physical demands of their professions to compose. Alfred Einstein declared in 1923, "Today I know creative musicians of high rank who, crushed in a mind-numbing occupation, mostly in the banking industry, have not written a note for years and years."[8] He asked why such composers should even bother when no publisher would print their work, no opera would stage it, and no conductor would program it. The only composers in Germany who could support themselves through their works, he concluded, were those

[8] Alfred Einstein, "Die Not der deutschen Musiker," *Anbruch* 6, no. 1 (1924): 26.

(like Strauss, and to a lesser extent Pfitzner and Schreker) who were already famous before the war. Observing this bleak situation were younger composers like Krenek and Hindemith, both of whom – following Strauss's model of the composer as artisan – adapted their early compositions to match the economic realities they encountered. For both, opera remained the primary avenue for making money, and both intentionally sought to engage popular audiences through their works, especially Krenek's *Jonny spielt auf* and Hindemith's *Neues vom Tage*. Hindemith lobbied for music education reform and composed large amounts of educational music for young ensembles, partly out of conviction and partly out of a recognition that a thriving market existed for that type of music. The large stylistic shifts in the early music of these composers reflect a willingness to adapt to an ever-changing musical landscape.

The figure of the composer was complex during Strauss's long life, trapped between the nineteenth-century ideal of unfettered inspiration and the often-ugly economic and social reality of the twentieth century. Publishing arrangements and copyright laws made it difficult for composers to make money on their works, causing them to rely increasingly on other forms of income such as conducting and teaching. Although the vast majority of composers struggled under this system, composers like Strauss managed to succeed, and some lobbied intensely to improve conditions for less talented and less successful composers in Germany, arguing that the composer deserves a wage just the same as the baker. The struggle of Strauss and others to redefine the composer as a craftsman who assumed his place in society is critical to our understanding of the discipline of composition during this period.

CHAPTER 20

The Conductor

Raymond Holden

Fêted by musicians and non-musicians alike, Richard Strauss worked at the highest level as a conductor for much of his long and remarkable life. The son of one of Germany's most renowned orchestral musicians, the redoubtable horn player Franz Strauss, Richard had the sounds of the lyric theater and the concert hall ringing in his ears from his earliest years. Although those sounds were heavily censored by the notoriously conservative Franz, they were fundamental to the ways in which he perceived, received, and shaped his musical environment. They were also the bases for his activities as a mature artist and affected his methods, both as a composer and as a performer. While Strauss was recognized early on as a creative musician of tremendous invention, his activities as an interpretative musician were somewhat less revolutionary. Consequently, his route to the podium was not dissimilar to that of his German-speaking contemporaries and was formed largely by the needs of the central European opera house system.

Strauss's family background and music education stood in sharp contrast to those of his famous colleagues, Arthur Nikisch, Gustav Mahler, and Felix Weingartner. Considered amongst the greatest and most influential performing musicians of their generation, Nikisch, Mahler, Weingartner, and Strauss knew each other personally, interacted professionally, and competed artistically. While all four had their roots in the German-speaking middle class, Strauss was the only one to come from an affluent family and the only one to be the son of a distinguished musician. He therefore benefited from an early insight into professional musical life that was relatively unique, both then and now. As a restless but bright student at Munich's Ludwigsgymnasium, Strauss supplemented his academic education with violin, piano, and composition lessons from members of the Munich Court Opera's music staff.

Nikisch, Mahler, and Weingartner were far less privileged musically during their childhoods and lacked Strauss's intense early musical training.

While Nikisch and Weingartner were the offspring of minor civil servants and were encouraged to pursue their love of music as children, Mahler's family was less supportive. A distiller by profession, Gustav's father was reluctant for his son to become a professional musician and only grudgingly allowed him to study at the Vienna conservatory as a 15-year-old. Unlike Strauss, the other three all attended major conservatories, were artistic renegades as students, and were committed Wagnerians at earlier ages. Their love of the Master's music remained with them for the rest of their lives and each was a noted interpreter of his works. As a young member of the Vienna Court Orchestra, Nikisch played under Wagner. Bowled over by his hero's approach to Beethoven's Third and Ninth Symphonies, Nikisch later claimed that those readings were "[decisive] for my conception of Beethoven as a whole, and, for my orchestral interpretation in general."[1] Strauss's epiphany as a *Zukunftsmusiker* (musician of the future) occurred somewhat later than those of Nikisch, Mahler, and Weingartner, and it was only as a young conductor at Meiningen in the mid-1880s that he began to explore Wagner's music in earnest.

Training to be a musician is one thing but earning a living as one is quite another. For an aspiring artist, his or her first leap into the professional dark can often be daunting. This is particularly true for conductors whose career paths can be uncertain at best. Today, the route to the podium might not be any easier than during the late nineteenth century, but opportunities for getting a foot on the bottom rung of the conducting ladder have increased exponentially with the advent of formalized conducting courses and the introduction of international conducting competitions. While conducting competitions are really a post–World War II phenomenon, conducting classes began towards the end of the nineteenth century with the Leipzig conservatory being amongst the first to offer such lessons. As a student at the conservatory, Weingartner attended its conducting classes but found them very rudimentary and was dismissive of them. For him, the best method of learning the craft of conducting was to be apprenticed to an established figure. And the artist to whom nearly all aspiring conductors wanted to be attached was Hans von Bülow.

Dubbed "the master conductor" by Weingartner, Bülow was the most celebrated performing artist of his age and conducted the most virtuosic

---

[1] Ferdinand Pfohl, "Arthur Nikisch," in *Arthur Nikisch: Leben und Wirken*, ed. Heinrich Chevalley (Leipzig: Theodor Althoff, 1922), 10–14.

orchestra of the period: the Meiningen Court Orchestra.[2] Unusually for the late nineteenth century, the ensemble was a touring chamber orchestra that was groundbreaking in its programming policy and influential in its performance style. An artistic magnet that attracted some of the leading orchestral virtuosos of the time, it inspired composers such as Brahms to write works for it. The orchestra's conducting staff were also much sought after and, when Franz Mannstädt resigned as Bülow's assistant at Meiningen to work with the Berlin Philharmonic in 1885, the Court Orchestra needed a new second conductor. Bülow was convinced that he had found the right man in Strauss and appointed him Musikdirektor the same year. Mahler and Weingartner were already employed as conductors in Kassel and Königsberg (Kaliningrad), but they coveted the position to which Strauss was ultimately appointed and never fully understood why Bülow had overlooked them. To have the chance of assisting a leading musician, and to learn the art and craft of conducting at the musical coalface, was a significant opportunity for the young Strauss. It is understandable, then, that his contemporaries were somewhat envious of his appointment. Strauss was happy and proud to be Bülow's apprentice, and the impact of that apprenticeship was both life-changing and lifelong. Even today, an important step on the road to becoming a maestro is learning from an established conductor.

When Strauss's earliest appointments are compared to those of Nikisch, Mahler, and Weingartner, it is clear that he was either very lucky, or extremely savvy, in his career choices. Unlike his three colleagues, Strauss's entire professional life as a tenured conductor was spent at either court- or state-run institutions. Conducting posts at these institutions, particularly those in major centers such as Munich, Berlin, and Vienna, were much sought after, attracted the most famous conductors, and paid the highest salaries. Nikisch was fortunate enough to work at Leipzig's commercially funded Stadttheater from 1877, but Mahler and Weingartner struggled to make ends meet by working at a string of provincial, commercial theaters that did little to advance them either musically or financially during their formative years. Commercial theaters often paid seasonally – a season generally lasted from September to May – while court theaters paid a secure annual salary. For musicians at early stages of their careers, the financial difference was striking. At the Duchy of Saxe-Meiningen, for example, Strauss was offered 2,000 Marks annually to remain as Bülow's replacement in 1886, while Weingartner was paid a meager 150 Marks per

---

[2] Bülow conducted the Meiningen Court Orchestra between 1880 and 1885.

month at the commercial Danzig Stadttheater for an eight-month season the same year. But, by the turn of the twentieth century, Strauss, Mahler, and Weingartner had released their musical and financial potentials and were paid sums that reflected their status as musical superstars. As Kapellmeister at the Berlin Court Opera from 1891, Weingartner earned 9,000 Marks annually; as Music Director of the Metropolitan Opera, New York, in 1908, Mahler received $30,000, forty times the average wage in America; while, as a guest conductor in London in 1909, Strauss was paid £200 per performance, the equivalent of two years wages for a skilled British laborer.

Money is not always the sole motivating factor for an artist: prestige, tradition, and conditions of service are also important. Unlike commercial and municipal theaters, court theaters offered greater rehearsal time for new productions and the chance to perform more challenging works. That said, all three types of theater generally operated as repertory houses, meaning that many established operas were staged with little or no rehearsal. Nevertheless, court theaters were still able to engage better singers and orchestral musicians, thanks to the higher, more stable, salaries they paid. Perhaps of greater interest to composer-conductors such as Strauss, Mahler, and Weingartner were the paid summer holidays that court theaters offered. This meant that they could work unhindered on their creative activities for at least part of the year.

During the first decades of the nineteenth century, it was common for composers to be conductors. Spohr, Weber, Meyerbeer, Mendelssohn, Liszt, and Wagner all acted as both. By the mid-nineteenth century, the situation had begun to change, with Bülow, Hans Richter, Hermann Levi, Anton Seidl, and Nikisch being amongst the first conductors to act primarily as performers. But the shift from creation to re-creation was not absolute by the end of the nineteenth century, and Mahler, Weingartner, and Strauss all pursued joint careers as composer-conductors. While they all made impacts with their youthful works, perhaps the least successful as a young composer was Mahler. Although his Second Symphony was more popular than either his *Das klagende Lied* or his First Symphony, it was not until the premiere of his Eighth Symphony at Munich in 1910 that he enjoyed an unqualified critical and public success. Weingartner fared somewhat better with his first opera *Sakuntala*, which premiered at the Weimar Court Theater in 1884, and his second opera *Malawika*, heard for the first time at the Munich Court Opera in 1886. Strauss was equally precocious and, after his Second Symphony was given first in New York under Theodore Thomas in 1884, he conducted the premiere of his

Suite for Winds at the Munich Odeon with the Meiningen Court Orchestra at the express wish of Bülow the same year. With that remarkable and somewhat nerve-wracking debut, Strauss not only took his first tentative steps on the road to becoming a professional conductor, he also began to pave the way for a career that saw him emerge as the most successful professional composer-conductor of the late nineteenth and early twentieth centuries.[3]

When Bülow resigned in a fit of pique from the Meiningen Court Orchestra at the end of 1885, Strauss decided to return to Munich, where he was appointed Musikdirektor, or Third Conductor, of the Court Opera in 1886. With this appointment, Strauss began his rise through the ranks of the central European opera-house system, a system that continues to this day to encourage and to exploit young musicians in equal measure. Something of a musical juggernaut that slows down to allow musicians and singers to hop on and hop off at various points in their careers, the system was, and is, the main employer of conductors in German-speaking countries. All those mentioned in this chapter were both beneficiaries and victims of that system, and Strauss was no exception. At the time of his Munich appointment in 1886, the conducting hierarchy of most German-speaking theaters was fixed from bottom to top: the Hof/Musikdirektor (Court/Third Conductor) conducted revivals and operetta; the Zweiter Kapellmeister (Second Conductor) took charge of more important works; the Hof/Erster Kapellmeister (Court/First Conductor) led some new productions and conducted some of the orchestra's subscription concerts; while the Generalmusikdirektor or Leiter (Director) was in overall charge of the theater and conducted most of its important concerts and new productions. Following his appointment as Musikdirektor in Munich, Strauss held increasingly important posts in Weimar (1889–94), Munich (1894–98), Berlin (1898–1918), and Vienna (1919–24). The siren call of Vienna was particularly alluring and it was as Director of the Court/State Opera that not only Strauss (1919–24) but also Mahler (1897–1907) and Weingartner (1908–11 and 1935–36) reached the heights of their fame. But each found that venerable institution something of a poisoned chalice and each left either disgruntled or under a professional cloud.

Strauss quickly made his mark in the opera house, but his abilities as a symphonic conductor were only recognized somewhat later.

<hr/>

[3] Strauss later recalled that, due to nerves, he conducted his work in "a state of slight coma"; Richard Strauss, "Reminiscences of Hans von Bülow," *Recollections and Reflections*, ed. Willi Schuh, trans. L. J. Lawrence (London: Boosey & Hawkes, 1953), 119.

Having started his podium career with Europe's most virtuosic chamber orchestra, Strauss built on those orchestral experiences at Weimar and later took charge of the Munich Court Orchestra's and Berlin Philharmonic's subscription series between 1894 and 1896. Strauss failed to impress at these concerts and was removed as principal conductor of the Munich series after two seasons and of the Berlin series after just one.

Clearly humiliated by his dismissals, Strauss gained some much-needed symphonic experience by taking charge of the less-than-prestigious Berlin Tonkünstler Orchestra in 1901, a post that did much to prepare him for his next orchestral appointment: principal conductor of the Berlin Court Orchestra's subscription series from 1908. As conductor of that series, he replaced his old nemesis, Felix Weingartner. Unlike Strauss and Mahler, Weingartner was generally regarded as a great symphonic conductor. After Berlin, Weingartner moved to Vienna in 1908, where he continued to impress in the concert hall. With the city's Philharmonic, his career went from strength to strength and he directed a remarkable 433 performances over the next 19 years with the orchestra. But Weingartner's prowess in the concert hall came at a price: he was considered by many to be less suited to the lyric theater than to the concert stage, and his tenures at leading opera houses often ended in acrimony. Conversely, Strauss was regarded as a consummate theater musician and led no fewer than 1,948 operatic performances as a tenured conductor between 1886 and 1924. While these statistics might seem high when compared to those of a modern music director, one must remember that, until the middle of the twentieth century, tenured conductors tended to be responsible for the majority of the performances given by the institution to which they were contracted. This was also true of Great Britain, where Sir John Barbirolli led 3,172 concerts with Manchester's Hallé Orchestra, the overwhelming majority of which he gave between 1943 and 1957 as the ensemble's "Permanent Conductor."

As musicians raised and educated in the German-speaking communities of central Europe, it is hardly surprising that Strauss and his contemporaries looked to that region's composers as the bases for their programming policies. For each, the composer who took pride of place in the opera theater was Wagner. By the end of the nineteenth century, the composer's stage works had taken on a near-cult status and often proved as divisive as they did enthralling. As a young Musikdirektor at Munich in 1888, Strauss was given the task of performing the composer's first opera, *Die Feen*, but was replaced at the last minute by his immediate superior, Franz Fischer. Disappointed and angry, Strauss had to wait until he was appointed

Kapellmeister at Weimar before he tackled a complete work by Wagner for the first time: *Lohengrin* on October 6, 1889. In all, Strauss conducted no fewer than 433 performances of Wagner's stage works in Weimar, Munich, Berlin, and Vienna.

Mahler was also a passionate champion of Wagner's works and, as Director of the Vienna Court Opera from 1897, his reputation as a Wagnerian reached its zenith. At that theater, he conducted Vienna's first uncut cycle of the *Ring* in the summer of 1897, two full years before Strauss's first complete reading of the tetralogy in Berlin. Mahler also collaborated with the Secessionist artist Alfred Roller (with whom Strauss would later work on a new production of *Parsifal* at Bayreuth in 1934) on a groundbreaking staging of *Tristan und Isolde* in 1903. For their ground-breaking *Tristan*, Mahler and Roller rejected the naturalism of earlier productions in favor of new sets, costumes, and lighting effects that were "truly overpowering in [their] effect, without in any way impairing [their] function through obtrusiveness."[4] Strauss, too, had caused a sensation with *Tristan* some years earlier when he gave an early uncut performance of it at Weimar. It seems that both Strauss and Mahler had fallen under the work's spell and would have agreed fully with their hero, Hans von Bülow, when he wrote that it was "as beautiful as the most beautiful of dreams ... [and] an experience beyond time and place."[5]

To be considered a Beethoven interpreter of distinction was a bench-mark of excellence to which all the conductors mentioned in this chapter aspired. Without question, Beethoven was the most frequently-performed composer at the major subscription concerts in German-speaking countries and was no less popular at similar series in London, Paris, and New York. Perhaps unsurprisingly, then, the first complete extant commercial recording of a symphony was the composer's Fifth under Nikisch with the Berlin Philharmonic in 1913. Strauss then set down the work with the Berlin Staatskapelle in 1928, two years after recording the composer's Seventh Symphony with the same orchestra. But it was Weingartner who was the first conductor to record all of Beethoven's nine symphonies as a group and the only conductor born in the nineteenth century to record the Fifth Symphony on four occasions, solely with London orchestras.

---

[4] Guido Adler, "Gustav Mahler," in *Gustav Mahler and Guido Adler: Records of a Friendship*, ed. Edward R. Reilly (Cambridge: Cambridge University Press, 1982), 26.

[5] Letter from Hans von Bülow to Eduard Lassen, July 31, 1865; in Kenneth Birkin, "'Une organisation musicale des plus rares': Hans von Bülow 1830–1894," *Richard Strauss-Blätter* no. 47 (2002): 17.

But it was Strauss's activities as a Mozart conductor that separated him from his contemporaries. Even though Mahler had led a series of critically acclaimed performances of the composer's operas at the Vienna Court Opera during the first decade of the twentieth century, it was Strauss who influenced three future generations of Mozartians. During his career, Strauss gave 470 performances of the composer's works and was the first to record Mozart's last three symphonies as a unit. Sir Henry Wood, Sir Thomas Beecham, Otto Klemperer, Fritz Busch, Herbert von Karajan, Sir John Pritchard, and Wolfgang Sawallisch all acknowledged the impact of Strauss's interpretations of Mozart on their readings of the composer's music, and all recognized Strauss's role as a pioneer in its dissemination.

The success or failure of a conductor can often come down to the ways in which he or she communicates with the musicians and the results that they draw from them. In a world that now values conducting gestures that excite the eye more than the ear, the podium styles of Nikisch, Weingartner, and Strauss might appear somewhat alien. From the cinematic and photographic evidence pertaining to those artists, it seems that they all began their careers standing on small podiums and conducting from chest-high music stands. The effect of these performance tools ensured little lower-body movement, greater emphasis on upper-body gestures, and increased eye contact. After the music stand was lowered to waist height during the third decade of the twentieth century, Strauss and Weingartner continued to use the left hand in a restrained manner. In the opera pit, Strauss and his colleagues originally performed at the apron of the stage with their backs to the orchestra. Later, they moved to the center of the pit before taking up the modern position at the pit wall.

From the cartoons and caricatures of Otto Böhler, and from the recollections of Bruno Walter, it seems that Mahler's physical conducting technique was somewhat different from that of his contemporaries. After being diagnosed with a heart condition in his forties, his podium style underwent a metamorphosis, changing from an exigent technique to a minimalist approach. What remained constant, however, was his often-hostile manner with the players, a manner not dissimilar to that of Arturo Toscanini in Italy. Nikisch took a markedly different stance and often developed relationships with the musicians that bordered on the familiar. Like Weingartner, Strauss was considerably less offensive than was Mahler, but much less chummy than Nikisch. Crucially, Strauss knew how to get the best out of the players by being courteous while keeping the necessary professional distance.

A defining characteristic of all the conductors considered in this chapter was their ability to balance tradition and innovation. For them, the conductor needed to act as both a curator and an iconoclast. Outwardly, this might seem something of a paradox, but the artistic culture from which they emerged thrived on such musical oxymora. While Bülow, Richter, Levi, and Nikisch no longer felt the need to compose, Strauss, Mahler, and Weingartner all continued to balance the symbiotic acts of creation and recreation and tried to tame the polycephaletic musical beast known commonly as the composer-conductor. In some ways, their activities acted as models for the next generation of podium artists – Bruno Walter, Otto Klemperer, and Wilhelm Furtwängler – who also aspired to the dual role of creator and re-creator. That these later figures were less successful in reaching their goal was not only a sign of the musical times but, also, a shift in how the conductor was perceived and received by the middle of the twentieth century. No longer was the conductor the holistic artistic-being that was best summed up by a nineteenth-century German *Kapellmeister*. Rather, he had become a specialist performer for an increasingly specialist age.

CHAPTER 21

The Orchestra

Scott Warfield

For Richard Strauss, the orchestra was his primary medium of expression. His nine tone poems are cornerstones of the symphonic repertoire, and more than a dozen other instrumental works are also heard frequently in concert halls. His 15 operas, moreover, often depend on orchestral forces for their effect, and Strauss even provided orchestral accompaniments for over three dozen of his Lieder. Part of the attraction in these works is the sheer sonic energy and the innumerable variegated timbres that arise from Strauss's expert command of large orchestral ensembles. He is rightly counted among the most proficient masters of orchestration, but, beyond that skill, Strauss's development and career reflect the transition from a classically oriented orchestra to the modern post-Wagnerian orchestra at the end of the nineteenth century.

Anyone attending a performance nowadays of a Strauss tone poem might expect to see a stage filled with as many as 100 professional musicians playing their individual parts expertly in a well-rehearsed ensemble. Novice listeners might even assume that similar groups existed as far back as the era of Mozart, Haydn, and Beethoven, which marks the beginning of the orchestral repertoire still played today. In fact, the modern symphony orchestra of 75–100 players did not come into existence until the last decades of the nineteenth century and only became fully established at the beginning of the twentieth century, the years of Strauss's greatest fame and influence. The typical orchestra of the early nineteenth century had five string parts (first and second violins, violas, celli, and double basses), woodwinds (flutes, oboes, clarinets, and bassoons) in pairs, and horns. More often than not, a pair of trumpets and timpani completed the ensemble and, occasionally, a few extra winds, trombones, or other percussion might be used. While orchestras of 50 or more were typical in larger cities, ensembles of only a few dozen regular musicians were also common in smaller and less affluent locales. Generally, the orchestra of the early- to mid-nineteenth century relied on the string ensemble – often referred to as the "quartet" – to carry the most important lines in a composition. Woodwinds reinforced the strings and added solo timbres, often in secondary or contrasting themes, while the brass provided weight at cadences and in *tutti* passages. This "double-wind" orchestra is the ensemble favored by Mendelssohn for most of his orchestral music, while R. Schumann and Brahms used nearly the same instruments plus three trombones, as did Saint-Saëns as late as his Second Symphony (1878) and Rimsky-Korsakov in his *Scheherazade* (1888), among others. Even Bruckner, often called the "Wagnerian symphonist," used only woodwinds in pairs and a regular brass section through his Seventh Symphony (1883).

Advances in orchestration in the mid-nineteenth century were not simply a matter of increasing numbers, but rather in how instruments were used, especially the brass. Among the most progressive of orchestrators in the 1850s was Liszt, whose 13 symphonic poems all call for a nearly uniform double-wind orchestra with full brass section, almost identical to the ensembles used by Schumann and Brahms. What is different, however, are the more prominent roles Liszt gave to the brass. In *Les préludes* (1856), for example, the first theme is announced by full brass and winds, while the strings are reduced to a negligible accompaniment and, later, the second theme is played by three horns. The return of the first theme in the closing pages is an orgy of brass, made even more thunderous by the addition of side drum, bass drum, and cymbals.

Even more important for the evolution of orchestration than Liszt, ultimately, was Wagner, whose treatment of the orchestra influenced a generation of composers, chief among them Richard Strauss. Wagner's concern for orchestral timbres began with his declaration of the funda-mental importance of the orchestra as the medium that carries the dramatic substance of an opera. To accomplish this task, Wagner ascribed to the orchestra the ability to "speak" in a metaphoric sense that conveyed to the audience the wordless essence of the drama.[1] Although Wagner wrote little about the techniques of orchestration, his scores became a veritable lexicon of new effects. Beginning with *Lohengrin* (1850), he expanded the woodwinds to three of each, plus the English horn and bass clarinet, and added both a tuba and a harp to the ensemble. For his *Ring* cycle, he called for quadruple woodwinds, including piccolo, English horn,

---

[1] Richard Wagner, *Opera and Drama*, trans. Edwin Evans (London: Wm. Reeves, n.d.), chapter IV, "The Orchestra in Illustration of the Poet's Intention," paragraphs 256, 273, 274, 277. 278, 281, *passim*, and chapter V, "The Mutual Vocation of Gesture and the Orchestra," paragraphs 304, 305, *passim*.

bass clarinet, and contrabassoon; a brass section of eight horns (four doubling on Wagner tubas), three trumpets, three trombones, tuba, and a bass trumpet; and percussion to include four timpani, cymbals, triangle, and other effects. The string section included a harp, and the numbers of regular strings were specified as 16 first and 16 second violins, 12 violas, 12 celli, and 8 double basses. While this immense ensemble was capable of great volume, the real innovation was the ability to create a wider range of expressive timbres. These included full brass choirs, *divisi* strings with as many as eight layers, and other unique timbres through novel combinations. He even had a new brass instrument, the "Wagner tuba," invented, with a timbre that fell midway between the French horn and trombone, to sound the "Valhalla" motif. The long gestation of the *Ring* cycle and the enormous demands required for a proper performance meant that Wagner's innovative orchestral techniques were heard only infrequently, even after the *Ring* premiered in 1876, and doubtless contributed to the reluctance of other composers to adopt them.

This is the musical world into which Strauss was born and raised, with the traditional double-wind orchestra as the accepted norm and Wagner's outsized ensemble a rarely heard curiosity. Even so, Strauss knew both ensembles, having attended performances of Wagner's operas as a boy, and he reported on them, often including details of the orchestration, in quite negative terms in letters to his friend and future composer, Ludwig Thuille. More important to Strauss's development were the conservative attitudes learned from his father, hornist of the Munich Court Opera. Franz Strauss was a practical musician, who valued experience over theoretical texts, as his son echoed in a letter to Thuille:

> So far as learning instrumental music is concerned, I can only give you one piece of advice – not to learn it from a book, since this, as my father says, is the worst thing. So I advise you not to buy a book, since even my papa knows only one by Hector Berlioz, who is a real scribbler and hack; instead ask Herr Pembauer for a table covering the range and best position of the various instruments that are used and learn the rest, that is the use and application of the same, from the scores of the great old masters . . .[2]

Richard's first experiences with an orchestra were with the Wilde Gung'l, an amateur orchestra that Franz Strauss directed. Richard played

[2] "Selections from the Strauss-Thuille Correspondence: A Glimpse of Strauss during His Formative Years," trans. Susan Gillespie, in *Richard Strauss and His World*, ed. Bryan Gilliam (Princeton, NJ: Princeton University Press, 1992), 198. Josef Pembauer was an Austrian composer and Thuille's teacher.

first violin for three years, and the group also performed several of his early compositions. Working with this small amateur group surely reinforced his father's notions of how an orchestra was constituted and scored.[3] The lessons learned under his father's guidance can be seen in Richard's earliest professional compositions, the Concert Overture in C Minor (1883), Symphony No. 2 in F Minor (1884), and even the *Burleske* (1886). All three make use of a traditional double-wind orchestra with modest brass.

Strauss began to learn the practical aspects of directing an orchestra when he assumed the duties of second conductor of the Court Orchestra at Meiningen in 1885. Hans von Bülow, one of the finest musicians of the era, had drilled the small orchestra into one of the best in Germany, if not all of Europe, but there were limits to what only 49 players could do. The already undersized string section was reduced in works like Beethoven's Fifth Symphony, which required three trombones, piccolo, and contra-bassoon, all of which were played by string players who doubled on those instruments. Similarly, one of the few Meiningen bassists, "who plays an E-string instrument," was also the bass trombonist, which created difficulties in some of Brahms's symphonies.[4] Compounding such matters, in the fall of 1885 the Duke cut the orchestra by ten musicians to only 39, Bülow tendered his resignation, and Strauss took charge of the orchestra through the spring. Strauss's year in Meiningen was also important for his regular conversations with an ardent Wagnerian, Alexander Ritter, who introduced the young composer to Wagner's philosophies, which would motivate Strauss's next orchestral works.

In the fall of 1886, Strauss returned to Munich, where he had been appointed third conductor at the Court Opera. More important in the next three years than his occasional opportunities to work with its large, first-class orchestra were Strauss's first programmatic orchestral compositions, in which he put Wagner's ideas into practice, first tentatively in *Aus Italien* (1886), and more fully in *Macbeth* (1888–91) and *Don Juan* (1888). These were his first scores to use triple-wind ensembles with full brass, although not without difficulties. *Aus Italien* was described by many critics as among the most demanding works ever composed for an

---

[3] On the Wilde Gung'l and its adherence to earlier performing traditions, see Scott Warfield, "The Autograph of Strauss's Festmarsch, o.Op. 87 (T 157)," *Richard Strauss-Blätter* no. 27 (1992): 60–81.
[4] Hans von Bülow, *Briefe und Schriften*, ed. Marie von Bülow, VII Bd. (Leipzig: Breitkopf u. Härtel, 1907), Bülow to Hermann Wolff, August 26, 1881, Letter 82, 82–83; and Bülow to Brahms, October 11, 1881, Letter 97, 95–96. In the later nineteenth century, two different kinds of double basses predominated, one with only three strings, whose lowest note was a G', and a four-string instrument that reached the low E'.

orchestra, and Bülow, the work's dedicatee, was concerned whether it could even be prepared for performance in the usual rehearsal time. Strauss himself seemed to doubt the wisdom of using a Wagnerian ensemble when he wrote to Bülow (August 24, 1888):

> Perhaps in the future there will come into bloom on both graves [*Macbeth* and *Don Juan*, both unperformed] that safe little flower to whose quiet poetry of woodwinds I am gradually trying to reconcile myself. But seriously: I promise you double woodwinds in my future work for certain! I'll also take the greatest trouble imaginable to limit the big technical difficulties.[5]

Despite those assurances, Strauss did not revert to a smaller ensemble, and *Macbeth*, his first tone poem, proved to be even more problematic, requiring multiple revisions before it reached its final form. In the first draft, Strauss changed his mind frequently and added several instruments to the ensemble as he wrote out the score. Following the mixed reception of *Macbeth*'s premiere (1890), he decided to re-orchestrate the work, urged especially by Franz Strauss, who pleaded with his son to ". . . throw out the excessive rolls of instrumental fat, and give the horns more favorable conditions so that what you truly want to say can be heard."[6] The third version of *Macbeth* (1892) was a success, even as it added still more instruments to the score.

Don Juan, unlike its two predecessors, was an extraordinary triumph at its premiere in Weimar (November 11, 1889). Strauss had only recently taken the position of second conductor at the Großherzogliches Hof (Grand Ducal Court), whose small orchestra was renowned for progressive musical attitudes that had been fostered during Liszt's residency. Despite limited resources, the Court's musical high point was undoubtedly the premiere of *Lohengrin*, which Liszt conducted with an orchestra of only 38 regular members and a handful of extra musicians.[7] The ensemble that Strauss inherited nearly 40 years later would not be much different, and he was concerned by the limited skills of some players but nevertheless pleased with the sound of his new work, as he wrote to his father (November 8, 1889):

---

[5] *Hans von Bülow and Richard Strauss: Correspondence*, ed. Willi Schuh and Franz Trenner, trans. Anthony Gishford (London: Boosey & Hawkes, 1955), 81. Translation emended.
[6] Richard Strauss, *Briefe an die Eltern: 1882–1906*, ed. Willi Schuh (Zurich: Atlantis Verlag, 1954), 134.
[7] Daniel J. Koury, *Orchestral Performance Practices in the Nineteenth Century* (Ann Arbor, MI: UMI Research Press, 1986), 134–35.

Yesterday I held the first rehearsal for *Don Juan* ... Everything sounded splendid and came out magnificently, even if it is frightfully difficult. The poor horns and trumpet ... blew with such effort that they were completely blue in the face ... In particular, the oboe solo in G with the fourfold divided basses, the divided celli and violas, all with mutes, and also the horns all with mutes sounded absolutely magical, just like the crazy place with the harp *bisbigliando* and the violas *sul ponticello*. Our first trumpet ... had never before been expected to play such moving notes around high B ... Our first clarinet has also never played passages above high F-sharp, just as our contrabasses have never dared [go] above high B, which nevertheless sounds just wonderfully characteristic. Yesterday's rehearsal was to me a success, in which I saw that I again had made progress in handling the orchestra ...[8]

While the success of *Don Juan* may be attributed in part to Strauss's ever-improving skills as an orchestrator, the composer's concern with who played his music also mattered. The well-received premiere of Strauss's next tone poem, *Tod und Verklärung* (1889), at the 27th meeting of the Allgemeine Deutsche Musikverein (General German Music Society; ADMV) on June 21, 1890, was just that sort of carefully managed success. While Strauss's Weimar ensemble formed the nucleus of the ADMV orchestra, it was augmented to twice its normal size with handpicked players. Strauss's desire for such a large orchestra was undoubtedly motivated by the large Wagnerian orchestra he had heard the previous summer at Bayreuth.

In fact, the augmented ADMV ensemble was not unusual. Throughout Germany, "strengthened" (*verstärkte*) orchestras were becoming quite common, especially in smaller cities and not always for Wagnerian repertoire. The *Neue Zeitschrift für Musik* (*NZfM*) regularly included concert reports, many of which in the late 1880s indicated the numbers of players used. Such numbers had rarely appeared previously in the *NZfM*, which suggests that the size of orchestras was becoming a point of interest. Reports of Weimar orchestra performances, for instance, frequently mentioned the "strengthening" of the ensemble with students from the local music school. More significantly, many notices suggested that extra players were also being used for double-wind repertoire. In 1886, concerts in Wiesbaden and Elberfeld used "strengthened" orchestras of 60–70 for performances of Brahms's Third Symphony, Mendelssohn's Overture to *A Midsummer Night's Dream*, Beethoven's Symphony in F, and similar repertoire.

---

[8] Strauss, *Briefe an die Eltern*, 119.

In Germany's largest cities, supporting an orchestra of proper size was a matter of civic pride, as Otto Neitzel wrote after reviewing a concert of Cologne's orchestra that required the strings to be reinforced in the city's large Gürzenich Hall. In 1888, the city began to provide financial support for the orchestra, and the difference was apparent a year later. As Neitzel wrote in a subsequent review, there was a great difference between a musician hired for a single concert and a regular third wind player, especially as it affected the orchestra's beauty of tone and the precision of the ensemble. In 1886, Hamburg, Germany's second-largest city, also reorganized its orchestra along Wagnerian lines, which would make the orchestra "among the most important in Germany."

In the 1890s, the increasing availability of triple-wind orchestras with large string sections almost certainly contributed to Strauss's orchestral successes and growing reputation. Beginning with *Till Eulenspiegels lustige Streiche* (1895), his next group of tone poems – including *Also sprach Zarathustra* (1896), *Don Quixote* (1897), and *Ein Heldenleben* (1898) – carried Strauss to the pinnacle of symphonic music at the turn of the century. The critical response to each new tone poem was strongly favorable, and Strauss's masterful handling of the orchestra was widely praised, even as his demands on the individual players increased. The size of Strauss's orchestra also grew with these works, with a brass section that included eight horns, five trumpets, three trombones, and two tubas for *Ein Heldenleben*. Also, beginning with *Till Eulenspiegel*, at the front of his scores, Strauss indicated the precise disposition of the string section, with numbers that mirrored Bayreuth's large orchestra almost exactly.

Strauss's fame as an orchestral composer was such that the publishing house of C. F. Peters asked him to update Berlioz's *Grand traité d'instrumentation et d'orchestration modernes* (1843, published in English as *Treatise on Instrumentation*), a task Strauss completed late in 1904. He did not rewrite any of Berlioz's prose; rather, he added commentary to a few dozen spots, generally to acknowledge advances in instrument design and usage. For example, Strauss dismisses Berlioz's explanation of valveless horns with a single sentence: "Up to this point, Berlioz's text is obsolete and is only of historical value," before adding his own commentary on the modern valved horn.[9] Strauss also added numerous score examples, nearly all of which come from Wagner, because, as Strauss wrote in his Foreword, "Richard Wagner's scores ... embody the only important progress in the

---

[9] *Treatise on Instrumentation by Hector Berlioz*, enlarged and revised by Richard Strauss, trans. Theodore Front (New York: Edwin F. Kalmus, 1948), 257, 260.

art of instrumentation since Berlioz." He then described the score of
Lohengrin as "a basic textbook for the advanced student" before recommending Wagner's later operas for further study. Strauss also cautioned
that the beginning orchestrator would do better to start with simple string
quartets and small orchestral works before attempting to use a Wagnerian
ensemble.

Strauss's work on Berlioz's *Treatise* was reflected in his next three scores
with orchestras: *Symphonia domestica* (1903), *Salome* (1905), and *Elektra*
(1908). Studying the history and advances of instruments apparently
encouraged Strauss to expand his ensembles to a quadruple-wind band.
Symphonia domestica calls for 106 players, including the oboe d'amore, an
instrument last favored by J. S. Bach, and a group of four saxophones – his
only use of that instrument. Both operas expand their orchestras even
more, adding the newly invented Heckelphone – a bass oboe first proposed by Wagner, but not built until 1904 – and even more brass
instruments. *Elektra*, Strauss's largest and most complex score, expands
nearly every instrumental family to its maximum, such as eight clarinets
(including two basset-horns), extended brass (including six trumpets, four
trombones, and four Wagner tubas), and a battery with six to eight
timpani. Most remarkable is Strauss's transformation of the traditional
five-part string ensemble into three groups of violins, three of violas, two of
celli, and the double basses, which reflects similar *divisi* passages in
Wagner's *Ring*.

Although Strauss never again called for an orchestra as large as that of
Elektra, he retained a taste for triple winds and striking timbres to his final
years. It is rare to find a Strauss orchestral score from after 1900 without a
few of the Wagnerian third winds or extra brass. Through the 1890s, only
Mahler, among Strauss's peers, had regularly called for similarly large
ensembles, but the end of the twentieth century's first decade saw a
noticeable increase in symphonic works scored for triple-wind (or larger)
orchestras. Among the best known of these new works are: Debussy, *La
mer* (1905), Glazunov, Symphony No. 8 (1907), Elgar, Symphony No. 1
(1908), Rachmaninoff, Symphony No. 2 (1908), Ravel, *Rapsodie espagnole*
(1908), Skryabin, *Prometheus: Poem of Fire* (1910), Stravinsky, *L'oiseau de
feu* (1910), Nielsen, Symphony No. 3 (1911), and Vaughan Williams,
A London Symphony (1913). Remarkably, nearly all of these composers had
written symphonic works previously, but only for double-wind orchestras,
which suggests that a significant change had taken place in the constitution
of the modern orchestra shortly after 1900. While it may be too much to
credit Strauss alone for this shift, as with so many other advances in music

around 1900, he was certainly in the mix and conspicuous at the forefront. Even those who might not have accepted Strauss's programmatic audacities or his harmonic language that tested the bounds of tonality admitted to being dazzled by his command of orchestration. Debussy, in a review of Strauss's music conducted by its composer, summed up that equivocation best: "One may not care for certain experiments . . ., but almost instantly one is struck by the prodigious variety of orchestral effects."[10] How many other listeners since have said the same thing?

[10] Claude Debussy, "Musique," *Gil Blas* (March 30, 1903), 2.

CHAPTER 22

Program Music

Jonathan Kregor

When Richard Strauss set to work in 1886 on what would become *Macbeth*, a *Tondichtung* ("Tone Poem") for large orchestra "after Shakespeare" that premiered four years later to lukewarm reception in Weimar, he could hardly have known that by the end of the century he would become the undisputed representative of a genre of music that had been breeding controversy for more than a generation: program music. Indeed, with subsequent single-movement orchestral works like the metaphysical *Tod und Verklärung* (1889), the roguish *Till Eulenspiegels lustige Streiche* (1895), the fantastic variations of *Don Quixote* (1898), and the quasi-autobiographical *Ein Heldenleben* (1898), Strauss significantly expanded the means by which a piece of music could engage with poetry, literature, the theater, and even its own composer. At the same time, while Strauss's program music was and remains undeniably original – rivaled in quality only perhaps by that of his friend Mahler – it was very much a product of its time. This chapter explores the environment of programmatic music-making that centered on the so-called "progressive" composers Liszt, Wagner, and their acolytes, contextualizes the ongoing debates between absolute music and program music that they occasioned, and considers various programmatic compositions outside of that narrow tradition in order to better situate Strauss's own aesthetic orientations and musical products.

Program Music and the New German Imagination

Sporadic examples of program music had appeared in Europe since the sixteenth century, with Johann Kuhnau, Vivaldi, Haydn, Carl Dittersdorf, and Beethoven writing occasional instrumental music that referenced extra-musical material. And while Schumann, Berlioz, and Mendelssohn, respectively, excelled in the character piece, programmatic symphony, and concert overture, Strauss and his contemporaries primarily looked to the program music of Liszt.

In an effort to revitalize a German tradition that he believed had peaked with Beethoven but in recent decades had languished, in the 1850s Liszt embarked on an ambitious plan of orchestral composition that resulted in 12 symphonic poems, two programmatic symphonies, and several programmatic compositions for solo piano. Alongside these compositions, which bore evocative titles and often carried descriptive or explanatory prefaces, Liszt promoted his ideas in print. Soon after he retired from the concert stage as a virtuoso pianist and moved to Weimar, he published a series of essays on the music of Chopin (1851/52), Beethoven (1854), Weber (1854), Mendelssohn (1854), Schumann (1855), and especially Wagner (1849; 1851) and Berlioz (1855) that collectively gave program music a distinct definition, whereby form was the result of musical content, exceptional figures should function as subjects for modern musico-poetic elaboration, and a program offered "the precise definition of the psychological moment which prompts the composer to create his work and of the thought to which he gives outward form."[1]

Liszt's compositional and journalistic efforts were supplemented by his students and adherents, including Franz Brendel, Hans von Bronsart, Hans von Bülow, Peter Cornelius, Richard Pohl, Joachim Raff, Alexander Ritter, Carl Tausig, and (briefly) Joseph Joachim. Even Wagner offered a vigorous, if vague, defense of the program music coming out of Weimar. Collectively, Brendel grouped these diverse musicians together as "New Germans," the ostensible true heirs to Germany's hallowed music tradition.

These composers had, for the most part, produced their seminal instrumental works without the aid of programs or other extra-musical stimuli (e.g., poems, artworks, sculptures), an approach famously encapsulated by the critic Eduard Hanslick as *tönend bewegte Formen* ("forms moved by tones"). For Hanslick, instrumental music existed completely unto itself, devoid of externals. By extension, then, music could not be subjective, for it could "undertake to imitate objective phenomena only, and never the specific feeling they arouse."[2] Hanslick laid out this theory of so-called

---

[1] Liszt and Marie von Sayn-Wittgenstein, "Berlioz and His 'Harold' Symphony," in *Source Readings in Music History*, ed. Oliver Strunk, rev. ed. Leo Treitler (New York: W. W. Norton & Company, 1998), 1168.

[2] Eduard Hanslick, "Vom Musikalisch-Schönen (1854)," in *Musical Aesthetics: A Historical Reader. Volume II: The Nineteenth Century*, ed. Edward A. Lippman (Stuyvesant, NY: Pendragon Press, 1988), 279.

autonomous or "absolute" music in his book, *Vom Musikalisch-Schönen* (*On the Musically Beautiful*), which went through ten editions – often with unacknowledged revisions – between 1854 and 1902. Thus, for almost the whole of the second half of the nineteenth century, the German-speaking musical world was sharply divided among those who promoted absolute music and those who promoted program music.

Strauss's move to Meiningen in 1885 resulted in a considerable change to his aesthetic orientation. The city boasted one of the finest orchestras in Europe, thanks almost exclusively to the transformative efforts of its conductor Bülow. Bülow had been Liszt's star piano student in the early 1850s, Wagner's most trusted conductor in the 1860s, an early devotee of Brahms's orchestral music in the 1870s, and an advocate for new music in general. Despite Bülow's catholic tastes, Strauss clearly sought to ingratiate himself with his mentor by making an unambiguous confession of New German faith, as evidenced in a famous letter from August 24, 1888:

> If you want to create a work of art that is unified in its mood and consistent in its structure, and if it is to give the listener a clear and definite impression, then what the author wants to say must have been just as clear and definite in his own mind. This is only possible through the inspiration by a poetical idea, whether or not it be introduced as a programme. I consider it a legitimate artistic method to create a correspondingly new form for every new subject ... [P]urely formalistic, Hanslickian music-making will no longer be possible, and we cannot have any more random patterns, that mean nothing either to the composer or the listener.[3]

Strauss actively cultivated connections with other New German associates, including Eduard Lassen, who had succeeded Liszt as Kapellmeister in Weimar, and whom Strauss succeeded in 1889; Cosima Wagner, who had taken over operations of her late husband's music festival in Bayreuth and occasionally engaged the young Strauss as assistant conductor; and especially Alexander Ritter. Wagner had met Ritter in 1849, and it was Alexander's mother, Julie, who backed up her words of encouragement to the struggling opera reformer with generous financial assistance. In 1854, Alexander married Wagner's niece and moved from Dresden to Weimar, where he worked in Liszt's orchestra and became an integral member of the composer's inner circle. Peregrinations around Germany landed Ritter in Bülow's Meiningen (1882), where he first met Strauss, who in turn

---

[3] Hans von Bülow and Richard Strauss, *Correspondence*, ed. Willi Schuh and Franz Trenner, trans. Anthony Gishford (New York: Boosey & Hawkes, 1955), 82–83.

invited Ritter to join his Munich orchestra in 1886. In short, Strauss's access to the New German imagination was unparalleled.

Program Music between Liszt and Strauss

By the time that Liszt began his musical reforms in Weimar, a solid canon of program music was in place. Beethoven's Sixth Symphony (1808) had remained and would remain popular among concertgoers and composers looking to emulate its characteristic pastoral sounds, spawning imitators that included Berlioz (*Symphonie fantastique* [1830] and *Harold en Italie* [1834]), Raff (Symphony No. 3, "Im Walde" ["In the Woods"; 1869]), Strauss himself (*Eine Alpensinfonie* [1915]), and Ferde Grofé (*Grand Canyon Suite* [1931]). Beethoven's *Leonore* No. 3 (1806), *Coriolan* (1807), and *Egmont* (1809/10) overtures paved the way for Mendelssohn's overtures to *A Midsummer Night's Dream* (1826) and "Hebrides" (ca. 1832), among others, which the composer created explicitly for performance on the concert stage instead of as a curtain-raiser for an opera or play. It was Beethoven's model that also inspired similar compositions by Berlioz (ten overtures between 1826 and 1863), Schumann (on Byron's *Manfred* [1848]), Wagner (on Goethe's *Faust* [1839; 1844; 1855]), and even Liszt, whose early symphonic poems had begun life as overtures.

While New German propagandists abundantly wrote about program music, few beyond Liszt actually composed it. Indeed, only a handful of compositions stand out for their proximity to Liszt and for the ways in which they attempt to develop his programmatic theories and compositional approaches. The first is Bronsart's *Frühlings-Fantasie*. Premiered in Leipzig in January 1858 and dedicated to Bronsart's piano teacher Liszt, the spacious Fantasy surveys topics long associated with the season of spring over the course of five titled movements. The bleakness of winter (movement I) yields to the coming of spring (II), which in turns gives rise to dreams of love (III). The storms (IV) that interrupt this idyll are swept away by a barrage of melodies in the finale (V), including an instrumental setting of a late sixteenth-century hymn, and a collection of musical items from the preceding movements. Beyond the obvious and obligatory nods to Beethoven, the Fantasy largely owes its musical style, formal structure, and orchestral sound to Liszt, especially *Les préludes*, which had been written only a few years earlier and published in 1856.

The second such composition came from one of Strauss's early mentors, Bülow. In April 1854, Bülow began to conceive of an overture in B minor, which within a few months had become attached to Carl Ritter's five-act tragedy, *Ein Leben im Tode*. As the work approached its first performance in early 1859, Liszt recommended that Bülow title it as a "Symphonic Prologue" either after Friedrich Schiller's *Die Räuber* (1781) or Lord Byron's *Cain* (1821). Bülow chose Byron for the premiere, but devised a completely new title for its publication seven years later: *Nirwana*. By explicitly connecting his work to the tenets of Schopenhauer's *The World as Will and Representation* – particularly as the Buddhist idea is unpacked in Book 2, chapter 41 – Bülow turned away from the poets that had proved so decisive in Liszt's development as a programmatic composer in favor of a figure who was to have decisive influence on Wagner, Nietzsche, Mahler, and Strauss himself.

Likewise, few of Liszt's students followed their teacher's model by calling their works "symphonic poems." Draeseke completed two in the early 1860s (*Frithjof* and *Julius Caesar*), but these remain unpublished. After a hiatus of composing for the genre that lasted two decades, *Das Leben ein Traum* after Calderón and *Penthesilea* after Kleist appeared in print with the generic title of "Prelude." With the unpublished *Erotische Legende* of 1890, Ritter returned to the symphonic poem after the *succès de scandale* of Strauss's early tone poems. However, his *Olafs Hochzeitsreigen* was published in 1892 as a "symphonic waltz," and *Sursum Corda!* appeared one year later as a "Sturm und Drang" Fantasy. And Raff – by far the most prolific of Liszt's former students, with eight programmatic symphonies on his compositional vita – seems never to have entertained the idea of composing a symphonic poem.

While these titular decisions may have been encouraged by the ongoing controversy associated with Liszt's music, by the 1880s program music had moved beyond its singular association with the symphonic poem. Overtures might sport qualifiers like "heroic," "pathetic," "dramatic," or "festive." Audiences could be treated to *Märchen* ("fairy tales"), *musika-lische Charakterbilder* ("musical character pieces"), *Tonbilder* or *Tonge-mälde* ("tone pictures"), *tableaux musicaux*, *peintures musicales* ("musical paintings"), and ballads. Orchestral suites and symphonies routinely featured titles or mottoes that tipped interpretation toward the programmatic, such as Karl Goldmark's popular "Ländliche Hochzeit" ("Rustic Wedding") Symphony from 1875, whose five movements respectively feature a march and variations, a wedding song, a serenade, an idyll, and a folk dance, or Anton Rubinstein's "Ocean" Symphony, which went through a number of versions between 1851 and 1880. At the same time, the extent to which composers actually structured their works according to professed programmatic content – per Liszt's original instructions – appears to have been minimal. Indeed, most exhibit mildly modified sonata types that rarely tax the analyst's faculties.

On the other hand, generic hybrids were also possible, and usually were structurally more inventive. Bülow, following the model of Wagner's *Faust* Overture, had published *Nirwana* as a *Symphonisches Stimmungsbild* ("Symphonic Mood Picture") in 1866, but re-published it 15 years later as a "Fantasy in Overture Form," a designation that privileged the work's structural design over its poetic elements. Tchaikovsky released *The Tempest* as a Symphonic Fantasia in 1873, *Hamlet* as an Overture-Fantasia in 1888, and settled on the subtitle of Fantasy-Overture for the third and final version of *Romeo and Juliet* in 1880. All three works challenge foundational components of sonata form; *Hamlet*, for instance, dispenses with the expected development section, possibly in an effort to capture something of the titular hero's personality. Raff's Overture to *Ein' feste Burg ist unser Gott* (dedicated to Bülow) began life in 1855 as a "Heroic Dramatic Work in the Form of an Overture," but ended up as an Overture "to a Drama from the Thirty Years' War" when it was published a decade later. Despite the change in title, the appearance of Martin Luther's famous hymn toward the end of the development superimposes a decisive narrative onto an otherwise straightforward sonata structure.

From a practical perspective, evocative or unique titles could help compositions stand out in a crowded market. But for composers grappling with the ontological implications of the New German School, hitting on the proper title for a programmatic work was artistically indispensable. Consider the long gestation of Mahler's First Symphony. Premiered at Budapest in 1889 as a symphonic poem in two parts without program, its failure caused Mahler to withdraw the work. Almost four years later, it resurfaced in Hamburg as a "Tone Poem in Symphonic Form" called *Titan*, where the composer distributed a long prose program that provided titles for all five movements. A performance at Weimar in June 1894 saw the fifth movement retitled as "From Hell to Paradise" instead of the earlier "From Hell," a change perhaps made to pay homage to the first movement of Liszt's "Dante" Symphony. Yet, when Mahler presented the definitive version of the Symphony almost two years later in Berlin, neither program nor titles appeared; moreover, what had been a five-movement work was now reduced to four.

Like Mahler, Strauss entered a robust yet fractured environment of program music. His orchestral works from the 1870s and early 1880s fall neatly into the characteristic overture tradition that went back to Beethoven and Mendelssohn. But with the "symphonic fantasy" *Aus*

Italien of 1886 and especially the three tone poems begun two years later, he attempted to reach an equilibrium between formal ingenuity and programmatic gloss. Strauss seems to have understood the merger of music and literature as the best means of achieving this lofty New German goal, hence his sustained work on *Don Juan* (Nikolaus Lenau), *Tod und Verklärung* (Ritter), and *Macbeth* (Shakespeare). On the other hand, the next, arguably most orchestrally inventive phase of Strauss's career saw the birth of *Till Eulenspiegel, Don Quixote, Ein Heldenleben*, and *Symphonia domestica*, in which his individual programmatic voice as regards genre, form, and even content is so omnipresent as to render moot any deference to tradition. Instead, these programmatic works openly parody, deform, and antagonize all that has come before them – all signs of Strauss clearly embracing an ultra-modern artistic attitude.

Geographies of Performance

The many layers of revisions that Mahler gave to his First Symphony illustrates the significant role that geography could play in determining the reception of programmatic compositions. No city was reliably hospitable to program music. Arguably the most recalcitrant was Vienna, where Hanslick wielded enormous influence as music critic and, after 1870, as professor of music history and aesthetics. Hanslick had railed against Liszt's program music after hearing *Les préludes* in 1857, so it came as little surprise that he took the conductor Hans Richter to task for programming the *Faust* and "Dante" Symphonies and various symphonic poems during the 1880s and 1890s. Hanslick's wholesale dismissal of these genres associated with the New German School was abetted by Max Kalbeck, who routinely pilloried such music in the Viennese press after becoming music critic at *Die Presse* in 1886. However, Vienna was large and diverse enough to accommodate other perspectives, such as those of the composer and critic Hugo Wolf, who upheld Liszt and Wagner as antidotes to the ossification of musical tradition that was ostensibly unfolding before him with the likes of Brahms and Hanslick. Yet despite the presence of well-positioned musicians sympathetic to the programmatic cause in cities like London, Berlin, and Leipzig, program music would continue to fight an uphill battle well into the early twentieth century.

However, other metropolitan cities looking to distinguish themselves as progressive or up-and-coming – or attempting to distance themselves from Germanic influences – seemed more receptive to programmatic repertoire.

Following its loss to Prussia in the Franco-Prussian War of 1870–71, France actively encouraged the production of music that could legitimately be deemed "French," or at least "non-German." The founding of the *Société Nationale de Musique* in 1871 provided a sympathetic environment for Saint-Saëns, Franck, and others to experiment compositionally, while concerts organized by Jules Pasdeloup, Édouard Colonne, and Charles Lamoureux in Paris regularly offered French programmatic works like Saint-Saëns's *Le rouet d'Omphale* (*Omphal's Spinning Wheel*) and *Danse macabre*, Berlioz's *Symphonie fantastique*, or Gustave Charpentier's *Impressions d'Italie*. At the same time, these groups did not categorically deny works of foreign composers: Lamoureux gave the French premiere of Strauss's *Don Juan* on November 29, 1891; his competitor Colonne presented *Tod und Verklärung* and *Till Eulenspiegel* six years later.

For cities lacking a critical mass of native composers, program music was simply imported. In Madrid, Saint-Saëns's symphonic poems – all variously modeled on Liszt's works – jumpstarted local interest in program music in the mid-1870s, such that the composer was welcomed as a celebrity when he visited the city in 1880. Native Spanish composers were slower to compose program music than, say, those in New York City (e.g., George Whitefield Chadwick, Edward MacDowell, or John Knowles Paine), allowing a flurry of foreign works and conductors to populate the programs and podiums of the Sociedad de Conciertos de Madrid and the Unión Artístico Musical for the remainder of the century. Strauss participated in this one-sided cultural exchange when, in 1898, he conducted the Madrid premieres of *Don Juan*, *Tod und Verklärung*, and *Till Eulenspiegel*. To be sure, many outbursts of program music composition were the result of nationalist impulses in the second half of the nineteenth century and early twentieth century, such as the Mighty Five in Russia (Balakirev, Borodin, Cui, Mussorgsky, and Rimsky-Korsakov) or the Young Poles (especially Mieczysław Karłowicz and Karol Szymanowski); but their works would only serve to underscore program music's fundamentally cosmopolitan nature.

One important group not attached to a specific locale that could help shelter program music from such vitriolic criticism was the Allgemeine Deutsche Musikverein (General German Music Society), or ADMV. Founded by Liszt and several associates in 1861, the ADMV organized annual festivals around Germany in order to promote music that aligned with New German precepts. Between 1859 and 1886 (the year of Liszt's death), the ADMV – which counted Bülow and Bronsart among its board members – not only presented program music of German composers, but

208

JONATHAN KREGOR

also introduced that of composers living abroad, including Balakirev, Borodin, Ödön Mihalovich, Rimsky-Korsakov, Saint-Saëns, and Robert Volkmann. Strauss was featured for the first time in 1887 with his Piano Quartet in C Minor, Op. 13, marking the beginning of a visibility within the group that culminated in him being named president in 1901.

Conclusion

Even though program music had made important inroads into concert halls and had been the subject of much critical discourse for at least a generation by the time that Strauss came on the scene, there remained considerable doubt that music could legitimately draw on, reference, or connect with the extra-musical world, at least insofar as the practice had manifested in Liszt's orchestral music. Strauss's early years as conductor in Meiningen, Weimar, and Munich reveal him to have been open toward, but also healthily suspicious of everything attached to the German music-making tradition – program music included. Indeed, as conductor he presented Liszt's symphonic poems, selections from Smetana's *Má vlast*, Bülow's *Nirwana*, and program music by Ritter and Draeseke alongside Beethoven, Raff, Rheinberger, and Brahms, thus laying the foundations for trendsetting compositions that gave him his first major successes.

Even though Strauss reinvigorated a practice that had been without an acknowledged leader since Liszt, few contemporaries followed his lead with similar resolve. In fact, the repertory of new program music suffered from significant attrition in the early years of the new century, and in the wake of the World War I increasingly met with outright hostility from critics and composers alike. (Notably, Strauss's last overtly programmatic orchestral work, *Eine Alpensinfonie*, dates from 1915.) In bounding over nineteenth-century music, the "neo-classical" music of trendsetting composers like Stravinsky and Schoenberg rejected the tenets that had allowed program music to grow in prestige and quantity.

At the same time, while program music increasingly suffered on stage, it began something of a second life on screen. Indeed, it is in film that the most innovative program-musical experiments occurred during the middle half of the twentieth century, with film scores by Gottfried Huppertz, Max Steiner, Erich Korngold, and others taking cues from Liszt, Wagner, and of course Strauss. In many ways, program music's migration to this new medium should not have come as a surprise, for arguably one of its most resilient and progressive features was the openness it had always shown to breaking down artistic boundaries.

CHAPTER 23

Post-Wagnerian Opera

Morten Kristiansen

When Richard Wagner died in 1883, he had become a towering icon whose nearly irresistible influence extended far beyond Germany and permeated all areas of cultural life, as seen in the many extensions of the *Gesamtkunstwerk* in literature, painting, sculpture, and arts and crafts. In France, for example, the literary *Revue wagnérienne* was dedicated to Wagner, who became the most frequently performed composer at the Paris Opéra after 1890, and attending the Bayreuth Festival was highly fashionable during the 1890s. A few French operas were even closely modeled on those of Wagner: Vincent d'Indy's *Fervaal* (1897) on *Parsifal*, and Ernest Chausson's *Le roi Arthus* (1895) on *Tristan und Isolde*. But while French composers and critics divided into highly polarized Wagner supporters and detractors, opposition to a national icon was not a legitimate option for German opera composers, whose only available paths were imitation or escape. The impact of Wagner's paralyzing presence on German opera seems clear; of the works composed between *Parsifal* (1882) and Richard Strauss's *Salome* (1905), only one opera has survived without needing revival: Engelbert Humperdinck's *Hänsel und Gretel* (1893). "Post-Wagnerian" thus refers in this chapter to the mostly forgotten Germanic operas written ca. 1882–1905 rather than opera after Wagner in general.

Wagner's Legacy

Especially significant to an understanding of post-Wagnerian opera is the disparity between music and the arts as a whole during the latter half of the nineteenth century. While the other arts had generally moved from Romanticism toward Realism, starting around mid-century, music shielded itself from non-metaphysical, contemporary values by clinging to the idealism that had granted music transcendental powers since the beginning of the century. Crucial to maintaining this insulation was the belated but intense reception of Schopenhauer's *The World as Will and Representation* (1818, rev. 1844) that ranked music as the highest among the arts and bestowed upon it the ability to access the most elevated metaphysical realms. The otherwise pessimistic philosophy resonated strongly with Wagner, who read Schopenhauer's work four times in 1854–55 and incorporated its ideas into many of his dramas, most notably *Tristan*. In his essay "Religion and Art" (1880) and in *Parsifal*, Wagner created an influential fusion of Schopenhauer's philosophy and Christian dogma that reinforced and even expanded the idealistic mission of music. A few critics and composers, Strauss among them, advocated for the music world to relinquish this idealism and instead embrace the more "modern" ideas of Friedrich Nietzsche and other facets of contemporary culture (such as satire, sexual freedom, and nervousness), but they were decidedly in the minority. Although Nietzsche's popularity peaked during the second half of the 1890s, it is hardly surprising that his polemic against pessimism, Christianity, and metaphysics was less attractive to composers than the idealism of Wagner/Schopenhauer, which remained dominant and undisturbed by fin-de-siècle culture and philosophy.[1]

The core idealistic concept around which German operas of the time revolved was Wagner's redemption through love. So many librettos recycled this theme that "redemption opera" became a category in its own right, and one commentator even noted the "redemption fog" that had enveloped the music drama. In many cases, redemption requires the sacrifice of the character who redeems another, the models being Senta and Elisabeth in *Der fliegende Holländer* and *Tannhäuser*, but in cases involving Christian compassion, most prominently *Parsifal*, the redeeming agent need not die. Frequently, the path to redemption requires a heroic act of renunciation and includes a conflict between physical and ideal love (or related binaries such as worldly/ideal and sacred/profane), again with *Parsifal* as the central template. *Tristan* supplied a gloomy and much imitated redemption variant through its famous *Liebestod* ("love-death") that allows Isolde to unite with Tristan in death and redeems both from an unbearable life of unfulfilled love. While Schopenhauer identified saints and ascetics who renounce all worldly matters as those most likely to be redeemed from life's misery, the fact that he believed in redemption

---

[1] Although Wagner's metaphysics overwhelmingly served to perpetuate Romanticism in opera, it was nonetheless integral to the development of Viennese modernism; see Kevin C. Karnes, *A Kingdom Not of This World: Wagner, the Arts, and Utopian Visions in Fin-de-Siècle Vienna* (Oxford: Oxford University Press, 2013).

neither through the agency of another nor through uniting in death suggests that Wagner's adaptations of Schopenhauer were more influential than the philosopher's own writings.

Since contemporary commentators focused more on the texts than on the music, the emphasis on the former in this chapter is intentional. Discussions of Wagner's works treated them more as literary works than musical ones and engaged in endless interpretive debates, and the most significant question asked of each new German opera was which *Weltanschauung* it expressed – not what its musical virtues might be. Nonetheless, the following Wagnerian stylistic features were as frequently emulated as the textual ones, if not always as successfully:

1. Large, polyphonic, colorful orchestra;
2. Tristanesque chromaticism;
3. Web of leitmotifs;
4. Avoidance of choruses, ensembles, and text repetition;
5. Archaic language, often using Wagnerian alliteration (*Stabreim*); and
6. Composer doubles as librettist.

Although the last feature was essential to the most committed Wagnerians, only a few composers consistently wrote their own libretti (Felix Weingartner, Alexander Ritter, Siegfried Wagner, Wilhelm Kienzl). Several wrote the first one or two, then left the text to someone else (Eugen d'Albert, Richard Strauss), and others never attempted to author one (Max von Schillings, Hans Pfitzner, Humperdinck, Ludwig Thuille).

The genres available to German composers entering the operatic arena during the 1890s were essentially limited to music drama, comic or lighthearted opera, and fairy tale. While the last two genres did not appear to invite imitation of Wagner, his *Die Meistersinger von Nürnberg* (1868) continued to exert a strong influence on comic opera, and fairy tales were not sufficiently different from myth to offer a likely escape route. In a statistical study of the 520 German operas that premiered in 71 cities between 1883 and 1913, Edgar Istel noted that the years 1893–99 exhibited the most intense activity, with 141 premieres, and that the works divided into 271 serious (but not always tragic) operas (52%), 176 comic or lighthearted ones (34%), and 73 drawn from fairy tale (14%).[2] Every new work was measured against Wagner, and examining representative examples from each genre gives us a sense of the extent to which German composers imitated or, more rarely, were able to bypass Wagner.

[2] Edgar Istel, "Eine deutsche Opernstatistik 1883–1913," *Die Musik* 55, no. 18 (1915): 260–66.

Music Drama

Not surprisingly, the Wagnerian music drama attracted the most earnest and worshipful followers whom contemporary critics often referred to as "epigones" in its uncharitable meaning of less distinguished imitators. The most extreme cases of emulation were those of the quickly forgotten August Bungert and the celebrated conductor and composer Weingartner, who both vainly desired a custom-built opera house à la Wagner's Bayreuth Festspielhaus for their multi-evening cycles. Bungert's *Homerische Welt* (*World of Homer*) consisted of *Die Odyssee* (four operas) and *Die Ilias* (five operas), of which he only completed the four works of *Die Odyssee* that premiered in Dresden between 1896 and 1903. Emulating Hans von Wolzogen's *Ring* motive guide and *Bayreuther Blätter* newsletter, Bungert supplied labeled leitmotifs in the vocal scores and later founded a journal to support his ideas. Weingartner, who had already contributed the redemption operas *Sakuntala* (1884) and *Genesius* (1892), published a proposal for a never to be finished trilogy of Biblical mystery plays titled *Die Erlösung* (*Redemption*) in 1895.[3] He prefaced the summaries of the dramas (of which one lasts two evenings, thus matching Wagner's tetralogy) with elaborate ideological justification, combining Wagner, Schopenhauer, and Buddhism, and with a plea for financial support that explicitly paralleled Wagner's in the private printing of the *Ring* texts of 1853.

Two music dramas by Strauss's slightly younger contemporaries and devoted Wagnerians, Schillings and Pfitzner, *Ingwelde* (1894) and *Der arme Heinrich* (1895), respectively, exemplify less extreme and more typical Wagner imitation. Both are operatic debuts that mostly adhere to the stylistic characteristics listed here, except that neither composer wrote his own text. Set to a libretto by Ferdinand Graf Sporck and based on a Nordic saga, *Ingwelde* is a gloomy tale of redemption and *Liebestod*. Viking chieftain Klaufe wins Ingwelde, daughter of the enemy tribe's leader, as a prize of war, but she will only return his love if the perpetually warring tribes reconcile. He agrees but is killed when Ingwelde betrays him. She then marries her foster brother Gest, and, during a quiet moment, they compare the joy of love to death. Her guilt causes paranoid visions of Klaufe and, when his brother Bran arrives to avenge her betrayal, Gest blocks the axe blow and dies. Filled with the ecstasy often associated with

---

[3] Felix Weingartner, *Die Lehre von der Wiedergeburt and das musikalische Drama, nebst dem Entwurf eines Mysteriums "Die Erlösung"* (Kiel: Lipsius & Tischer, 1895).

death in post-Wagnerian opera, they board the "death ship" serving as Gest's burial and go down with it whilst singing of "glorious death" (Act III, Scene 4). A brief excerpt from the preceding scene exemplifies Wagnerian alliteration:

Nornen, Nornen	Norns, Norns
helfet uns nun!	help us now!
Weiset uns hilfreich den Weg!	Be helpful and show us the way!
Daß Liebe lösche	So that love may erase
des Schicksals Schuld	the guilt of fate
und Tod der Liebe Leid!	and death the agony of love!

This grandiose act of redemption grants Ingwelde *Liebestod* (Bran even uses the term) through her reunion with Gest, allows both to atone for their guilt, and brings about the peaceful union of the tribes.

Representing a less common variant, Pfitzner's non-tragic *Der arme Heinrich*, adapted from the medieval legend by librettist James Grun, arrives at redemption with everyone still alive. God has punished the knight Heinrich's attachment to worldly glory with agonizing disease from which only the willing sacrifice of a pure maiden (as in *Der fliegende Holländer* and *Tannhäuser*) can redeem him. The young Agnes watches over the sick knight and uses the example of Christ's sacrifice to convince him and her parents to allow the gruesome ritual, but just as she is about to suffer her "most blissful *Liebestod*," Heinrich renounces his own salvation, is healed by a lightning bolt, and prevents the doctor from cutting out Agnes's heart. His newfound Parsifalian compassion has redeemed him, saved Agnes, and transformed him into a devout Christian with a future as a wandering preacher.

Strauss knew these works and supported both composers. He and Schillings became close friends during Strauss's second term in Munich (1894–98), and Strauss conducted the local *Ingwelde* premiere in 1897. Although he never performed *Der arme Heinrich*, the Berlin Opera produced it during Strauss's tenure there in 1900, and he wrote to Pfitzner in 1912 that he wanted to conduct it. He later attended the world premiere of Pfitzner's best-known opera *Palestrina* in Munich in 1917. Set to his own libretto, Strauss's first opera *Guntram* (1894) fell mostly in line with those of his colleagues. A tale of a Christian minnesinger who leaves his beloved in order to atone for killing her evil husband, the work employs the themes that populated the music dramas of the time: compassion, renunciation, physical vs. ideal love, and redemption. And yet, his atypical treatment of some of these themes caused several contemporary critics to view him as

oddly poised between Schopenhauerian orthodoxy and Nietzschean individualism, and the libretto even caused a serious rift between Strauss and
his arch-Wagnerian mentor, Alexander Ritter.

Fairy Tales

Viewed by some contemporaries as merely a lighter and thus derivative
version of Wagner's myths and by others as a promising new path leading
away from Wagner, the fairy tale opera (*Märchenoper*) is often mentioned
as a significant post-Wagnerian development (although operatic fairy tales
were nothing new). No one considered it a distinct genre until the
resounding success of Humperdinck's *Hänsel und Gretel*, however, and
even then it remained unclear whether inclusion in the genre required
merely a supernatural component or more features of fairy tales proper,
such as simple characters and moral, an unspecified time and place, and a
happy ending.

Many pointed to Bayreuth insider Ritter as the originator of this
particular resurgence of fairy tale elements. Wagner had reportedly advised
Ritter to avoid heroic myths and favor the smaller genres of saga, legend,
and fairy tale, and in the one-act operas *Der faule Hans* (1885) and *Wem
die Krone?* (1890), works Strauss conducted several times between
1890 and 1892, Ritter endeavored to present Wagnerian style and ideology in a lighter, more palatable packaging. In *Der faule Hans*, the lethargic
protagonist spends his time daydreaming about old times when his mother
read fairy tales to him, but when the kingdom and its queen come under
attack by foreigners, he single-handedly vanquishes the enemy and wins
both queen and crown after transforming into "young Siegfried." Along
the way Ritter sneaks in the Wagnerian themes of transient vs. eternal, the
truth content of dreams, the transfigurative power of love, and German
nationalism (the final line directly echoes *Die Meistersinger*: "Blessed be
German ways, preserved with faithful purity").

Also closely associated with the Bayreuth circle, Humperdinck produced an instantly successful and lastingly popular mixture of a scaled-
down Wagnerian style (chromaticism, orchestral polyphony, leitmotifs)
and folklike simplicity in *Hänsel und Gretel*. Like Ritter, he and librettist
Adelheid Wette smuggled in a few suitably-diluted Wagnerian features by
adding a religious component (a dream during which angels protect the
children and the final lines: "When distress is at its worst, the Lord God
lends a hand") and the redemption of the children turned into cookies by
the witch. Strauss greatly admired the work and conducted the Weimar

world premiere along with numerous later performances. Nationalists hailed the work as the salvation of German opera, newly threatened by the influx of Italian *verismo* spearheaded by the German premieres of Mascagni's *Cavalleria rusticana* and Leoncavallo's *Pagliacci* in 1891–92: "Then Humperdinck's wonderful German fairy tale *Hänsel und Gretel* appeared. Overnight the radiant Italian sun shining on adultery, murder, and killing went down behind the German whispering pines, behind the magic of German forest bliss: the latest Italian opera invasion had been repelled."[4] This was wishful thinking, however; the popularity of Italian opera continued unabated.

Wagner's only son, Siegfried, with whom Strauss had a strained relationship and whose works he never conducted, studied composition with Humperdinck in 1889–90 and later followed in his teacher's footsteps with his first and most successful opera *Der Bärenhäuter* (1899). His libretto combines two different fairy tales with a historical episode and treats religion and redemption within a lighter mood and more popular style. The soldier Hans Kraft returns from the Thirty Years' War and finds employment guarding souls in Hell, but when he loses them to a disguised St. Peter in a game, the Devil condemns him to wander the earth filthy in a bearskin, and only a woman who remains faithful to him for three years during his absence can redeem him. In a small village, he meets Luise, whose compassion accomplishes this, and everyone praises God in the final pages. These three composers were trying to have their cake and eat it too by appropriating Wagner while forging a path away from him, but many observers also viewed their lighter works as part of a movement away from Wagnerian gravitas toward a more down-to-earth *Volksoper* (people's opera). In a letter of 1896 to Humperdinck, Siegfried Wagner expressed just that: "The return to simplicity! The small scale! It remains forever to your credit to have embarked on this path and have shown it to us. Only this way can we prove ourselves true Wagnerians. A harmless, thoughtful, German *Lustspiel* [comedy] is really what remains to us."[5]

Comic Opera and Hybrids

In spite of the desire for lighter subject matter, however, German composers had produced few comic operas since mid-century. Until the success of *Hänsel und Gretel* appeared to trigger a wave of comic works

---

[4] Walter Niemann, *Die Musik seit Richard Wagner* (Berlin: Schuster & Loeffler, 1913), 101.
[5] Peter P. Pachl, *Siegfried Wagner: Genie im Schatten* (Munich: Nymphenburger, 1988), 142.

during the second half of the 1890s, the most notable examples were *Der Barbier von Bagdad* (1858) by Peter Cornelius and *Die Meistersinger* (1868). Apart from hybrid works that somewhat inorganically mixed seriousness and pathos with comic plots, such as Emil Nikolaus von Reznicek's *Donna Diana* (1894) and Hugo Wolf's *Der Corregidor* (1896), the new crop of comic operas polarized into *Meistersinger* spinoffs and bourgeois idylls that shunned Wagnerian features at all cost.

In both musical style and ideology, *Der Pfeifertag* (1899) by Schillings, of which Strauss attended a performance in 1899 and later conducted productions in Berlin, most closely followed Wagner's model. Piper king Duke von Rappoltstein has banished his son Ruhmland for joining the pipers and his son's friend Velten for wooing his daughter Herzland so as not to lose another child to the musicians. As the minstrels gather for their annual festival, Ruhmland and Velten plot to trick the Duke into letting them marry Herzland and Velten's sister Alheit, respectively, and to convince him to end the piper tax and recognize them as equals. The libretto comments on the 1890s musical landscape; one character mentions the great piper Kühnrad (obviously Wagner) who overshadowed everyone and made room for the current preference for foreign music when he died, and another laments that "in the piper forest foreign parasites and burs proliferate as seldom before; the native tree can barely save itself" (Act II, scenes 6–7). The Duke eventually recognizes their nobility, admits the divine nature of music and especially love songs, abolishes the tax, and sanctions both marriages. The *Meistersinger* parallels are abundantly clear: a historical musicians' guild, the elevated status of the musician, the metaphysical power of music and its connection with love, and German nationalism – all embedded within a comic love story.

With its diatonicism, small and transparent orchestra, and dance tunes, d'Albert's *Die Abreise* (1898), which Strauss conducted in 1899 and 1903, represents the opposite pole, a harmless escape track onto which some felt that Wagner's presence had forced comic opera. A one-act work with a trifling plot set in a small palace during the late eighteenth century, it generated more commentary than any other comic opera of the period. Gilfen is about to leave on a trip, but when his friend Trott is overly eager to help him depart, he senses that Trott is interested in his wife Luise and sends him on all sorts of errands before canceling the trip. The marriage had cooled, but the threat of Luise being left alone with Trott brings them back together – with no hint of emotional depth or pathos.

The internationally successful and still occasionally revived operas *Tiefland* (1903) by d'Albert and *Der Evangelimann* (1895) by Kienzl show that the genres discussed above were not the only available options. A failed nationalist effort to foster a competitive German *verismo*, the competition of Saxe-Coburg in 1893 had received about 200 one-act entries, but *Tiefland* remained the sole German hit in the genre. Blending Italian and German stylistic features, it adapted a Spanish drama about the pure mountain shepherd Pedro who descends to the sinful lowlands to marry Marta, then kills her evil lover and oppressor and returns to the mountains with her. Based on the memoirs of a police inspector and subtitled "a musical play," the sentimental *Der Evangelimann* also contained elements of *verismo*, but its mixture of scattered Wagnerian gestures and veristic passion with periodic phrasing, simple accompaniment, closed numbers, children's choruses, and hymns created an eclectic, colorful, and very popular concoction viewed by some as a viable style for a new *Volksoper* beyond Wagner. Mathias loves Martha, but his brother Johannes also loves her and frames Mathias for setting a fire. After 20 years in jail and 10 as a wandering lay preacher, Mathias returns and forgives (redeems?) his dying, guilt-ridden brother out of Christian compassion. The moral is sung numerous times: "Blessed are those who are persecuted for righteousness' sake" (Matthew 5:10). Strauss conducted it four times during 1899–1901.

No particular genre or hybrid created a widely adopted alternative to Wagner, however. Although it was not clear at the time, *Salome* (1905) was the light at the end of the tunnel for this uncertain period in the history of German opera. While Strauss's second and moderately successful opera *Feuersnot* (1901) had mixed comedy and fairy tale in an awkward attempt to settle a score with his hometown, *Salome* was an act of liberation that allowed Strauss to incorporate, reject, and transcend Wagner all at once. Although its declamatory singing, leitmotifs, orchestral size and polyphony, and chromaticism owe a huge and obvious debt to Wagner, *Salome* is a decidedly un-Wagnerian tragedy that steers clear of heroic epic and myth, brushes ideology aside, and instead turns the camera inward in order to explore "modern" pathological urges and psychological states much like those being investigated by Strauss's pioneering contemporary, Sigmund Freud. Wagner's influence remained strong in the new century, but Germanic opera composers born during the 1870s and associated, like Strauss, with early Modernism, such as Zemlinsky and Schreker, no longer felt Wagner as a paralyzing presence and were able to absorb his influence with less anxiety.

CHAPTER 24

The Lied

Jürgen May
(Translation by Matthew Werley)

Any attempt to contextualize Richard Strauss's corpus of Lieder in a social, political, or music-historical sense is complicated from the outset by the fact that the subject itself has yet to be fully explored in a scholarly manner. The existing monographs on the topic have focused almost exclusively on musical details and biographical aspects and, to date, only a handful of analytical case studies have sought to understand his compositions within their relevant contexts.[1] What therefore follows is an attempt to illuminate individual aspects of the *Klavierlieder* (songs for voice and piano) while leaving aside the *Orchestergesänge* (those with orchestral accompaniment), terms Strauss used consistently throughout his oeuvre to differentiate two different genres.

Aesthetic and Generic Contexts

Given that Strauss's compositional output began in 1870, the year when he composed his first two pieces – one of which was, significantly, a Lied – it immediately becomes apparent just how closely the composer was connected (at least temporally) to the nineteenth-century Lied tradition. Strauss's conservative-minded father recommended to his son the early exponents of the Romantic Lied, such as Schubert, Mendelssohn, and Robert Schumann. Some of the prominent representatives of the genre, such as Peter Cornelius or Liszt, were still alive when Strauss took his first steps in this area, and he even knew Brahms personally and considered him an important model for his early works. If it was out of such diversity of styles that the youthful apprentice composed his Lieder before Op. 10,

---

[1] Prominent among publications aimed at a more general readership is Alan Jefferson's *The Lieder of Richard Strauss* (London: Littlehampton, 1971). Exemplary of a more focused, contextual study is Christian Schaper's "Von der Tiefe der Oberfläche: Zu zwei Liedern von Richard Strauss im ersten Jahrgang der Zeitschrift Jugend," in *Lied und Lyrik um 1900*, ed. Dieter Martin and Thomas Seedorf (Würzburg: Ergon, 2010), 141–63.

what unites them is that the models from which Strauss initially appropriated stylistic and aesthetic characteristics are easily recognizable.

The aesthetics of the Lied had always been closely associated with its social contexts, which include specific performance environments. It is no coincidence that its golden era occurred during the social upheavals of the early decades of the nineteenth century, namely, the delayed effects of the French Revolution and the increasing presence of industrialization in social life. This shift witnessed the passing of musical patronage from the nobility, whose importance was rapidly waning, to the economically strengthened and educated bourgeoisie. From its beginning, then, the Lied was not linked to the public stage but to the salons of this newly consolidated social class. More specifically, the domestic performance context of the song corresponded with its aesthetic ideals: simplicity, immediacy of expression, and, most significantly, its intimate character. As late as 1912, Siegmund von Hausegger (who was aesthetically quite close to Strauss) summarized this early paradigm thus: "The Lied is based on the *lyrical poem*. Born of the moment, its content is condensed into a singular emotional point. ... The language of the lyrical poem is that of intimate communication from person to person, a confession that needs no witnesses."[2] The public format we know today began to take root comparatively late, around 1870, when the Viennese tenor Gustav Walter initiated the first *Liederabende* (song evenings). In 1876, Walter established a series of *Liederabende* in Vienna's Bösendorfer Hall (which had a capacity of nearly 600 seats), followed by tours all over Europe. Considering the increasing importance of the urban space for late nineteenth-century social life, this new concert format may be understood "as a means to bridge the divide between high and not-so-high, or at least professional and domestic, art," or even as reflecting "the breaking down of social barriers between aristocracy and bourgeoisie."[3] This new performance context, the shift from the private salon to the public stage, bore consequences for the genre itself

Amidst these shifting social contexts, Strauss grew up in an environment in which domestic music making – comprised of repertoire from both Lieder and chamber music – constituted a fixed component of family and

[2] Siegmund von Hausegger, "Über den Orchestergesang (1912)," in *Betrachtungen zur Kunst: Gesammelte Aufsätze von Siegmund von Hausegger*, ed. Arthur Seidl (Leipzig: C. F. W. Siegel's Musikalienhandlung, 1921), 207.
[3] Laura Tunbridge, *The Song Cycle* (Cambridge: Cambridge University Press, 2010), 46.

social life. His early biographer, Max Steinitzer, reported that "also some of his [Strauss's] little songs" were sung at gatherings of family and friends.[4] As far as is known, the young Strauss never considered publishing any of the Lieder he wrote before Op. 10. There must be a reason why he sought to go public as a composer of Lieder in 1887, and with works he composed two years prior at that. That the eight Op. 10 Lieder hardly signaled a "qualitative jump from the previous songs," as Elisabeth Schmierer has claimed, may be correct, at least concerning formal design and harmony, but the gesture and design of their musical details already appear characteristically "Straussian." Most of these songs convey extroverted gestures that consciously flaunt their public appeal, such as the pathetically rising sixth at the conclusion of "Zueignung" (No. 1), the humorous endings of "Nichts" (No. 2) and "Die Verschwiegenen" (No. 6), or the raising of tension by stretching melodic phrases and interrupting them with precisely inserted rests in "Die Nacht" (No. 3). Thus, the Op. 10 Lieder strove to find new ways to reach beyond the confines of the private sphere into the larger public stage. This approach may be rooted in the fact that there was a palpable aesthetic shift in the air that favored bold expressivity above Romantic inwardness, one that seemed to foreshadow the approaching century. This shift is also clearly evident in a wider context; construction of the Eiffel Tower began in Paris in 1887, van Gogh commenced his rapid succession of famous late-style paintings in 1888, and, in the same year, Nietzsche completed his book *Der Antichrist*, for example.

Contemporaries

It is no coincidence that Hugo Wolf also upset the well-established paradigm of intimacy in his Mörike-Lieder around the same time as Strauss did. To challenge the listening expectations of his contemporaries, Wolf contrasted the expressive vocal line (rich in unconventional intervals, chromaticism, and rhythmic idiosyncrasies) with a piano accompaniment of high musical independence. His approach to the Lied was so unusual that the writer Detlev von Liliencron, in his poem "To Hugo Wolf," described it as "petrifyingly new."

While there is no evidence to suggest that Strauss and Wolf influenced each other in a mutually productive manner, that is not the case with Gustav Mahler and Max Reger, both of whom held varying stances toward Strauss. It is well known that Strauss's and Mahler's approaches to the

---

[4] Max Steinitzer, *Richard Strauss* (Berlin: Schuster & Loeffler, 1911), 17.

symphony were diametrically opposed – Mahler once recalled Schopenhauer's image of two miners digging from opposite sides of the same mountain to describe Strauss's orchestral works in relation to his own – but their approaches to the Lied were also vastly different. Directly evoking the Schubertian tradition, Mahler followed a path where simplicity and frugality (e.g. manifesting in "song-like" qualities) remained guiding principles of the genre. From the outset, his (piano) Lieder formed the genetic core of his symphonic works, where the material subsequently underwent creative expansion and development through orchestral reworking. To a large extent, this synchronization between genres permeates Mahler's entire oeuvre, where two originally disparate mediums, Lied and symphony, appear as different poles of a larger artistic whole.

With regard to songwriting, there is probably no other composer who has been compared to Strauss more frequently than Reger, both in scholarly writings and in contemporary reviews.[5] This is not least due to the fact that Reger had arranged some of Strauss's songs for piano and also set a number of poems previously taken up by the older composer. That it was apparently a conscious decision on Reger's part is supported by the fact the he chose texts to "re-compose" based on his previous arrangements of Strauss's songs for piano. Had Reger wanted to instigate a public competition with Strauss, he might well have pulled it off. Hardly any contemporary critic of Reger's settings seemed capable of avoiding comparisons with those by Strauss. In 1899, for instance, a reviewer for the *Heidelberger Tageblatt* praised Reger's version of "Traum durch die Dämmerung," Op. 35/3 (Strauss, Op. 29/1) as "an extremely interesting composition that can boldly place itself next to the Strauss setting of this text, perhaps even surpassing it as far as the interpretation of the text is concerned; but where it loses, by contrast, is in its facile comprehensibility." In 1902, Karl Straube took Reger's 1899 setting of "Glückes genug," Op. 37/3 (Strauss, Op. 37/1) as an opportunity to substantially distinguish Reger's style from that of Strauss. For Straube, Reger resisted "the temptations of his texts to paint a dramatic picture" and refrained "from all external descriptions of the situation ... in order to reproduce only what

5 Eberhard Otto, "Richard Strauss und Max Reger in Liedern nach gleichen Texten," *Musik in Bayern* 31 (1985): 71–93; Wolfram Steinbeck, "Hommage als Wettstreit: Regers Liedern nach Strauss," *Reger-Studien*, no. 6 (2000): 213–34; Jürgen Schaarwächter, "Enfants terribles der deutschen Musik: Bunte Blätter zu Strauss und Reger," *Richard Strauss-Blätter*, no. 49 (2003): 8–46; Alexander Becker, "'Ich habe kolossal viel von Richard Strauss gelernt': Max Regers Verhältnis zu Strauss," in *Richard Strauss-Jahrbuch 2011*, ed. Günter Brosche and Jürgen May (Tutzing: Hans Schneider, 2011), 23–37.

had been experienced inwardly and emotionally." This separated "him, for example, from Richard Strauss in the strongest sense of the word. ... While Richard Strauss represents – Reger feels."[6]

Interestingly, such early reviews already evoke the cliché, still present today, of Strauss as a composer of the external, of the superficial, as one who lacks a true depth of feeling. In as much as it is undeniable that Strauss's Lied settings were composed much more with the audience in mind, it should be critically questioned whether Strauss's highly effective musical surfaces conceal any deeper layers below. Whatever the case may be, it remains to be seen whether Reger's "Lieder after Strauss" (as described by Wolfram Steinbeck) constituted a conscious attempt to place himself in the context of his competitor's work, as a kind of public act of self-affirmation, one that simultaneously sought to underline a point of demarcation between the two.

Society and Politics

As already mentioned, Strauss began to compose Lieder during a period of technological, political, and social upheaval. But the subsequent decades were also marked by massive political and social fault lines. Not only international political conflicts, which eventually resulted in the outbreak of the World War I, but also social trends, such as worker and feminist movements, profoundly influenced the times. Artistically speaking, this period of upheaval at the turn of the century found its expression, *inter alia*, in Naturalism. The Naturalists, in brief, were concerned with depicting reality (and hence also political, social, and technical change) rather than artistically idealizing the aesthetic object. Drawing from the field of literature, Strauss set works by its representative poets, namely Otto Julius Bierbaum, Richard Dehmel, Karl Henckell, and John Henry Mackay.

It is difficult to assess to what extent Strauss perceived temporal shifts except for those that directly affected his own sphere of life, such as technological developments or the effects of war. Ostensibly untouched, Strauss cultivated a bourgeois lifestyle that rarely questioned societal and familial structures. In this respect, it must be asked what correlation Strauss's Lied compositions even had with his own idea of bourgeois life on the one hand and with ongoing social change on the other. The simple fact that Strauss was married to a singer must be recalled, as it repeatedly manifests itself like a knot in the methodological slippage between

---

[6] Both quotations from Schaarwächter, "Enfants terribles der deutschen Musik," 38 and 40.

biographical details and his Lied production. To be sure, his marriage to Pauline de Ahna in 1894 triggered in him a veritable creative surge. While his interest in composing Lieder had been in decline and even dried up completely for a period of two years, the wedding marked the beginning of a new period of productivity that reached its apex in 1900, which saw 14 compositions (Op. 46, Nos. 1, 4, 5; Opp. 47 and 48; and Op. 49/6). A striking number of song cycles and individual works from this period (Opp. 27, 32, 37, 41, 43) are directly or indirectly related to Strauss's new role as husband and father.

Yet one would be mistaken to suspect that Strauss limited himself to the selection of subjects that affirmed love or bourgeois family. In at least a few cases, he turned to poems that do not fit these criteria, most notably Richard Dehmel's "Der Arbeitsmann" (Op. 39/3) and Karl Henckell's "Lied des Steinklopfers" (Op. 49/4), both examples of "social poetry" from the field of Naturalism. The latter in particular is workers' poetry in a narrower sense. Henckell's obituary in the social democratic newspaper *Volksrecht* (August 3, 1929) described him as a "workers' poet" who had come "from the middle classes as a fighter and communicator to the proletariat." Accordingly, "Das Lied des Steinklopfers" ("The Song of the Stonebreaker") describes the misery of the proletariat in all its blemishes. Strauss takes this into account with a clear, declamatory setting in the vocal line and a dissonance-rich, almost machine-like piano accompaniment.

The situation is somewhat different with "Der Arbeitsmann" ("The Worker"). It is doubtful that Strauss was aware of the fundamentally Marxist bias of Dehmel's poem. Although he seems to grasp its core message by weighting the dramatic climax precisely to the relevant passage in the text, musically, he leaves the text's prescribed social milieu behind when he dramatizes the entire song with altering colors and moods. Here lies the bone of Dehmel's critique, who complained that "Der Arbeitsmann" was "not understood in its simplicity; it's too convulsive." Although Strauss and Dehmel were personally acquainted, the poet had previously expressed the fear that the composer was essentially "a disguised literary Naturalist with Romantic tendencies. The latter brings me no praise, Romanticism lies behind us."[7]

Strauss was hardly alone among professional composers who failed to grasp the nuances of socialist poetry. The task of setting such texts – which

---

[7] Richard Dehmel to Paula Dehmel, February 26, 1902; and Richard Dehmel to Willy Seibert, December 11, 1900, in Richard Dehmel, *Ausgewählte Briefe aus den Jahren 1833 bis 1902* (Berlin: Fischer, 1923), 405 and 359.

had nothing to do with traditional songs with piano accompaniment – fell to the next generation of composers such as Paul Dessau, Hanns Eisler, and Kurt Weill, all of whom were born at the turn of the twentieth century. The bourgeois concert hall was hardly suitable as a platform for songs that served up political agitation. Thus, the preoccupation with socio-critical poetry remained marginal to the genre in general.

Commentary on Contemporary Events?

Whether the hiatus in Strauss's Lied output between 1906 and 1918 had anything to do with the composer's strong gravitation to opera, his wife's withdrawal from public concerts, or yet another reason altogether, remains a matter of pure speculation. It is nevertheless noteworthy that Strauss resumed his Lied production during a time when profoundly ominous political storms were brewing. The end of the futile Great War in November 1918 had shaken the foundations of German society, leaving it with a deeply demoralized population. Like most of his contemporaries, Strauss shared in the enthusiasm for an inevitable victory during the war's early days, but changed his mind quickly thereafter. Finally in June 1918, he demanded that the politicians end "this dreadful war."[8] Perhaps more telling, however, is that later that summer he was photographed in a contemplative pose atop the Loser in Austria, a peak remarkably close to the summer residence of the Habsburg monarchy – the "war's epicenter" in 1914.[9] Here Strauss presented himself as a detached observer, a figure who viewed world events from an elevated position, perhaps even as one who commented on them in his music.

That Strauss reverted exclusively to historical poetry (aside from *Krämerspiegel*) during these years gives the false impression of an inward retreat to the aesthetic. To the contrary, seen against the landscape of the war, a few of these settings actually demonstrate a high degree of contemporary historical relevance. The three Goethe settings from Op. 67/4–6, for example, invite listeners to hear them as a searing commentary on the current political situation.

---

[8] Richard Strauss to Fürstner, June 27, 1918, Richard Strauss-Archiv.
[9] Matthew Werley, "The Architecture of Trauma: Richard Strauss, Salzburg and the Great War," in *Music, Modern Culture and the Critical Ear*, ed. Nicholas Attfield and Ben Winters (London: Routledge, 2018), 115.

Furthermore, at least one additional song from his 1918 Lied output relates explicitly to the everyday events of the war (though the composer's shortening of the title veils its true meaning): "Lied der Frauen," Op. 68/6. When one considers the complete title of Clemens Brentano's poem, "Lied der Frauen, wenn die Männer im Kriege sind" ("The Song of Women, When Men are at War"), which Strauss set at the beginning of May, the resonances become entirely clear. Viewing these Lieder against the period of upheaval at the war's end and the revolution that followed sheds light on facets of Strauss's personality that do not easily square with existing clichés. The picture that emerges from the details is of a composer who attentively observed historical events and even reflected upon them within his works.

Ausklang

After 1918, Strauss's productivity in the Lied waned. In the years that followed he set several texts by Johann Wolfgang von Goethe, a poet whose works had hardly featured in his early song corpus (with a few exceptions, of course) but whose poems had recently captured his attention in the Drei Lieder, Op. 67/4–6. The Goethe texts he set between 1919 and 1942, such as "Sinnspruch" (1919), "Durch allen Schall und Klang" (1925), and "Zugemessne Rhythmen" (1935), have more to do with poetic dictums than lyrical poetry in the strictest sense. Indeed, these settings display an aphoristic compactness and concentration of form marked by clear declamation and a wholesale avoidance of musical padding of any kind. More "musical reflection" than pure songs, they pose the question as to whether the generic label of "Lied" even applies.[10]

That Strauss occupied himself musically with Goethe during his later years, and that he did so in ways that placed the texts within musical "quotation marks" (thus suggesting such poems did not serve primarily as a stimulus for his own creativity) complements the way in which the aging Strauss engaged intellectually with Goethe's work and personality more generally – that is, as a figure with whom he not only identified, but one from whom he took his bearings when looking back across "3,000 years of cultural development." As a universal artistic personality,

---

[10] Dieter Borchmeyer, "'Die Genies sind eben eine große Familie . . .': Goethe in Kompositionen von Richard Strauss," in: *Goethezeitportal* (1999), 9–12. www.goethezeitportal.de/db/wiss/goethe/borchmeyer_strauss.pdf.

Goethe appeared as the ideal embodiment of a figure who had perfectly united life and work, the artist and the universe. Ultimately, the construction of a musical and cultural history, which Strauss laid out for himself during the final decades of his life, formed the larger autobiographical and ideological contexts not only of his late song compositions but perhaps of his late style as a whole.

In History

CHAPTER 25

Modernism

Peter Franklin

A History Emerges

Across Europe, "modernism" meant many things during Strauss's lifetime. Much depended upon class and politics, upon how old, and when and where you were. The outwardly settled 1890s, the chaotic and battle-scarred meltdown of the 1914–18 war, or the turbulent social and political cross-currents of the following inter-war period – all had their particular modernisms and "secessionist" movements. Whether in art, design, and architecture, in music and literature, or in fashion and lifestyle, these advertised their challenging embrace of the new. They opposed what seemed outmoded and irrelevant to a changing world of urban consumerism, technical progress, and political turmoil, variously threatening and exciting.

Of course, the nineteenth-century institutions of culture – theaters, concert halls, and opera houses – were "modern" in the sense that they depended upon an expanding audience of paying consumers. Yet as the influence of the old aristocracy over taste and manners had, by the century's end, waned in response to the political and cultural pressure of an economically powerful, entrepreneurial middle class (the bourgeoisie or *Bürger*), so in the twentieth century that same middle class came to seem hidebound by its own investment in the values of a fading world of imperial, colonial, and economic power over "others" (women, the working class, the "masses" and "undeveloped" native peoples). Those others were deliberately, if conflictedly, referenced in the works of a new generation of modernists, from Stravinsky's *Rite of Spring* (1913) to the African-mask-inspired stylization of a painter like Picasso. Modernism of one kind could undoubtedly be found in attractive new consumer products and entertainments; but for political and intellectual radicals it entailed the renewal of a Romantic idealism that *rejected* consumerism and sought, whether satirically or seriously, something beyond the pleasurable or the conventionally communicative, even beyond "art" as formerly construed. When Marcel Duchamp exhibited a urinal in 1917 (titled *Fountain*), it seemed deliberately to mock the art-establishment and its self-appointed connoisseurs.

The "context" of modernism in Strauss's case is complex. It was continually evolving, its character and protagonists different in different cultural centers: in Vienna, Berlin, or Munich; in Paris, London or New York. Critical writing about current exhibitions, the latest theatrical premiere, or launch of a new literary star was widely discussed. Far from representing a fixed background to the drama of Strauss's career, modernism was about simultaneities, criticism, and contestation, be it between French "impressionism" and German "expressionism" or, more specifically, in music, between the lush, post-Wagnerian tonal language of Strauss's early symphonic poems and the experimental atonalism of the youthful Second Viennese School (Schoenberg, Berg, and Webern). These manners were subsequently overlaid in Germany by competing post–World War I styles: New Objectivity, Brecht's didactic political theater (with its pared-down, vernacular music), and the hard-edged, sometimes "neo-classical" manners of Hindemith, Pfitzner, and the later works of Schreker.

Partisan critical writing took the lead in newspapers and journals with widely differing circulation numbers and agendas. Interwar books by younger critics eagerly fabricated a "history" of musical modernism that often focused, in admiration or disbelief, on Schoenberg's pre–World War I "expressionism" and interwar development of the so-called serial technique of composition with 12 tones, in which dissonances were systematically privileged over the compromisingly pleasurable consonances and the perhaps self-indulgent richness of late-Romantic textures. Strauss's longevity meant that he survived widely fluctuating assessments of his contribution, sometimes reacting in print to the way he figured as a modernist around 1900, thereafter as an irrelevance, his apparent conservatism construed as both politically and stylistically compromised. For him (and many in the audiences for Strauss's music in the old, still energetically functioning concert halls and opera houses), the subsequently canonized modernists merely represented a fashionable, evanescent froth on the surface of a more traditionally-based and "naturally" evolving cultural practice.

For the post–World War II generation, however, their "histories" of modernism had become tendentious narratives of change, presented as "progress" – narratives fashioned by prominent critics into an emergent, "official" account of twentieth-century modernism and its representatives. After 1945, it solidified into doctrine. In 1969, Schoenberg biographer H. H. Stuckenschmidt's paperback guide to *Twentieth Century Music* (its back cover emphasized that "modern" was meant) could make up for imprecision about the geographical location of its subject with the apparent certainty of its pronouncements:

> After *Elektra*, Strauss felt he could no longer continue on the same course and he abandoned it. The calmer language of *Der Rosenkavalier* is the first instance in post-Wagnerian music of a regressive tendency ...[1]

Just two years later, Joan Peyser in the United States published *The New Music* (by 1980 it had been reissued as *Twentieth Century Music*) and offered a more specifically contextualized assessment:

> With *Der Rosenkavalier*, which Strauss composed in 1911, the latter repudiated the advances he had made in *Salome* (1905) and the wildly dissonant *Elektra* (1909). At the same time Schoenberg continued to move ahead.[2]

Both of these writers might have referenced the German Marxist philosopher Theodor Adorno, whose biting critique of Strauss marked what would have been the composer's 100th birthday in 1964. Published in English translation over two issues of the high-octane Princeton journal *Perspectives of New Music* (in 1965 and 1966), it proposed a distinction between the modern*ist* and the modern, between the shocker of the bourgeoisie and the supplier of its latest technological novelties. That, Adorno implied, is what Strauss's innovations really amounted to:

> His music soars, yet it is down to earth; a product of the dawn of aviation, it dupes the *bourgeoisie* into believing it to be both better than and different from what it is. [...] The life which celebrates itself in this music is death; to understand Strauss would be to listen for the murmur beneath the roar, which, inarticulate and questioning, becomes audible in the final measures of *Don Juan* and is its truth-content.[3]

Here the "evolutionary" narrative of music's advance revealed its critical claws. Strauss, in company with composers like Pfitzner, Elgar, or Rachmaninoff, was judged against an idealized modernism, represented by Schoenberg (supposedly "anticipated" by Liszt, Wagner, and Mahler),

[1] H. H. Stuckenschmidt, *Twentieth Century Music*, trans. Richard Deveson (London: Weidenfeld & Nicolson, 1969), 12–13.
[2] Joan Peyser, *Twentieth-Century Music: The Sense Behind the Sound* (New York: Schirmer, 1980), 28.
[3] Theodor Adorno, "Richard Strauss: Born June 11, 1864," trans. Samuel and Shierry Weber, in *Perspectives of New Music* 4, no. 1 (1965): 14 and no. 2 (1966): 129.

that was assumed to be ideologically anti-bourgeois, opposing Strauss's "old" dominant class, its art, and the politics that sustained it into the Nazi era. However, the intentionally shocking distance from the bourgeoisie of that idealized modernism was driven by the same horror of the wider public, of popular music and entertainment, that had underpinned the bourgeois construction of serious Classical Music completed by Romantic criticism. By 1835, both E. T. A. Hoffmann and Schumann had defined the classical as "great" because ineffable, its principles and techniques a guild-secret of the professionally musical, its proper criticism an act of worship.

The continuation of Stuckenschmidt's 1969 estimation of Strauss's move from *Elektra* to *Der Rosenkavalier* is revealing: "The turning-point in Strauss's creative career came to light with the first performance of *Der Rosenkavalier* at Dresden in 1911. The world-wide success of the work justified him." It was the *success* of *Der Rosenkavalier* after the supposedly bourgeois-discomforting shocks of *Salome* and *Elektra* that marked Strauss as an apostate of official modernism, with its critical insistence upon the "collapse" of tonality and root-and-branch stylistic renewal. Less violent critical models of development influenced Alfred Kalisch's article on Strauss in the 1928 edition of *Grove's Dictionary*, written when Strauss was very much alive and heading for the sad debacle of his spell in the service of National Socialism. Kalisch was happier to accept the composer's changing stylistic affiliations, anticipating a late flowering, like that of Verdi, while regretting that, in present-day criticism "more stress is always laid in a new work on the startling features, which may be more external than the essentials."[4] But what was essential and what "external" about the fact that Strauss, as President in 1933–35 of the aggressively *petit bourgeois* and populist Reichsmusikkammer (Reich Music Chamber), played his part in encouraging fantasies of the *völkisch* Germany projected in Wagner's *Die Meistersinger von Nürnberg*, its stratified classes celebrating unity under a populist leader obsessed with race and "foreign degeneracy"?

Strauss's Alternative

Whatever the determinants of Strauss's capitulation to Nazi pressure to serve the Party's cause in 1933, even given his already hostile rejection of the "mad" Schoenberg, it is worth questioning the depth of his support for

---

[4] *Grove's Dictionary of Music and Musicians*, 3rd ed., ed. H. C. Colles, Vol. 5 (London: Macmillan, 1928), 166–67.

the Nazis' *anti*-modernism that inspired the Munich exhibition of "Degenerate Art" (1937) and that of "Degenerate Music" in Düsseldorf (1938).[5] Strauss's own previous work from the *Salome* and *Elektra* period should really have fallen into the "degenerate" category of the kind of modernism considered as decadent and "Jewish" by anti-Semitic conservatives. Relevant here might have been Strauss's 1907 essay "Is there an Avant-Garde in Music?" ("Gibt es für Musik eine Fortschrittspartei?"), reacting to the context in which he then found himself.

The original German title merits comment. "Fortschrittspartei," which L. J. Lawrence translated as "Avant-Garde" for Willi Schuh's 1953 English edition of Strauss's *Recollections and Reflections* (published in German in 1949, the year of Strauss's death), might have been rendered as "Progressive Party" in 1907.[6] Strauss's "Party" (or Faction) emphasizes its political implications, later buried beneath the widely-used term "Avant-Garde." For a post–World War II audience that term signified a supposedly objective and critically validated body of "modern" (commonly suggesting "difficult" or "classical") European new music, from Schoenberg and Stravinsky to Varèse and early Boulez or Stockhausen.

Strauss's 1907 essay was designed to introduce a series of articles on contemporary music that he was editing for the weekly journal *Der Morgen*. Exasperation colored the parodic self-consciousness with which he alluded to his conservative critics:

> Now I am usually credited with a good nose for sensational matters and, as certain clever contemporaries have long since found out, I spend my day speculating like a kind of musical tailor how best to satisfy next year's fashions.

He nevertheless claims that the journal had enlisted him as "Head of the Progressive Party." Such a designation, which he may once have been as pleased to acknowledge as he was now self-consciously to mock it, led him to question what "progress" might actually mean. Strauss noted that Wagner's cultural-historical triumph had been supported by an influential group of critical disciples, but that they alone did not "make" Wagner

---

[5] Strauss described Schoenberg, whom he had initially supported, as "mad" in 1920; see *Richard Strauss-Franz Schalk: Ein Briefwechsel*, ed. Günter Brosche (Tutzing: Hans Schneider, 1983), 164.
[6] Richard Strauss, "Gibt es für die Musik eine Fortschrittspartei? (1907)," in *Betrachtungen und Erinnerungen*, ed. Willi Schuh (Zürich: Atlantis, 1949), 12–19; and "Is There an Avant-Garde in Music?," in *Recollections and Reflections*, ed. Willi Schuh, trans. L. J. Lawrence (London: Boosey & Hawkes, 1953), 12–17.

famous or "modern" through essays like those about to be published in *Der Morgen*:

> The main thing is the compelling contact between the creative genius and the mass of listeners willing to appreciate progress, who far exceed the limits of any possible "Fortschrittspartei."

Accepting that the public also had an undeniable taste for "easily digestible stuff, commonplaces and banalities," Strauss suggested that one of its "two souls" refused to accept "art which is neither immediately comprehensible nor eminently forceful."

Strauss's attitude toward the "multitude of naively receptive listeners" who, he believed, had recognized in Wagner's modernism what many conservative critics were stubbornly blind to, was far from stable. But in 1907, welcomed and supported by those same listeners, Strauss was prepared to see in them "the Voice of God" – an historical force to counter the dead weight of traditional authority:

> [A]lthough there is not, and need not be, such a thing as a "Progressive Party," in the proper meaning of the word, it is necessary to protect the natural sound judgement of the unprejudiced against the onslaught of those who are forever reactionary, and who labour unceasingly out of ignorance, inability, complacency or self-interest to stifle the public's innate flair for progress.

Opting for a non-partisan notion of advance in cultural life as part of a "great organic development" in which the significant works of a given period were seeds planted "in the souls of our descendants, to inspire [. . .] ever higher and more perfect creations," Strauss sought to de-factionalize the notion of "progress." Of course he too was being idealistic, imagining creators and consumers of art united in mutually beneficial development; he nevertheless astutely re-engaged the political with his final, modernist exhortation, directed at critics rather than the bourgeois public: "may the reactionary party perish!"

Strauss and Modernity

The instability and negotiability of critical definitions of modernism, both before and after the World War I, was exemplified in key studies published between 1912 and 1930. In Adolf Weissmann's 1922 *Die Musik in der Weltkrise* (literally "Music in the World Crisis," but tendentiously translated as *The Problems of Modern Music* by M. M. Bozman in 1925), the German critic still regarded Strauss, *with* Debussy and Schoenberg,

Figure 25.1   Heading of the first chapter of Arthur Seidl's *Moderner Geist in der deutschen Tonkunst* (1901), dedicated to Strauss.

as one of the three "peaks" of a period rich in many more or less notable composers in many countries. Around 1900, Strauss's friend Arthur Seidl had already dedicated to Strauss a series of four lectures on "The Modern Spirit in German Music" (published in 1912 as *Moderner Geist in der deutschen Tonkunst*). Individually titled "What is modern?," "The modern spirit in dramatic and instrumental music," "Thus sang Zarathustra," and "Modern musical lyricism," the lectures celebrated not only the modern, Nietzschean spirit of Strauss's works but also the *modernity* of their internal technology – the technology of harmonic and orchestral complexity and lyrical extension to which Wagner had so significantly contributed.[7]

Later that conceptual binary would turn to Strauss's disadvantage. Julius Korngold in Vienna famously questioned the "sensational" elements in *Salome*, but could still guardedly celebrate the composer of the even more extreme *Elektra* as "more than a mere technician." Sensationalism and technical facility nevertheless dogged Strauss's European reputation as signifiers less of modernism than of his *modernity*, in Adorno's sense, exemplified by his "nose for sensational matters" (as he had self-defensively joked). European critics disapproved of his willingness to commodify himself, as when he conducted in the Wanamaker Department Store in New York in 1904. Strauss impressed American audiences as a modern master precisely because of his down-to-earth character and good business sense. Where other European visitors affected superiority or decadence,

---

[7] References in this and in the start of the following paragraph to Adolf Weissmann, *Die Musik in der Weltkrise* (Stuttgart: Deutsche Verlags-Anstalt, 1922) and *The Problems of Modern Music*, trans. M. M. Bozman (London: J. M. Dent & Sons, 1925); Dr A[rthur] Seidl, *Moderner Geist in der deutschen Tonkunst* (Regensburg: Gustav Bosse, n.d. [1912]); and Julius Korngold, *Deutches Opernschaffen der Gegenwart* (Leipzig & Vienna: Leonhardt, 1921); Korngold's *Salome* and *Elektra* reviews are on pp. 136–55.

Strauss (as Olin Downes later put it) seemed an "unassuming man . . . desirous of plain communication with plain people."[8] Of course, the Americans' taste for Strauss was seized upon by his European detractors as *negating* his modernist credentials. Alma Mahler's account of the 1902 Vienna premiere of *Feuersnot* had emphasized that when the composer joined them in the restaurant, he had tormented Mahler with his materialism:

> [. . .] with calculations of the exact royalty on successes, good or middling, with a pencil in his hand the whole time that he now and then put behind his ear, half in jest, and behaved in fact just like a commercial traveller.[9]

This might of course have been a self-parodying performance at Mahler's expense (Strauss's – for the period – conventional anti-Semitism did not blind him to Mahler's genius, although he was not above describing him as "the Jew Mahler"). Strauss's public embrace of his own German *bürgerlich* side, ostensibly part of his "modernity," became *too* public, too blatant. Its affront to a certain notion of decency suggests that it might almost have earned him added credit as a modern*ist* of that period. However, older-generation bourgeois taste already relished self-critical, self-parodying humor as a "modern" trait – in operetta, in journalistic *feuilletons*, in *Der Rosenkavalier* – and one that implicitly short-circuited the opposition between the "dangerous" and the "conservative" phases of Strauss's subsequently mythologized development.

Rebellious Conservatism

Strauss's career spanned a tumultuous period of change and renewal across Germany and Austria. At its outset, *Jugendstil* and "art nouveau," inspired by related movements in Britain and France, had vied with the French impressionists and post-impressionists as sources for the galleries and design schools associated with modern art in Paris, Berlin, and Munich. Before 1914, sculptors and painters like Klinger and Böcklin were being viewed in uncluttered spaces designed by followers of Charles Rennie Mackintosh or Henry van de Velde. The latter was a close friend of Harry Kessler, the aristocratic diplomat and modern art connoisseur who would

---

[8] Included in a report on the 1927 Strauss Festival in Frankfurt, see *Olin Downes on Music*, ed. Irene Downes (New York: Simon and Schuster, 1957), 128.

[9] Alma Mahler, *Gustav Mahler: Memories and Letters*, ed. Donald Mitchell and Knud Martner, 4th ed. (London: Cardinal, 1990), 27–28; for Strauss's following reference to Mahler, see Christopher Morris, *Modernism and the Cult of Mountains* (Farnham: Ashgate, 2012), 52.

enter Strauss's world as co-collaborator with Hugo von Hofmannsthal on both *Der Rosenkavalier* and the 1914 ballet *Josephslegende*.

Around 1900, Strauss had been setting the poetry of Bierbaum and Richard Dehmel, published by Kessler in the modernist journal *Pan* – yet his villa in Garmisch was later heavily adorned with Bavarian bric-à-brac of the kind that Kessler would have mocked as *he* acquired paintings by Seurat and up-to-the-minute van de Velde furniture for his own apartments in Berlin and Weimar. In Weimar (1903–06) Kessler was briefly responsible for the Grand Ducal Museum of Arts and Crafts, where he followed a modernizing policy of resisting the German Emperor's tendency, in the words of an official he quotes, to "judge art only from the patriotic point of view ... only as a tool of the state." The official added, "since modern trends are not suited for this, he will fight them with all his might."[10]

Strauss, before 1933, was as little likely to sympathize with the Emperor as with Kessler's more doctrinaire modernism. Recent scholarship has read even his most "modern" early works, in Adornian fashion, as fundamentally bourgeois beneath their iconoclastic, Nietzschean surface. Yet Strauss's continuing ability to shock even his supposedly unshockable critics by *affirming* and celebrating his bourgeois worldview and outlook in *Symphonia domestica* and the proto-cinematic autobiographical opera *Intermezzo*, advertised his continuing sympathy with the musical philosophy embraced by Vienna's short-lived Vereinigung schaffender Tonkünstler (Alliance of Creative Musical Artists, 1904–05). Modeled by Schoenberg and others on the Secession of Klimt and his circle, it sought not to shock the liberal bourgeoisie so much as to educate it in the ways of the new, seeking to advance *with* that audience, in the spirit of Strauss's 1907 "Fortschrittspartei" essay. But, by 1918, Schoenberg's severe and elitist Society for Private Musical Performances signaled an irrevocable rift in that short-lived alliance. Strauss became a modernist has-been, but his legacy proved one that modern mass media could gratefully explore and exploit.

---

[10] *Journey to the Abyss: The Diaries of Count Harry Kessler 1880–1918*, ed. and trans. Laird M. Easton (New York: Vintage Books, 2011), 306.

CHAPTER 26

Traditionalism

Leon Botstein

Our modern music suffers from self-indulgence [*Masslosigkeit*]. And that will lead to the death of an art that has become intensely overwrought [*hypersthentisch*]. The way things look now, it appears that we are not at the beginning of a glorious epoch of new music, but have come to the end of music altogether.[1]

August Wilhelm Ambros, the eminent critic and music historian, came to this conclusion on the occasion of an 1873 all-Bruckner concert. Ambros was 57 years old; Richard Strauss was 9. Ambros's conjuring of the specter of death for a cherished art that had, in the early nineteenth century, been the exclusive province of landed aristocrats and an elite of educated urban amateurs had become commonplace by the mid-1870s. Ambros spoke for the entrenched custodians of culture. Music seemed doomed by an imminent collapse in aesthetic norms and standards, the first symptom of a broad decline in culture. At mid-century, the allegation of cultural decline sought to refute the belief in the inevitability of progress in civilization as a consequence of material advances; the spread of literacy, including musical literacy, and the democratization of culture spurred by demographic and economic expansion threatened normative aesthetic standards. Connoisseurship would be rendered irrelevant by mere fashion. Alluring but purely decorative novelty, audible in readily grasped sonorities and narrative structures in new music, matched the massive industrial scale and vulgarity of contemporary life. Past became pitted against present, ancients against moderns.

Ambros's lament (fueled no doubt by his distaste for Wagner) would be repeated in subsequent accusations of decline. New music came to be haunted by ethical and aesthetic criticism rooted in a glorified memory of eighteenth-century classicism and early romanticism. Lack of aesthetic

---

[1] August Wilhelm Ambros, *Musikaufsätze und -rezensionen 1872–1876*, Vol. 1, ed. Markéta Štědronská (Vienna: Hollitzer, 2017), 524. The literal translation of *Masslosigkeit* is lack of moderation. My terminology suggests the implied cause.

restraint justified moral condemnation framed in nostalgia. Long before Strauss emerged as a composer, the rapidly growing public for music was confronted with the idea that it had come too late to the party, forcing amateurs and listeners to defend apostles of the new from the charge of being subversive and inferior to the unimpeachable standards set by a history still fresh in the collective memory.

The spirit of Ambros's critique would reappear in the mid-1890s in the contempt and outrage expressed (among others) by the Viennese critic Robert Hirschfeld, one of Mahler's most articulate detractors, directed at Strauss's orchestral music. What set Strauss apart, however, was that, although he was castigated as self-indulgent, his brilliance as a composer was not in dispute (unlike Mahler). And he was embraced by the public, enthralling the expanded audience for music.

Strauss at the turn of the century was still seen as an *enfant terrible*. His radicalism stemmed from his insistence on music as an instrument for the candid, unsentimental, and realist exploration of the human experience. His narrative ambitions were said to have led him astray (even though the tone poems made sophisticated use of sonata and variation form) into the "unmusical" and "un-representable." Contemporaries found Strauss glib and shallow, content with superficial surface drama, punctuated periodically by a desire to shock.

Yet Strauss's success was decisive. The split his generation inherited – between the New German School and its opponents, including Brahms – had been overcome. Strauss's forward-looking synthesis, audible in *Salome* and *Elektra*, boasted a radical, anti-metaphysical literary and philosophical apparatus of expression marked by intensity, irony, humor, and disarming candor about human nature. There seemed nothing complacent or conservative about Strauss even though his music was accessible. Ambitious and conceited as he may have been, Strauss nonetheless harbored more of Ambros's pessimism about the era he was living in than his music suggested. Like Brahms, Strauss suspected he was at the very end of the great era of European arts and letters.

A tour of America in 1904 cemented the 40-year-old Strauss's reputation as the leading composer in the West. Although the 1903 *Symphonia domestica* outraged Charles Ives, Strauss's influence on younger contemporaries in particular was astonishing. There are echoes of Strauss in Bartók's *Kossuth* (1903), Elgar's *In the South* (1904), Glière's *Ilya Muromen* (1911), Schoenberg's *Gurrelieder* (1900–11), Szymanowski's *A Concert Overture* (1913), Korngold's *Sursum Corda* (1919), and even Othmar Schoeck's smaller-scale and idiosyncratic *Gaselen* (1923).

So dominant was Strauss that Rimsky-Korsakov could hardly stop berating him as "wretched" despite the ephemeral brilliance of his superficial, albeit virtuosic writing.[2] The older group of Strauss's now-forgotten contemporaries whose work reveals Strauss's stature and influence at the turn of the century includes Siegmund von Hausegger, especially his tone poem *Wieland der Schmied* (1904), and Max von Schillings, whose opera *Mona Lisa* (1915) was performed over 1,500 times between 1915 and 1934.

In the years following World War I, the tables turned. Strauss found himself marooned and abandoned by cultural politics. Both the extreme left and extreme right dismissed his lush, hyperrealist aesthetic (despite its fierce rejection of music as a metaphysical art) as a relic of a bygone era in which monarchists and a smug urban upper middle class held sway. The new right lamented that Strauss was too cosmopolitan; in their eyes, Max Reger had died too soon, before forging a lasting connection to the soul of the German Volk. The left ignored Strauss as benignly irrelevant, or hinted at some more sinister complicity. A contemporary poem by Walter Hasenclever had the refrain: "The murderers are in their seats at *Rosenkavalier.*"[3] In the 1920s, a new generation of futurists in musical composition successfully seized the limelight.

Strauss, who was proud of the daring innovation in his collaboration with Hofmannsthal on *Ariadne*, reacted to being sidelined after the war by articulating his own version of Ambros's pessimistic condemnation: he decried the decline in the quality of new music, accusing his contemporaries of Ambros's "self-indulgence." Some, like Pfitzner, were all too proud of an aesthetic conservatism and were content to write "superfluous" symphonies, concerti, and variations. Worst of all were the abandonment of tonality and the decade's enthusiasm for novel vulgarities in popular music, particularly jazz. Julius Brammer and Alfred Grünwald, in their lyrics to the prologue finale of Emmerich Kálmán's 1928 operetta *Die Herzogin von Chicago*, poked fun at the prevailing taste of the decade that so alarmed Strauss: "It's now the fashion, always only jazz! It's the rhythm we follow, always only jazz! It's what we breathe, it's the tempo of our new, wild and fast paced age." The future of music was in peril.

In 1922, Strauss conceded to Rudolph Reti that he may have given the new music of the era its first "push," but that the 1920s displayed an

---

[2] Tatiana Rimsky-Korsakov, *Rimsky-Korsakov: Letters to His Family and Friends*, ed. Malcolm J. Crocker and Margarita Maksotskaya, trans. Lilia Timofeeva (Milwaukee: Amadeus Press, 2016), 238.

[3] Walter Hasenclever, *Die Mörder sitzen in der Oper: Zum Andenken an Karl Liebknecht* (Berlin: Verlag die schöne Rarität, 1919), 2.

unwarranted arrogance by abandoning the richest source of the new: the past. Strauss, from the start of his career, saw himself as the beneficiary of a glorious past. Modernists in the 1920s believed they were on the threshold of a new great era without a history. To Strauss, this all seemed too self-serving. "Why do you compose like that?" Strauss once asked Paul Hindemith – whose talent he admired despite finding his music "ill-mannered and crazy." "You don't need to. You have talent!"[4]

Between 1918 and 1928, in works ranging from *Der Bürger als Edelmann, Die Frau ohne Schatten,* and *Intermezzo* to the *Gesänge des Orients* and *Die ägyptische Helena,* Strauss sought to acknowledge the new era (through forays into neo-classicism, condensed operatic structures, adventuresome harmonies, and exotic instrumentation) while asserting the power and relevance of tradition. The useful musical inheritance began with Mozart and included Liszt, Bruckner, and above all Wagner. In the context of the premiere of *Die ägyptische Helena,* Strauss predicted that "atonality will have fundamentally burned out, and possibly been entirely defeated. When the public and the press truly have had enough of decadent jazz ... the right time will have come for music and melody to rise up, like the phoenix out of the ashes of atonality, through *Helena.*"[5]

Strauss's expectations were not met. Writing to Joseph Gregor in 1935, he confided a sense of failure that would stay with him until his death. He observed that "past heights of a thousand-year-old cultural achievement – like *Tristan* and *Die Meistersinger* – can no longer be equaled ... perhaps only a modest new world can be won."[6] In Strauss's 1941 *Capriccio,* the Director muses, "I preserve the good that we possess, I hold high the art of our forbearers, with reverence I guard the old, and patiently I await the fertile new, expecting works of genius from our time! ... Where are they? ... Only pale aesthetes stare at me, ridiculing the old and creating nothing new." *Metamorphosen* (1945) was the composer's epitaph for music; the words "In Memoriam," placed under the *Eroica* funeral march quotation after more than twenty minutes of a magisterial display of inherited compositional practices, marked the end of a tradition and signaled Strauss's confirmation of Ambros's "end of music altogether."

---

[4] Norman Del Mar, *Richard Strauss: A Critical Commentary on His Life and Works,* Vol. 3 (New York: Cornell University Press, 1986), 225.
[5] Walter Werbeck, "Revolution und Musik," in *Musikkultur in der Weimarer Republik,* ed. Wolfgang Rathert and Giselher Schubert (Mainz: Schott, 2001), 74.
[6] *Richard Strauss und Joseph Gregor: Briefwechsel 1934–1949,* ed. Roland Tenschert (Salzburg: Otto Müller, 1955), 17–18.

The musical modernism that dominated the late 1920s violated three axioms of Strauss's artistic credo. First and foremost, he believed in the inexhaustible resilience and objective validity of tonality. As the younger Austrian composer Hans Gál put it, tonality was as natural as gravity. As a normative system, tonality provided the only proper grammar of music, and the harmonic extremes Strauss flirted with in the 1920s demonstrated its inexhaustible potential. One might imagine, as Gál put it, existence without gravity, but with the exception of Hindemith and Schoenberg, by abandoning tonality, as Strauss wrote in his diary in 1941, modern composers revealed "mediocrity" and "impotence." Thomas Mann, in a 1951 letter to Hans Heinz Stuckenschmidt, complimenting the author of the first postwar biography of Schoenberg, echoed Strauss's guiding premise: "I understand the New Music only very theoretically. Though I know something of it, I cannot really enjoy and love it."[7]

Second, music was at its core for Strauss a medium of human expression and expressiveness. Music was not, strictly speaking, a language, but its purpose and function were akin to language. Music generated a magical interaction between meaning, understood through language, and meaning beyond language that inspired unique sensibilities still tied to everyday experience. Music, with and without words, transfigured the quotidian, transcended the mundane and the rational without implying or justifying a metaphysical realm. There was, therefore, a necessary link between the making of music and the understanding of reality.

Third, music needed to captivate and sustain a public. Strauss harbored little respect for critics, but he was not aggressively hostile to the audience. The much-maligned 1922 ballet *Schlagobers* was written to entertain and to amuse. Its sparkling gestures and ironic allusions to musical tradition also had their polemical purpose: to mock the tendentious art and politics of the age that championed the birth of a new era of politics and culture. Strauss made his point by enchanting the audience with seductive, nostalgic evocations of childhood, outraging critics enamored of a modernist conceit. *Schlagobers* luxuriated in the mundane and trivial while elevating them by pitting them against the contemporary penchant for the self-consciously weighty and tragic.

The vibrancy and political and cultural significance of musical life in German-speaking Europe before World War I persisted during the 1920s. This bears repeating. By 1905, when *Salome* saw its premiere, Strauss's

---

[7] Hans Heinz Stuckenschmidt, *Arnold Schoenberg*, trans. edith Temple Roberts and Humphrey Searle (New York: Grove Press, 1959), 12.

unchallenged pre-eminence as Europe's most admired and emulated composer was within a crowded and competitive field. Two popular volumes of short biographies of leading contemporary composers were published in 1906–07. As the editors realized, Strauss towered above the rest: his "works are the accompaniment to the spiritual journeys of our time."[8] Of the 37 composers given entries, only Mahler, Delius, Reger, Pfitzner, Humperdinck, Wolf-Ferrari, and d'Albert have retained, in decreasing significance, a presence in music history, besides Strauss.

A similar compendium by Arthur Seidl appeared in 1926. He covered 52 individuals, including many who appeared in the 1906–07 volumes, but also a new generation of composers, some of whom were regarded as leaders of a disruptive "modernist" movement. Among them were Schoenberg, Krenek, Hindemith, Korngold, Schreker, Conrad Ansorge, and Schoeck.[9] Although Strauss's position in 1926 was no longer that of first among equals, Seidl observed that Strauss not only continued to innovate but also had become the leader in a counter-revolutionary cause directed against the fashionable modernists. Strauss's continued productivity in the 1920s and 1930s placed him at the forefront of contemporaries who shared his resistance against the abandonment of tonality, the rejection of melodic beauty, and the explicit use of the rhetoric of expressiveness inherited from nineteenth-century Romanticism.

Music by early and mid-twentieth-century composers once deemed "conservative" and out of step with history has, since the mid-1970s, made its way back to the repertory and tastes of musicians and audiences. Works written by Strauss from 1918 to 1945, before his celebrated "Indian Summer" (1945–49), have led this revival. They include the return of *Schlagobers* to the ballet and concert stage, the successful revival of *Intermezzo*, *Die ägyptische Helena*, *Die Liebe der Danae*, and *Capriccio*.

The mid-twentieth-century composers with whom Strauss's music from the 1920s and 1930s can be compared include Zemlinsky, Korngold, Schreker, Pfitzner, Schoeck, Braunfels, and Martinů. In each case, works written after 1918 bear resemblances to Strauss's and point to his prominence as a symbol of the power of continuity over change in European musical culture. Before the outbreak of World War II, not only among partisans and sympathizers with fascism, but also among victims of Nazism

---

[8] Max Hehemann, "Die Musik unsrer Tage," *Monographien moderner Musiker*, Vol. 2 (Leipzig: C. F. Kahnt, 1907), 3.
[9] See Arthur Seidl, *Neuzeitliche Tondichter und zeitgenössische Tonkünstler* (Regensburg: Gustav Bosse, 1926).

and proponents of liberal and left-wing politics, this allegiance to the aesthetics of tradition was widespread. Post-1918 traditionalists included victims and anti-fascists such as Paul Dessau, Paul Ben-Haim, Adolph Busch, and Jerzy Fitelberg. A significant but neglected work that forces a closer analysis of the intersection between aesthetics and politics in the mid-1930s is Dessau's collaboration with Max Brod, a cantata setting of the Passover Haggadah, the *Haggadah shel Pesach* composed in the shadow of fascism in 1936.

A disturbing affinity between fascism and aesthetic conservatism was undeniable. In 1921, the Austrian composer Joseph Marx, who embraced Austrofascism and thrived under Nazi rule, wrote the striking *Eine Herbstsymphonie*, an orchestral essay on nature evocative of Strauss's earlier *Alpensinfonie*. Then there were the fascist sympathizers who were hacks, such as Paul Graener, and more talented collaborators who appropriated aspects of interwar modernism into their brand of traditionalism even after 1933; that list includes Schoeck, Orff, and Werner Egk.

Zemlinsky, brother-in-law of Schoenberg and teacher of Korngold, wrote his one-act masterpiece, *Der Zwerg*, based on a short story by Oscar Wilde, in 1921. Its drama, pathos, and orchestral fabric demonstrate the influence of Strauss. As had been the case with Zemlinsky's 1917 setting of another Wilde text, *Eine florentinische Tragödie*, there was the inevitable critical comparison with Strauss. *Der Zwerg* lacks Strauss's languid irony and contains a Mahlerian emotional intensity, but it delivers a dramatic punch worthy of *Elektra*, particularly in its final scene. Zemlinsky's 1924 Lyric Symphony, a work clearly indebted to the past, deserves a place alongside Mahler's *Das Lied von der Erde*.

Korngold's 1927 masterpiece, *Das Wunder der Heliane*, has an intense lyricism and self-conscious lyric beauty that shows his lifelong emulation of Strauss, but Korngold's musical language remains clearly his own. A resemblance is also audible in Braunfels's 1924 *Don Juan Variations*, Op. 34 when placed alongside Strauss's *Don Quixote*. Both composers shared a veneration for Mozart, whose music forms the basis of Braunfels's work. But despite Strauss-like uses of the orchestra and an allegiance to classical variation form, Braunfels too shapes his own sound world. Braunfels was part Jewish and retreated from public life under the Nazis.

Pfitzner was perhaps the German contemporary whose reputation and fame came closest to rivaling Strauss's. Pfitzner's most famous work, the opera *Palestrina* (1917), was greeted with acclaim and won distinguished advocates, Mann and Bruno Walter among them. But Pfitzner was considerably more conservative than Strauss, both in politics and aesthetics.

Strauss remained playful and adventuresome in the 1920s while Pfitzner assumed the mantle of a reactionary and engaged in open polemics against modernism, advocating a rigid adherence to tradition. Indeed, his 1923 Violin Concerto was hailed as the greatest foray into the genre since Max Bruch. It shows none of the grace, transparency, and fluidity of Strauss but rather transmits Pfitzner's dark intensity and sonic intricacy. Despite its early success, the concerto has disappeared, together with most of Pfitzner's music, in part on account of the composer's outspoken support of the Nazi regime.

The most successful German-language opera composer of the 1920s apart from Strauss was Schreker. Like Braunfels he was half Jewish. Schreker was celebrated as an "expressionist" in whose work constantly shifting harmonies, overlapping rhythms, and dream-like sensuous sonorities formed a continuous fabric whose imagery seemed ever changing. His opera *Irrelohe* (1924) was well received by the public, but critics, eager for a bolder departure from past practice, attacked him, as they did Strauss, for becoming an apologist for the old-fashioned and superficial. The Debussy-like texture of Schreker's music was quite distinct from Strauss's, but Schreker shared with Strauss the expansive use of tonality and strategies of thematic elaboration.

In the 1920s, the Swiss composer Schoeck drifted more toward modernism in his musical language. But at no moment did he travel beyond experimenting with tonality and with the possibilities of linking words to music in the service of expression, just as Strauss sought to do. Schoeck's 1926 song cycle *Lebendig begraben* is a work of symphonic proportions for baritone and orchestra. Schoeck, who studied briefly with Reger and admired him, drew from Strauss not only in terms of orchestral colors but also in approaches to declamation and word setting, although he avoids Straussian ironic suggestions of nostalgia. Tonal and post-Wagnerian in sonority, Schoeck's setting is arresting, varied, and unique. James Joyce heard a radio broadcast of the cycle and promptly sought the composer out to congratulate him on writing the finest work of contemporary music he had heard.

Martinů, a Czech patriot and ardent foe of both fascism and communism, witnessed the premiere of his finest opera, *Julietta*, in Prague in 1938. Offering a surrealist vision, Martinů's score, like its libretto, seems a world apart from Strauss's *Danae* from the same period. Although the music often sounds closer to Stravinsky and Ravel, and despite the use of Czech materials, the persistent lapses into searing tonal eloquence and lyricism are reminiscent of Strauss. While Martinů went much farther than

Strauss in forging a dialogue between tradition and modernism, the use of devices from late Romanticism remains audible, as does the evocation of the heritage of operatic drama and convention.

When the proverbial curtain fell on the era of preeminence enjoyed by radical musical modernism during the later twentieth century, two neglected historical realities came into view. First, the attention paid to Schoenberg, Stravinsky, and modernism during the interwar era and the war years in criticism masked the continuity of distinctive late-Romantic practices after World War I. It was far greater than imagined. Second, and even more striking, is the resilience of tradition after World War II. These twin realities justify a reassessment of the high art musical culture of the twentieth century. In that reassessment, Strauss' innovations and compositional experiments suggest an alternative formulation of the modern, one that can be regarded as a having helped define the trajectory of twenty-first-century contemporary music.

Coda

Strauss' ideology celebrated not only continuity with the past, but its evocation through irony, fragmentation, quotation, and allusion. Tonality made music expressive in a commonsense manner linked to language. Strauss rejected categorical claims about music's "autonomous" abstract and formal essence. Music's function was to entertain and cultivate an aesthetic sensibility at the highest level (and therefore in an especially German manner). As a consequence, the music Strauss wrote between 1918–45 demonstrated a different concept of the modern, one obsessed with history, skeptical about the present, and yet committed to tonality, expressiveness, and accessibility.

This mix of invention, sense of loss, and ironic distance has permitted Strauss to emerge from the shadows as the most representative figure in twentieth century music precisely on account of his rejection of a belief that one could break free from history and begin anew. Strauss's pessimistic view of the present as marking the end of a golden age of culture and civilization fueled his disdain for the more experimental music of the interwar era. The late twentieth-century's rejection of modernism may have proved him right. Strauss' fierce ambition to stay the course after 1918 certainly emboldened others to resist the allure of revolution in terms of form, sonority, and musical materials. The imaginative traditionalists will end up defining the twentieth century.

CHAPTER 27

World War I

Philip Graydon

Inter Arma Silent Musae ("when society is under any kind of stress or in an extreme situation, creativity suffers") may have been a veritable catch-cry in some combatant nations in 1914, but the nexus between artistic expression and war was far more nuanced during the ensuing four-year conflict. Sparked by the assassination of the Austro-Hungarian Archduke Franz Ferdinand and his wife, Sophie, at the end of June of that year, the Viennese press was abuzz with discussion of how to offset an approaching "World War," implying that any new conflagration would be on an unprecedented scale.

Of that, their suppositions were not displaced, but those engaged in artistic endeavor were faced with a dilemma: could art and aesthetics be coincident with war? The answer was resoundingly in the affirmative, perhaps most strikingly so in Germany. Music had long held a central role in the cultural politics of Wilhelmine Germany, and it was called upon to provide the *Volk* with moral and spiritual fortitude, especially during what many in Germany viewed as, on the one hand, a cultural war between German values and Anglo-Saxon materialism and, on the other, French formalist rationalism. In a speech delivered in Heidelberg in December 1915, the German poet, Rudolf Borchardt, was strident in his defense of the German *Kulturnation*: "Culture is a purely German notion," he proclaimed, "not translatable into any other European language. As truly as God lives our victory must finish off this 'civilization', this 'European civilization', once and for all."[1]

As the present essay attests, many prominent German musicians and composers (not least, Strauss) subscribed to such cultural chauvinism,

---

[1] Rudolf Borchardt, *Der Krieg und die deutsche Selbsteinkehr* (Heidelberg: R. Weissbach, 1915), 10 ff, cited in Wolfgang J. Mommsen, "German Artists, Writers and Intellectuals and the Meaning of War, 1914–1918," in *State, Society, and Mobilization in Europe during the First World War*, ed. John Horne (Cambridge: Cambridge University Press, 1997), 29.

resulting in the production of wartime works that were, in some cases, nationalist in the extreme. But, in the post-war period, the essentially-outmoded cast of such music would only serve to contextualize the continuing crisis of an art form caught between its nineteenth-century heritage and an ever-evolving modernist aesthetic. In many ways, German music became characterized by this dichotomy, personified by a diffuse avant-garde determined on transcending post-Romanticism whose obverse was a nationalist-conservative rump hell-bent on perpetuating it. That such positioning bespoke wider cultural (and, furthermore, political) concerns serves to highlight the continued centrality of German music to such discourse through the 1920s and into the fateful decade that followed.

During the World War I, however, most German intellectuals shared the tenets of Borchardt's belief. Though less stentorian in tone, they signed manifestos declaring the innate ascendancy of German culture as a justification for their country's cause and the attendant, expansive military objectives being pursued by its army's high command. An early example was issued in response to claims of acts of barbarism perpetrated by German soldiers in occupied Belgium in October 1914. The entreaty, the "Manifesto of the Ninety-Three," carried the names of some of the leading lights of Germany's intelligentsia, including the writer Gerhart Hauptmann, the painter Max Liebermann, the historian Friedrich Meinecke, and Strauss's slightly older contemporary, the composer Engelbert Humperdinck. At base, the "Manifesto" was an out-and-out repudiation of Allied anti-German war propaganda, which it held to be perniciously false. Moreover, its signatories claimed that Germany had in no sense precipitated the War and that it had been foisted upon the country, which was now engaged, as a result, in an existential crisis; they also averred that German militarism had been responsible for the welfare of German culture, which would have perished some time before without such a lifeline. By the autumn of 1916, any notions of a cultural rebirth from the spirit of war were put to rest by the harsh realities of trench life at the front and food, fuel, and financial shortages at home.

In music, the practical exigencies of sustaining careers and revenue during the fighting may have caused some composers and institutions to simultaneously question the cost of war while answering the call to (artistic) duty. Others were, by comparison, less circumspect: mere months after the commencement of hostilities, Siegfried Wagner's *Der Fahnen-schwur* (*A Pledge of Allegiance*) for male-voice choir and orchestra premièred at Berlin's Philharmonic Hall on October 24, 1914, the score dedicated to the imperial army and its commanders. At the same time,

Figure 27.1   Commemoration of victory in the 1870 Battle of Sedan (Berlin, 1914).
Photographer unknown

Max Reger was at work on *Eine vaterländische Ouvertüre* (*A Patriotic Overture*) – a patently-jingoistic piece of limited value, similarly dedicated to the imperial forces. By the end of 1915, the music critic Arthur Seidl could list some 670 composers who had written patriotic music in what amounted to a catalogue of such output published in a series of articles in the *Allgemeine Muzikzeitung*. Less clear-cut was the case of the veteran composer Max Bruch; a witness to the Franco-Prussian War (1870–71), he wrote to his daughter Margaretha that "streams of blood will be the price for justifying our cause, for the shocks and horrors of this war will be greater than any other hitherto."[2] Nevertheless, with the outbreak of war, Bruch, like Strauss, was cut off from his foreign royalties and was thus minded to compose a number of works that would appeal to the wartime public. With titles such as *Heldenfeier* (*Heroes' Celebration*) for six-part chorus and organ (1915) and *Die Stimme der Mutter Erde* (*The Voice of Mother Earth*) for mixed chorus, organ, and orchestra (1916), their overtly-patriotic inspiration is clear.

---

[2] Letter from Max to Margarethe Bruch, July 31, 1914, cited in Christopher Fifield, *Max Bruch: His Life and Works*, 2nd ed. (Woodbridge, Suffolk: Boydell Press, 2005), 306.

Strauss himself was not averse to such posturing, taken up by artistic matters on the eve of the War, having traveled first to Paris and then on to London to conduct the premières of *Josephslegende* (with the Ballets Russes) on May 14, and June 23, 1914, in turn. By August 1 (with the composer ensconced back in Garmisch), Germany had officially entered the fray. In response, Strauss's entry in his Writing Calendar for the next day reads: "War and Victory! Hail Germany! We will not be beaten!" He likewise inscribed at the top of the manuscript of the short score of Act I of *Die Frau ohne Schatten*: "the day of the victory at Saarburg. Hail to our brave troops. Hail to our great German fatherland."[3] Writing on August 22 to Gerty, wife of his longest-serving librettist, Hugo von Hofmannsthal, he similarly enthused about other, early German successes on the battlefield: "These are great and glorious times … One feels exalted, knowing that this land, this people … must and will assume the leadership of Europe." Ever striking a contradictory pose, Strauss then refused to sign the "Manifesto of the Ninety-Three" when asked to do so in September, proclaiming that "declarations about things concerning war and politics are not fitting for an artist, who must give his attention to his creations and to his work." He evidenced such determination once more at the end of that month in a letter to Reger:

> To think that the Duke of Meiningen has thrown out his old and famous orchestra on the street: whoever heard of such a thing – *that* is German vandalism! How are we innocent citizens to summon up enthusiasm for all the fearful sacrifices this war demands of us if the Emperor's own sister [the Duchess of Meiningen] sets an example like that![4]

By October 8, 1914, he had vacillated again, demonstrated by his comment to Hofmannsthal, "We're bound to win, of course." Over the course of early 1915, his intermittent bellicosity would become tempered with a resurgence of an instinctive Nietzcheanism that found such striking expression in *Eine Alpensinfonie* (which premièred later that year): "As far as the war itself is concerned we have, I think, every reason to view the future serenely" (February 1915); "But as for politics: I think we'll view them from a little way off, and leave them to the care of those concerned with them; only hard work can console us; only hard work can bring us

---

[3] First citation from Richard Strauss, *Schreibkalender*, entry for August 2, 1914, in Franz Trenner, *Richard Strauss: Chronik zu Leben und Werk*, ed. Florian Trenner (Vienna: Verlag Dr Richard Strauss, 2003), 358 (my translation); second citation in Michael Kennedy, *Richard Strauss: Man, Musician, Enigma* (Cambridge: Cambridge University Press, 2006), 188.

[4] The first two citations are in Michael Kennedy, *Richard Strauss* (New York: Schirmer, 1996), 58; the third is in Kennedy, *Strauss: Man, Musician, Enigma*, 189.

victory" (March 1915).[5] The noumenal power as vested by Strauss in the Alpine mountains was underwritten by his evocation of its physicality. As George Mosse asserts, the mountain had stood since time immemorial as a German cultural trope, representative of national-collective determination and virtue. Indeed, during World War I, this metaphor strengthened to the point where it stood for nothing less than "the revitalization of the moral fiber of the Volk and its members."[6]

Other German composers expressed similar sentiments, if less outré manifestations of a national-mythological stance. Like Strauss, Ferruccio Busoni distanced himself from politics, but was, at base, pessimistic about what outcome the War would bring. He wrote to his wife from the United States in early 1915 (the distance offering some slim sense of hope): "There will be no end to the War … The wonderful thing about art is that in spite of everything it is still alive and creative."[7] Though Busoni penned the first draft of the libretto for his unfinished magnum opus *Doktor Faust* during the War, his principal project was the one-act opera *Arlecchino*, completed in Zurich in August 1916 upon his return to Europe, and premièred in that city as part of a double-bill with his two-act work *Turandot* on May 11, 1917. The Austrian writer Stefan Zweig noted the uneasy balance between tragedy and farce. As he wrote: "Arlecchino … finally becomes the philosophic mocker and *raisonneur* of the World War. The whole is a caprice, a play of moods, but of a humour which tries to conceal deadly earnest."[8]

This underlying war-weariness also led the German wartime public away from military musicals to operetta. Mindful of morale, the authorities lambasted popular forms of art and entertainment that encouraged a slipping in moral standards, an increase in self-indulgence, and the wanton waste of resources both material and spiritual. Possibly by way of consequence, the benefit concert gained traction as a public event in Germany and Austria. While the mainstay of the conventional subscription concert had been the symphony heretofore, the repertoire of the typical benefit

---

[5] Citations from Strauss to Hofmannsthal, October 8, 1914; February [undated], 1915; and March 30, 1915, *The Correspondence between Richard Strauss and Hugo von Hofmannsthal*, trans. Hanns Hammelmann and Ewald Osers (Cambridge: Cambridge University Press, 1980), 211, 216, and 218.

[6] George L. Mosse, *Fallen Soldiers: Reshaping the Memory of the World Wars* (Oxford: Oxford University Press, 1990), 114.

[7] Cited in Arnold Whittall, "The Great War: A Documentary," *The Musical Times* 106, no. 1462 (1964): 895.

[8] Cited (and translated from) the *Neue Freie Presse*, Vienna, May 4, 1918, in Antony Beaumont, *Busoni the Composer* (Bloomington: Indiana University Press, 1985), 237.

concert included the national anthem, popular songs, and popular (recognizably German) orchestral pieces, such as Beethoven's *Egmont* and Wagner's *Tannhäuser* overtures. On September 18, 1914, Strauss conducted the first in a series of such concerts in Munich. Perhaps predictably, the program consisted of Beethoven's *Egmont* and Fifth Symphony, in addition to Weber's *Euryanthe* Overture, before closing with Strauss's *Tod und Verklärung*. The second concert was even more militaristic in tone, sporting Beethoven's *Leonore* Overture No. 3, Haydn's Symphony No. 100 ("The Military"), Liszt's *Les préludes*, Wagner's *Rienzi* Overture, the Prelude from *Lohengrin*, and ending with the latter's *Kaisermarsch*.

Albeit infrequent prior to 1914, orchestral concert tours also became regular on the German and Austrian home fronts during the conflict. In July 1917, the Vienna Philharmonic toured Switzerland performing works by Beethoven, Berlioz, and Tchaikovsky in order to underline Austria's pluralist attitude with regard to culture. Even still, a Beethoven-only program was played in Lausanne, and, in a similar manner, the Berlin Philharmonic played Beethoven-only programs for some 66 concerts from 1914 to 1918. "Wagner Evenings," Bach-Beethoven-Brahms festivals, and a steady diet of Mozart, Strauss, Schubert, Weber, Gluck, and Mendelssohn became standard wartime fare in the German capital, leavened occasionally by the infrequent programming of non-German composers such as Liszt and Tchaikovsky.

Opera was largely "business-as-usual" despite the gaping chasm caused by the forced closure of events such as the Bayreuth Festival and the encroaching lack of funds. In Strauss's case, the war years witnessed the premiere in Vienna of the revised version of *Ariadne auf Naxos* (October 4, 1916) and the completion of *Die Frau ohne Schatten* in 1917 – the year in which he cofounded The Salzburg Festival Society with Hofmannsthal, Max Reinhardt, and Alfred Roller. The wartime period was not bereft either of other high-profile opera premières by composers such as Max von Schillings, Erich Wolfgang Korngold, Alexander von Zemlinsky, Hans Pfitzner, and Franz Schreker.

On a more general level, the effect of the World War I on the reputation of German music was profound, both at home and abroad. As a consequence, there were many examples of composers of international repute other than Bruch or Strauss who fell afoul of enemy proscription and the resultant loss of income. Perhaps more damaging in the longer term was the general removal of German music from foreign concert programs, thereby signaling the end of a hegemonic presence that had endured for well over a century. In a wider sense, the Western art music tradition had been shared across national lines for centuries before the War; numerous works were produced and performed across Europe, regardless of precise origin. The nationalist sentiment brought on by the conflict only served to heighten difference by pointing obliquely to its role as a cultural marker. Such divisiveness abroad bred a distinct intensification of the politicization of music on the domestic scene in Germany, not least in cultural commentary. Beethoven was duly conscripted by the popular imagination, his will imbuing German soldiers with preternatural courage and strength as they readied themselves for battle (according to letters published in the national press). One notable account from 1915 detailed the specifics of Beethoven's Fifth Symphony, the formal architecture of its first movement providing the backdrop to the development of the German military effort on the French front. Entitled "Beethoven's C minor Symphony in the Trench," its anonymous author enthused:

> Recently during the night I have gone through the C-Minor in my mind: that is truly the symphony of war. The introductory measures in fortissimo are the mobilization orders. Then the measures in piano: anxiousness before the tremendous [events ahead]. Then the crescendo and again fortissimo: the overcoming of all terror and fear and the summoning of courage and unity, rising to a unified will to victory. The second theme represents our loved ones at home, their worries, their pain, and their loving favors. In the bass of this section, the first theme [is recalled]: the faraway thunder of the battle on the border; the rise to fortissimo: the rejoicing of victory in the Fatherland. The second part of the first movement is the war itself, the great battles. The measures with the half-notes [describe] the long waiting in fortified positions, intermittently broken by the short first theme: the violent battles for the fortified positions, like those we go through here.[9]

In August 1918, as the endgame approached and German defeat seemed ever-imminent, musicologist Hugo Riemann sought to contextualize his introduction to a volume of Beethoven piano sonatas by proffering that German soldiers were analyzing the scores in the trenches – ample evidence for him of the ramifications for German *Kultur*. By November 9, Strauss (for one) had reason to be less sanguine about conditions on the ground; planning to travel to Munich from Berlin, events swiftly overtook him as an absent train, the already-simmering German Revolution, the

---

[9] Cited (and translated) from "Beethovens C-moll-Sinfonie im Schützengraben," *Deutsche Militär-Musiker-Zeitung* 37 (1915): 4; in David B. Dennis, "'*O Freunde, nicht diese Töne*': First World War Beethoven Reception as Precedent for the Nazi 'Cult of Art'," in *Musik bezieht Stellung: Funktionalisierungen der Musik im Ersten Weltkrieg*, ed. Stefan Hanheide, Dietrich Helms, Claudia Glunz, and Thomas F. Schneider (Göttingen: V&R Unipress, 2013), 257–58.

abdication of the Emperor, and the *de facto* creation of a new German Republic happened in quick succession. Two days later, Strauss started a brief spell as an interim director of the Berlin Opera – which he likened to a "nuthouse" (*Narrenhaus*) – but would agree to terms shortly thereafter for the position of codirector of the Vienna State Opera, a role he held from 1919 to 1924.

Unsurprisingly, this tendency toward introspection was also evident in compositional endeavor long before the end of the War. Reger's Requiem was performed on July 16, 1916 in Heidelberg as part of a memorial concert for its composer, who had died some two months previously. A more overt example of nationalist conservatism appeared during the following year in the form of Pfitzner's opera *Palestrina*, which premièred in Munich in 1917. Promoted by figures of such national prominence as the writer Thomas Mann, the plot centers on the fictional story of the sixteenth-century Italian composer Palestrina safeguarding music from being eviscerated by the edicts of the Council of Trent. As a testament to his vision, Pfitzner prefaced the score of his post-Wagnerian opera with a quotation from the nineteenth-century German philosopher, Arthur Schopenhauer, that made direct reference to the latter's expressed distinction between the purity of intellectual individualism and the "noise" of quotidian existence. It is telling that the opera's first production was taken to Switzerland by Bruno Walter on what the conductor termed a "propaganda tour" during the War in a bid "to demonstrate to the world the high level of German operatic art."[10]

Like his idol Wagner, Pfitzner was no stranger to controversy, and he produced some decidedly polemical writings underlining the trenchancy of his artistic credo. In 1917, his article "Futuristengefahr" ("Futurist Danger") directly confronted the claims Busoni had made in his 1907 book, *Entwurf einer neuen Ästhetik der Tonkunst* (*Sketch of a New Esthetic of Music*). As a resolute anti-Wagnerian, Busoni naturally set himself apart from his contemporaries, and his clarion call for a return to pre-romantic aesthetics (a move toward what he termed "Young Classicism") would find its greatest expression amongst the generation of composers that came to prominence after the War. Amongst Busoni's ideas in his *Entwurf* were advocacy of the development of a system of 113 heptatonic modes and a proposal that music could be predicated on the use of non-standard scales and sub-chromatic intervals.

[10] Bruno Walter, *Theme and Variations: An Autobiography* (London: Hamish Hamilton, 1947), 247.

In response, Pfitzner used his later article as a platform to denounce what he saw as the calamitous condition of contemporary music in Germany (largely the result of an overly-influential cadre of "international groups and the Jews," he claimed); he even proffered that the "atonal chaos" perpetrated by some composers was tantamount to bolshevism. By the end of the War, that sense of alienation would become even more acute for Pfitzner, particularly when faced with the German defeat, the dissolution of the Empire, and the severe terms exacted by the Treaty of Versailles. His 1920 cantata, *Von deutscher Seele* (*Of German Soul*), on texts by the nineteenth-century poet Joseph von Eichendorff, gave expressive voice to Pfitzner's soul-searching and represents an extended meditation on "Man and Nature" and "Life and Singing" (such were the titles of each half of the cantata).

Although Pfitzner embodied that brand of protective hyper-nationalism still celebrating a glorious prewar past while yearning for its restoration, that very conservatism pointed to the caesura in the German sense of self wrought by the War that irrevocably changed its relationship with that past. After, music would take an ironic "turn" against the elevated meta-physical claims and earnest modes of musical expression that the nineteenth century had bestowed to pre-war modernism. But the latter phenomenon only strengthened the resolve of those sympathetic to Pfitzner's stance – thus, it acted as a decisive factor in the later history of the Weimar Republic, as that feeling of societal and cultural chasm became more pronounced and the political landscape became ever more amenable to the rise of National Socialism.

CHAPTER 28

Nazi Germany

Erik Levi

Few composers lived through such cataclysmic changes as Richard Strauss. Born during the final years of the Bavarian monarchy, he witnessed the rise and fall of the German Empire, the Weimar Republic, the Third Reich, two World Wars, and the post-1945 division of Germany. Throughout most of these periods, Strauss remained determinedly aloof from the crises besetting Germany. Focusing on composition and conducting, he refrained from taking a political stand or aligning himself to a particular political party. Such a position, however, became far less tenable in 1933 after Hitler and the Nazis came to power. This chapter examines musical life during the Nazi era, seeking to contextualize Strauss's problematic relationship with the regime and the ways in which Nazi cultural policies affected his career.

In order to understand Strauss's position, this narrative begins in 1930 when the composer was working on *Arabella* and an adaptation of Mozart's *Idomeneo*. Burying himself in these creative projects shielded him to a certain extent from the dire situation that faced Germany. As a result of the Wall Street Crash, the economy was in meltdown, and the performing arts were hit particularly hard. An emergency decree, passed by Chancellor Brüning in December 1930, resulted in slashed subsidies for state-run organizations such as theaters, opera houses, orchestras, and conservatoires with consequent reductions in employment prospects for musicians. Composers also suffered, finding it increasingly hard to secure commissions or persuade performing institutions to promote their latest work. Concurrently, the introduction of the newly arrived sound film dealt a further blow, since the new technology caused the immediate dismantling of the numerous cinema orchestras that had been thriving.

By the summer of 1932, unemployment was so widespread that an estimated 30,000 of approximately 80,000 professional musicians were out of work.[1] A number of orchestras in Osnabrück and Münster, as well as the Berlin Symphony Orchestra (unrelated to later orchestras with similar name), had already fallen by the wayside. Even the survival of the Berlin Philharmonic was not assured. Speaking on the occasion of the orchestra's 50th anniversary in 1932, its principal conductor, Wilhelm Furtwängler, acknowledged that the crisis facing Germany was of a magnitude that the modern world had never experienced, one not only "encompassing economics and immediate life necessities," but also "artistic and spiritual matters." Furtwängler was adamant that music had to be protected at all costs, warning that if the Berlin Philharmonic ceased to exist, German musical life would suffer irreparable damage.[2]

The National Socialist Party, which swept to power in a right-wing coalition government in January 1933, capitalized on the fears and uncertainties of a thoroughly demoralized music profession. By instigating a protectionist program of national renewal, it promised to overcome the chaos and instability of the early 1930s through state control of the arts. Its plea for the revivification of German musical life appealed to a wide swath of musicians of a more conservative disposition, including Strauss, who felt alienated from much of the music written in the 1920s and had become increasingly disillusioned by the democratic experiment of the Weimar Republic. Strauss, in particular, longed for a return to the political system and status quo that had existed before the World War I. Like many, he believed that state control of the arts might be a price worth paying if it achieved cultural regeneration, and that the more proscriptive aspects of Nazi cultural policy, such as its virulent anti-Semitism, would be tempered in time.

Unfortunately, such hopes were dashed in the aftermath of Hitler's appointment as Reich Chancellor. Throughout February and March 1933, Nazi storm troopers were frequently on the streets threatening to disrupt cultural events featuring artists deemed aesthetically and racially unacceptable. Intimidation proved a successful tactic for hastening the departure of a number of high-profile musicians, such as conductor Bruno Walter, composer Kurt Weill, and pianist Artur Schnabel. A more systematic purge of conductors, orchestral players, and music conservatory teachers swiftly followed. Formerly employed as civil servants, these

[1] Michael H. Kater, "The Revenge of the Fathers: The Demise of Modern Music at the End of the Weimar Republic," *German Studies Review* 15, no. 2 (1992): 303.
[2] Elisabeth Janik, *Recomposing German Music: Politics and Musical Tradition in Cold War Berlin* (Leiden: Brill, 2005), 59.

musicians were now deprived of work as a result of the enactment of the *Gesetz zur Wiederherstellung des Berufsbeamtentums* (Law for the Restoration of the Civil Service) on April 7, 1933.

Although the Nazis celebrated the removal of many leading cultural figures in early 1933, the most effective way of carrying forward the so-called national revolution was less clear, in part due to the bitter struggle between rival factions in the Nazi hierarchy seeking to exert their influence on the *Gleichschaltung* (enforced conformity) of cultural life. Initially, the task was assigned to the Kampfbund für deutsche Kultur (KfdK; Fighting League for German Culture) founded in 1928 by Alfred Rosenberg. In its original guise, the KfdK drew support from a limited number of figures in the musical, artistic, and literary world of a nationalist and conservative disposition who felt strongly alienated by the cultural climate of the Weimar Republic. But after the Nazi take-over, it could no longer be regarded as a fringe organization with a membership that increased dramatically from 6,000 in January to 38,000 in October 1933.[3] Yet Rosenberg's hopes of supervising culture on a national scale were soon thwarted by the ambitions of his archrival, Joseph Goebbels, who had persuaded Hitler that culture would be best served by being absorbed into his newly created Ministry of Enlightenment and Propaganda. He moved quickly to create a special music and theater division within the Ministry in May 1933. As Goebbels pressed ahead, Rosenberg's influence declined. Nonetheless, the spat between the two political leaders destabilized musical life, not least because Rosenberg exploited every opportunity to berate the more pragmatically inclined minister whenever his policies appeared to deviate from hardline Nazi ideology.

One of the most notable achievements of the KfdK was to set up a Reichskartell der deutschen Musikerschaft (Reich Cartel of German Musicians) in the summer of 1933. Under one umbrella, this association united performers from various music trade unions that were no longer permitted to function under Nazi law. Establishing a cartel or music chamber that could represent the legal, economic, and professional interests of all musicians had in fact been a long-standing preoccupation. It surfaced at meetings held by the Allgemeine Deutsche Musikverein (ADMV), of which Strauss was a leading member just before the World War I.[4]

[3] Alan E. Steinweis, *Art, Ideology & Economics in Nazi Germany* (Chapel Hill: University of North Carolina Press, 1993), 32.

[4] *Materialien zur Gründung einer Zentralstelle für die Wahrnehmung der gemeinsamen Interessen aller Musiker ("Musikerkammer")* (Berlin: Allgemeiner Deutscher Musikverein, 1912). See also Oskar

Goebbels turned the ADMV's aspirations into reality. With the unveiling of the *Reichskulturkammergesetz* (Reich Chamber of Culture Law) on September 22, 1933, the Propaganda Minister established guilds of practitioners within the different branches of culture at the national level as a means of exerting greater control. This bureaucratic organization was headed by Goebbels as its President, who established separate chambers devoted to theater, film, visual arts, press, radio, literature, and music.

The administrative design of the Reichsmusikkammer (RMK; Reich Music Chamber) was somewhat labyrinthine. At its epicenter was an inner council consisting of a President, Vice-President, Business Manager, and a standing committee of eight members. A second layer embraced officials working in the areas of press, propaganda, information, finance, management, and law. Below this were seven sectors focused on the various branches of the music profession, namely composers, performers (largely drawn from the former Reich Cartel), concert organizers, choral singers and folk musicians, music publishers, music dealers, and the musical instrument industry. In line with the Nazi commitment to the *Führerprinzip* (leader principle), leaders were appointed to each sector. Cultural administrators were also created at a regional level, and somewhat later, in February 1936, municipal music officers were appointed to oversee local program planning. Anyone seeking employment as a professional musician in Germany from late 1933 onwards was obliged to join the RMK. But following the strictly racist and protectionist policies, membership was denied to Jews and to those whose political affiliations were deemed anti-Nazi.

Goebbels demonstrated considerable acumen in his choice of musicians appointed to the most significant RMK positions. Rather than selecting Nazi loyalists, he chose the politically unaffiliated Strauss to be President as well as leader of the Fachschaft Komponisten (Council of Composers), with Furtwängler as Vice-President. Appointing two of Germany's leading musicians to serve in a state-controlled corporate organization secured a huge propaganda coup for the regime, legitimizing and enhancing the status of the Nazi cultural program while demonstrating an apparent commitment to embed musical life in the Third Reich within the German tradition.

Goguel, *Musikerkammern: Ein Vorschlag zur Gesundung des deutschen Musiklebens* (Heidelberg: Reiher & Kurth, 1929).

Figure 28.1   Detail of the Reichsmusikkammer organizational chart.
Official publication of the RMK, 1934.

Strauss initially viewed the RMK favorably since he believed it enabled him to forge a better future for German musical life. In a speech delivered during the opening ceremony of the RMK in February 1934, he signaled his approval. Strauss was convinced "that the National Socialist government was able to breathe life into such an entity as the Reich Music Chamber," and this fact alone offered proof that "the New Germany is not inclined to allow artistic developments to more or less simply come as they may and stand on their own, but rather that there is a desire to pursue targeted means and methods for intervention that will provide new impetus for the life of our musical culture."[5] His appointment also enabled him to realize a number of domestic and international ambitions. Given his lifelong concern for improving working conditions for German composers, he urged Goebbels to approve the creation of a new state-controlled body known as STAGMA (Staatlich genehmigte Gesellschaft zur Verwertung musikalischer Aufführungsrechte), responsible for collecting and distributing copyright royalties. Strauss also successfully persuaded him to apportion a much higher percentage of these fees to serious compositions than to popular music. Another significant achievement, enacted in December 1934, was a redraft of the copyright law that extended the period of protection for composers' works from 30 to 50 years after their deaths.

Strauss's eminence and position at the RMK were also useful for the Nazis in the area of international music diplomacy. In May 1933,

5 "Richard Strauss: Speech at the Opening of the Reich Music Chamber," in *The Third Reich Sourcebook*, ed. Anson Rabinbach and Sander L. Gilman (Berkeley: University of California Press, 2013), 529.

the composer had attended the Maggio Musicale in Florence where he engaged in extensive discussions with Italian colleagues on a proposal to create an organization that would promote international exchange amongst more conservative composers than the existing Internationale Gesellschaft für Neue Musik (International Society for Contemporary Music or ISCM), which generally sponsored avant-garde music. Following Strauss's appointment to the RMK and Germany's withdrawal from the ISCM in late 1933 on the grounds that it was a leftist organization dominated by Jews, this idea gained greater traction, particularly after a selected number of foreign musicians received an invitation from Strauss to attend the first German Composers Conference in Berlin in 1934. Discussions held there and later in the same year at the ADMV Festival in Wiesbaden established what was to become the Ständiger Rat für die internationale Zusammenarbeit der Komponisten (Permanent Council for International Cooperation amongst Composers). The organization was formally inaugurated in Venice in November 1934, with Strauss as President. Its main task was to organize international festivals of stylistically accessible contemporary music. Inevitably, the Permanent Council's claim to support international co-operation and tolerance was illusory, not least since the Germans would never sanction the performance of music by Jewish composers. To its enemies, therefore, it was little more than a *Blut und Boden* (blood and soil) music festival.

Strauss soon became disillusioned by Nazi interference in the organization and programming policies of the Permanent Council, refusing to attend its first Festival held in Hamburg in June 1935. Nor was he interested in the day-to-day business of overseeing a whole raft of bureaucratic policy directives from the RMK, preferring to leave his assistants to take on this work. Furthermore, he steadfastly refused to sign any anti-Semitic measures proposed by RMK officials.

A combination of circumstances eventually brought Strauss's relationship with the RMK to breaking point. One major factor was undoubtedly the continued backbiting over cultural matters between Rosenberg and Goebbels. Throughout 1934, Rosenberg was not only sharply critical of some of Goebbels's appointments but also sought to expose those whose outlook he believed to be incompatible with National Socialist ideology. Initially, Goebbels managed to fob off Rosenberg's objections. But he could not afford to ignore evidence of insubordination, particularly when emanating from a leading figure in the RMK such as Furtwängler. In November 1934, Furtwängler fell foul of the regime by becoming embroiled in a public support for the composer Paul Hindemith, whose reputation he defended in a national newspaper. The conductor was particularly concerned by the Rosenberg faction's sustained attack on Hindemith and its branding of him as a degenerate composer. Furtwängler's plea for a more tolerant attitude toward the composer was interpreted as a direct challenge to Nazi authority, and he was forced to resign from the RMK on Goebbels's orders in December 1934.

Further resignations followed as Goebbels realized that he needed to rein in any official who failed to fall in line with prescribed policies. Two major casualties from the RMK in the summer of 1935 were Gustav Havemann, formerly a KfdK activist and director of the Association of German Performers, and the RMK's press officer, Friedrich Mahling. Havemann's misdeed was to continue to express his support for Hindemith, whereas Mahling was dismissed on the grounds of "cultural-political" unreliability for hiring a non-Aryan assistant.

It seemed only a matter of time before Strauss's own position would come under greater scrutiny. The Rosenberg wing of the Nazi party had campaigned aggressively against the composer once it became aware that Strauss had chosen the Jewish writer Stefan Zweig as the librettist for his next opera, *Die schweigsame Frau*. Rosenberg told Goebbels that Strauss's partnership with a non-Aryan disqualified him from being President of the RMK. Goebbels initially resisted demands to unseat Strauss, and the work premiered in Dresden in June 1935, albeit without the Propaganda Minister in attendance. Goebbels's absence at such an important cultural event signaled his growing realization that Strauss had outlived his usefulness as the principal musical figurehead of Nazi Germany. A contributory factor was undoubtedly the hostile attitude shown toward him by RMK bureaucrats. For example, the RMK's business manager, Heinz Ihlert, complained to Goebbels that the composer was only interested in self-promotion and acted like a "completely detached bystander" when it came to overseeing political and structural issues.[6] The final nail in the coffin, however, was a letter to Zweig, intercepted by the Gestapo and sent directly to Hitler, in which the composer made scathing remarks about his role at the RMK. This signaled an intolerable degree of disloyalty, and in July 1935, Strauss was forced to resign.

Utterly humiliated, Strauss experienced a severe crisis of confidence, further exacerbated after Zweig decided that the current political climate in Germany precluded any possibility of continuing their collaboration. In

---

[6] Bryan Gilliam, "'Friede im Innern': Strauss's Public and Private Worlds in the mid-1930s," *Journal of the American Musicological Society* 57, no. 3 (2004): 579.

addition, Strauss became much more anxious about the vulnerability of his immediate family, given that his daughter-in-law was Jewish and her children, according to the Nuremberg Race Laws, therefore *Mischlinge* (of mixed Aryan and Jewish parentage). At first, Strauss believed that his career as a composer was finished, although, remarkably, he composed more works during this difficult period than in the previous decade (he completed the operas *Friedenstag, Daphne, Die Liebe der Danae*, and *Capriccio* between 1938 and 1942).

Despite his falling out with Goebbels, the latter still recognized the propaganda value of Strauss's presence at important cultural events, such as the 1938 *Reichsmusiktage* in Düsseldorf where the composer conducted his *Festliches Präludium*. Furthermore, the regime still relied on him to serve as musical ambassador for Germany, a task he undertook with some degree of success, for example during a visit of the Dresden Opera House to London in 1936 when the composer was also awarded the Royal Philharmonic Society's Gold Medal. Four years later, Goebbels negotiated the commission with the Japanese government for Strauss to compose the orchestral work *Japanische Festmusik* in celebration of the 2,600th anniversary of the Japanese Empire, while the opera *Capriccio* premiered in Munich in 1942 under the direct sponsorship of the Propaganda Ministry.

By the time Strauss was removed as RMK President and replaced by the more malleable musicologist and conductor Peter Raabe, German musical life was far more stable than in the early 1930s. A sizeable upturn in the economy enabled the state to offer higher wages and standardized work hours to musicians. Furthermore, increased state subsidies resulted in a notable enhancement of concert and operatic activity and a resultant decline in unemployment. A good barometer of the relative buoyancy of music-making from the mid-1930s onwards was the enormous increase in the number of music festivals throughout Germany. During the years of depression, such events were limited affairs mainly confined to big metropolitan centers and operating under severely restricted budgets. Yet by 1938, almost every significant German town hosted a music festival and was in a position to offer performing opportunities while at the same time boosting tourism.

Despite the outbreak of war, musical activity continued with the same or even an increased degree of intensity. The Nazis used music as a powerful weapon of cultural imperialism in the occupied territories where they tried to impose the same ideological restrictions on programming as on the home front, invariably supporting the primacy of Austro-German music. At home, the intention was to shift the public's attention away

ERIK LEVI

from the battlefield by encouraging orchestras and opera houses to program "accessible" and "optimistic" music. The disastrous losses suffered by
German troops on the Eastern front from 1943 onwards, coupled with the
increased Allied bombing raids on home soil, which led to the destruction
of many significant German opera houses and concert halls, merely
strengthened Nazi resolve to maintain as full a concert and operatic
program as possible. Only after Goebbels's declaration of "Total War" in
the summer of 1944 was this policy abandoned. Yet even after most
orchestras and opera houses were no longer able to function, it was deemed
necessary to boost morale in the German capital during the last months of
the war by ordering the Berlin Philharmonic to continue giving concerts
for as long as possible.

Perhaps the most salient characteristic of music-making during the Nazi
era can be encapsulated in the words "Honor your German masters" – a
reference to Hans Sachs's closing address in Wagner's *Die Meistersinger*,
which Goebbels tellingly appropriated during a rabble-rousing radio
broadcast to the nation in August 1933.[7] Accordingly, Nazi leaders not
only emphasized the great achievements of German music, but also their
reinterpretation in elaborate festivals commemorating specific composers,
notable examples being the Bach, Handel, and Schütz celebrations of
1935. No festival was more lavishly organized than the nationwide events
held in conjunction with the 150th anniversary of Mozart's death in 1941.
The culminating festival in Vienna (Mozartwoche des deutschen Reiches)
in December featured all of Mozart's major operas, including Strauss
conducting his arrangement of *Idomeneo*, as well as speeches in honor of
the composer from Goebbels and Baldur von Schirach. In every respect,
the program was designed to create a sense of national pride while also
deflecting attention away from the harsh realities of war.

As a result of the exodus of so many important composers from
Germany after 1933, the Nazis were desperate to fill the void. Accordingly,
the call went out to every orchestra and opera house that performing
institutions had a duty to promote new music. Yet despite state-sponsored
encouragement, which resulted in the premieres of over 150 new operas
between 1933 and 1945, there was far less consensus than might have been
expected as to what exactly constituted the acceptable and unacceptable
face of contemporary music. Furthermore, only a handful of contemporary

---

[7] David B. Dennis, "'The Most German of all German Operas': *Die Meistersinger* through the Lens of
the Third Reich," in *Wagner's Meistersinger: Performance, History, Representation*, ed. Nicholas
Vazsonyi (Rochester, NY: University of Rochester Press, 2002), 110.

works enjoyed anything approaching widespread dissemination. Statistics drawn from German opera houses between 1933 and 1939 confirm that Strauss remained by some distance the most frequently performed living composer in Nazi Germany, and that *Arabella* far outstripped other new operas in number of performances.

CHAPTER 29

Lateness

Giangiorgio Satragni

In March 1954, nearly five years after Richard Strauss's death in Garmisch at the age of 85, the German author Gottfried Benn gave an address, first for the radio station Süddeutscher Rundfunk at Villa Berg in Stuttgart and then at the Bavarian Academy of Fine Arts in Munich. Titled *Altern als Problem für Künstler* (*Aging as Problem for Artists*), Benn's address focused broadly on aging in relation to the creativity of the artist. The 68-year old Benn had begun to reflect along these lines with regard to the late periods of a number of writers, painters, and musicians. He himself was aging, but his own work was not the basis of his address; he chose instead to discuss the long-lasting creativity of twentieth-century composers such as Emil Nikolaus von Reznicek, Jean Sibelius, Hans Pfitzner – and Strauss. They were contemporaries, and all engaged in prolonged artistic activity into their late years. Reznicek, a friend of Strauss, wrote operas, one ballet, and several songs in the 1930s before the Nazi regime interrupted the work of the 80-year-old musician by confiscating his manuscripts in 1940. Pfitzner, born in 1869, composed intensively during World War II and until 1949, when he died three months before Strauss at the age of 80; Pfitzner thus shared with Strauss a late musical flourishing during the same period and at some of the same locations. Sibelius, on the other hand, gradually abandoned composition during the 1930s and outlived the others, dying in 1957 at the age of 92.

Benn was 22 years younger than Strauss and passed away in 1956 at the age of 70. While his own late period was not as long as that of Strauss, who composed several masterpieces after reaching that milestone, Benn's reflections on artists and aging nonetheless provide a context for Strauss's own late years, which Benn himself witnessed. He was attracted to the theme of lateness as a broadly defined artistic field and discussed aging not in the biological sense but in terms of introspection, referring specifically to the inner, creative sphere of activity.[1] Using an imaginary artist as an example, he explained his idea of lateness as follows:

> And if he has not entirely quenched the volcanic element in himself, not entirely lost the dash and vigor of youth, what it comes to is that the critics nowadays exclaim: "Good heavens, why can't the man be quiet? Isn't it time he got down to writing something classical and preferably with something of a Christian tinge? Surely it's high time for him to ripen and mellow as befits his years!" But if, for once, he does write something more mellow and glowing and, so far as he has it in him, classical, the cry is: "Oh, the fellow's completely senile! He was moderately interesting when he was young, in his storm-and-stress period, but how he's a mere hanger-on desperately trying to keep up with himself. He hasn't anything to say, so why can't he have the decency to shut up?"

As this excerpt illustrates, Benn adopts an ironic style in writing about the perceived dichotomy of aging artists: whether they are active or weak and retrospective in their later years. He places Strauss's long creative life alongside other artists – Titian and Michelangelo in particular and, in the twentieth century, Max Liebermann – and in doing so, transforms a potentially negative interpretation into a positive one by emphasizing the importance of late works and of late style. In this light, Strauss's creative output in his old age is seen as a response to new challenges. In this vein, Benn quotes an aphorism by Goethe: "Growing old means entering into a new business; all the circumstances change, and one must either entirely cease to act or take over the new role with purposefulness and deliberation." Strauss identified a new role for himself in his final decade as a guardian of myth, classicism, and the humanistic heritage of Western Europe. From this viewpoint, his late style exemplifies Benn's descriptions of clarity in many works by aging composers. For many decades after his death, Strauss's late work was perceived as suffering from epigonism and repetition (the negative aspect about which Benn writes in ironic terms). For some, he was the image of a musician incapable of treading new creative paths. By the 1980s, however, Norman Del Mar had already positioned Strauss's late instrumental works as part of an "Indian Summer," or an unexpected burst of late creativity after he had given up writing opera.[2]

---

[1] Letter of October 30, 1953, in *Gottfried Benn–Wilhelm Oelze: Briefwechsel 1932–1956*, Vol. 4, ed. Harald Steinhagen and Holger Hof (Göttingen: Klett-Cotta & Wallstein, 2016), 235; and Gottfried Benn, "Artists and Old Age," trans. Ernst Kaiser and Eithne Wilkins, in *Primal Vision: Selected Writings of Gottfried Benn*, ed. E. B. Ashton (Norfolk, CT: New Directions, N.D. [1960]), 185–87.

[2] Norman Del Mar, *Richard Strauss: A Critical Commentary on His Life and Works*, Vol. III (Ithaca, NY: Cornell University Press, 1986), 179–245 and 405–77.

Strauss stated in 1941 that it is only possible to write one last testament, telling the conductor Clemens Krauss he would not compose another opera after *Capriccio*. Strauss tended to diminish the importance of his subsequent works, facetiously defining them as "wrist exercises." In a letter to his biographer Willi Schuh during World War II, he writes: "I sent Krauss a 3-movement 'sonatina' for 16 wind instruments ('from the workshop of an invalid') and am now writing a similar introduction and finale as a wrist exercise – all 'for the estate', meaning music superfluous to music history."[3] After the Sonatina No. 1 for wind instruments (1943), Strauss composed a second work for a similar ensemble, which he completed in 1945 just after the end of the war. Hardly superfluous, they represent the zenith of a two-century-old tradition in this genre, linking the spirit of Mozart with modern harmony. In this sense, the idea of an Indian Summer is appropriate. While Strauss was true to his word and did not write another opera, he did provide another "last testament" for the voice and orchestra, one that included references to several of his previous works. The *Vier letzte Lieder* (*Four Last Songs*; 1948), in the sequence of the posthumous edition ("Frühling," "September," "Beim Schlafengehen," "Im Abendrot"), collectively convey a farewell to life in the guise of natural description and allegory leading to the final sunset and the beginning of the night. The songs are rich with musical symbols. "Im Abendrot" features trilling flutes imitating the song of larks (referenced in Eichendorff's poem). The larks, morning birds rather than nocturnal nightingales, already announce a new day following the night, a rebirth of light in the eternal cycle of nature. The soprano voice sings the question "Ist dies etwa der Tod?" ("Is this perhaps death?"), and the orchestra answers with the transfiguration melody Strauss composed more than a half century before for his tone poem *Tod und Verklärung* (1889). In the more youthful work, the theme symbolizes the achievement of the artistic ideal. Here, it seems to answer the question posed in the text by calling to mind a creator who transfigures himself in the realization of his own artistic ideal. For him, there is no death.

Rather than termination, some of Strauss's late works can thus be viewed as reflecting eternity through a symbolic regeneration of nature and life. He explored such musical symbolism in the final scene of the opera *Daphne* (1937) with the maiden's transformation into a laurel tree. The tree is animated by birds trilling in the woodwinds, which represent

---

[3] Richard Strauss, *Briefwechsel mit Willi Schuh* (Zürich: Atlantis, 1969), 57. See also *Richard Strauss – Clemens Krauss, Briefwechsel: Gesamtausgabe*, ed. Günter Brosche (Tutzing: Schneider, 1997), 407.

voices of nature conveying eternity not only for Daphne but even more so for the laurel, sacred to Apollo as a symbol of the art work. The eternity of the artwork postulated by the wordless ending of *Daphne* occurs again at the end of "Im Abendrot," suggesting the eternity of the creative spirit, which transforms and regenerates itself, like nature. Akin to Nietzsche's concept of the "eternal return" in *Also sprach Zarathustra*, such musical moments exemplify the essence of Strauss's late style – an aesthetic affirming that nature, like beauty, is everlasting.[4]

As previously noted, Strauss's late works are often defined by clarity. This is evident not only in the chamber-like quality of the works for wind instruments but also in the *Vier letzte Lieder* and substantial passages in *Capriccio* (scored for a large orchestra). This clarity exemplifies a central affirmation of Benn, who draws a parallel in his writing to East Asian philosophy: "The Master Kung Dsi, speaking of painters, says: 'He is crude in whose work the meaning has more weight than the line'. In other words, for him, too, the higher thing is the manipulated thing, the manufactured thing, style."[5] Applied to music, compositional transparency and purity may be viewed as transcending the work itself to encompass the absolute and the eternal. Examples of Strauss's sense of proportion and his refined melodic style include the Oboe Concerto (1945) and the Duet Concertino for Clarinet and Bassoon (1947), both written for a small orchestra.

In his own deliberations on late style, published posthumously, Edward Said recalls Adorno's comments concerning late Beethoven. According to Adorno, "lateness is the idea of surviving beyond what is acceptable and normal; in addition lateness includes the idea that one cannot really go beyond lateness at all, cannot transcend or lift oneself out of lateness, but can only deepen the lateness. There is no transcendence or unity." (All quotations of Said are cited in footnote six.) This is essentially the opposite of late Strauss, who transcends his own musical language and continues to live on through his music. Referring to the dialectic between timeliness and lateness, Said writes: "Lateness therefore is a kind of self-imposed exile from what is generally acceptable, coming after it, and surviving beyond it." Even if Strauss ironically described his late instrumental work as wrist exercises, and he was obliged to leave Germany, his late years were not a self-exile in a cultural sense. During this period he wrote for posterity,

---

[4] Giangiorgio Satragni, *Richard Strauss dietro la maschera: Gli ultimi anni* (Torino: EDT, 2015), 262–73, 285, 336–45; for commentary on Strauss's metaphorical world see 177–273.
[5] Benn, "Artists and Old Age," 204.

communicating through his music an everlasting beauty that lingers for generations after the destructive impacts of World War II.

The chapters of Said's book *On Late Style* were assembled after his death from different materials, so we do not know if his view of Strauss – mainly negative and influenced by Adorno – would have changed had he completed this project. Nevertheless, some of his observations concerning the composer's late style draw attention to the importance of eighteenth-century models to modern composers:

> It is this persistent embrace of and return to twentieth-century versions of eighteenth-century idioms and forms that distinguishes Strauss's style as we look at it in its wider cultural setting, at a time when the modern movement in music simultaneously produced those more characteristically advanced or realistic styles we associate with dodecaphonism or serialism, polytonality, and in composers like Varèse, concrete music.

Said notes that Strauss was not the only opera composer of this era who chose historical settings; in addition to *Capriccio*, he refers to Weill's *Threepenny Opera* (1928), Britten's *Peter Grimes* (1945), and Stravinsky's *The Rake's Progress* (1951). But he offers no commentary on Strauss's late musical language, which itself reflects earlier influences, and he draws no comparisons between Strauss and Stravinsky in their respective applications of historical models. Strauss did not share the objectivity of Stravinsky, for whom the forms and idioms of the past were *objets trouvés*. Strauss apparently had greater faith in the music of the eighteenth century, for instance, which he reworked imaginatively using the harmony of the twentieth century; language drawn from the past is presented again to the future. Neither Weill, Stravinsky, nor Britten are comparable to Strauss in this regard. More alike is Respighi, who gave new life to Italian and French Baroque music in the earlier suite for small orchestra, *Gli uccelli* (1927), and who previously transcribed Renaissance lute music in his *Antiche arie e danze* (1917 and 1923; a third suite followed in 1931). While Strauss was aware that these were to be his final compositions, Respighi died much younger, at the age of 57, in 1936.

In the context of twentieth-century music, Said observes a "stubborn artificiality" in Strauss's works and characterizes the composer himself as a musician "resolutely committed to a tonal language and traditional form" while conceding that he later formulated a more balanced approach:

> Far from being an easily accessible and replicable world, the eighteenth century for Strauss in his last years is a sort of sustained second nature, a musical ethos so accomplished and so responsive to the atonality all around

him as to acquire not just a utopian but an oddly historical profile. You hear late Strauss, I think, as a counterpoint to Berg's *Lulu* or to Zimmermann's *Die Soldaten.*

Despite this clear statement on Strauss's historical position as an alternative to the radical avant-garde, but not as a trivial conservative, Said in his final verdict condemns Strauss as a survivor together with the philosopher who had previously condemned Strauss, Adorno:

> Like Adorno, Strauss is a figure of superannuation, a late-nineteenth-century essentially romantic composer living and writing well past his real period, exacerbating his already-unsynchronized idiom by moving stubbornly even further back in time to the eighteenth century.[6]

In his book *The Force of Character*, philosopher and psychologist James Hillman identifies this quality of being a "survivor" as a positive aspect of aging: "We find right off that what we value most about things called old is precisely their deathless and ageless character. Old masters' paintings, old manuscripts, old walls do not bring to mind dying but everlastingness." This corresponds well to the sense of eternity in Strauss's late works, both in terms of subject matter (e.g., in the operatic and musical myths that explore an ever-regenerating nature) and in the music itself (e.g., through his engagement with historical styles and forms along with the aforementioned focus on clarity). Hillman for his part contends, "If 'lasting' means remaining true to form, then what lasts is our character – and this can long outlive our life, because its influence and originating force are prior to the body's life and thus not altogether dependent upon it." He then concludes, "Old age means arrival at the condition of an image, that unique image that is your character." For some, this perspective might explain why "less is more" in Strauss's late works, and why his essence survives. For Hillman, "Since it is not age but character that is to blame for the intensification of peculiarities in later years, then the work of prolongation should focus on the main cause, the force of character, rather than on the 'Arithmetic' of longevity."[7]

Strauss's lateness demonstrates such a force of character: it does not mean for him to be "late" (as Adorno and Said claim) but to be wiser. Strauss, after the end of World War II and the destruction of Germany, began to reinforce the cultural heritage of the humanities – in particular,

---

[6] Edward W. Said, *On Late Style: Music and Literature against the Grain* (New York: Pantheon Books, 2006), 13, 16, 30–31, 43, 44, 45.
[7] James Hillman, *The Force of Character: And the Lasting Life* (New York: Random House, 1999), 40, 12, 48, 20.

music's position of prestige alongside classical and classicizing literature by figures such as Homer or Goethe. In a letter to Ernst Reisinger penned in the summer of 1945, Strauss envisioned the return of an educational system where music is taught to new generations alongside the other humanistic disciplines: "May the *Humanistische Gymnasium*, in the competent hands of experienced friends and enriched by music, soon be resurrected in its pristine glory as the benevolent guardian of European culture."[8] Strauss himself embodied that culture in his late years, his music reflecting the purity and proportions of classicality. Along these lines, Benn also mentioned Auguste Rodin as a long-productive artist who created works until late age before dying at 77. The French sculptor and painter, like Strauss but 24 years older, had a special affinity for antiquity. In his article *La leçon de l'antique* (*The Lesson of Antiquity*), he writes:

> In the first place, the Antique is Life itself. There is nothing more alive and no style in the world has ever been capable of rendering Life as it has done. [. . .] Life could be rendered by Antiquity because the ancients' consummate observation of Nature enabled them to perceive what was essential in it [. . .] and since that is where truth itself is to be found, the figures they constructed could never be weak.

Essence and eternity are cited as characteristics of the old masters from antiquity, and they are also the traits of late Strauss. Classicality, shaped from antiquity, is a virtue of old age that for Rodin belongs to maturity and lateness:

> It is a bad thing to set the Antique before beginners, and a mistake to begin with the Antique, for it should come last. [. . .] Well then, if you want to teach someone sculpture, set him face to face with Nature, and when he excels at working from Life, you can say to him: Now see how it was done in Antiquity, and the Antique will then become a source of new energy for him . . . It is not the artist's alphabet, but the reward of his work. The real command it gives us is not to copy or interpret it, but to proceed in the same way – which is not the same thing.[9]

Strauss attained classicality by reshaping earlier models with a sense of purity derived from antiquity through the force of character. For Hillman, "old brings out character, gives character"; late Strauss arrives at the condition of an image, and his lateness is the image of character.[10]

---

[8] Richard Strauss, *Recollections and Reflections*, ed. Willi Schuh, trans. L. J. Lawrence (London: Boosey & Hawkes, 1953), 93.
[9] Auguste Rodin, "The lesson of Antiquity" (1904), trans. Maev de la Guardia, in *Rodin: The Zola of Sculpture*, ed. Claudine Mitchell (Burlington, VT: Ashgate, 2004), 141–42.
[10] Hillman, 44.

CHAPTER 30

Reception

Franzpeter Messmer

While well-known conductors, orchestras, and opera houses performed Richard Strauss's compositions after his death, many critics considered his music backward-looking. This perspective was perhaps most vociferously expressed by Theodor Adorno. Negative assessments of Strauss's music were linked to comments on his personal life. Adorno, for instance, derided Strauss for having "the air of a great industrialist," while Fred K. Prieberg condemned his involvement in the Nazi regime.[1] Musicological interest in Strauss beyond such perspectives was largely non-existent until the 1990s, when the horizon of Strauss research and reception widened and the composer's contributions to musical modernity and postmodernism were recognized.[2]

This chapter seeks to understand Strauss reception at an earlier time – during his life. Critical perspectives are presented within the context of contemporary developments in music, the visual arts, literature, philosophy, science, and relevant historical events. While contemporary reception lacks historical distance, it nonetheless presents unique opportunities for assessing the immediate impact of music as it was first heard.

Strauss Reception in a New Age

While Strauss spent the early years of his career in a courtly context, a new, urban musical life developed rapidly from the 1880s onwards. The large number of newly established orchestras reflected this trend. Apart from the

---

[1] Theodor W. Adorno, "Richard Strauss: Born June 11, 1864," trans. Samuel and Shierry Weber, *Perspectives of New Music* 4, no. 1 (1965): 14–32, and 4, no. 2 (1966): 113–29; and Fred K. Prieberg, *Musik im NS-Staat* (Frankfurt: Fischer Taschenbuch Verlag, 1982), 203ff.

[2] For example: *Richard Strauss und die Moderne: Konzertzyklus der Münchner Philharmoniker*, ed. Bernd Gellermann (München: Münchner Philharmoniker, 1999); *Richard Strauss und die Moderne*, ed. Bernd Edelmann, Birgit Lodes, and Reinhold Schlötterer (Berlin: Henschel, 2001); and Michael Walter, *Richard Strauss und seine Zeit* (Laaber: Laaber-Verlag, 2001), 257ff.

royal orchestras, which played both operas and symphonic concerts, there were ensembles that focused on concert repertoire such as the Berlin Philharmonic (1882) and the Munich-based Kaim Orchestra (1893; renamed Munich Philharmonic in 1928). The rise of these public-oriented orchestras was a direct response to a rapidly growing audience. Around 1900, the number of performances exploded so that in Munich, for example, people spoke of a "flood of concerts." Through the introduction of lower ticket prices, these concerts aimed to provide opportunities not just for the wealthiest to hear classical music, but for the growing middle class as well. Later, in the 1920s, radio orchestras were established in Germany, France, and Great Britain. This broadening of concert life brought with it a new form of reception, shaped by sensationalism on the one hand and by the new bourgeoisie's thirst for education on the other.

The expansion of concerts also transformed musical performance. Strauss and other important conductors of his time, such as Bülow, Levi, Richter, Nikisch, Mottl, Mahler, Weingartner, Toscanini, and Walter, raised the level of orchestras, notably through exploration of diverse timbres and rhythmic precision during faster tempos.

There were also significant developments in the realm of music theater during Strauss's lifetime. The art of staging was not acknowledged as an independent art form until around the turn of the century, after which directors and stage designers assumed increasingly prominent roles. Figures such as the director Max Reinhardt and the stage designer Alfred Roller, both of whom collaborated with Strauss, revolutionized the performance of operas.

The high level of public interest in Strauss's oeuvre is closely connected to the proliferation of musical journalism at the turn of the century. The written word played an essential role in reception for educated audiences. Introductions to the tone poems, such as those provided by writer and composer Wilhelm Mauke, presented narrative programs, intellectual background, and individual musical themes with examples. They were issued as booklets in the series *Der Musikführer* (*The Musical Guide*), which many concert-goers brought to performances. Similar opera guides were published in the Schlesinger'sche Musik-Bibliothek series and were likewise directed at an educated, musically literate audience. Prepared by Otto Singer, piano reductions of Strauss's works allowed for an even more intense preparation, offering piano-playing amateurs the possibility of engaging with new music during an era before radio.

An important section of many daily newspapers, the feuilleton, focused on culture, literature, art, music, and philosophy, typically written in an entertaining literary style. Interested readers further educated themselves through dedicated cultural papers such as *Hochland, Illustrierte Zeitung,* and *Roland von Berlin.* Newspapers devoted entirely to music included, for example, the *Neue Zeitschrift für Musik* (established in 1834 by Robert Schumann), the semi-monthly *Die Musik* (since 1901), and in Austria, *Der Merker: Österreichische Zeitschrift für Musik und Theater.*

In his hometown of Munich, Strauss found critical opposition in the teacher and music writer Paula Reber as well as Oskar Merz, who wrote for the influential *Münchner Neueste Nachrichten.* Other critics like Rudolf Louis, Oskar von Pander, Anton Würz, and Wilhelm Zentner were influenced by the so-called Munich School of composers, led by the Academy professor Ludwig Thuille, who was a friend of Strauss. Their attitude was generally conservative and was especially positive toward Strauss's early works.

There were naturally many influential commentators on music and theater in Berlin, where Strauss worked for two decades. There Fritz Jacobsohn wrote for *Die Schaubühne,* Arthur Neisser (author of an early Mahler biography) for the *Neue Zeitschrift für Musik,* and Erich Urban for *Die Musik.* Oscar Bie and Hans Joachim Moser, professors in Berlin, also authored music reviews and books for the general public.

Vienna was also a central location for the reception of Strauss. The notorious music critic Eduard Hanslick appreciated Strauss's youthful violin concerto but pointedly attacked him once Strauss aligned himself with the Wagnerian camp. Others who intensively explored Strauss's music in Vienna include Theodor Helm, Julius Korngold (father of the composer Erich Wolfgang Korngold), Ludwig Karpath (who later worked in theatrical administration and to whom Strauss dedicated his ballet *Schlagobers*), Richard Specht (playwright, poet, music writer, and professor at the Imperial Academy of Music and the Performing Arts), composer Egon Wellesz, music historian Paul Stefan, and musicologist Roland Tenschert.

In smaller cities as well, there were numerous critics of nationwide importance who contributed to the greater dialogue on Strauss's music. In Dresden, for instance, Eugen Schmitz served as music editor at the *Dresdner Nachrichten* and later as Professor of Musicology at the Technische Hochschule (from 1918). Paul Bekker left Berlin in 1911 to write for the *Frankfurter Zeitung,* and in that city's liberal climate, he later coined the term *Neue Musik* (new music) in 1919. Karl Holl succeeded him as music critic in Berlin, while Bekker went on to become an influential director of the state theaters in Kassel (1925) and Wiesbaden (1927).

Other significant figures who commented on Strauss's music include Friedrich Brandes, director of music at the university in Leipzig, the dramatic adviser Arthur Seidl in Leipzig and Dessau, Heinrich Chevalley in Hamburg, and Oscar Schröter, president of the Stuttgart Conservatory. Lastly, Willi Schuh became particularly important after Strauss relocated to Switzerland in 1945. Schuh had worked as a music critic since 1928 and served as music editor of the *Neue Zürcher Zeitung* in 1944. Strauss entrusted him with the publication of his *Betrachtungen und Erinnerungen* (*Recollections and Reflections*), and Schuh later wrote the first basic, but unfinished biography of Strauss after the composer's death.

Perspectives on Strauss's Innovations

Assessments of Strauss's music during his lifetime often centered on his mastery of orchestral sound, undisputed throughout his long career. Beginning with the first tone poems, commentators wrote positively about the colorfulness of the Strauss orchestra. Around the time of *Salome*, however, some contended that Strauss's scores displayed something less than true art – mere technical virtuosity. For example, composer and *Schaubühne* critic Georg Gräner wrote: "The flickering beauty of the orchestra is admirable, but its powerlessness to crystallize even one vivid musical thought from the colorful chaos is deplorable."[3] Some commentators acknowledged such orchestral virtuosity as outward progress but condemned what they heard as an imbalance between content and expenditure. Earlier, Urban likened the use of a tone poem orchestra in *Feuersnot* to "cracking a nut with a sledgehammer" (25). Changes to the Strauss orchestra in *Ariadne auf Naxos*, *Intermezzo*, and *Capriccio* yielded Mozart-like reductions and produced a more transparent *Konversationston* (conversational tone), which was well received by many critics during Strauss's life but did not influence the dominant opinion of him as an artisan-like composer after his death. Adorno perceived this *Konversationston* as merely an outward stylistic shift but not a substantial development: "The late works disgrace the earlier ones by caricaturing them."[4]

Some observers recognized that Strauss was searching for a new form of musical theater, but many viewed this with a critical eye. Munich-based

---

[3] *Kritiken zu den Uraufführungen der Bühnenwerke von Richard Strauss*, ed. Franzpeter Messmer (Pfaffenhofen: W. Ludwig Verlag, 1989), 39. Page numbers in parentheses all refer to this volume.
[4] Adorno, "Richard Strauss," 126.

critic Merz described *Guntram* as a "psychological proceeding in one act with two prologues" (13); for Merz, it was a testimony to Strauss's inadequacies as a playwright. The adoption of the "Überbrettl tone" in *Feuersnot* (referring to Ernst von Wolzogen's *Überbrettl* cabaret in Berlin) was acknowledged and praised by some as a new form of realism. Conversely, Strauss's adaptation of Oscar Wilde's tragedy *Salomé* (with nearly the original text) on the heels of Debussy's *Pelléas et Mélisande*, one of the earliest examples of "literature opera," was deemed "one of the most fatal errors" (31) by Chevalley in Hamburg. Opinions were sharply divided concerning *Der Rosenkavalier* as to whether or not it represented a new form of musical comedy. One critic admired the enchanting *Lustspielton* (sound of comedy) and what he heard as an overcoming of the "spirit of gravity" (88, 78) while Otto Sonne of the *Leipzig Illustrierte Zeitung* labeled it "a cuckoo's egg of an operetta – albeit a smart and brilliantly disguised one," unworthy of comparison with the now less-known musical comedies of Ermanno Wolf-Ferrari, let alone those of Mozart (89).

The union of play and opera in *Ariadne auf Naxos* attracted great public interest, in part because Strauss collaborated with Reinhardt. But in the Berlin journal *Bühne und Welt*, Neisser judged it a "failed experiment" (124) and lamented an "unbelievable lack of style stemming from expecting interest in a symbolic-romantic love fantasy in the style of the twentieth century from a late-seventeenth-century French marquise" (124). Not all reviews were negative. Berlin critic Felix Vogt deemed Strauss's ballet *Josephslegende* a successful "cross between musical drama and symphony" (165), and after the premiere of *Intermezzo*, Holl wrote that Strauss had found a new form of musical theater through the "amalgamation of all previous ways of mixing words and music" (227). The "synthesis of new and old opera forms" in *Die Frau ohne Schatten* was seen as "a higher unity" (199) by a critic writing for the *Illustriertes Wiener Tagblatt*. And after the premiere of *Die ägyptische Helena*, Hugo von Hofmannsthal's libretto was widely discussed. Alfred Dressler (*Breslauer Zeitung*) saw it as "lowering the level" of Euripides (230) and Stefan (*Neue Zürcher Zeitung*) as "a great and beautiful libretto" that, however, demanded "too many transformations, changes, catharses" (234).

Pulling back the lens, Strauss's search for new forms of stage music coincided with a broader revolution in theater that attempted to move beyond nineteenth-century naturalism. There were many new impulses, from the expressive dance of Sarah Bernhardt to Reinhardt's new production concepts. As the above critical snippets illustrate, Strauss's responses to his own inherited traditions earned a mixed reception.

Debating Strauss: On Progress and History

In the age of the industrial revolution, people experienced technological progress to a degree never seen before. Music, of course, was not excluded from broader philosophical and practical questions concerning innovation and progress. During his time as Kapellmeister in Munich, Strauss was labeled *Zukunftsmusiker* (musician of the future), a term associated with Wagner and linked to composers of the New German School.[5] But even some who favored Wagner, such as the Munich critics Reber and Merz, rejected Strauss, to say nothing of Hanslick in Vienna, who condemned the Bavarian as "a great talent for false music, for the musically ugly" after hearing a performance of *Don Juan* in 1892.[6] *Don Quixote* was also condemned by many, with some lambasting Strauss's inclusion of a wind machine. The greater scandal stemmed from the tone poem's dissonances, however, which the critic Paul Hiller of the *Neue Zeitschrift für Musik* (1898) mocked as "caterwauling." In general, as noted, Strauss was often dismissed as a composer who, in comparison to Wagner, made "progress in superficial features" (namely in instrumentation) but not in the "idea" or in "invention" (52).

Some years later, the Berlin critic and composer Heinz Tiessen observed a modern classicism in *Der Rosenkavalier* (104) but cast the operas that followed, especially *Die ägyptische Helena*, as regressive (249). While critics such as Walter Schrenk, Jacobsohn, and especially Bekker judged Strauss as a composer of an old era, others like Schmitz, Stefan, and Pander argued that Strauss maintained tradition "in middle of the high tide of atonality and in spite of the 'theses' hurled at romantic opera," as Alfred Burgatz wrote (246).

Although Strauss also selected historical themes for his first four operas, *Guntram, Feuersnot, Salome,* and *Elektra,* his depiction of history was only viewed negatively from *Der Rosenkavalier* onwards. Reflecting on that opera, Louis found its "unhistorical historicizing," such as the juxtaposition of eighteenth-century Viennese Rococo with the nineteenth-century waltz, unbearable for an educated public (96). Regarding *Ariadne,* Neisser considered the inclusion of an ancient form of theater, the *commedia dell'arte,* as problematic because the figures do not seem "alive" (132). Strauss's collaboration with the avant-garde Ballets Russes that resulted in

---

[5] Emil Peschkau, "Auch ein Zukunftsmusiker," *Münchner Neueste Nachrichten,* October 6, 1886. This satirical tale appeared a few days after Strauss had conducted the orchestra of the Court Opera.
[6] Eduard Hanslick, *Fünf Jahre Musik* (Berlin: Allgemeiner Verein für Deutsche Literatur, 1896), 180.

Josephslegende was also controversial. Neisser rejected the modern stage set, arguing it was not a historically correct "reconstruction of those wonderful banquet paintings of Paolo Veronese," but rather "a consciously stylized Russian blend of half-understood Veronese and totally misunderstood Palladio" (171).

Strauss's treatment of history was perceived and judged in the context of turn-of-the-century historicism in architecture and history painting as well, represented for example by the artist Karl Theodor von Piloty. With their ahistorical combination of eras and styles, the works of Strauss (with his collaborators Hofmannsthal, Reinhardt, and Roller) broke with existing practices that originated in nineteenth-century historicism and naturalistic manifestations in painting and theater. Furthermore, they drew upon developments in contemporary art and literature around 1900, which broke from realism and representation in favor of exploring unconscious phenomena through symbolism, for example. Just as Oscar Wilde's *Salomé* was inspired by the images of the symbolist painter Gustave Moreau and the dance of Sarah Bernhardt, the critic Brandes argued that Strauss's music too was inspired by contemporary artistic developments (34–35).

Music and Psychology

Contemporary interest in psychological states was an important context for critical discussions of Strauss's music. The term *Ausdruckskultur* (culture of expression) circulated in the literature of the time. The journal *Der Kunstwart*, for instance, published by Ferdinand Avenarius, had from 1907–12 the subtitle *Halbmonatsschau für Ausdruckskultur in allen Lebens-gebieten*, referring to the expression of culture in all facets of life – including the psychological. Sigmund Freud (together with Josef Breuer) initially developed his ideas of psychotherapy in his *Studies in Hysteria* (1895), and works by figures such as Arthur Schnitzler in literature and Gustav Klimt and Egon Schiele in painting further explored aspects of the subconscious. In music, *Ausdruckskultur* was extended to encompass the relationship between sound and the psyche.

For example, after the premiere of *Tod und Verklärung*, one critic described its musical representation of psychological processes as "soul painting."[7] But the intensification of expression in *Guntram*, which Strauss

---

[7] Dr. O. [Kürzel], "Die 97. Tonkünstlerversammlung des Allgemeinen Deutschen Musikvereins in Eisenach, Dritter Tag (Uraufführung von *Tod und Verklärung*)," *Neue Zeitschrift für Musik* 86, no. 3 (1890): 327.

completed five years later, was criticized for its "extreme harmonic, rhyth-mic, and instrumental excess" (13). *Salome* was both praised and derided for its musical depiction of eroticism and the hysterical female (the term "hysteria" was applied at the turn of the century to various pathologies, particularly those diagnosed in women). Critics also observed musical reflections of pathological anomalies in *Elektra*; as with *Salome*, its disso-nant harmonies were directly associated with representations of the mind. Even in *Der Rosenkavalier*, the Breslau critic Albert Geiger found a similar "perversity," although "sweetened" (81).

Some considered such works to be "on the brink," where all composi-tional rules disintegrate into the uncertain. Strauss supporters heralded these operatic and orchestral compositions as new and progressive, while opponents saw them as harbingers for the "degeneration of music" (35). It must be noted that terms such as degeneration and pathology, in this context and others, bear anti-Semitic associations: Jewish decadence, sul-triness, half-rotten eroticism, and cacophony. Decades later, after the premiere of *Friedenstag* (1938), the critic Karl Laux (who was known for his loyalty to the national-socialist party) noted that Strauss had left the "cacophonies of *Elektra*" behind (282).

On Heroism, Irony, and Satire

As noted, Strauss reception was influenced by perceptions of his person-ality. Some critics interpreted his melodic climaxes as a metaphor for the "artist prince" who owned a mansion in Garmisch and later a palatial home in Vienna. For example, after the 1924 premiere of the ballet *Schlagobers* (an Austrian word for whipped cream) in which a boy has nightmares after overindulging in a Viennese bake shop, the Austrian critic Emil Petschnig attacked Strauss's "materialistic behavior" and drew atten-tion to the fact that Strauss was "building a magnificent villa on a property offered free of charge by the municipality" (219). In the nineteenth century, the artist-as-prince was an archetype exemplified by figures such as Franz von Lenbach and Franz von Stuck in Munich and by Wagner in Bayreuth. Strauss, however, seemed to take a step further by portraying himself in *Ein Heldenleben*, *Symphonia domestica*, and *Intermezzo*. Bekker interpreted *Ein Heldenleben* as the self-portrait of a "careless aristocrat."[8] Romain Rolland found it remarkable that Strauss "had the audacity to write, after Beethoven, an Heroic Symphony, and to imagine himself the

[8] Paul Bekker, "Richard Strauß zu seinem 60. Geburtstage," *Der Kunstwart* 37, no. 9 (1924): 96.

hero." For Rolland, Strauss embodied the new type of German artist at the time of Emperor Wilhelm II: initially determined by idealism, he secludes himself, disgusted by the world, into a "frenzy of pride, a belief in self, and a scorn for others" asking himself "Why have I conquered?"[9]

Other contemporary writers recognized that Strauss often infused his heroic depictions with elements of humor, irony, and satire. Bekker observed the composer's "strong natural disposition toward humor" in the tone poems *Till Eulenspiegel* and *Don Quixote* as well as in the musical comedy *Feuersnot* (103), and also considered parody a central trait of *Der Rosenkavalier*. Nonetheless, this side of Strauss was judged ambivalently. His witty musical inventions in *Till Eulenspiegel* were complimented, but the satire in *Feuersnot* was roundly criticized: "Where is all the bile coming from?" asked the writer and critic Karl Söhle (29). The self-portrait in *Intermezzo*, in which Strauss ironically shattered the presentation of himself as an artist prince, was described as a "self-surrender" (226) by Holl in the *Frankfurter Zeitung*. This ambivalence was criticized during the Nazi era. For this reason, some viewed *Friedenstag* as Strauss's first heroic work; its libretto by Joseph Gregor opened up hitherto distant realms of heroism whereas "the Half-Jew Hofmannsthal and the Jew Zweig" had inhibited Strauss from exploring the truly heroic (279).

In sum, heroism was an important topic within the context of the foundation of the German Reich in 1871 and beyond. In 1897, a luxurious volume titled *Unser Heldenkaiser* (*Our Hero-Emperor*) was published to celebrate the 100th anniversary of the birth of Emperor Wilhelm I, and around this time, popular posters with photos of Emperor Wilhelm II, Bismarck, and various officers bore the caption "Our heroes of 1870." But this new heroism was attacked by satirical publications like *Simplicissimus* and in cabarets such as Wolzogen's *Überbrettl*.

A rich variety of cultural contexts informed the contemporary reception of Strauss's oeuvre in Germany. Developments in music such as the advent of atonality and new frontiers in musical theater certainly shaped critical perspectives, but so did modern conceptions of history, advancements in science, such as those in the area of psychoanalysis, and political developments relating to the rise and fall of the German Empire.

---

[9] Romain Rolland, "Richard Strauss" (1899), in *Musicians of To-Day*, trans. Mary Blaiklock (New York: Holt, 1914), 139 and 164–67.

PART VI

Artifacts and Legacy

Publishers and Editions

Andreas Pernpeintner and Stefan Schenk
(Translation by Margit L. McCorkle)

It is well known that Richard Strauss was self-assured in dealing with his publishers, and as such, he was able to drive a hard bargain and command high fees. He lobbied for composers' rights to share in performance proceeds, and he comically and spitefully read the riot act to the most significant music publishers in his song cycle *Der Krämerspiegel* (1918). Drawing upon primary source materials, including anecdotes from the many volumes of Strauss correspondence, this chapter outlines his relationships with key publishing firms and discusses various editions of his works spanning from the late nineteenth century to the present. The examples discussed illuminate the often complex relationship between composer and publisher as well as various issues that arose in music publishing during Strauss's lifetime and after his death in 1949.

Publishers

The first publishing partner of the ambitious composer was Eugen Spitzweg of the Munich publishing house Jos. Aibl (founded 1825), whose catalog also included works by Hans von Bülow, Max Reger, Josef Rheinberger, and Alexander Ritter. Strauss's only previous publication, which was financed by his uncle, the beer brewer Georg Pschorr, was the Festmarsch, Op. 1. That score was issued by the venerable Leipzig house Breitkopf & Härtel (the world's oldest music publishing company, founded in 1719, whose catalog included works by Haydn, Schubert, Mendelssohn, and Robert Schumann).[1] The collaboration with Spitzweg started the same year (1881) with the String Quartet, Op. 2 and lasted until 1898; all orchestral works up to *Don Quixote* as well as choral, piano, and chamber music, Lieder, and the opera *Guntram* were published by Aibl.

---

[1] Letter from Richard Strauss to Breitkopf & Härtel, February 8, 1881; in *Richard Strauss: Dokumente. Aufsätze, Aufzeichnungen, Vorworte, Reden, Briefe*, ed. Ernst Krause (Leipzig: Reclam, 1980), 272 f.

Spitzweg's personal involvement in the advancement of Strauss's fledgling career resulted in a friendship that managed to stand up to the business acumen of the increasingly successful composer. This relationship is probably not comparable to the deep personal bond between Brahms and his publisher, Friedrich August Simrock, but it was close enough that Strauss could convince Spitzweg to publish compositions by Max Reger as well. It was not until the turn of the century, with the dispute over copyright, that the collaboration between Strauss and Spitzweg came to an end. In 1904, the aging Spitzweg sold Aibl to Universal Edition, founded in 1901 in Vienna. Although Strauss was not happy about the change, from today's vantage point, his work fit perfectly with Universal who, with Mahler and Schoenberg, had in its catalog other key representatives of musical modernism (later also Berg, Webern, Zemlinsky, Bartók, Szymanowski, Kodály, Weill, Schulhoff, Schreker, and Eisler).

In 1890, Strauss collaborated with the Berlin publishing house Adolph Fürstner for the first time on the publication of the *Mädchenblumen* Lieder, Op. 22. Ten years later, Fürstner became Strauss's primary publisher.[2] The collaboration with Fürstner would last even longer than that with Spitzweg. Strauss benefited from the fact that Fürstner had excellent contacts abroad and considerable experience with stage works (he carried in his catalog, among others, the Wagner operas *Rienzi, Der fliegende Holländer,* and *Tannhäuser,* along with a selection of pieces by Liszt), and thus, from *Feuersnot* (1901) on, Strauss began to publish his operas with Fürstner. The composer first signed with Fürstner exclusively for a period of three years, and even later, when he took greater liberties in his choice of publisher, he usually offered new works to Fürstner first. From *Arabella* (1932) on, however, Strauss self-published his operas, consigning them to Fürstner only on commission, meaning that the publisher oversaw distribution but assumed no economic risk.

His fruitful business relationship with Fürstner endured when the publishing business passed to Adolph Fürstner's son, Otto, a partner in the company since 1911 and sole owner from 1922. Strauss's break with the house finally occurred during the Third Reich. Otto Fürstner fled to England in 1935, escaping the Nazi regime's reprisals against Jewish publishers, and leased the rights for German works to his proxy, Johannes

---

[2] Strauss wrote to his friend Spitzweg: "My new publisher, I recently forgot to tell you, is Fürstner." Letter to Eugen Spitzweg, March 22, 1900; Münchner Stadtbibliothek, Monacensia, Strauss, Richard A I/69.

Oertel, who in 1939 became the owner of Fürstner's German publishing division during the course of the so-called *Arisierung* (Aryanization). Following Austria's annexation into the German Reich in 1938, Fürstner's Austrian business was also transferred to Oertel. Fürstner wanted to take legal action while Strauss, perhaps less sensitive politically, took Oertel's side. Even when Strauss and Fürstner resumed contact after the war, Strauss was in favor of its German division remaining in the hands of Oertel, who also remained Strauss's agent for the self-published works. Only after the composer's death did Fürstner recover all publishing rights.

Unaffected by this reassignment were the international publishing rights to the Strauss works Fürstner had sold in 1943 to the British firm Boosey & Hawkes, who had in its catalog works by prominent nineteenth-century composers such as Rossini, Bellini, Donizetti, and Verdi. During World War II, Boosey & Hawkes moved to the USA and added pieces by Britten, Stravinsky, and Copland. Even independent of this transfer of rights, Boosey & Hawkes became very important. Strauss and his wife lived in Switzerland from 1945 to 1949, a period during which his royalties were blocked abroad and musical life in Germany and Austria had come to a standstill. Strauss's role as former president of the Reichsmusikkammer (Reich Music Chamber) was examined in the framework of the denazification law, and he was acquitted in 1948. As an authorized representative of the publishing house (who at times even took it over), Ernst Roth visited Strauss on multiple occasions in his Swiss exile, acquired the rights to publish most of the post-war works, including the Second Horn Concerto and *Metamorphosen*, and also prepared numerous piano scores and arrangements.[3]

Strauss maintained contact with other publishers throughout his career, as the following examples illustrate. The Opp. 15 and 17 Lieder were published by Daniel Rahter (Hamburg, Leipzig, and London), the tone poems *Ein Heldenleben* and *Eine Alpensinfonie* along with various Lieder and choral pieces by F. E. C. Leuckart (Leipzig), and *Symphonia domestica* by Bote & Bock (Berlin). Other publishers came into play even without Strauss's direct involvement, such as from the aforementioned sale of Jos. Aibl to Universal Edition in 1904. From this firm, in turn, the C. F. Peters publishing house (Leipzig), which had already published the Op. 57 military marches and the *Instrumentationslehre* (Strauss's update of

---

[3] See Dominik Rahmer, "Strauss and his publishers," in *Richard Strauss Handbuch*, ed. Walter Werbeck (Stuttgart: Springer, 2014), 54–64.

Berlioz's orchestration treatise), acquired in 1932 the tone poems once published by Aibl – an irony of history, because as early as 1890 the young Strauss had unsuccessfully tried to sell his first tone poem *Macbeth* to Peters.[4] After Strauss's death, acquisitions and sales led to the Fürstner publishing house becoming part of Schott Music (Mainz), as it remains today. Other important publishers that produced first editions of Strauss's compositions during his lifetime include Steingräber (Hannover, later Leipzig), Rob. Forberg (Leipzig), C. A. Challier (Berlin), and P. Cassirer (Berlin). Franz Trenner's catalog of Strauss's works provides a detailed overview of these editions.[5]

The interaction between Strauss and his publishers, as documented by the extant letters they exchanged, involved both business matters and musical content. In his dealings with publishing houses, Strauss (after initial subservience with his Op. 1) soon became more of an equal partner in these discussions and proved to be a tough and skillful negotiator. When his goal was to make the tone poem *Macbeth* attractive to his early publisher Spitzweg, Strauss pitched it by referencing a competing offer by C. F. Peters: "if you do not want it and Peters wants to pay well for it, then I don't quite understand why I should not let it be published by Peters."[6] After almost a year, the strategy paid off as a satisfactory agreement with Spitzweg was reached. This was fortunate for Strauss, because the interest from Peters that Strauss repeatedly mentioned was in no way specific.

As his prominence increased, Strauss was able to elevate his publishing fees. After the great success of *Salome* (1905) that enabled Strauss to build his Garmisch villa from the income, he received a spectacular sum of 100,000 Marks from Fürstner for *Elektra* (1908).[7] By comparison, the fee for his first opera, *Guntram*, had amounted to a mere 5,000 Marks in 1894–95. Strauss also recognized the great business potential of performing rights, for which the publishing houses previously paid only a one-time fee. Thus in 1903, on the initiative of Strauss, Hans Sommer, and Friedrich Rösch, the Genossenschaft Deutscher Komponisten (Association of German Composers) founded the Anstalt für musikalisches

---

[4] Letter to C. F. Peters, May 13, 1890; Sächsisches Staatsarchiv Leipzig, inventory 21070 C. F. Peters, Leipzig, No. 2154. This letter contains an offer by Strauss to Peters, who would later evade response to a subsequent request.

[5] Franz Trenner, *Richard Strauss Werkverzeichnis*, 2nd ed. (Wien: Verlag Dr. Richard Strauss, 1999), 369–73.

[6] Letter to Eugen Spitzweg, December 19, 1889; Münchner Stadtbibliothek, Monacensia, Strauss, Richard A I/31.

[7] Richard Strauss, 1908 Schreibkalender [writing calendar], April 22, 1908 (p. 28), Richard-Strauss-Archiv.

Aufführungsrecht (Institute for Musical Performance Rights), a forerunner of modern licensing organizations.

Strauss collaborated closely with his publishers in the production of his printed music, often directly participating in the process of proofreading scores and parts. For instance, he was in direct contact with the C. G. Röder lithograph company in Leipzig, the production firm, concerning the string parts in *Also sprach Zarathustra*. As one would expect, Strauss also paid meticulous attention to the layout of his scores. For *Don Juan*, he prompted Spitzweg to print the full score in a larger format than *Aus Italien*, and for *Till Eulenspiegels lustige Streiche*, he demanded that the full score adhere as closely as possible to the pagination of his engraver's copy.[8]

Despite Strauss's desire for control over the process, his publishers sometimes made decisions independently or without his consent. Fürstner, for example, invited the American composer Otis Bardwell Boise to make "a few insignificant changes" to Strauss's *Mädchenblumen* Lieder. Boise added an English translation of the vocal texts as requested, but he also altered the piano part – in red ink directly in the autograph. This incensed Strauss. Ultimately, he accepted some interventions, but others, as he wrote to Fürstner, he would have "to reject most firmly." Nonetheless, this "compromise" version of the *Mädchenblumen* Lieder appeared in print. Strauss's request to Fürstner to produce a revised edition that corresponded exactly to the original manuscript remained unfulfilled until the publication of the critical edition in 2016 (see the penultimate paragraph of this chapter).[9] Another example is Ernst Roth's influence on the late works, notably his handling of the three *Gesänge von Hermann Hesse für hohe Singstimme mit Orchester* ("Frühling," "September," and "Beim Schlafengehen") and the setting of Eichendorff's *Im Abendrot*. Roth not only produced the piano reduction after Strauss's death but was also responsible for grouping the Lieder together and titling them *Vier letzte Lieder (Four Last Songs)*, which today are counted among Strauss's most significant compositions.

Strauss created a musical monument to his sometimes contentious relationships with music publishers in his *Krämerspiegel* song cycle, Op. 66. In 1906, Strauss had contractually promised 12 Lieder to Bote & Bock, but since he only delivered six (Op. 56), he still owed the publisher another half

---

[8] Letters to Eugen Spitzweg, October 27, 1896 and January 15, 1890; Münchner Stadtbibliothek, Monacensia, Strauss, Richard A I/92, and Strauss, Richard A I/44. Instructions to the publishing house and music engraver are pasted into the autograph score of *Till Eulenspiegels lustige Streiche*.

[9] Letters from Adolph Fürstner to Richard Strauss, November 6, 1890 and January 13, 1891, and Strauss to Fürstner, January 11 and 25, 1891, Richard-Strauss-Archiv.

dozen. Strauss composed no more Lieder until 1918, however. When he resumed song composition in that year, he refrained from offering the publishing house the six Brentano Lieder (Op. 68) due to a conflict with Hugo Bock regarding copyright issues. Instead, he set 12 satirical poems commissioned from the Berlin theater critic Alfred Kerr and aimed at music publishers, which became the *Krämerspiegel*. Bote & Bock, however, refused to accept them, and other music publishers showed solidarity. Even the public presentation of *Krämerspiegel* was banned for several years. Strauss was legally obliged to deliver "six proper Lieder." The songs he finally submitted, of the mad Ophelia from Shakespeare's *Hamlet* and from the *Buch des Unmuts* (*Book of Disgust*) from Goethe's *West-östlicher Diwan*, in their awkwardness, likely also displeased the publishing house. This time, however, Bote & Bock could raise no objections because Strauss Lieder on texts by Shakespeare and Goethe would be perceived as "proper" by all. The rejected *Krämerspiegel* finally came out in 1921, furnished with etchings by Michel Fingesten in a deluxe edition from Paul Cassirer, who, as an art publisher, was outside the music world.[10]

Editions

Lieder, one of Strauss's most important creative outlets, appeared in a variety of editions over the decades due to their great appeal to performers and music lovers. Whereas the early prints were restricted to the original language and vocal range, transposed versions and editions with poetic translations in other languages, especially English, soon appeared. Later printings often contained editorial modifications to the musical text. From time to time, there were special publications of individual Lieder, such as prints in magazines and bibliophile facsimile albums. (Large works, such as *Tod und Verklärung*, also appeared in such facsimiles.) Along with the editions of specific Lieder came anthologies; Universal Edition's Lieder albums I–IV achieved an especially wide circulation with numerous printings. During the 1940s, Strauss was personally involved in the preparation of a complete edition of his Lieder for C. F. Peters and Universal Edition, but the project was left incomplete.[11]

---

[10] See Hartmut Schick, "Musikalische Satiren über Kunst und Kommerz: Richard Strauss' Liederzyklus Krämerspiegel op. 66," in Bayerische Akademie der Schönen Künste, Jahrbuch 26 (2012) (Göttingen: Wallstein, 2013), 107–27.

[11] See the Richard Strauss correspondence with Kurt Soldan and with C. F. Peters and Universal Edition; Münchner Stadtbibliothek, Monacensia, Strauss, Richard A III/7–13, Richard-Strauss-Archiv; Universal Edition Vienna, Sächsisches Staatsarchiv Leipzig, inventory 21070 C. F. Peters.

Also for large-scale operas and instrumental works, publication was by no means exhausted by the first editions. The early tone poems were already issued in pocket scores (i.e., re-engraved in small format) by the Eulenburg publishing house; examples include *Macbeth* and *Don Juan* in 1904. Hence, it would have been possible to rectify errors from the first prints and to involve Strauss in that process, but whether such collaboration took place is unknown. It is certain, however, that Strauss himself used these small scores, since in 1908 he asked Ernst Eulenburg to send him the entire Strauss catalog for his personal library in Garmisch.

Numerous arrangements of works also circulated. Strauss undertook some Lied orchestrations himself, while others were completed by Felix Mottl or Robert Heger. Added to this are the well-known Lied transcriptions for piano by Reger, Otto Taubmann, and Walter Gieseking, as well as Lied arrangements for instrumental ensembles (for salon or mandolin orchestras, for example). Instrumental works were also rearranged, such as the Serenade for Winds, Op. 7 for harmonium and piano. Strauss scores intended for music connoisseurs, such as the series *Musik für Alle* (*Music for All*), contained tone poem excerpts arranged for piano (for example the opening of *Also sprach Zarathustra*), original piano pieces, Lied transcriptions, and opera excerpts for solo piano (notated with vocal texts). Also quite attractive were various arrangements of tone poems for smaller orchestras; *Don Juan*, for instance, was arranged for chamber and salon orchestra by Emil Baur.

Strauss himself prepared orchestral arrangements of some stage works, such as the widely performed *Rosenkavalier* suite. Both the major orchestral pieces and the operas appeared in complete piano reductions, many arranged by Otto Singer, with some others by Strauss's friend Ludwig Thuille in the early years. Since Strauss composed many of his operas for very large ensembles, scaled-down versions were produced for smaller opera houses. In some instances, as with Singer's *Elektra* reduction, we know that Strauss collaborated in the process. In others, this is difficult to determine. Revised editions to correct well-known errors also appeared, such as the *Rosenkavalier* edition by the conductor Clemens Krauss, published in 1938 with the claim that Strauss was involved.

Some of the pieces Strauss considered as part of his estate of unpublished works, such as the *Vier letzte Lieder* and the Second Horn Concerto, came on the market soon after his death. Subsequent anniversaries in the decades that followed gave rise to important publications. Franz Trenner produced a four-volume Lieder edition for what would have been Strauss's 100th birthday, supplemented in 1968 by Willi Schuh's *Nachlese*; together, they contain nearly all of the Strauss Lieder, even the juvenilia.

Various editions of hitherto unpublished works and other manuscripts appeared later, frequently also as facsimiles, such as *Wir beide wollen springen, Wer hat's gethan?*, *Malven*, the *Particell* of *Im Abendrot*, the composer's late handwritten copies of the *Till Eulenspiegel* score, Introduction, Theme, and Variations in E Flat and Andante (both for horn and piano), Zwei kleine Stücke for piano, and so on.

The *Richard-Strauss-Edition* appeared 50 years after Strauss's death, combining in 50 volumes the bulk of his oeuvre in a large, impressive edition, but merely reproducing the old prints for the most part. The fact that no complete scholarly edition existed may be related to the fact that postwar music research largely ignored Strauss, likely due to his traditional style and seemingly ambivalent role during the Third Reich. After the turn of the millennium, Christian Wolf generated several first editions of Strauss's piano works as well as the first edition of the youthful Lied *Aus der Kindheit*.

Underway since 2011 as a project of the Bayerische Akademie der Wissenschaften (Bavarian Academy of Sciences and Humanities) has been the *Kritische Ausgabe der Werke von Richard Strauss* (*Critical Edition of the Works of Richard Strauss*). This long-term project is producing edited volumes of Strauss's main works for the first time using the methods of modern critical scholarship while also making other hitherto unknown pieces and versions publicly available. The edition is based on evaluation of all accessible sources from the composer's lifetime: autographs, transcriptions, prints of full scores and orchestral parts, piano reductions, and historical performance materials that Strauss himself used, some of which contain informative handwritten annotations. Another indispensable resource in this process is the composer's extensive correspondence; the editors are consulting the many thousands of letters to and from publishers, poets, friends and relatives, conductors, musicians, and concert promoters to inform their work. Some of the most interesting documents, including historical reviews and the texts of his vocal works, appear on the online platform www.richard-strauss-ausgabe.de.

Following the expiration of the copyright term at the end of 2019, other editions are likely to come onto the market. Even publishers who previously had no rights to print Strauss's music will have the opportunity to add works by the globally popular composer to their portfolio. This has already occurred in some countries, as demonstrated by the complete edition of Strauss's Lieder by the Japanese firm Zen-On. The Munich publisher G. Henle followed in early 2020 with new editions of works, such as the Violin Sonata, Op. 18. Seventy years after his death, it is an interesting time for Strauss and his music.

CHAPTER 32

Letters

Claudia Heine and Adrian Kech
(Translation by Margit L. McCorkle)

Flowing through Strauss's letters is the fresh air of objectivity that includes the simply apt word, the most succinct expression. This objectivity is arguably the most prominent characteristic of the Straussian letter. [...] The letters, however, only seldom offer glimpses into the intellectual-spiritual experience. Discussing insights and feelings, retrospectively analyzing inner experiences, or explaining his intellectual development was never Strauss's thing (7–8, 11).

Willi Schuh concluded thus in the introduction to his 1954 edition of Richard Strauss's *Briefe an die Eltern*. Schuh, a Swiss music journalist whom Strauss himself appointed as his biographer, here named two essential points that still to this day define the framework for assessing the composer's written correspondence. On the one hand, the Strauss letter language is clear, straightforward, simple, often pointed, and provocative. For these reasons, it is entertaining and enjoyable in passages, well suited for public readings, and convenient to quote (still done extensively in research and elsewhere). On the other hand, most of the Strauss letters reveal the inscrutability described by Schuh. Apart from the fact that "Strauss's own statements could be very contradictory and were either impulsive in nature or arose from strategic considerations," they do, generally speaking, dispense with any kind of introspection.[1] Even Strauss's private memoranda, in contrast to his utterances to others, display the composer's sense of objective distance from himself and his work despite his partisanship for certain aesthetic or politico-cultural positions.

Quantitatively, Strauss's written correspondence consists of many thousands of documents. The publicly-known portion is extensive indeed, even without approximating the total inventory: edited today are some 8,000 letters, postcards, and telegrams to and from the composer. Hitherto

---

[1] Wolfgang Rathert, "Strauss und die Musikwissenschaft," in *Richard Strauss Handbuch*, ed. Walter Werbeck (Stuttgart: Metzler, 2014), 540.

untapped, however, is more than that amount of material held in various archives and libraries. Particularly noteworthy here is the family-owned Richard-Strauss-Archiv (RSA) in Garmisch, which houses the largest share of Straussiana worldwide, including the greatest quantity of letters written to the composer. An official, even if only fairly complete catalog of Strauss's correspondence, both published and unpublished, is still an urgent research desideratum.[2] This chapter aims to contextualize the extant materials by focusing on issues such as access, chronology, editorial standards, and dissemination.

Published Correspondence

Publication of Strauss's correspondence, of which only a small portion has been translated from German, began already during his lifetime (see the Appendix for a list of published correspondence organized alphabetically by correspondent). The first proper edition of Strauss's letters, significant apart from the disclosure of occasional individual letters (or excerpts from them), was his correspondence with Hugo von Hofmannsthal, provided in 1926 by his son Franz Strauss. Hofmannsthal summed up the authors' objectives on May 4, 1925: "to make evident, on the one hand, the seriousness of our joint labours; to avail ourselves, on the other, of the casual commentary provided by the letters to remedy the lack of understanding still shown for some of our works" (538).[3] Publishing the exchange of letters of "living authors operating within the brightest light of the public eye" (6), of course, necessitated some restrictions. Confining themselves to a selection of letters from 1907–18, they removed everything that, as Hofmannsthal stressed, could have provided "ammunition for stupidity and malice" and furnished "fuel for fresh misunderstandings" (540–41). Provided that certain letters were not completely withheld,

---

[2] Whereas a research project carried out in the 1990s at the University of Bochum to prepare a catalog of Strauss letters did not get beyond the initial unpublished approaches, the *Richard-Strauss-Quellenverzeichnis* (rsi-rsqv.de; published in 2011) created a new standard in the area of Strauss source documentation. Its focus is not on the correspondence documents, however, but on musical sources such as scores and sketches. *Kalliope* (kalliope.staatsbibliothek-berlin.de) supplies some 1,700 hits for Strauss (query data: "richard strauss" as of May 2019).

[3] *The Correspondence between Richard Strauss and Hugo von Hofmannsthal*, trans. Hanns Hammelmann and Ewald Osers (Cambridge: Cambridge University Press, 1980), 401–2. Since this most current English edition, first published in 1961 by William Collins Sons & Co., is a translation of the second German edition of 1955, the remaining quotations and all parenthetical page numbers are from Richard Strauss and Hugo von Hofmannsthal, *Briefwechsel*, ed. Willi Schuh (Munich & Mainz: Piper & Schott, 1990), which uses the text of the fifth and most recent German edition of 1978.

"numerous passages of a mostly personal nature were deleted, certain names omitted or disguised, harsh remarks toned down, and much else" (6). Another edition from Strauss's lifetime is his correspondence with Hermann Bahr, published – including drafts of *Intermezzo* – by Joseph Gregor in 1947 as part of Anna Bahr-Mildenburg's estate that had entered the collection of the Austrian National Library.

Strauss's *Betrachtungen und Erinnerungen* (*Recollections and Reflections*) was published by Schuh in 1949, still before the composer's death. For this volume, Schuh collected memoranda, some of which were extant only in manuscript form, as well as articles, prefaces, open letters, and other opinion pieces by Strauss that had appeared elsewhere over the course of half a century. Expanded in 1957, the volume stands today as essential research material. Strauss himself did, however, criticize the publication, complaining to Schuh that he had "completely uncritically" edited "such and such" hitherto unpublished records, "written absolutely *carelessly* and *not ready for publication*, [...] which I would have heavily revised and would possibly not even have included in the little book."[4]

The first years after Strauss's death yielded numerous editions, including the so-called *Werkstattbriefe* (workshop letters): the composer in written dialogue with his librettists Hugo von Hofmannsthal (1952), Joseph Gregor (1955), and Stefan Zweig (1957). Published in addition to the above-mentioned selection of letters to his parents (1954), which Schuh had already prepared in 1942, were also various correspondences with prominent contemporaries, such as Romain Rolland (1951), Ernst von Schuch (1952), Hans von Bülow (1953), Johann Leopold Bella (1955), Franz Wüllner (1963), and Clemens Krauss (1963) – the latter Strauss's coauthor of the *Capriccio* libretto. Then followed the anthology *Die Welt um Richard Strauss in Briefen* (1967), published by Franz Grasberger in collaboration with Franz and Alice Strauss, Alfons Ott's edition of Strauss's letters to Ludwig Thuille (1969), which includes a wealth of facsimiles, and the correspondence with Willi Schuh (1969), edited by Schuh himself. Important additions to the editions of letters were the collection *Richard Strauss: Dokumente seines Lebens und Schaffens* (1954), edited by Franz Trenner, and the comprehensive, three-volume works catalog by Erich H. Mueller von Asow (1959–74). Heavily augmented by letter quotations, the latter was completed posthumously by Trenner and Ott.

In summary, the letter editions up to the end of the 1960s can be described as pioneering. Striking here is the central role of Willi Schuh,

---

[4] Richard Strauss, *Briefwechsel mit Willi Schuh*, ed. Willi Schuh (Zurich: Atlantis, 1969), 179f.

who was directly or indirectly involved in many of the publications. Although most of the editions fall short of today's editorial standards, some, for lack of better alternatives, remain indispensable for the foreseeable future. In this regard, the Hofmannsthal correspondence is paradigmatic. Though there is still no critical edition, the "complete edition" – it was conceived as such and so declared from the outset – has over time been subject to ongoing additions and corrections resulting from newly discovered documents. From 1952 to 1978 the correspondence went through five editions, with the third edition of 1964 unquestionably signifying the largest breakthrough. Schuh, only the editorial arranger of the correspondence in the previous issues published by Franz and Alice Strauss, officially became the editor and produced a quantitatively as well as qualitatively improved edition. Added to the 532 already published letters were another 86; Schuh, moreover, who until then had worked mainly from transcriptions, now had access to the originals. His handling of these still not easily accessible documents illustrates both the value and the limitations of his edition. It is true that "careless copying errors, misread words, and other errors, but also inadvertent omissions" (7) are corrected on the basis of the originals, but at the same time "the spelling is modernized to current usage, and minor careless errors were tacitly corrected. Proper names are always spelled correctly" (9). In short, the original text of the documents, available for the first time, immediately fell victim to editorial smoothing.

In publishing the correspondence, the interests of Strauss's descendants still had (and have) to be considered. For instance, Schuh points out in the third edition of the Hofmannsthal correspondence that the "passages hitherto suppressed out of personal considerations – among them many rather extensive ones – are now included" (7), but "excluded again this time, according to the wishes of Dr. Franz Strauss, were the passages relating purely to business matters" (8). Whereas Schuh at least identified these omissions with ellipses, some passages were tacitly omitted from letters published three years later in *Die Welt um Richard Strauss in Briefen.*[5] After all, it was not primarily a scholarly edition, but, according to Franz Strauss's preface, intended to commemorate his father's "comprehensive personality, touching all realms of an intellectual life" (ix).

The *Veröffentlichungen der Richard-Strauss-Gesellschaft München* headed by Trenner provided new impetus from 1977. Born in Munich, he was a high school teacher and thus not a full-time musicologist, but like Schuh, a spare-time researcher in the best sense. He also belonged to the circle of

[5] Walter Werbeck, *Die Tondichtungen von Richard Strauss* (Tutzing: Hans Schneider, 1996), 5.

those "unperturbed by the zeitgeist" who published about Strauss at a time when scholars avoided him as a subject of academic inquiry in the aftermath of World War II.[6] In collaboration with Wolfgang Sawallisch and Alfons Ott, Trenner founded the Richard-Strauss-Gesellschaft (RSG) in Munich in 1976; with the new series of publications, he laid the foundation for more professional editions of letters and other Strauss materials. As the programmatic starting volume, he published a summary of the Strauss sketchbooks in Garmisch, but due to Sawallisch's preferences, the focus from the outset was on Strauss's correspondence with his contemporaries. Over the following decades, different editors published the correspondence with Cosima Wagner (1978), Ludwig Thuille (1980), Franz Schalk (1983), Rudolf Hartmann (1984), Max von Schillings (1987), Romain Rolland (1994), Ernst von Schuch (1999), and various conductors and composers (three volumes: 1996, 1998, and 2004). There were also inventories of Strauss autographs in Munich and Vienna (1979), Lied texts (1986), reviews of the premieres of the stage works (1989), and a works catalog updated by Trenner (1993). Added later were the proceedings of Strauss conferences held in Munich (2001) and Bochum (2005) and, more recently, *Richard Strauss: Sein Leben und Werk im Spiegel der zeitgenössischen Karikatur* (2009) and *Späte Aufzeichnungen* (2016).

Important independent editions (that is, outside of the RSG series) were Strauss's correspondence with Gustav Mahler (1980 and 1988), Clemens Krauss (1997), and Karl Böhm (1999). The new edition of the Krauss correspondence rectified a situation typical of many earlier editions; whereas the 1963 first edition by Götz Klaus Kende and Schuh had still eliminated everything "that cannot claim any general interest and contribute to our understanding of the relationship between the two men" (5), Günter Brosche now presented the available documents "in an absolutely unabridged and unaltered form" (6) and furthermore in the original orthography. Also appearing in 2003 was Trenner's extensive Strauss chronicle, the publication of which its author did not live to see. Trenner died in 1992, and his son Florian took over the editing of the volume, drawing its information largely from the correspondence.

Not to be overlooked are three other groups of editions. First, a considerable portion of the Strauss correspondence was edited as contributions to periodicals, notably in the publications of the Internationale Richard-Strauss-Gesellschaft (IRSG) in Vienna (now based in Salzburg). For instance, the correspondence with Ludwig Karpath (1975–76),

---

[6] See Bernd Edelmann, "Gegen Strauss' Verdammnis," *Akademie Aktuell* 37, no. 2 (2011): 36–39.

Gerhart Hauptmann (1983), Alfred Kerr (1998), and Hugo Reichenberger (2004) was published in the *Richard Strauss-Blätter* while several newly discovered letters to Ernst von Schuch as well as the correspondence with Karl Lion (both 2012) appeared in the *Richard Strauss-Jahrbuch*. Second, some letters only appear – partly listed, partly transcribed – in the catalogs of Strauss exhibitions, especially in the publications from Vienna (1964) and Munich (1964 and 1999). And third, there are the publications of correspondence in writings and works not concerned primarily with Strauss but focusing on his respondent, especially the critical Hofmannsthal edition with its volumes for *Arabella* (1976), *Rosenkavalier* (1986), *Elektra* (1997), *Frau ohne Schatten* (1998), *Ägyptische Helena* (2001), and *Ariadne auf Naxos* (first version, 2006; second version, 1985).

New musicological editions emerged after 1980 as interest in Strauss as a subject of scholarly inquiry increased. But in many cases, the documentation of sources concerning the correspondence and other written material remained imprecise; editions with evidence for each individual document – such as the Schuch correspondence presented by Gabriella Hanke Knaus or the *Späte Aufzeichnungen* edited by Marion Beyer, Jürgen May, and Werbeck – are exceptions that prove the rule. The evidence in other editions is merely general or can be derived only indirectly at best; for example, the Trenner chronicle lists a multitude of sources but rarely indicates from where a specific piece of information was gleaned. Trenner thus perpetuated what already had been rightly criticized in Schuh's Strauss biography of 1976, namely, that verification of his information without specific source evidence was occasionally quite tedious, if not impossible.[7] One type of information in this Trenner source is an exception according to its preface: the citations are, unless otherwise noted, taken from Strauss's own calendars.

Unpublished Correspondence

Taking into account only previous editions and other published evidence, Strauss's correspondence partners would seem to number about 400. In reality there are many more, as evidenced by an internal, semi-official card index in the RSA. Created and maintained by Strauss's daughter-in-law Alice, who ran the archive until her death in 1991, this index contains a wealth of information, primarily about on-site correspondence, but also concerning letters located in reproduction in the RSA whose originals are kept elsewhere. Alice Strauss indexed the vast correspondence alphabetically by person or

[7] Werbeck, 5.

institution – whether in direct communication with Richard Strauss or simply mentioned in the correspondence. For many people, she recorded data on their occupation, location, and the like in keywords, while noting for those only mentioned where they are named. The completeness of the index is unknown, but it proves direct written contact with Strauss for about 1,600 names. It is important to note that this is an index focused on the RSA holdings; what exists unedited elsewhere is not necessarily covered by it.

The number of previously unpublished documents from the RSA varies widely from one correspondent partner to another. Whereas for some people the existing material is sparse, others involve large inventories. Amongst the vast correspondence not yet edited is that with his family and his publishers, especially with the Fürstners (Adolph and Otto) and with Johannes Oertel. Based on RSA catalogs and personal on-site inspection, the total volume can be estimated at least roughly.[8] Archived in 31 folders, the family correspondence in which Strauss directly participated comprises about 4,800 documents (specifically: letters to or from his parents Franz and Josephine, sister Johanna, wife Pauline, son Franz, daughter-in-law Alice, and grandsons Richard and Christian). By comparison, printed editions and catalogs currently hold slightly more than 700 family letters – just 15 percent of the total inventory estimated here – and the letters from Strauss's direct milieu, such as Pauline's correspondence with her parents, are not even considered. Strauss's letters to Fürstner and Oertel together fill six folders with almost 1,600 documents from 1885 to 1949. In addition, there are another 2,000 letters from the Fürstner publishing house to Strauss from the same period (although the inventory before 1910 is full of gaps). Though mentioned in the Alice Strauss card index, these letters, which are mostly copies of typescripts, could not be located at the RSA until the summer of 2016. According to the card index, they arrived there from "Frau Ursula Fürstner in 1970 as a gift." In addition to the extensive holdings of the RSA, a large quantity of unpublished correspondence is located in Munich, including partly unpublished volumes at the Bavarian State Library (siglum: Ana 330) and the Munich City Library.

The total quantity of previously unpublished Strauss correspondence worldwide is thus plainly inestimable, owing to the lack of catalogs.[9] Aside

---

[8] Insofar as the Strauss family and publishing-house correspondence could be examined by the authors, it was usually as paper copies since, with a few exceptions, the originals were previously inaccessible.

[9] See Claudia Heine, "Objekte von ideellem und materiellem Wert. Wege der Überlieferung von Strauss-Autografen in die USA," in *Richard Strauss. Der Komponist und sein Werk. Überlieferung, Interpretation, Rezeption. Bericht über das internationale Symposium zum 150. Geburtstag, München,*

from the fact that an uncertain number of original documents are in unknown private possession, Strauss sources, including letters, postcards, etc., are still being traded at auctions and via antiquarian booksellers. Estimating reliably the number of items is not possible for the time being. If these documents are not purchased by public institutions or by the Strauss descendants for the family archive, they become quite difficult to trace, with many available only at auctions and through catalogs and meta-catalogs such as the *Jahrbuch der Auktionspreise* and *American Book Prices Current*. Further, a certain percentage of Strauss sources must simply be considered lost or destroyed. Important stages of Strauss's life, such as relocations, his extensive travel in Europe and overseas, and historical events such as the two world wars certainly led to some irrecoverable losses.

Outlook

Wolfgang Rathert rightly stated in the *Richard Strauss Handbuch* of 2014 that the "evaluation of the extensive and complex source situation [. . .], pertaining to primary texts (letters, autographs) and reception documents, is still far from complete."[10] Currently, Strauss research is in an upheaval phase stemming, on the one hand, from technical advancements in editing. Following the online publication of the *Richard-Strauss-Quellenverzeichnis* (rsi-rsqv.de) of 2011, the *Kritische Ausgabe der Werke von Richard Strauss*, established the same year, now presents part of its data in a digital format. Whereas the music volumes appear in classically printed form, the project's online platform (richard-strauss-ausgabe.de), activated in 2017, offers an accompanying inventory of selected documents, the scope of which is expected to increase with the growing number of edited volumes.[11] On the other hand, the scholarly discourse around Strauss has gained considerable momentum, and this has had an indirect effect on the demand for quality editions of writings and letters. The *Richard-Strauss-Ausgabe*, for example, discloses the basis of its transcription for each individual letter edited and, if it is a singular document (original

---

26.–28. *Juni 2014*, ed. Sebastian Bolz, Adrian Kech, and Hartmut Schick (Munich: Allitera, 2017), 533–39, especially 535, with a preliminary and yet incomplete listing of the holdings in New York, Chicago, Washington, D.C., and New Haven (Yale University).

[10] Rathert, "Strauss und die Musikwissenschaft," 540.

[11] The *Richard-Strauss-Ausgabe* thus stands alongside other hybrid editions, such as the *Carl-Maria-von-Weber-Gesamtausgabe* (weber-gesamtausgabe.de), which is likewise published in a printed as well as digital edition. Both aim to increase data networking, for example, within the context of *correspSearch* (correspsearch.net).

or reproduction), its location and examination date as well. This sets a new standard of source transparency for later editions with academic aspirations.

How many "unimportant" letters were discarded in earlier editions – whether to limit the quantity of published documents or to give the edition a better reading flow – is hard to gauge. Which letter is important and which is not is always context-dependent. A brief note in which Strauss informs the addressee of his current whereabouts may at first glance seem less interesting than the detailed description of a concert experience, and some people may find less enjoyment from reading a conductor's friendly refusal than from a pointed rant. But even insignificant particulars, such as location details or a conducting refusal, can indirectly inform other events, by elucidating, for instance, the course of a particular time or events. From a scholarly point of view, it is therefore of the utmost relevance that in the future also the "unimportant," that is, the superficially insignificant letters and notes, are made accessible according to modern edition principles – no matter the media, whether in print or online.

CHAPTER 33

In Performance

Raymond Holden

Whether it be *Ein Heldenleben* or *Salome*, *Metamorphosen* or *Ariadne auf Naxos*, *Eine Alpensinfonie* or *Der Rosenkavalier*, Richard Strauss's works are benchmarks of orchestral and vocal excellence that are now central to many artists' repertoires. Audiences flock to be touched and thrilled by their beauty and daring, orchestras and opera houses love the technical challenges they present, and recording companies clamor for the opportunity to include them in their discographies. It is a fascinating exercise, therefore, to examine the frequency with which Strauss's works were performed by his contemporaries and successors and to explore the role his compositions played within the performance aesthetics of individuals and institutions. This chapter examines performance data relating to selected musicians, orchestras, opera houses, and recording companies and the ways in which it reflects trends in Strauss performance.[1] To understand the genesis and context of that process fully, it is essential to consider how the composer-conductor placed these works within his own programming policy.

Orchestras and Opera Houses

Accused wrongly of simply being interested in marketing his own musical wares at the expense of others, Strauss did much to promote the next generation of composers and was a passionate advocate of Mozart, Beethoven, and Wagner. Given Strauss's undeniable credentials as a podium artist and the remarkable popularity of his music, he was almost inevitably in constant demand to perform his symphonic works as a guest conductor.

[1] Several venues and ensembles with rich histories of performing Strauss's works maintain digital archives of performances. See for instance the Vienna State Opera (https://archiv.wiener-staatsoper .at), Metropolitan Opera (http://archives.metoperafamily.org), Vienna Philharmonic (www .wienerphilharmoniker.at/converts/archive), and New York Philharmonic (https://archives.nyphil .org/performancehistory).

Such requests were undoubtedly flattering and lucrative but quickly lost their appeal. Bored by the prospect of being asked constantly to conduct his music as a visiting artist, he ensured that his own works were an integral, rather than a dominant, part of the subscription series he led as a tenured musician. At his 27 concerts with the Munich Court Orchestra and the Berlin Philharmonic (1894–96), for example, Strauss programmed only two works of his own creation. Of the 125 concerts with his beloved Berlin Court Orchestra (1908–20), only 30 featured his music. This might seem a relatively high figure, but he also gave a staggering 36 first performances and an impressive 18 premieres by 15 composers. In the opera house, Strauss again balanced his own interests with his wider responsibilities; during his time at the Berlin Court/State Opera, 165 of the 922 operatic performances were of his own works.

As a court orchestra, the Berlin Court Orchestra divided its time between the opera pit and the concert stage. Subject to the artistic whim of the notoriously conservative Emperor, and conducted previously by Strauss's professional nemesis, Felix Weingartner, the Court Orchestra presented just three of Strauss's works between 1891 and 1908. Across town at the Berlin Philharmonic, Strauss's music fared only marginally better. During its early years, the subscription concerts were directed by the composer's great friend and mentor, Hans von Bülow. While he recognized Strauss's obvious talent, he struggled with his protégé's emerging compositional style and was reluctant to include Strauss's works in his Berlin programs. That was also true of his subscription concerts in Meiningen, Bremen, and Hamburg, where he performed Strauss's compositions on only six occasions.[2]

When Arthur Nikisch took the helm of the Berlin Philharmonic in 1895, Strauss's music was programmed more regularly with 28 of the 258 concerts containing a tone poem, but of the 569 concerts he conducted with the Gewandhaus Orchestra in Leipzig, only four contained one. At his earlier appointment as Music Director of the Boston Symphony Orchestra, Nikisch conducted just two performances of *Don Juan* at the 190 performances of 95 programs he gave in the city between 1889–93.

Strauss worked as a tenured conductor in Berlin for more than two decades, but Vienna occupied a special place in his personal and professional affections. While Strauss was never in charge of the Vienna

---

[2] This figure does not include Bülow's activities as a touring musician or concerts he gave with the Meiningen Court Orchestra on tour.

Philharmonic's subscription concerts, he did perform with it on 106 occasions between 1906 and 1944. After Mahler took up the Philharmonic baton in 1898, the Bavarian's works were sidelined; consumed by the need to champion his own music, Mahler only performed extracts from *Guntram* and *Aus Italien* with the orchestra. When Weingartner took over its subscription concerts in 1908, he bowed to popular pressure by giving at least 17 performances of nine works by Strauss during his 19-year engagement. These included all of the tone poems and an increasingly rare performance of the F-minor Symphony. In 1930, Clemens Krauss became the last of the Vienna Philharmonic's tenured conductors and a close friend of Strauss. For many, Krauss was Strauss's true musical heir and the conductor who best reflected the composer's artistic intentions, and yet their Vienna recordings of the tone poems differ markedly. Nevertheless, Krauss was proud to have been associated with Strauss and conducted his works on 121 occasions with the Philharmonic.

By the time of Strauss's conducting debut with the New York Philharmonic in 1904, the orchestra already had a long association with his music. The American orchestra gave the world premiere of his Symphony in F Minor under Theodore Thomas on December 13, 1884, and in the following decades, performances of the Serenade Op. 7, *Macbeth, Tod und Verklärung, Till Eulenspiegel,* and *Ein Heldenleben* were given by a string of conductors. With Mahler's appointment as Music Director in 1909, Strauss's works attained a more prominent place on the Philharmonic's Carnegie Hall and touring schedules. In contrast to the paucity of Strauss performances that Mahler gave in Vienna, he conducted at least 28 performances of eight works during his two-year tenure. When Willem Mengelberg took charge of the orchestra in 1922, Strauss's artistic profile rose still further. A joint dedicatee of *Ein Heldenleben,* Mengelberg had a strong personal connection with the composer's music. As principal conductor of the Concertgebouw Orchestra of Amsterdam, he programmed Strauss's music at 591 concerts between 1895 and 1945. While that staggering figure was not replicated in New York, Mengelberg did direct 130 performances of Strauss's works with the Philharmonic.

This stands in sharp contrast to the activities of Arturo Toscanini, who struggled with Strauss's personal and artistic *Weltanschauungen.* From 1928–37, he led 60 Philharmonic performances of six works by Strauss, 21 of which were of *Tod und Verklärung.* When Toscanini moved to the NBC Symphony Orchestra in 1937, he conducted only 25 performances of the same six compositions: *Don Juan, Tod und Verklärung, Till Eulenspiegel, Don Quixote, Ein Heldenleben* and *Salome's* dance. His response to the composer's stage works revealed his true feelings about Strauss's music: having given an early performance of *Salome* at Milan in 1906, Toscanini refused to conduct any of the later operas and was particularly scathing about *Arabella*.

During the immediate pre-war years, Bruno Walter, Otto Klemperer, and Wilhelm Furtwängler dominated Berlin's musical landscape. As Generalmusikdirektor at the Städtische Oper, the Kroll Opera, and the Berlin Philharmonic, respectively, they represented something of a golden period for the city. While Walter and Klemperer performed multiple readings of most of the composer's tone poems and a handful of his operas, they shied away from *Ein Heldenleben*. Whether they found the tone poem itself or the idea of Strauss as hero unpalatable, the composer's perceived relationship with Germany's emergent fascist regime did much to color their personal and professional responses to him. Conversely, Furtwängler seems to have openly embraced *Ein Heldenleben* and programmed it at his concerts in Berlin, Leipzig, and New York. He also confirmed his affinity with Strauss by adopting *Don Juan* as his musical calling card, performing the work at his debut with the Berlin Philharmonic in 1917 and at his first performances with the Royal Philharmonic Society in London and the Philharmonic in New York in 1924 and 1925.

With the fall of fascism and the advent of the jet age, a new breed of global superstar conductors emerged. Among them, Herbert von Karajan and Leonard Bernstein dominated this brave new world and used the fast-moving advances in audio and televisual technology to spread their artistic messages and champion the music they cherished most. Despite their very different cultural and personal backgrounds, they both performed a Strauss tone poem at their professional debuts.[3] Their aesthetics diverged as their careers progressed, however, and Karajan was later increasingly associated with the music of Strauss. Having performed *Elektra* from memory in the presence of the composer in Berlin in 1940, Karajan was quickly recognized as a Straussian of standing and eventually directed some 450 performances of the composer's works. Bernstein peppered his New York Philharmonic concerts with Strauss's music but performed only one of his works with the Vienna Philharmonic, the orchestra with which Bernstein became increasingly associated from the late 1960s. That said,

[3] Karajan conducted *Don Juan* with the Salzburg Mozarteum Orchestra on January 22, 1929 and Bernstein conducted *Don Quixote* with the New York Philharmonic on November 14, 1943. While Karajan conducted *Don Juan* by choice, Bernstein famously substituted at short notice for an indisposed Bruno Walter in a program that already contained *Don Quixote*.

he did give eight memorable performances of *Der Rosenkavalier* at the Vienna State Opera (1968–71) that were the bases for a remarkable CBS recording of the work.[4]

Munich, Berlin, and Vienna can all lay artistic claim to Strauss, but London attracted him as guest conductor for an unparalleled 50-year period: 1897–1947. During that time, he worked closely with three of its most distinguished conductors – Sir Henry Wood, Sir Thomas Beecham, and Sir Adrian Boult – and performed at its leading institutions. As a passionate advocate of new music, Wood quickly recognized the importance of Strauss's works and was instrumental in arranging the local premieres of *Ein Heldenleben* and *Symphonia domestica*. Beecham staged the first British performances of *Feuersnot*, *Salome*, *Elektra*, *Ariadne auf Naxos* (1912 version), and *Der Rosenkavalier*, and with Ernst Roth of Boosey & Hawkes, he later organized a Strauss festival in London at which the composer shared the podium with Boult.

Of the next generation of British conductors, Sir John Pritchard and Norman Del Mar did most to disseminate Strauss's compositions. Del Mar wrote a much-discussed three-volume study of the composer's music, while Pritchard gave many critically acclaimed performances of Strauss's works with orchestras and opera houses on both sides of the Atlantic.[5] But not all British conductors have found the composer's music totally convincing, and no doubt some would agree with Sir Mark Elder when he opined:

> Did [Strauss] write a truly great work? Even though he was a brilliant purveyor of beautiful sounds, and dressed up his ideas with consummate skills, I think that his importance lies in a series of very great moments rather than whole works ... He was like a head-waiter who knew how to serve with ease and panache ... [Of] course, orchestras love playing [his] music, as he not only writes marvellous parts for individual instruments but knows how to integrate them into the whole.[6]

Whether or not Strauss was simply "a head-waiter who knew how to serve with ease and panache" is of little importance to opera companies. Outside the German-speaking countries, Britain's opera houses were amongst the first to recognize the importance of Strauss's stage works with

---

[4] Currently available as Sony 7527322.
[5] Norman Del Mar, *Richard Strauss: A Critical Commentary on His Life and Works* (London: Faber & Faber, 1986).
[6] Raymond Holden, *Elder on Music: Sir Mark Elder in Conversation with Raymond Holden* (London: Royal Academy of Music Press, 2019).

the Royal Opera House, Covent Garden, performing them regularly from the end of the first decade of the twentieth century. From the start, Strauss's operas were not only popular but also lucrative financially, resulting in a total of 93 performances divided among *Der Rosenkavalier* (45), *Salome* (21), *Elektra* (20), the 1916 version of *Ariadne auf Naxos* (3), and *Arabella* (4) between 1910 and 1938. From those statistics, the clear favorite was *Der Rosenkavalier*, and Lotte Lehmann dominated the Covent Garden stage as the Marschallin during that period. In the years following the World War II, the Royal Opera House gave 10 of Strauss's 15 operas, extending its repertoire to include *Die Frau ohne Schatten, Die ägyptische Helena, Die schweigsame Frau, Daphne*, and *Capriccio*. But *Die ägyptische Helena, Die schweigsame Frau, Daphne*, and *Capriccio* were only heard on one occasion each, with the latter two given as concert performances. Of the 306 performances of Strauss's operas at Covent Garden from 1947, the clear favorite was again *Der Rosenkavalier* with 104 performances. *Elektra* and *Salome* also proved popular, with 53 and 58 performances respectively.

At the Vienna Court Opera, the first Strauss opera to be given was *Feuersnot* in 1902 followed by *Elektra* in 1909. *Der Rosenkavalier* was heard in Vienna for the first time in 1909, and, in 1916 and 1919 respectively, the company staged the world premieres of *Ariadne auf Naxos* (the 1916 version) and *Die Frau ohne Schatten*. After its scandalous first performance at the Dresden Court Opera in 1905, *Salome* proved too shocking for Vienna's local censor, resulting in its first appearance at the Court Opera being delayed until 1918. Consequently, its Austrian premiere was given at provincial Graz in 1906 and conducted by the composer. As of early 2019, the Vienna Court/State Opera has staged a staggering 3,067 readings of 12 Strauss operas, of which 999 have been of *Der Rosenkavalier*.

Across the Atlantic at the Metropolitan Opera, Strauss's operas also proved contentious and, after *Salome* was heard for the first time there in 1907 with Olive Fremstad in the title role, it was considered so shocking that it was not performed again until 1934. Surprisingly, *Elektra* was not heard at the Met until 1932, and *Ariadne auf Naxos* (1916 version) did not appear until 1962. In all, 911 performances of eight Strauss operas have been staged by the company and, as in London and Vienna, *Der Rosenkavalier* has proved most popular with 393 performances. Missing from the schedules of all three theaters are *Friedenstag* and *Die Liebe der Danae*, works that have yet to fire the imaginations of conductors, directors, and audiences.

Recordings

With an eye focused firmly on the bottom line, record companies realized early that Strauss's more popular works often meant sure-fire sales. That being so, it might seem strange that his own commercial recordings of his stage music are restricted to excerpts from *Salome, Ariadne auf Naxos* (1912 version), *Josephslegende*, and *Feuersnot* on piano rolls, and *Salome* and *Der Rosenkavalier* on shellac. But one must remember that Strauss was most active during the recording industry's earliest years, and that sets of complete operas were prohibitive financially at that time. Since those pioneering days, Deutsche Grammophon, Decca, EMI, Hänssler, and others have filled many of the gaps in this repertoire by having major Strauss interpreters, such as Karajan, Karl Böhm, Sir Georg Solti, Wolfgang Sawallisch, Giuseppe Sinopoli, and Semyon Bychkov document the composer's better-known operas. In keeping with the statistics mentioned above, the most frequently recorded operas have been *Der Rosenkavalier, Salome*, and *Elektra*, with Solti and Böhm recording all three works for Decca and Deutsche Grammophon respectively.

The *Vier letzte Lieder* (*Four Last Songs*) were first recorded by the BBC at a concert given by Kirsten Flagstad, Wilhelm Furtwängler, and the Philharmonia Orchestra at the Royal Albert Hall, London, on 22 May 1950. Currently available on Testament Records, it is a fascinating souvenir of the cycle's world premiere. Organized as a group by Ernst Roth, the songs have since become some of Strauss's most performed lyric pieces. Whilst Flagstad was a dramatic soprano, the *Vier letzte Lieder* have increasingly become the province of lyric sopranos, such as Dame Elisabeth Schwarzkopf, Lucia Popp, Dame Felicity Lott, and Renée Fleming. Amongst the earliest recordings of Strauss's Lieder by a male singer must be those by Heinrich Schlusnus. Documented by Deutsche Grammophon with Strauss as accompanist in 1921, and now available through The Intense Media company, "Das Geheimnis," "Ich liebe dich," "Zueignung," "Heimkehr," "Die Nacht," and "Ruhe, meine Seele" are now some of the composer's most frequently performed and recorded songs. When compared to the more comprehensive overview of Strauss's Lieder made by Dietrich Fischer-Dieskau and Gerald Moore for EMI (1967–70), the discs offer valuable insight into the shifting trends in vocal style and technique during the twentieth century. Equally interesting are the recordings that Strauss made of his Lieder for Reichssender Wien (1942–43) with Anton Dermota, Hilde Konetzni, Alfred Poell, Maria Reining, and Lea Piltti. With these leading singers from the Vienna State

Opera, Strauss documented 37 recordings of 31 songs, five of which he also recorded with Schlusnus. Not always faithful to the printed texts, Strauss's readings reveal a performer who valued musical pragmatism over artistic dogma. But when Glenn Gould later adopted Strauss's freer approach to textual fidelity while recording some of the composer's Lieder with Schwarzkopf for CBS in 1966, the singer objected and refused to continue. It seems that historically informed performance practice has its limitations.

Of particular personal significance to Strauss was his Violin Sonata (1888), a demanding work for both violinist and pianist that he continued to play publicly until 1936. Unquestionably the most performed and recorded of all his chamber works, it was documented twice by Jascha Heifetz, first with Arpád Sándor in 1934 and later with Brooks Smith in 1954. Since then, it has been recorded by leading violinists such as Ginette Neveu, Gidon Kremer, Kyung-Wha Chung, Vadim Repin, and Sarah Chang. Strauss's earlier chamber works, solo piano compositions, and melodramas have fared less well and are rarely heard. But an engaging recording was made of the melodrama, *Enoch Arden*, by Claude Rains and Glenn Gould for CBS in 1962 and an equally engaging rendition of Strauss's youthful piano works by Gould for the same company 20 years later. More recently, ARTS Music documented all of Strauss's chamber and solo piano works, including his melodramas and concertos with piano accompaniment, which have since been re-issued by Brilliant Classics. With the exceptions of the horn concertos, the Oboe Concerto, and the *Burleske*, Strauss's works for solo instruments and orchestra have largely failed to find a place in the concert hall or the recording studio. The most frequently performed and recorded are the two horn concertos while the *Burleske* can now be heard conducted by Strauss on Testament. Recorded at London's Royal Albert Hall on October 19, 1947 with Alfred Blumen and the Philharmonia Orchestra, the performance was the composer's last public concert.

Strauss can also be heard conducting all his major symphonic works on a variety of labels. He documented *Don Juan* most frequently with his first dating from 1916 and his last from 1947. Not all were studio recordings, and at least two have cuts and orchestrational changes. As his 1916 discs with the Berlin Court Orchestra for Deutsche Grammophon and his 1922 discs with the London Symphony for Columbia UK were acoustic recordings, some cuts were necessary so that the work could be released on

---

[7] As Strauss was late for the 1916 session, his assistant, George Szell, recorded the first two sides of the set.

four sides of a 78-rpm set.[7] Similarly, some changes had to be made to the orchestration so that the recording's limited acoustic range could be accommodated. Common to all of Strauss's recordings is his carefully crafted approach to tempo. Where multiple recordings of works exist, such as *Don Juan*, *Till Eulenspiegel*, *Don Quixote*, and *Ein Heldenleben*, the composer is strikingly consistent in his choices. As tempo is the skeleton of any performance, listeners are left in no doubt as to Strauss's interpretative wishes. This stands in sharp contrast to Stravinsky's recordings of his own music, which vary markedly from disc to disc. It is something of a curiosity, then, that modern conductors have yet to explore fully Strauss's recordings as authoritative sources.

As Strauss's discs were not all made in the studio, it fell to the next two generations of conductors to document these works commercially. Fritz Busch, Fritz Reiner, George Szell, and Böhm all worked closely with the composer and made iconic recordings of selected tone poems. Rudolf Kempe and David Zinman then went on to document more comprehensive overviews of Strauss's symphonic music with the Dresden Staatskapelle and the Zurich Tonhalle Orchestra in the 1970s and the 2000s for EMI and Arte Nova Classics respectively. Sawallisch embarked on a similar project with the Philadelphia Orchestra for EMI in the 1990s, but it ended for commercial reasons before completion. While the appetite for such ventures might not be as great as it once was, it does not mean that major recording companies have lost faith completely in Strauss's music. But faith is often dependent on commercial success and artistic credibility. Of the conductors active today, Christian Thielemann perhaps best meets these criteria. His ever-increasing profile and position as the preeminent German conductor of his generation have captured not only the public's imagination, but also the attention of Deutsche Grammophon and Decca. Together, they continue to disseminate the great Central European conducting tradition and fly the flag for Strauss's music.

CHAPTER 34

Influence

Ben Winters

Historically, influence has been something of a problem for Strauss scholarship. For many years, a modernist suspicion of the composer's later works ensured his music was regarded as more or less moribund in terms of twentieth-century historiography. A dead end that led nowhere, it could be contrasted with the music of Mahler who, unlike Strauss, garnered the respect of arch-modernist critic Theodor Adorno. Although the rather one-dimensional view of modernism that underpins this view of Strauss is thankfully now more obviously open to critique, there is a sense in which the concept of influence itself still carries the ideological charge of that very same brand of modernism that Strauss's music consistently problematizes and challenges. In a musicology now more aware than ever of the forces that shape its endeavors, it is arguably no longer desirable to trace a composer's influence amongst, on the one hand, a series of lesser epigones, unable to cope with the attractive power of a forebear's language, and, on the other, those in whom a Bloomian struggle with a composer's influence takes place, final mastery over which results in the creation of a unique creative voice.[1] Instead, when we hear Strauss's voice in the music of others, we might recognize that the connection is as dependent on our position as listeners as it is on any historical causal link between composers. We may thus each construct our own postmodern Straussian "text" from music encountered in a variety of contexts without some over-arching notion of historical progress to find value in the connection.

Such a text may recognize a common stylistic attribute to bring Strauss and other music into dialogue, whether it be the modernist qualities of *Elektra* and *Salome* that along with Mahler's musical language undoubtedly formed an important part of the Second Viennese School's cultural

---

[1] Harold Bloom's concept of the "Anxiety of Influence" in which a (usually male) creator struggled to overcome the legacy of his forebears characterizes much modernist historiography. See Michael Klein, *Intertextuality in Western Art Music* (Bloomington: Indiana University Press, 2005), 17–21.

background, or – more obviously perhaps – the lush harmonic language and orchestration of Strauss's tone poems and operas that found a sympathetic ear amongst a group of late romantics. This group might include not only near contemporaries like Max von Schillings and, in America, perhaps George Chadwick and Henry Handley, but also representatives of a younger generation of European composers such as Béla Bartók (at least in early works like *Kossuth*), Franz Schreker, Joseph Marx, Franz Schmidt, Julius Bittner, Mieczysław Karłowicz, and – youngest of all – Erich Korngold (1897–1957). This chapter traces the weave of one particular Straussian text for which Korngold appears to be a chief nodal point with the aim of hearing Strauss in the sound world of Hollywood film scores. Historically, this is partly – if not principally – a result of Korngold's role alongside others with a similar European background (such as Franz Waxman, Max Steiner, and Dimitri Tiomkin) in establishing a narratively-driven kind of Hollywood film score. This tradition of scoring is both shaped by the expressive potential of Strauss's harmonic language and influenced by his dramaturgy, but, crucially, it is also reliant on us being prepared to listen to both Strauss and film in wider contexts. As a result, we might hear in the commercial film typified by Hollywood a natural home for the composer's brand of late romanticism, and hear in Hollywood films in turn a closer connection with other twentieth-century repertories. As such, it is a text that persists across a broad span of the twentieth century and continues to the present. After briefly outlining Korngold's historical connection with Strauss, this chapter explores how one can hear Strauss in the film scores of Korngold and his contemporaries, before demonstrating how aspects of that connection can be traced in more recent film music, including the output of John Williams (b. 1932).

Strauss, Korngold, and Others

The idea of placing Strauss and cinema in dialogue is not a radical one. Indeed, the composer's own actions offer compelling evidence for doing so, as indicated by his provision of a silent film version of *Der Rosenkavalier* (albeit to better publicize the "real thing") and his description of the interludes from *Intermezzo* as "cinematic." Even Eduard Hanslick's 1893 review of *Tod und Verklärung* was eerily prescient in its mocking recognition of the potential theatrical resonances of the symphonic poem form, something that found its ultimate expression in the scores of Korngold et al. in the 1930s and 1940s:

The realism lacks only the final step: the dimly lighted sickroom with the dying man upon a real stage, his death struggle, his visions, his death – all in pantomime – plus Strauss's music in the orchestra. That would be no more than consistent and may, in time, actually be tried.[2]

The potential for orchestral special effects and for the orchestra to have a "speaking ability" (*Sprachvermögen*) can be traced, at least in part, to Wagnerian music drama and, before that, to the descriptive sounds of Berlioz's *Symphonie fantastique*. Strauss's use of overt musical imagery in tone poems such as *Don Quixote* and *Till Eulenspiegel* – which prompted Mahler to contrast his style of programmaticism – also finds parallels, however, in the denotative musical depiction of Classical Hollywood. Thus, the *Naturlaut* (sounds of nature) that characterized *Eine Alpensinfonie* seem tailor-made for the natural environments encountered in the German expressionist-inspired Universal horror pictures of the 1930s, as heard in Franz Waxman's score for *Bride of Frankenstein* (1935). Moreover, the stylistic plurality that Strauss employs in his operas – which embrace the historical settings of their narratives – is directly relevant to the skills required of a Hollywood film composer working in the studio system of the Classical period (ca. 1930–60). Composers were required (to a degree) to subordinate individual compositional style to the specific demands of the film project at hand, and often opted to create a deliberately archaic soundworld when working with historically distant narratives. In so doing, they were drawing on traditions of musical narrativity familiar from opera and the Straussian tone poem. Undoubtedly, though, it is through Erich Korngold that Strauss's impact on the cinema is most clear, given Korngold's own prominent role in the history of the medium.

Korngold's respect and admiration for the older composer were unwavering, despite the problems that Strauss encountered with Korngold's music-critic father, Julius. Korngold's wife, Luzi, recounts in her memoirs a telling episode from their youth:

> One evening Rudi D put Richard Strauss's *Elektra* on the piano. Erich would not have needed the piano score. He had grown up with Strauss's works, had, as it were, absorbed them with his mother's milk; no bar, no note was strange to him. He jumped with rapture at the chance to play this masterwork, which he so admired.[3]

[2] Eduard Hanslick, *Music Criticisms 1846–99*, ed. and trans. Henry Pleasants (London: Penguin Books, 1963), 294.
[3] *Erich Wolfgang Korngold: Ein Lebensbild von Luzi Korngold* (Vienna: Elisabeth Lafite, 1967), 28. Translation by the author.

The debt can also clearly be heard in Korngold's music to such an extent that the word "influence" is indeed tempting to apply. His youthful Sinfonietta, Op. 5 of 1912 – a misnomer given its scope and scoring for large orchestra – has many Straussian harmonic and orchestrational touches: the chromatic fugal introduction to the finale, for instance, has unmistakable overtones of the "Von der Wissenschaft" episode from *Also sprach Zarathustra*. At the Berlin premiere, the teenage Korngold sat next to Strauss, whom Luzi refers to as his "protector," and the admiration the young composer felt was further reflected in the dedication to the older composer of his Op. 13 symphonic overture, *Sursum Corda*, a work that was later recycled in his score for the 1938 Warner Bros. swashbuckler, *The Adventures of Robin Hood*. *Sursum Corda*'s orchestration is also particularly significant in sharing many of the instrumentation choices of *Elektra*: like Strauss, Korngold uses the rare bass trumpet as the foundation of the section, and divides his violins into three groups rather than the customary two, as part of an extended division of string parts.

The impact of Strauss's music on Korngold's operas is also striking, however. To give one brief example, the Viennese waltz culture and orchestrational sheen of *Rosenkavalier* is apparent throughout Korngold's third opera *Die tote Stadt* (1920), while the characterization of Faninal's Act II anger in high woodwinds and piccolo can also be heard in the ecstatic fury of the Messenger's music at the end of Scene 2 in Act III of Korngold's 1927 opera, *Das Wunder der Heliane*. Korngold's extensive employment in his operas of keyboard percussion instruments such as celesta, harmonium, glockenspiel, glockenklavier, xylophone and his use of both wind machine effects and, once again, the elusive bass trumpet in *Die tote Stadt*, also reflects the extended orchestral palettes of the Straussian operatic orchestra. Harmonically, too, there are resonances. The chains of parallel distantly-related triads common to *Elektra* are found in, for example, the opening to *Das Wunder der Heliane*, whose first scene also features a falling whole-tone phrase in parallel chords associated with the stranger's suffering that bears a striking resemblance to a falling motive in parallel chords from Act III, Scene 2 of *Die Frau ohne Schatten*. Such allusions are easy enough to identify and evince that harmonic language that Korngold had absorbed, as Luzi put it, "like mother's milk."

Given that it is possible to hear Strauss in Korngold's operas if one wishes, it should not be surprising that this Straussian text extends to the younger composer's film scores. The love scenes between Maria and Denis in *Anthony Adverse* (1936), one of Korngold's earliest scores, are unmistakably Straussian in tone while the music for the Errol Flynn swashbuckler *The Sea Hawk* (1940) is suffused at times with the spirit of *Rosenkavalier*, despite being set in England, Panama, and on the high seas around the time of the Spanish Armada. Indeed, the film features a celesta-filled scene of courtly love set in an English rose garden that could conceivably have triggered the association. In particular, Korngold appears to reimagine the Act II fanfare-like calls announcing the arrival of Octavian bearing the silver rose as a signaling hail between Geoffrey Thorpe's ship *The Albatross* and the Spanish galleass *Santa Eullàlia del Monte* while he accompanies a *misterioso* scene – in which the chief antagonists gather around a globe – with the kind of parallel-triad writing and chromatic transformations familiar from the subsequent presentation of the rose scene. One could continue such games of allusion spotting. *Die Frau ohne Schatten* reminiscences, for instance, are apparent in *Captain Blood* (1935), *The Adventures of Robin Hood*, and *Juarez* (1939), and one might hear in the falling fourths that dominate the expressionist score to *The Sea Wolf* (1942) Jochanaan's prophecy motive from *Salome*.

At times, Korngold's contemporaries and successors also seemed to draw upon Strauss's gestural and harmonic palette. Nathan Platte has noted a typical allusion to "Von den Freuden und Leidenschaften" from *Also Sprach Zarathustra* in the cascading chromatic lines of Franz Waxman's score to *The Paradine Case* (1947), and *Till Eulenspiegel* has often been cited as a precursor for Max Steiner's humor-inflected score for *The Big Sleep* (1946).[4] Some, too, have identified a general Straussian tone to Alfred Newman's scores for *Wuthering Heights* (1939) and *The Prisoner of Zenda* (1952). Furthermore, the orchestration and harmonic character of *Salome*'s "Dance of the Seven Veils" appears to have been a prominent model for everything exotic in film and television, from Steiner's *Casablanca* score (1942) to the music from the 1936 *Flash Gordon* serial – not forgetting George Duning's music for the 1953 *Salome*, and eventually Alexander Courage's music for Vina's slave dance from the 1965 pilot television episode of *Star Trek*.

Parallel Triads, Third Relations, and Chromatically Modulating Cadential Resolutions

One particular Straussian harmonic signature, though, is ever-present in Korngold's film-score language: a progression of distantly-related parallel

[4] Nathan Platte, *Musical Collaboration in the Films of David O. Selznick, 1932–1947* (Ph.D. dissertation, University of Michigan, 2010), 267, n72.

triads (sometimes flavored with added sevenths and ninths). In the case of triads related by tritones – an octatonic chordal sequence that features heavily in *Elektra* and also in works as varied as the *Alpensinfonie, Intermezzo, Die Liebe der Danae,* the Oboe Concerto, and Second Horn Concerto, to name but a few – Korngold uses the progression on a number of occasions. It is heard in *A Midsummer Night's Dream* (1935) in the scene after Bottom discovers his "transformation," and during the escape scene from *The Sea Hawk,* where muted brass present chords of B-flat and F-flat major in successive descending octaves; other examples can be found in *Escape Me Never* (1947) and *The Private Lives of Elizabeth and Essex* (1939). Subsequently, the progression can be found in Bernard Herrmann's scores for *The Day the Earth Stood Still* (1951) and *North by Northwest* (1959) and in John Williams's score for *Raiders of the Lost Ark* (1981), where alternating chords of C minor and F-sharp minor make up the motive for the eponymous Ark of the Covenant. More recent examples in film can be heard in the music of James Newton Howard, James Horner, and Alan Silvestri – often in connection with fantastical narratives, as Scott Murphy has outlined.[5]

Far more commonly used in Strauss, though, are third-related triadic sequences – a class of chord progression that also includes the specific Tarnhelm progression from Wagner's *Ring* (minor triads a major third apart). These progressions became indicative of a typical Hollywood approach to harmonic richness in the mid- to late twentieth century and have continued into the early twenty-first century, albeit with varying degrees of functionality depending on the stylistic idiom chosen. They are found throughout Strauss's output, from the major third progressions of the Second Horn Concerto and the Oboe Concerto, the ending of *Tod und Verklärung* and the close of "Im Abendrot" from the *Four Last Songs,* to those related by the minor third found in *Salome* around Rehearsal number 27 and *Till Eulenspiegel* around number 34. They are particularly prominent in the *Alpensinfonie.* Korngold, too, uses these kinds of third progressions in many of his film scores. In the escape scene in *The Sea Hawk,* for instance, he uses a chain of ascending major triads a major third apart (C, E, A flat). He also frequently harmonizes important thematic melodies with parallel chords, and third-related triadic progressions form part of this: Essex's fanfare-like theme in *The Private Lives of Elizabeth and Essex* is based on a progression from D minor to B major, while the

---

[5] Scott Murphy, "The Major Tritone Progression in Recent Hollywood Science Fiction Films," *Music Theory Online* 12, no. 2 (2006). Open access at www.mtosmt.org.

Queen's own fanfare involves root position A-flat, F, and B-major chords – a progression that was also used to announce the Queen in *The Sea Hawk*. Branwell's drunken music at the Inn in *Devotion* (1944) likewise consists of parallel triads that include the progression B flat, G, and E flat; and Dr. Gordon's theme in *Kings Row* (1942) consists almost entirely of third-related triads, while a B major to G major progression forms part of that film's main title.

These kinds of octatonic and hexatonic triadic progressions are also found in the music of Korngold's contemporaries such as Bernard Herrmann and Hugo Friedhofer and continue to feature in more recent film scores (e.g. those of James Horner, James Newton Howard, David Arnold, and Alan Silvestri) though such scores have little else in common with Korngold's style. In particular, though, they are prominent in John Williams's scores to the *Star Wars* films, whose debt to Korngold is openly acknowledged by the composer. The "rebel fanfare" motive of *Star Wars* (1977), for instance, consists of interlocked major triads a minor third apart, much like the Queen's fanfares in *The Private Lives of Elizabeth and Essex* and *The Sea Hawk*. Partly as a consequence of its reuse in other films of the series scored by Williams, including *Star Wars: The Last Jedi* (2017), it is one of the score's most recognizable aural signatures. It is even quoted to notable effect in Michael Giacchino's score to the *Star Wars* spin-off film, *Rogue One* (2016). Such chord progressions are not restricted to Strauss's music, of course; indeed, Williams's repeated use of the Tarnhelm progression in "The Imperial March" from *The Empire Strikes Back* (1980) might be cited as evidence of a broader late-nineteenth- or early-twentieth-century harmonic palette, though one could also point to a specific Tarnhelm progression at the beginning of Strauss's *Four Last Songs*.

Williams's stylistic forebears are admittedly manifold; however, other compositional traits can link him more overtly with Strauss, if we so choose. Tom Schneller, for instance, has noted similar processes of teleological genesis – the gradual emergence of an extended melody from motivic fragments – in *Tod und Verklärung* and Williams's scores to *E.T. the Extra-Terrestrial* (1982) and *Close Encounters of the Third Kind* (1977), while *Tod und Verklärung*'s use of I–II# harmony is found throughout Williams's scores, most obviously in the love theme from *Superman* (1978).[6] Moreover, similarities in the use of chromatic harmony for dramatic effect can be found in the music of both composers. As Frank

---

[6] Tom Schneller, "Sweet Fulfillment: Allusion and Teleological Genesis in John Williams's *Close Encounters of the Third Kind*," *Musical Quarterly* 97, no. 1 (2014): 98–131. On *Superman*, see Ben

Lehman has outlined, Williams is "perhaps the most prolific employer" in contemporary film music of a kind of sudden chromatic modulation in which the expected tonic cadential resolution is replaced by a non-diatonic chord that asserts itself as a new tonic – a gesture that is capable of generating awe and wonder.[7] Lehman labels this as a Chromatically Modulating Cadential Resolution (CMCR) and finds prior examples in the film music of Max Steiner from the early 1940s. Although it is somewhat rarer in Korngold's film music – though prominent examples occur in the title music from *The Sea Hawk* and *Elizabeth and Essex* – CMCRs can also be heard in the music of Strauss: for example, the G-flat major cadence preparation at Rehearsal number 23 of the *Rosenkavalier* suite, which resolves to A major; bar 114 in the first movement of the Oboe Concerto (F major instead of the expected A); or figure O in the second movement of *Aus Italien* (C major instead of the expected G flat).

Straussian Texts

To hear Strauss in Korngold and John Williams is just one way to construct a Straussian cinematic text. That there is also a myriad of other possible Strauss texts is undeniable. A Straussian text may also encompass those composers noted by Leon Botstein, for whom Strauss's conception of the relationship between music and theater is of greater significance than any aspect of his musical language; and it may embrace composers who responded to the quasi-postmodernist attitude evident in the historicist style of many of his operas.[8] Strauss's legacy as a conductor, codirector of the Vienna State Opera between 1919 and 1924, and a founder of the Salzburg Festival, should not be overlooked. Moreover, one could make a case for the primary importance of Strauss's role in contributing to the discursive text of musical modernism, given it once used his music as a foil to better define for what it stood, and now sees in him the gateway to a more pluralistic conception – one that allows for varying musical responses to modernity beyond questions of mere tonality. Strauss's influence (if indeed one chooses to use such a term) may thus be recognized in much of

---

Winters, "*Superman* as Mythic Narrative: Music, Romanticism and the 'Oneiric Climate'," in *The Music of Fantasy Cinema*, ed. Janet K. Halfyard (Sheffield: Equinox Press, 2012), 111–31.
[7] Frank Lehman, "Hollywood Cadences: Music and the Structure of Cinematic Expectation," *Music Theory Online* 19, no. 4 (2013). Open access at www.mtosmt.org.
[8] Leon Botstein, "The Enigmas of Richard Strauss: A Revisionist View," in *Richard Strauss and His World*, ed. Bryan Gilliam (Princeton, NJ: Princeton University Press, 1992), 3–32.

the twentieth century in terms of compositional creativity, musical practice, and critical discourse alike. As an example of constructing a listening
text, though, hearing Strauss in the music of Korngold and Williams is a
testament to the power of seeking to encounter the composer's music in
varied and often surprising contexts.

CHAPTER 35

2001: A Space Odyssey *and Beyond*

Charles Youmans

On November 9, 1968, the soundtrack album of Stanley Kubrick's *2001: A Space Odyssey* peaked at number 24 on the *Billboard 200* album chart, outpacing that week's sales of *Johnny Cash at Folsom Prison*, Simon & Garfunkel's *Sounds of Silence*, the debut album by The Doors, and *Sgt. Pepper's Lonely Hearts Club Band*. For a total of 60 weeks, "popular music" would include the likes of Ligeti (*Lux aeterna* and the Requiem), Khachaturian (the Adagio from his *Gayane* Suite No. 3), and Johann Strauss, Jr. (*The Blue Danube*), thanks to a rare artist willing and able to integrate high culture and marketability.

The musical engine of this 500,000-LP phenomenon was of course the opening of Strauss's *Also sprach Zarathustra* (1896), an easily detachable two-minute tour de force that in its second life would reach a level of cultural saturation rivaling the motto of Beethoven's Fifth. First transferred to other suitably majestic contexts (the BBC's television coverage of space missions), then deployed openly as kitsch (the introduction of Elvis Presley's stage show), and finally wallpapered into baseball parks (e.g. by the Durham Bulls, made famous in Hollywood's *Bull Durham* [1988]), discotheques (via Eumir Deodato's jazz-funk arrangement, which reached no. 2 on the *Billboard* Hot 100 singles chart in 1973), and cell phones (first by Nokia, among a selection of monophonic public domain melodies pre-loaded into cell phones beginning in 1996), this fanfare proved itself both endlessly malleable and irresistibly arresting to the senses.

Presumably Kubrick did not anticipate what he would unleash; after all, these secondary appropriations hover in the consciousness, like it or not, when one returns nowadays to *2001*'s dizzying mythological heights. Yet spontaneity, and a healthy appreciation for the value of unanticipated meanings, were central to Kubrick's creative process. He had an eye, and an ear, for rich symbols, and he sought them everywhere. The *Blue Danube* cue, for example, was apparently a projectionist's experiment, after which Kubrick, characteristically open to his collaborators' inspiration, turned to the others in the room and asked, "would it be a stroke of genius, to use that?"[1] Indeed it was, as Camille Paglia elaborates: "[In] that first moment, where we see the space station outlined against the inky blackness of infinite space, you hear the music of *The Blue Danube*, and you recreate in your mind everything most beautiful, everything most elegant, everything most precious about the entire history of art, and manners, courtliness, ritual – everything is rehearsed in your mind."[2] Kubrick knew, as did Sergei Eisenstein before him, that mere juxtaposition of interesting fragments would prompt his viewers to construct meaning.

With a score of "temp tracks," then – excerpts of pre-existing music normally used as placeholders for newly composed cues – the main question is not simply what Kubrick thought he was doing, but what interpretive possibilities were created, whether or not he foresaw them. In choosing music already loaded with meaning, he invited readings that he could not control. And in the case of Strauss's *Zarathustra* those reach to an uncanny depth.

Kubrick's film was based on a book, as was Strauss's tone poem, though the director had a considerable hand in producing his source. In March 1964, he approached Arthur C. Clarke to propose a collaboration. The next month they met in New York City and began developing a prose treatment, which reached 50,000 words when completed in December 1965 and later became a novel. Kubrick remained at least an equal partner throughout; when he insisted on changes, they were made. (It was Kubrick, for example, who decided that Dr. Dave Bowman should be the only surviving member of Discovery's crew.)

Notwithstanding his coauthorship, however, Kubrick took important steps to distance the film from the novel. Most strikingly, after a screening for MGM executives in March 1968 he removed a lengthy set of voice-overs providing background details, to the alarm of a skeptical Clarke. Viewers unfamiliar with the novel thus have no idea that the monolith in the Dawn of Man sequence has been placed there by extra-terrestrials as what Clarke called a "teaching machine," to supply the starving hominids with the idea of using weapons to obtain meat; nor that the spaceship at the famous match cut from the shot of the hurtling bone is actually an atomic bomb (i.e., another tool that has become a weapon); nor that the

---

[1] Related by Andrew Birkin, Kubrick's uncredited assistant, in an interview excerpted in Tyler Knudsen, *How Kubrick Made 2001: A Space Odyssey*, https://youtu.be/StZ2fmWYom4 (accessed 20 October 2019).

[2] Paul Joyce, dir., *2001: The Making of a Myth* (London: Atlantic Celtic Films, 2001).

Star Child hovering above the earth in the film's last moment intends to detonate the entire collection of orbiting weapons, thus raising the possibility of an ending similar to that of *Dr. Strangelove*. Kubrick disputed that inference, but Clarke was not so sure: "Why would we expect any mercy from a returning Star Child?"[3] Knowledge of such details would seem essential to the viewing experience, and Clarke certainly thought so. But Kubrick saw an advantage in the resulting uncertainty, for reasons he articulated explicitly: the film was to be "an intensely subjective experience that teaches the viewer at an inner level of consciousness, just as music does."[4]

Did Kubrick know about Strauss's experience with similar challenges? Possibly so, probably not – but in any case the common ground is more interesting than who knew what. The difficulties and opportunities of transferring a verbally rendered story to a symbolic art were much on the mind of the young composer of *Macbeth* and *Don Juan*, not to mention *Tod und Verklärung*, for which he developed the story collaboratively with his mentor Alexander Ritter and helped write the poetic text appended to the score. The physical details embedded in that program – heartbeats, sighs, and the like – would be a distraction for some listeners, especially those who believed in music's power to render an ideal content in a Wagnerian sense. Strauss's abandonment of detailed verbal programs such as he used in *Tod und Verklärung* thus reflects a conclusion similar to Kubrick's, namely that the possibilities of "intensely subjective experience" increased as the density of plot detail fell.

To communicate "just as music does," Kubrick made the apparently unprecedented choice to forego newly composed music entirely. (That the studio allowed a major film without a score by a major composer is a measure of Kubrick's clout.) He took that step late in the process, however, Alex North having composed a set of cues that were recorded at Anvil Studios (Denham, England) in January 1968. This score fell so miserably short that Kubrick could not bring himself to break the news to North directly, or indeed to have anyone else do it before the premiere. Elsewhere, however, he explained the decision with merciless candor: "However good our best film composers may be, they are not a Beethoven, a Mozart or Brahms. Why use music which is less good when there is such

---

[3] Arthur C. Clarke, *The Lost Worlds of 2001* (London: Sidgwick and Jackson, 1972), 239.
[4] Eric Norden, "The Playboy Interview: Stanley Kubrick," *Playboy*, September 1968, 94; quoted in Alison Castle, ed., *The Stanley Kubrick Archives* (Cologne: Taschen, 2005), 398.

a multitude of great orchestral music available from the past and from our own time?"[5]

Defining what Kubrick meant by musical "greatness" poses a challenge, for the criteria seem in conflict. On one hand he required immediacy, a reliable impact on the "inner level of consciousness" that he hoped to reach visually and dramatically. But the music must also be symbolically malleable, for the sake of a subjectivity that "teaches," in other words, that is felt so powerfully it seems to convey truth. The music must fit the image and the drama in a believable way, even as it encourages the discovery of unexpected meanings. By this standard, North could not measure up to Strauss; the three *Zarathustra* cues resolve the conflicting demands as well as any moment in the director's oeuvre.

The first acknowledges Nietzsche's pictorial impression on Strauss, as if to salute the composer's ability to capture a sight in sound. Unafraid to play the big-budget showman when the moment called for it, and obviously aware that the first section of Nietzsche's prologue appeared at the front of the score, Kubrick provides a visual sunrise as stunning as Strauss's musical one. Our ears are prepared for the incandescent ur-tonality by three minutes of Ligeti's signature clusters over a dark screen, before Strauss's C pedal eases our transition from the studio logo into the diegesis (i.e., the film's story world). Sun and moon then cross earth's horizon precisely at the fall from major to minor, and minor becomes a reenergized major just as the sun moves halfway above the moon. From there the credits enter neatly synchronized to musical events: the studio first, at the final trumpet motto, and then Kubrick's own name leaping shamelessly to the screen in a luminous shower of subdominant sparks. The title then soaks up the final cadence, after which six seconds of black silence provide space for contemplation of the spectacle – and perhaps to wonder whether, as in the tone poem, the work's best moment has come and gone. Finally, to allow the energy to dissipate, the sunrise replays itself without music in a series of shots of an African landscape in the grip of a ten-million-year drought.

The immediate appeal, and its commercial promise, can hardly be missed. Yet Kubrick, like Strauss, could play the crowd-pleaser and the thinker at once. True, the images merely paint what the words describe: Zarathustra's view as he addresses the sun. But this literal reading invites a deeper look into Nietzsche's text: it focuses our attention on the

[5] Michael Ciment, *Kubrick*, trans. Gilbert Adair (New York: Holt, Rinehart, and Winston, 1983), 177.

fundamental confrontation – nature and individual, object and subject, physics and metaphysics, earth and heaven, the phenomenal and the noumenal – and for a moment the search for knowledge yields a glimpse of how an answer would feel. The alignment of earth, moon, and sun draws on the disorienting inquisitiveness of a 90-degree shot, a quality Michel Chion calls "frontality," to which Kubrick returns often, for example, when we search Hal's machine eye for signs of malice, or Dave's face for clues of what he is experiencing as he passes through the monolith near Jupiter, and finally the Star Child as it prepares we-know-not-what in the film's last moment.[6] We are driven to contemplate the unknowable, with Nietzsche's Zarathustra and Strauss's.

Evolution was the heart of the matter for Kubrick, and he did know Strauss's widely quoted public characterization of the tone poem, which suggested a similar goal: "I did not intend to write philosophical music or portray Nietzsche's great work musically. I meant rather to convey in music an idea of the evolution of the human race from its origin, through the various phases of development, religious as well as scientific, up to Nietzsche's idea of the *Übermensch*."[7] That Kubrick felt a special kinship with Strauss's reading of Nietzsche is suggested by his abandonment of an initial plan to use a portion of Mahler's Third Symphony, after encountering the Strauss in a *Time-Life* documentary about World War I (he also considered music of Mendelssohn, Chopin, Vaughan Williams, and Orff, even contacting the latter personally). What particularly interested Kubrick and Clarke were the transitions between phases; the monolith serves as a tool by which extra-terrestrials help earth-dwellers negotiate difficult moments of passage. Thus, the second appearance of Strauss's prologue marks not a confrontation but an epiphany, facilitated by aliens: a single hominid recognizes a bone's potential as a weapon and crosses the Rubicon. In this new context Kubrick opted for a less slavish synchronization, with one exception, the subdominant liquidation. At the C–G–C preparation of this moment we see a slow-motion shot of a hand wielding the bone-weapon, and this is followed by a cut, at the change of harmony, to a vantage point flat on the ground looking up at the ecstatic, bloodthirsty celebration. Thus, the moment of truth drew from Kubrick a subtle

[6] Chion notes that "*there is not a single shot – reverse shot of two close-ups of human characters*" [emphasis in original], the goal being to frustrate the viewer with the sphinx-like opacity of what we see. Michel Chion, *Kubrick's Cinema Odyssey*, trans. Claudia Gorbman (London: British Film Institute, 2001), 82–83.
[7] Henry T. Finck, *Richard Strauss: The Man and His Works* (Boston: Little, Brown and Company, 1917), 181. This English version of the quotation is the earliest known source.

musical insight – the fanfare's dual character as genesis and final cadence – and we hear, as well as see, that the dawn of a new age is simultaneously the culmination of the old one.

What could follow such splendid, triumphant, conclusive music? Judging from the tone poem's lukewarm reception (to this day), Strauss did not find a satisfactory answer. But just this weakness allowed Kubrick to use the segment a third time, in the last moment of the film, when the Star Child slowly rotates toward the viewer and, in the final shot, looks us straight in the eye. By ending the film at the prologue's unsurpassably emphatic cut-off, Kubrick took a step Strauss could not: he left the question unanswered. Nietzsche's Zarathustra had broken down at the realization that he could not transcend his humanity, that he could not reach the state of the *Übermensch*. By the same token, Kubrick acknowledges both the impossibility of knowing the next stage and the certainty that something must come. And so Strauss's beginning becomes also the end, and is equally at home there, forcing the responsibility for confronting the paradox back on us.

Beyond the Nietzsche connection and Strauss's comment on evolution, there is little evidence that Kubrick knew of, or had interest in, the composer's own creative dilemmas. Still, a wide range of creative similarities seem worthy of note without pressing claims of witting engagement. Certainly Kubrick was by no means ashamed of his films' financial success; already in 1968 he would brag that *2001* was "well on its way to becoming the greatest money-maker in MGM's history," and he felt no danger to artistic integrity in that fact.[8] Some critics saw it differently, most infamously Pauline Kael, who would play his Adorno: "If big film directors are to get credit for doing badly what others have been doing brilliantly for years with no money, just because they've put it on a big screen, then businessmen are greater than poets and theft is art."[9]

These accusations were as predictable in the 1960s as in the 1890s, and Kubrick argued for the aesthetic legitimacy of Hollywood corporate cinema just as forcefully as did the young Strauss in the case of program music. Strauss's publicity efforts, especially for the tone poems from *Zarathustra* through *Symphonia domestica*, included interviews, commissioned guidebooks, tidbits dropped to reporters, and so on. Kubrick followed the same playbook, with public self-advocacy (e.g., a lengthy

---

[8] Castle, ed., *The Stanley Kubrick Archives*, 398.
[9] Pauline Kael, "Trash, Art, and the Movies," in *Going Steady* (Boston: Little, Brown and Company, 1970), 124.

interview published in *Playboy*) that showed a Straussian penchant for stating as fact the result he was hoping to bring about (e.g., "film has until recent years been exempted from the category of art – a situation I'm glad is finally changing").

Likewise, Kubrick would follow Strauss in keeping certain facets of his creative work strictly private and even working actively to obscure them. Suppressing the voice-overs, and later cutting 19 minutes of dialogue-heavy footage did more than any other step to create the pregnant obscurity that would become the film's hallmark. A similar good instinct led Strauss to omit a verbal program for five of the six tone poems after *Tod und Verklärung* (the exception being *Zarathustra*) and to leave the details to the authors of *Erläuterungen* (musical guidebooks) – thus rendering those details deniable. Why, then, did Kubrick allow the novel to be published? Good faith with Clarke was surely part of it, but perhaps also a realistic assumption that the novel would remain no better known to most viewers than Nietzsche's book is to Strauss's listeners. "Free after Clarke" seems a fair characterization (playing on "free after Nietzsche," the tone poem's subtitle), considering the freedom Kubrick enjoyed to modify his source or ignore it altogether.

Adapting a verbal source for a non-verbal medium brought with it certain challenges, then, that the two artists tackled in similar ways. In the matter of genre, both saw an advantage in taking a hybrid approach, which would convey in filmic or musical ways a sense of newness appropriate to the subject matter. In the interview quoted in note 1, Steven Spielberg saw in *2001* an entirely new genre: "not a drama, not a documentary, not science fiction, but science eventuality." Kubrick undercut his generic allusions with various tools. Musical choices removed the film from the norms of science fiction. The suppression of text, including a prologue comprised of interviews with scientists on the possibility of extraterrestrial life, eliminated a flirtation with the documentary. And the Star-Gate sequence leaned so strongly toward visual abstraction that narrative became an afterthought.

Intentionally or not, the film replayed the bold formal experimentation of Strauss's *Zarathustra*, in which isolated moments suggest connections to the past – a typical sonata-form main theme, a lyrical contrasting theme in a non-tonic key, a fugal development, a reverse recapitulation – but play out in a structural context so distorted as to be uncategorizable. Those traces of the past are what tell us that the past is over, and that something new must emerge. In the end they communicate with more nuance than the Ligeti curtain-opener, which comes across merely as unexplained strangeness. Allusion, the confrontation of past and present, provides context that makes a reading possible.

One connection that Kubrick certainly cannot have known is particularly revealing of the artists' common instincts and interests. In her *Filmguide to 2001: A Space Odyssey*, Carolyn Geduld situates the film within the director's broader exploration of human nature in the cold war, and specifically the question of whether intelligence or feeling predominates in modern humanity. *Dr. Strangelove* answers in favor of intelligence and renders the verdict that humanity should die, while *2001* asks how it is that intelligence triumphed over feeling. The answer, somewhat less damning, is that outside agency was required, and further that perhaps in the long run a reconciliation is possible, albeit in a being at a higher stage of evolution.

Remarkably similar issues occupied Strauss during the composition of his early tone poems, and they came to the surface in an 1890 debate with Cosima Wagner about *Don Juan* and *Tod und Verklärung*. In a frank assessment of *Don Juan*, Cosima cautioned Strauss to "listen closely to your heart, and here and there command your intelligence, which is always at the ready, to be quiet."[10] Essentially, she asked for less tone-painting and more music that would be amenable to symbolic interpretation. Strauss resisted, holding that in a true artist "the unconscious and the instincts [...] will always be more powerful than the intellect, however highly developed the latter may be." But Cosima's warning about "the play of the intelligence against the emotions" lingered in his ear through the remaining seven tone poems, and the wisdom of leaving his listeners freedom for interpretation became ever clearer to him. Never did that impulse play out more strongly than in *Zarathustra*, where it resonates with the B/C duality at the end and its implied tensions between physical and metaphysical, human and superhuman, past and future, programmatic and absolute, literal and figurative. These are not meant to be solved by intelligence but contemplated by a creative combination of intelligence and feeling.

In the opening sequence of *Toy Story 2*, Buzz Lightyear makes his way across a chasm in a massive space station while we hear a playful arrangement of the *Zarathustra* opening. The sight of an unimaginably huge, human-created structure, a man-made planet, had already become de

---

[10] See letters of February 25, March 3, and March 6, 1890; in *Cosima Wagner – Richard Strauss: Ein Briefwechsel*, ed. Franz Trenner assisted by Gabriele Strauss (Tutzing: Hans Schneider, 1978), 26–34.

rigueur in science fiction films by 1987, when Mel Brooks parodied it in *Spaceballs* – playing on *Star Wars*, which played on *Forbidden Planet* (1956), which played on *Metropolis* (1927). The Pixar scene thus juxtaposes two references, one visual and one musical, that are now so deeply ingrained in the western popular consciousness as to be tests of cultural literacy. But that staying power does not imply semiotic stability. Over time such moments drop meanings and acquire new ones, for better or worse, as when Leni Riefenstahl's *Triumph des Willens* found its way, surely for stylistic reasons alone, into Lucas's *Star Wars* films (for the good guys and the bad) and Michael Jackson's *HIStory*. And so the history of an appropriation can tell us a great deal about visceral impact, but not much about meaning, which evolves. That insight, a central one of the twentieth century, pointed the way in Strauss and Kubrick toward a new era of art and artists.

CHAPTER 36

Scholarly Directions

Matthew Werley

The preceding 35 chapters have richly demonstrated the depth, width, and complexity of research on Strauss and his times. Given that the composer was active in every conceivable musical genre and remained in full possession of his powers from the age of 4 until 85, this is hardly surprising. Neither is the fact that his creative imagination was able to take root and find resonance with the public throughout five successive periods of German political history: the Kingdom of Bavaria, German Empire, Weimar Republic, Third Reich, and Federal Republic. Nevertheless, such vibrancy of approaches to the contextual study of Strauss conceals just how long genuine academic research into the composer has been overshadowed by the work of dilettantes, whose work still dominates the tone of public discussion in many sectors.[1]

One need only look at the number of doctoral dissertations written on Strauss, and when they were written, to see that interest in the composer within German and English-language universities in particular has become something of a cottage industry. As of 2019, no fewer than 96 dissertations that focus solely on Strauss have been successfully carried out (a list appears at the end of the chapter).[2] As Figure 36.1 reveals, 68 have appeared since 1980 alone, indicating that Strauss clearly remains a vital subject of academic interest.[3] Dissertations are but one form of research, yet surveying their contents collectively can reveal trends that emerge over time in terms of topics and methodologies that have captured the interest of

[1] For discussions of the scholarly reception of Strauss, see Richard Wattenbarger's 2000 dissertation and Wolfgang Rathert, "Strauss und die Musikwissenschaft," in *Richard Strauss Handbuch*, ed. Walter Werbeck (Stuttgart: Metzler, 2014), 531–47.
[2] This list is restricted to Ph.D. dissertations. A more comprehensive catalog that includes DMA research as well as studies that feature but do not focus exclusively on Strauss (undoubtedly dozens more) may be assembled by searching WorldCat, RILM, and the dissertation database maintained by the American Musicological Society (www.ams-net.org/ddm).
[3] The majority of these were undertaken at English-speaking universities.

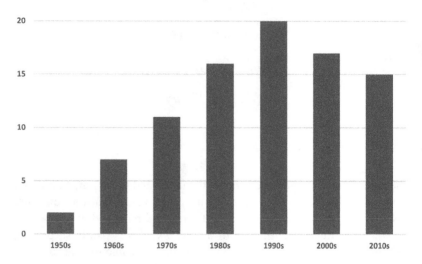

Figure 36.1   Ph.D. dissertations on Strauss by decade.

emerging scholars. The first ever dissertation on Strauss (from 1923) concentrated on his operas and was something of a harbinger.[4] Since then, the operas have remained the bread and butter of Strauss scholarship. Ranked in quantity, there have been nine dissertations each on aspects of *Elektra* and *Salome*, eight on *Die Frau ohne Schatten*, four on *Ariadne auf Naxos*, and three on *Der Rosenkavalier*. Nearly two dozen others examine one or more of the tone poems; many of these dissertations are analytical in approach and come from the discipline of music theory. Other common themes include critical reception, the creative process, and collaboration; on the latter, a staggering 17 dissertations assess Strauss's partnership with long-time librettist Hugo von Hofmannsthal. Collectively, while the bulk of research concerns more than individual works, the documents listed in this chapter largely center on the works themselves rather than broader, contextual topics.

Strauss scholarship, dissertations and beyond, is not merely defined by the issues it addresses and questions it puts forward, but also by those it ignores or unwittingly pushes to the margins of discussion. The remainder of this chapter samples topics and approaches largely absent in existing Strauss scholarship, many of which have been more thoroughly explored in

---

[4] It is noteworthy that eight dissertations were written during Strauss's lifetime, and that the first one in English did not appear until 1962.

related fields. While far from comprehensive, this discussion suggests some potentially fruitful paths for future research.

Lieder

Certainly one of the most neglected areas of research, if one considers the significant proportion of space it occupies within his oeuvre, is the Lied. The publication of Barbara Petersen's 1977 doctoral thesis (German translation 1986), highly valuable if sorely dated, remains the only critical study of his 200+ contributions to the genre. A critical analysis of the Lieder, which would allow one to access overlooked biographical details of Strauss's relationship with various singers (above all, his wife) and the personal relationships he cultivated with poets (from Richard Dehmel to Josef Weinheber) has the potential to cast new light on the state of the German Lied in the early twentieth century (Lodato, 1999) as well as reveal new aspects of Strauss's prolific activities as a Lied accompanist.

Even more neglected still are the orchestral Lieder.[5] The composer's anachronistic appropriation of his own "back catalog" and the ill-defined aesthetic issues that come into play with new performing mediums (instrumentation, timbre, staging, dramatic vocal demands, etc.) require nuanced methodological sensitivity. Their political side, to take two examples, also appears to be a factor: Strauss's first compositional activity of any kind during the initial weeks of the Weimar Republic in 1918 was to orchestrate his socialist "Der Arbeitsmann" (1898) for Leo Kestenberg, and in June 1948, while waiting out the final hours of his denazification trial (in absentia), Strauss orchestrated his "Ruhe, meine Seele" (1894), originally conceived as a wedding present to Pauline. Such factors aside, what generic expectations the orchestral Lieder evoked for concert-going audiences, and what new shades of meaning he attempted to give to his original settings (for voice and piano), are questions that pose methodological and aesthetic challenges long addressed in Mahler scholarship but have appeared critically tractionless in the case of Strauss.

Influence

Also neglected is Strauss's influence on contemporary composers and those of subsequent generations. The sound worlds his hyper-technically

---

[5] An exception being Laura Tunbridge, "Versioning Strauss," *19th-Century Music* 40, no. 3 (2017): 283–300.

orchestrated works opened up inspired a younger generation of imaginative composers, such as Béla Bartók, Mieczysław Karłowicz, and Franz Schreker (to name but three) and prompted many to radically rethink what was possible in the world of sound. The need to map that influence is a project that has long been hinted at by commentators such as Glenn Gould, Leon Botstein, and Alex Ross, but has not been systematically taken up by any one scholar. It is easy to imagine why, as the challenges to carrying it out are daunting. For example, how does one begin to square that there are references to *Salome* in the Anglican setting of the *Magnificat in D* by George Dyson, composed in Dresden in 1906? Or, for that matter, that around the same time Edgard Varèse composed several large-scale Straussian tone poems (Strauss supported their premiere in Berlin in 1909) but later destroyed them during the 1960s when it was fashionable to view Strauss as the postwar scapegoat? In this vein of sound innovators, moreover, there has also been no study of how Strauss's music and conducting aesthetic also influenced younger conductors known for developing new recording technologies and formats, such as Georg Solti, Fritz Reiner, and especially Herbert von Karajan. The materiality of Strauss's rich sound canvases has left its own imprint on our contemporary experience of music through technological mediums, about which little has been written.

Administrator

Long before the premiere of *Salome*, Strauss could have lived comfortably off the royalties of his compositions alone. That he concomitantly pursued the career of a Kapellmeister, which involved not only conducting duties but also responsibilities as a cultural administrator, has not been addressed within the field. Indeed, the fact remains that while nineteenth-century institutional and economic conventions shaped the pragmatic structure of his dual career path, later-day scholars have, in all but a few exceptions, separated out the composer from the Kapellmeister. Aside from a few empirical studies on his podium activities (*passim* Holden), this is not the same as a study of his creative influence at the helm of various opera houses, his negotiating strategies with internal and external colleagues, and his capacity to marshal institutional forces (often outdated) to serve his vision of German culture. The interaction of these sides has rarely been scrutinized in tandem, though much of Strauss's correspondence reveals that such distinctions among his musical and administrative roles were charged with historical and political overtones (Hottmann, 2005).

Archives in Munich, Berlin, Salzburg, Regensburg (Donaueschingen), and Vienna hold vast amounts of unseen primary source materials that have the potential to radically refine our understanding of just how Strauss viewed his mission as a cultural figure. A closer analysis of such documents holds promise not only to reveal the social-aesthetic drive behind Strauss's programming and selection of interpreters, but also his thinking behind the opera as a business enterprise. The resulting study would re-frame any future discussion of Strauss's (notorious) relationship to money within the discursive framework of institutional histories, and as such, provide valuable nuance and context to longstanding arguments (*passim* Adorno).

Material History

Arguably one of the most astonishing if enigmatic aspects of Strauss's artistic personality, outside his music, is the villa the architect Emanuel von Seidl designed for him in Garmisch-Partenkirchen between 1906–08. Thanks to Garmisch's sheltered position in the Bavarian Alps, the structure and its contents remain more or less intact since 1949 (this is not the case for other major cultural figures in Europe, whose estates were destroyed or dispersed by the ravages of two world wars). Strauss had a hand in the design and selection of artwork. He initially procured decor and paintings through Brakls Kunsthaus in Munich, run by the former opera-tenor-turned-art-dealer Franz Josef Brakl, and over the years gradually amassed a substantial private collection of paintings, sculptures, local folk art, and bric-a-brac. How the visual surroundings of his everyday life inspired his musical imagination, or were seen as a para-textual extension of a deeper cultural project, remain fascinating lines of inquiry for future scholars to catalog and situate within a broader interdisciplinary setting. Indeed, how one approaches the apparent contradiction that Strauss could acquire works by Tintoretto and El Greco for the interior of his villa, but also have Seidl crown the external turret with two grotesque unicorn heads (since removed), would necessitate an explanatory framework drawing just as much from art and architectural history as from musicology and ethnomusicology.

As a counterpoint to this, one might also note that no scholarship has addressed the vast amounts of photographic documentation of Strauss's life. Moving beyond dilettantism (Kurt Wilhelm, *An Intimate Portrait*) and old-fashioned empirical iconography, there is scope to develop a sophisticated, philologically sound analysis of the ways in which Strauss allowed himself to be captured by the camera lens. The desire to display a certain image when in front of the camera was also a hallmark of the increasingly hyper-industrialized society of the German Empire and was especially exploited by his employer Emperor Wilhelm II, only five years his senior. A systematic, critically reflective study – such as one encounters in dance studies, art history, or film studies – would help to provide context to his perception in the mass media, a platform Strauss consciously exploited equally in his life and music.[6]

His People

Finally, there is the thorny matter as to who exactly has spoken for Strauss scholarship over the last century. Strauss himself had a hand in selecting individuals who would construct the public image of his life and works, both during his lifetime and after. Two individuals whose credentials and personal motivations to present the composer in the best possible light have hitherto escaped critical scrutiny. The first is Alice Strauss, from 1924 the composer's daughter-in-law, personal secretary, and curator of the Richard-Strauss-Archiv (Garmisch) until her death in 1991. To what extent she may have steered scholars away from certain (especially political) topics, destroyed or hid unflattering letters, published altered versions of source documents without editorial indications (the published letters are rife with un-notated omissions), or kept visiting scholars away from her ill husband (Franz) are questions long considered taboo in Strauss studies. Still, her tireless work, helpfulness, and meticulous organizational skills have had an enormous positive impact on Strauss studies, for which many living scholars are still grateful.

Less personally invested, but also far more influential within academic circles, is Strauss's self-appointed biographer, Willi Schuh. Schuh prepared three letter editions (parents, Hofmannsthal, and Zweig), knowing full well that he was reliant on family heirs (still living) to access and publish what at times amounted to intimate exchanges about daily life, artistic circumstances, money, and contemporary political affairs. His estate at the Zentralbibliothek Zürich contains illuminating correspondence with publishing houses, conductors, composers, and other prominent figures in Strauss's life, materials necessary for filling out the background of how Strauss scholarship took the shape it did during the unstable postwar

---

[6] Roswitha Schlötterer-Traimer's anthology of caricatures (*Richard Strauss im Spiegel der Karikatur* [Mainz: Schott, 2009]) provides an example of a print version of a project that would undoubtedly be best presented as an online database.

period and Cold War Era (a period when most serious critics were hostile toward the composer). Lastly, both Alice and Schuh were key members in establishing the pre- and postwar societies devoted to the promotion of the composer. Several were already in existence during the composer's lifetime, but little documentary evidence on them remains. In 1944 (the year of Strauss's 80th birthday), Gauleiter Baldur von Schirach and Mayor Hanns Blaschke attempted to establish a Richard Strauss archive in Vienna, but nothing came of it. Eight years later, Strauss's former colleague in the Reichsmusikkammer, Julius Kopsch, founded the Internationale Richard Strauss-Gesellschaft in Berlin. It still exists and publishes the only academic journal on Strauss (*Richard Strauss-Blätter*, now *Jahrbuch*), though little is known about its history, activities, aims, and members. Any examination of the society's files – on deposit at the Richard-Strauss-Institut (Garmisch), Bavarian State Library (Munich), and British Library (Boosey & Hawkes Estate; London) – would result in a more complete critical history of the research and trends that have characterized the discourse on the composer since his death.

PH.D. DISSERTATIONS ON RICHARD STRAUSS, 1923–2019

Mathis-Rosenzweig, Alfred. *Zur Entwicklungsgeschichte des Strauss'schen Musikdramas* (Vienna, 1923).

Wachten, Edmund. *Das Formproblem in den sinfonischen Dichtungen von Richard Strauss: mit besonderer Berücksichtigung seiner Bühnenwerke* (Berlin, 1932).

Krüger, Karl-Joachim. *Hugo von Hofmannsthal und Richard Strauss: Ihre Wege und ihre Begegnungen* (Marburg, 1935).

Röttger, Heinz. *Das Formproblem bei Richard Strauss, gezeigt an der Oper Die Frau ohne Schatten mit Einschluß von Guntram und Intermezzo* (Munich, 1937).

Becker, Gerhard. *Das Problem der Oper an Hand von Richard Strauss' Capriccio* (Jena, 1944).

Blessing, Carmen. *Das instrumentale Schaffen von Richard Strauss im Spiegelbild der Presse und der zeitgenössischen Kritik* (Munich, 1944).

Gatscha, Otto. *Librettist und Komponist: dargestellt an Opern Richard Strauss'* (Vienna, 1947).

Trenner, Franz. *Die Zusammenarbeit von Hugo von Hofmannsthal und Richard Strauss* (Munich, 1949).

Schopenhauer, Ruth. *Die antiken Frauengestalten bei Richard Strauss* (Vienna, 1952).

Wendhausen, Wilfried. *Das stilistische Verhältnis von Dichtung und Musik in der Entwicklung der musikdramatischen Werke Richard Strauss'* (Hamburg, 1954).

Schneider, June. *On Devices Employed by Richard Strauss in his Opera Salome in the Service of the Poetic Idea* (Johannesburg, 1962).

Murphy, Edward Wright. *Harmony and Tonality in the Large Orchestral Works of Richard Strauss* (Indiana, 1963).

Gerlach, Reinhard. *Tonalität und tonale Konfiguration im Oeuvre von Richard Strauss: Analysen und Interpretationen als Beiträge zum Verständis von tonalen Problemen und Formen in sinfonischen Werken und in der Einleitung und ersten Szene des Rosenkavalier* (Zurich, 1966).

Stiegele, Waltraud. *Hugo von Hofmannsthals Ariadne auf Naxos, zu spielen nach dem Bürger als Edelmann des Molière: Entstehungsgeschichte und Metamorphosen* (Munich, 1966).

Gruhn, Wilfried. *Die Instrumentation in den Orchesterwerken von Richard Strauss* (Mainz, 1968).

Gräwe, Karl Dietrich. *Sprache, Musik, und Szene in Ariadne auf Naxos von Hugo von Hofmannsthal und Richard Strauss* (Munich, 1969).

Lenz, Eva-Maria. *Hugo von Hofmannsthals mythologische Oper Die ägyptische Helena* (Frankfurt, 1969).

Schulken, Samuel Bernhardt. *Buffa and Seria: Musical Features in the Operas of Richard Strauss* (Florida State, 1970).

Thurston, Richard Elliott. *Musical Representation in the Symphonic Poems of Richard Strauss* (Texas at Austin, 1971).

Dinerstein, Norman Myron. *Polychordality in Salome and Elektra: A Study of the Application of Reinterpretation Technique* (Princeton, 1975).

Strickert, Jane Elizabeth. *Richard Strauss's Vier Letzte Lieder: An Analytical and Historical Study* (Washington St. Louis, 1975).

Erwin, Charlotte E. *Richard Strauss's Ariadne auf Naxos: An Analysis of Musical Style Based on a Study of Revisions* (Yale, 1976).

Lienenlücke, Ursula. *Lieder von Richard Strauss nach zeitgenössischer Lyrik* (Cologne, 1976).

McDonald, Lawrence F. *Compositional Procedures in Richard Strauss's Elektra* (Michigan, 1976).

Pantle, Sherrill Jean Hahn. *Die Frau ohne Schatten by Hugo von Hofmannsthal and Richard Strauss: An Analysis of Text, Music, and Their Relationship* (Colorado at Boulder, 1976).

Petersen, Barbara Ellingson. *"Ton und Wort": The Lieder of Richard Strauss* (New York, 1977).

Forsyth, Karen A. *Ariadne auf Naxos by Hugo von Hofmannsthal and Richard Strauss: Its Genesis and Meaning* (Oxford, 1979).

Velikay, Patricia. *Analyse des Briefwechsels Richard Strauss – Hugo von Hofmannsthal bis einschließlich der Frau ohne Schatten* (Vienna, 1979).

Lafenthaler, Günter. *Gedanken zum Begriff musikalischer Komik in den sinfonischen Dichtungen von Richard Strauss* (Vienna, 1980).

Wajemann, Heiner. *Die Chorkompositionen von Richard Strauss* (Mainz, 1980).

Birkin, Kenneth W. *Friedenstag and Daphne: An Interpretative Study of the Literary and Dramatic Sources of the Operas by Richard Strauss* (Birmingham, 1982).

Winterhager, Wolfgang. *Zur Struktur des Operndialogs: Komparative Analysen des musikdramatischen Werks von Richard Strauss* (Bochum, 1982).

Partsch, Erich Wolfgang. *Artifizialität und Manipulation: Studien zu Genese und Konstitution der "Spieloper" bei Richard Strauss, unter besonderer Berücksichtigung der Schweigsamen Frau* (Vienna, 1983).

Bales, Suzanne E. *Elektra: From Hofmannsthal to Strauss* (Stanford, 1984).

Gilliam, Bryan Randolph. *Richard Strauss's Daphne: Opera and Symphonic Continuity* (Harvard, 1984).

Wilde, Denis Gerard. *Melodic Process in the Tone Poems of Richard Strauss* (Catholic, 1984).

Kaplan, Richard Andrew. *The Musical Language of Elektra: A Study in Chromatic Harmony* (Michigan, 1985).

Splitt, Gerhard. *Richard Strauss 1933–1935: Ästhetik und Musikpolitik zu Beginn der nationalsozialistischen Herrschaft* (Freiburg, 1985).

Bailey, Shad Culverwell. *Harmony and Tonality in the Four Works for Mixed Wind Instruments of Richard Strauss* (Arizona, 1986).

Konrad, Claudia. *Die Frau ohne Schatten von Richard Strauss: Studien zur Rezeptionsgeschichte* (Hamburg, 1987).

Walshe, Robert Clive. *The Horn and Richard Strauss: Selected Aspects of the Horn Concertos; The Influence of the Natural Horn* (Fairfax, 1987).

Axt, Eva-Maria. *Musikalische Form als Dramaturgie. Prinzipien eines Spätstils als Auswirkungen von Librettoproblemen in der Oper Friedenstag von Richard Strauss und Joseph Gregor* (TU Berlin, 1988).

Jackson, Tim. *The Last Strauss: Studies of the Letzte Lieder* (CUNY, 1988).

Kissler, John Michael. *Harmony and Tonality in Selected Late Works of Richard Strauss, 1940–1948* (Arizona, 1988).

Stöckl-Steinebrunner, Karin Marianne. *"Wer glücklich ist wie wir, dem ziemt nur eins: schweigen und tanzen!" Kunst und Lebensbewältigung um 1900 am Beispiel der Elektra von Hofmannsthal und Strauss* (Freiburg, 1990).

De Wilde, Craig James. *The Compositions of Richard Strauss from 1871–1886: The Emergence of a "Mad Extremist"* (California Santa Barbara, 1991).

Boulay, Jean-Michael. *Monotonality and Chromatic Dualism in Richard Strauss's Salome* (British Columbia, 1992).

Salvan-Renucci, Françoise. *"Ein Ganzes von Text und Musik": Hugo von Hofmannsthal und Richard Strauss* (Aix-en-Provence, 1992).

Velly, Jean-Jacques. *Richard Strauss: l'orchestration dans les Poèmes symphoniques, langage technique et esthétique* (Sorbonne, 1992).

Knaus, Gabriella Hanke. *Aspekte der Schlußgestaltung in den sinfonischen Dichtungen und Bühnenwerken von Richard Strauss* (Bern, 1993).

Bayreuther, Rainer. *Richard Strauss' Alpensinfonie: Entstehung, Analyse und Interpretation* (Heidelberg, 1994).

Martinez Santafé, José Juan. *Una venganza inolvidable: Elektra de Richard Strauss* (Barcelona, 1994).
Holden, Raymond Warren. *Richard Strauss: The Origin, Dissemination and Reception of His Mozart Renaissance* (London, 1995).
Okada, Akeo. R. *Shutorausu "Bara no kishi" kenkyū: Ongaku, doramaturugī, jidaihaikei* (Osaka, 1995).
Sadrieh, Astrid. *Konvention und Widerspruch. Harmonische und motivische Gestaltungsprinzipien bei Richard Strauss am Beispiel ausgewählter Tondichtungen und Opern* (Bonn, 1995).
Warfield, Scott Allan. *The Genesis of Richard Strauss's Macbeth* (UNC Chapel Hill, 1995).
Bayerlein, Sonja. *Musikalische Psychologie der drei Frauengestalten in der Oper Elektra von Richard Strauss* (Würzburg, 1996).
Youmans, Charles Dowell. *Richard Strauss's Guntram and the Dismantling of Wagnerian Musical Metaphysics* (Duke, 1996).
Schmid, Mark-Daniel. *The Tone Poems of Richard Strauss and Their Reception History from 1887–1908* (Northwestern, 1997).
Seshadri, Anne Marie Lineback. *Richard Strauss, Salome, and the "Jewish question"* (Maryland, 1998).
Köhler, Michael. *"Jetzt endlich hab' ich instrumentieren gelernt!" Studien zur Instrumentation der frühen Opern von Richard Strauss* (Humboldt, 1999).
Lodato, Suzanne Marie. *Richard Strauss and the Modernists: A Contextual Study of Strauss's Fin-de-siecle Song Style* (Columbia, 1999).
Obermaier, Gerlinde. *Die Bühnenwirksamkeit der Symbole in Hugo von Hofmannsthals und Richard Strauss' Zauberoper Die Frau ohne Schatten: Ein Einblick in die Inszenierungsgeschichte des 20. Jahrhunderts* (Munich, 1999).
Steiger, Martina Michaela. *Die Liebe der Danae von Richard Strauss: Mythos, Libretto, Musik* (Mainz, 1999).
Kristiansen, Morten. *Richard Strauss's Feuersnot in Its Aesthetic and Cultural Context: A Modernist Critique of Musical Idealism* (Yale, 2000).
Wattenbarger, Richard Ernest. *Richard Strauss, Modernism, and the University: A Study of German-Language and American Academic Reception of Richard Strauss from 1900 to 1990* (Minnesota, 2000).
Wu, Janice P. *Richard Strauss: Heroism, Auto-heroism and the Musical Self* (Queensland, 2000).
Welling, Miriam Joelle. *Words, Music and Operatic Aesthetics in Richard Strauss's Capriccio* (Texas Austin, 2001).
Callaghan, Mary B. *Richard Strauss's "Geheimnisvolle Musik": Unveiling the Meaning of Salome* (Belfast, 2003).
Ganani, Uri. *Konvention und Emanzipation: Weibliche Stimmen in der Opernwelt von Richard Strauss und Hugo von Hofmannsthal* (Tel Aviv, 2003).
Holzmann, Hubert. *"Pygmalion in München": Richard Strauss und das Konzertmelodram um 1900* (Würzburg, 2003).

Hottmann, Katharina. *"Die andern komponieren. Ich mach' Musikgeschichte!":* *Historismus und Gattungsbewusstsein bei Richard Strauss: Untersuchungen zum späteren Opernschaffen* (Hannover, 2003).

Schütte, Jens-Peter. *Musik als Bekenntnis: Die Tondichtungen Einleitung und Allegro und Metamorphosen im Spätwerk von Richard Strauss* (Dortmund, 2003).

Cha, Jee-Weon. *Music, Language, and Tone Poem: Interpreting Richard Strauss's Tod und Verklärung, Op. 24* (Pennsylvania, 2004).

Gibson, Robert Raphael. *Parody Lost and Regained: Richard Strauss's Double Voices* (Oxford, 2004).

Graydon, Philip Robert. *Die ägyptische Helena (1927): Context and Contemporary Critical Reception* (Belfast, 2005).

Heisler Jr., Wayne. *"Freedom from the Earth's Gravity": The Ballet Collaborations of Richard Strauss* (Princeton, 2005).

Bayerlein, Sonja. *Verkörperte Musik: Zur Dramaturgie der Gebärde in den frühen Opern von Strauss und Hofmannsthal* (Würzburg, 2006).

Larkin, David John Paul. *Reshaping the Liszt–Wagner Legacy: Intertextual Dynamics in Strauss's Tone Poems* (Cambridge, 2006).

Jones, Joseph E. *Der Rosenkavalier: Genesis, Modelling, and New Aesthetic Paths* (Illinois Urbana-Champaign, 2009).

Wolf, Christian. *Studien zur Entstehung der Oper Salome von Richard Strauss* (Munich, 2009).

Sarver, Sarah K. *Embedded and Parenthetical Chromaticism: A Study of their Structural and Dramatic Implications in Selected Works by Richard Strauss* (Florida State, 2010).

Shirley, Hugo. *An Operatic Project in Collapse: A Critical Investigation of Hugo von Hofmannsthal's and Richard Strauss's Die Frau ohne Schatten* (King's College, 2010).

Werley, Matthew Michael. *Historicism and Cultural Politics in Three Interwar-Period Operas by Richard Strauss: Arabella (1933), Die schweigsame Frau (1935) and Friedenstag (1938)* (Oxford, 2010).

Price, Jonathan Meredith. *Richard Strauss's Choreographic Works in the Context of the New Baroque* (Belfast, 2011).

Høgåsen-Hallesby, Hedda. *Salome Ever and Never the Same: (Re)productions of a Canonized Opera* (Oslo, 2013).

Kech, Adrian. *Musikalische Verwandlung im Opernwerk von Hugo von Hofmannsthal und Richard Strauss* (Munich, 2013).

Woronecki, Stuart A. *The Harmonic Language of Richard Strauss's First Period Works: A Transformational Approach* (Connecticut, 2013).

Cöster, Christian. *Studien zu Intermezzo von Richard Strauss* (Dresden, 2014).

Enderlein, Olaf. *Die Frau ohne Schatten von Richard Strauss: Untersuchungen zur musikalischen Gestalt* (Berlin, 2014).

Reynolds, Michael. *The Theatrical Vision of Count Harry Kessler and Its Impact on the Strauss-Hofmannsthal Partnership* (London, 2014).

McHugh, Erik Rose. *The Vocality of the Dramatic Soprano Voice in Richard Strauss's Salome and Elektra* (Royal College of Music, 2018).

Ogburn, Christopher G. *Strauss and the City: The Reception of Richard Strauss's Salome, Elektra, and Der Rosenkavalier within New York City, 1907–1934* (CUNY, 2018).

Tan, Emily X. X. *Aspects of Richard Strauss's Late Aesthetic* (Oxford, 2018).

Becke, Carson. *Richard Strauss and the Piano* (Oxford, 2019).

Schaper, Christian. *Richard Strauss, Die Frau ohne Schatten: Studien zu den Skizzen und zur musikalischen Faktur* (Karlsruhe, 2019).

Further Reading

PART I: FAMILY, FRIENDS, AND COLLABORATORS

1   Family and Upbringing

Schuh, Willi. *Richard Strauss: A Chronicle of the Early Years 1864–1898.* Translated by Mary Whittall. Cambridge: Cambridge University Press, 1982.

Strauss, Richard. *Briefe an die Eltern 1882–1906.* Edited by Willi Schuh. Zurich: Atlantis Verlag, 1954.

Trenner, Franz. *Richard Strauss: Chronik zu Leben und Werk.* Edited by Florian Trenner. Vienna: Verlag Dr. Richard Strauss, 2003.

Walton, Chris. "Mad Mothers, Fractious Fathers and Fractured Cowbells: Richard Strauss Reconsidered." *The Musical Times* 157, no. 1934 (2016): 19–44.

Wilhelm, Kurt. *Richard Strauss persönlich.* Zurich: Ex Libris, 1985.

2   Formative Influences

Birkin, Kenneth. *Hans von Bülow: A Life for Music.* Cambridge: Cambridge University Press, 2011.

Hausegger, Siegmund von. *Alexander Ritter: Ein Bild seines Charakters und Schaffens.* Berlin: Marquardt, 1907.

[Interview with] "Richard Strauss." *The Musical Times* 44, no. 719 (1903): 9–15.

Schuh, Willi. *Richard Strauss: A Chronicle of the Early Years.* Translated by Mary Whittall. Cambridge: Cambridge University Press, 1982.

Walker, Alan. *Hans von Bülow: A Life and Times.* Oxford: Oxford University Press, 2010.

Youmans, Charles. *Mahler & Strauss: In Dialogue.* Bloomington: Indiana University Press, 2016.

Richard Strauss's Orchestral Music and the German Intellectual Tradition: The Philosophical Roots of Musical Modernism. Bloomington: Indiana University Press, 2005.

3   Pauline de Ahna

Birkin, Kenneth. "'Ihr thörichtes Kind: Ihre dankbar Ergebene': Pauline de Ahna to Hans Von Bronsart, Richard Sternfeld und Max Marschalk: Letters from

Strauss's Weimar and Berlin Years." *Richard Strauss-Blätter* no. 43 (2000): 116–48.

Frevert, Ute. *Frauen-Geschichte: Zwischen Bürgerlicher Verbesserung und Neuer Weiblichkeit.* Frankfurt am Main: Suhrkamp, 1986.

Hanke-Knaus, Gabriella. "Neuschöpfung durch Interpretation: Richard Strauss' Eintragungen in die Handexemplare seiner Lieder aus dem Besitz von Pauline Strauss-de Ahna." *Die Musiktheorie* 11, no. 1 (1996): 17–30.

Petersen, Barbara A. *Ton und Wort: The Lieder of Richard Strauss.* Ann Arbor: UMI Research Press, 1980.

Sauer, Edith. *Liebe und Arbeit: Geschlechterbeziehungen im 19. und 20. Jahrhundert.* Edited by Margareth Lanzinger. Vienna: Böhlau, 2014.

4   Close Friends

Edelmann, Bernd. *Ludwig Thuille.* Tutzing: Schneider, 1993.

Hofmeister, Michael. *Alexander Ritter: Leben und Werk eines Komponisten zwischen Wagner und Strauss.* Baden-Baden: Tectum, 2018.

Schlötterer, Roswitha. "Richard Strauss und sein Münchner Kreis." In *Jugendstil-Musik? Münchner Musikleben 1890–1918*, edited by Robert Münster and Renata Wagner, 13–24. Wiesbaden: Reichert Verlag, 1987.

Schmidt, Manuela Maria. *Die Anfänge der musikalischen Tantiemenbewegung in Deutschland.* Berlin: Duncker & Humblot, 2005.

Schwartz, Richard Isadore. "An Annotated English Translation of *Harmonielehre* of Rudolf Louis and Ludwig Thuille." Ph.D., Washington University, 1982.

Steinitzer, Max. *Richard Strauss.* Berlin: Schuster & Loeffler, 1911.

Youmans, Charles. *Richard Strauss's Orchestral Music and the German Intellectual Tradition: The Philosophical Roots of Musical Modernism.* Bloomington: Indiana University Press, 2005.

5   Hofmannsthal

Broch, Hermann. *Hugo von Hofmannsthal and His Time: The European Imagination, 1800–1920.* [German edition, 1964]. Translated, edited, and with an introduction by Michael P. Steinberg. Chicago: University of Chicago Press, 1984.

Hamburger, Michael. *Hofmannsthal: Three Essays.* Princeton: Princeton University Press, 1972.

Kovach, Thomas A., ed. *A Companion to the Works of Hugo von Hofmannsthal.* Rochester: Camden House, 2002.

Mayer, Matthias and Julian Werlitz, eds. *Hofmannsthal Handbuch: Leben – Werk – Wirkung.* Stuttgart: J. B. Metzler, 2016.

Sammons, Jeffrey L. *Hugo von Hofmannsthal, the Elusive Poet.* New Haven: Yale University Press, 1969.

Steinberg, Michael P. *The Meaning of the Salzburg Festival: Austria as Theater and Ideology, 1890–1938.* Ithaca, NY: Cornell University Press, 1990.

Vilain, Robert. *The Poetry of Hugo von Hofmannsthal and French Symbolism.* Oxford: Clarendon Press, 2000.

6 The Other Librettists

Birkin, Kenneth. "Feuersnot." In *Richard Strauss-Jahrbuch 2014*, edited by Günther Brosche, 5–64. Tutzing: Schneider, 2014.

Gregor, Joseph. *Clemens Krauss: Seine musikalische Sendung.* Wien: Walter Krieg Verlag, 1953.

Hösch, Rudolf. *Kabarett von Gestern*, Vol. 1: 1900–1933. Berlin: Henschelverlag, 1967.

Kristiansen, Morten. "Strauss's First Librettist: Ernst von Wolzogen Beyond Überbrettl." *Richard Strauss-Blätter* no. 59 (2008): 75–116.

Pander, Oscar von. *Clemens Krauss in München.* München: Verlag C. H. Beck, 1955.

Röslau, Walter. *Das Chanson im Deutschen Kabarett 1901–1933.* Berlin: Henschelverlag, 1980.

Wolzogen, Ernst von. *Wie ich mich ums Leben brachte: Erinnerungen und Erfahrungen.* Braunschweig & Hamburg: G. Westermann, 1922.

7 Stage Collaborators

Baker, Evan. *From the Score to the Stage.* Chicago: University of Chicago Press, 2013.

Gallup, Stephen. *A History of the Salzburg Festival.* Topsfield: Salem House Publishers, 1987.

Hartmann, Rudolf. *Richard Strauss: The Staging of His Operas and Ballets.* Translated by Graham Davies. New York: Oxford University Press, 1981.

Heisler, Wayne. *The Ballet Collaborations of Richard Strauss.* Rochester, University of Rochester Press, 2009.

Lesnig, Günther. *Die Aufführungen der Opern von Richard Strauss im 20. Jahrhundert: Daten, Inszenierungen, Besetzungen.* 2 vols. Tutzing: Hans Schneider, 2008.

Reinhardt, Max. *Leben für das Theater: Briefe, Reden, Aufsätze, Interviews, Gespräche, Auszüge aus Regiebüchern.* Edited by Hugo Fetting. Berlin: Argon, 1989.

8 Champions

Böhm, Karl. *Begegnung mit Richard Strauss.* Edited by Franz Eugen Dostal. Vienna: Doblinger, 1964.

Gregor, Joseph. *Richard Strauss, der Meister der Oper.* Munich: R. Piper, 1939.

Hartmann, Rudolf. *Richard Strauss: The Staging of His Operas and Ballets.* Translated by Graham Davies. New York: Oxford University Press, 1981.

Lehmann, Lotte. *Five Operas and Richard Strauss*. Translated by Ernst Pawel. New York: Macmillan, 1964.
Wilhelm, Kurt. *Richard Strauss: An Intimate Portrait*. Translated by Mary Whittall. London: Thames & Hudson, 1989.

PART II: CAREER STATIONS

9 Munich and Garmisch

Jelavich, Peter. *Munich and Theatrical Modernism*. Boston: Harvard University Press, 1996.
Makela, Maria. *The Munich Secession: Art and Artists in Turn-of-the-Century Munich*. Princeton: Princeton University Press, 1990.
Münster, Robert and Helmut Hell, eds. *Jugendstil-Musik? Münchner Musikleben 1890–1918*. Wiesbaden: Ludwig Reichert, 1987.
Prinz, Friedrich and Marita Krauss, eds. *München – Musenstadt mit Hinterhöfen. Die Prinzregentenzeit 1886–1912*. Munich: C. H. Beck, 1988.
Schwarzmüller, Alois. *Beiträge zur Geschichte des Marktes Garmisch-Partenkirchen im 20. Jahrhundert*. www.gapgeschichte.de.
Wolf, Christian and Jürgen May. *Bei Richard Strauss in Garmisch-Partenkirchen*. Munich: Prestel, 2008.

10 Meiningen and Weimar

Birkin, Kenneth. "Richard Strauss in Weimar. Part 1: The Concert Hall." *Richard Strauss-Blätter* no. 33 (1995): 3–36.
"Richard Strauss in Weimar. Part 2: The Opera." *Richard Strauss-Blätter* no. 34 (1995): 3–56.
Hofmann, Renate and Kurt Hofmann. "Johannes Brahms und das Herzogshaus Sachsen-Meiningen." In *Brahms-Studien* no. 15 (2008): 37–66.
Holden, Raymond. "Kapellmeister Strauss." In *The Cambridge Companion to Richard Strauss*, edited by Charles Youmans, 257–68. Cambridge: Cambridge University Press, 2010.
Koller, Ann Marie. *The Theater Duke: George II of Saxe-Meiningen and the German Stage*. Stanford: Stanford University Press, 1984.
Osborne, John. *The Meiningen Court Theatre, 1866–1890*. Cambridge: Cambridge University Press, 1988.

11 Bayreuth

Carr, Jonathan. *The Wagner Clan*. New York: Atlantic, 2007.
Edelmann, Bernd. "Strauss und Wagner." In *Richard Strauss Handbuch*, edited by Walter Werbeck, 66–83. Stuttgart: Metzler, 2014.
Hilmes, Oliver. *Cosima Wagner: The Lady of Bayreuth*. Translated by Stewart Spencer. New Haven: Yale University Press, 2011.

Spotts, Frederic. *Bayreuth: A History of the Wagner Festival*. New Haven: Yale University Press, 1994.
Trübsbach, Rainer. *Geschichte der Stadt Bayreuth 1194–1994*. Bayreuth: Druckhaus Bayreuth, 1993.
Wagner, Nike. *The Wagners: The Dramas of a Musical Dynasty*. Translated by Ewald Osers and Michael Downes. Princeton: Princeton University Press, 1998.

12 Berlin

Fischer, Jens Malte. "'Das Theater ist auch eine meiner Waffen': Die Hofoper im Zeichen des Kaiserreiches." In *Apollini et Musis: 250 Jahre Opernhaus Unter den Linden*, edited by Georg Quander, 117–46. Berlin: Propyläen, 1992.
Fritzsche, Peter. *Reading Berlin 1900*. Cambridge: Harvard University Press, 1996.
Paret, Peter. *The Berlin Secession: Modernism and Its Enemies in Imperial Germany*. Cambridge: Harvard University Press, 1980.
Restle, Conny and Dietmar Schenk, eds. *Richard Strauss im kaiserlichen Berlin: Eine Ausstellung im Musikinstrumenten-Museum SIMPK*. Berlin: Staatliches Institut für Musikforschung Preussischer Kulturbesitz, 2001.
Rühle, Günther. *Theater in Deutschland, 1887–1945: Seine Ereignisse, seine Menschen*. 2nd ed. Frankfurt am Main: S. Fischer, 2007.
Schenk, Dietmar. "Berlins 'Richard-Strauss-Epoche': Richard Strauss und das kaiserliche Berlin." In *Richard Strauss: Der Komponist und sein Werk – Überlieferung, Interpretation, Rezeption*, edited by Sebastian Bolz, Adrian Kech, and Hartmut Schick, 38–49. Munich: Allitera, 2017.
Schutte, Jürgen and Peter Sprengel. *Die Berliner Moderne, 1885–1914*. Stuttgart: Reclam, 1987.

13 Vienna

Botstein, Leon. "Strauss and the Viennese Critics (1896–1924)." In *Richard Strauss and His World*, edited by Bryan Gilliam, 3–32. Princeton: Princeton University Press, 1992.
Ebner, Paulus. *Strukturen des Musiklebens in Wien: Zum musikalischen Vereinsleben in der Ersten Republik*. Wien: Peter Lang, 1996.
Gruber, Helmut. *Red Vienna: Experiment in Working-Class Culture, 1919–1934*. Oxford: Oxford University Press, 1991.
Lindström, Fredrik. *Empire and Identity: Biographies of the Austrian State Problem in the Late Habsburg Empire*. West Lafayette: Purdue University Press, 2008.
Mühlegger-Henhapel, Christiane and Alexandra Steiner-Strauss, eds. *Richard Strauss und die Oper*. St. Pölten: Residenz Verlag, 2014.
Wagner-Trenkwitz, Christoph. *Durch die Hand der Schönheit: Richard Strauss und Wien*. Wien: Kremayr & Scheriau, 1999.

PART III: CULTURAL ENGAGEMENT AND MUSICAL LIFE

14 Strauss as Reader

Hottmann, Katharina. *"Die andern komponieren. Ich mach' Musikgeschichte!":* *Historismus und Gattungsbewusstsein bei Richard Strauss: Untersuchungen zum späteren Opernschaffen.* Tutzing: Hans Schneider, 2005.
Strauss, Richard. *Späte Aufzeichnungen.* Edited by Marion Beyer, Jürgen May, and Walter Werbeck. Mainz: Schott, 2016.
Youmans, Charles. *Richard Strauss's Orchestral Music and the German Intellectual Tradition: The Philosophical Roots of Musical Modernism.* Bloomington: Indiana University Press, 2005.

15 Antiquity

Geary, Jason. *The Politics of Appropriation: German Romantic Music and the Ancient Greek Legacy.* Oxford: Oxford University Press, 2014.
Gilliam, Bryan. *Rounding Wagner's Mountain: Richard Strauss and Modern German Opera.* Cambridge: Cambridge University Press, 2014.
Kramer, Lawrence. *Opera and Modern Culture: Wagner and Strauss.* Berkeley: University of California Press, 2004.
Marchand, Suzanne. *Down from Olympus: Archaeology and Philhellenism in Germany, 1750–1970.* Princeton: Princeton University Press, 1996.
Ward, Philip. *Hofmannsthal and Greek Myth: Expression and Performance.* New York: Peter Lang, 2002.

16 Philosophy and Religion

Behler, Ernst. "Nietzsche in the Twentieth Century." In *The Cambridge Companion to Nietzsche,* edited by Bernd Magnus and Kathleen M. Higgins, 281–322. Cambridge: Cambridge University Press, 1996.
Gatz, Felix M. *Musik-Ästhetik in ihren Hauptrichtungen: Ein Quellenbuch der deutschen Musik-Ästhetik von Kant und der Frühromantik bis zur Gegenwart mit Einführung und Erläuterungen.* Stuttgart: Ferdinand Enke, 1929.
Houlgate, Stephen. *Hegel, Nietzsche, and the Criticism of Metaphysics.* Cambridge: Cambridge University Press, 1986.
Magee, Bryan. *The Philosophy of Schopenhauer.* Oxford: Clarendon Press, 1997.
McGrath, William J. *Dionysian Art and Populist Politics in Austria.* New Haven: Yale University Press, 1974.
Safranski, Rüdiger. *Schopenhauer and the Wild Years of Philosophy.* Translated by Ewald Osers. Cambridge: Harvard University Press, 1990.
Williams, John R. *The Life of Goethe: A Critical Biography.* Oxford: Blackwell, 2001.

17 The Allgemeine Deutsche Musikverein

Deaville, James. "The Allgemeine Deutsche Musikverein: Forming German National Identity through New Music." In *Music's Intellectual History*, edited by Zdravko Blažeković and Barbara Dobbs Mackenzie, 481–94. New York: RILM, 2009.

"'. . . Nicht im Sinne von Franz Liszt . . .': Reger and the Allgemeine Deutsche Musikverein." In *Reger Studien 6: Musikalische Moderne und Tradition*, edited by Alexander Becker, Gabriele Gefäller and Susanne Popp, 121–43. Wiesbaden: Breitkopf & Härtel, 2000.

"The Forty-Second Tonkünstler-Festival of the General German Music Society, at Essen. May 24–8." *The Musical Times* 47, no. 761 (1906): 486.

Kaminiarz, Irina, ed. *Richard Strauss: Briefe aus dem Archiv des Allgemeinen Deutschen Musikvereins (1888–1909)*. Weimar: Böhlau, 1995.

18 The Genossenschaft Deutscher Tonsetzer

Bently, Lionel, Uma Suthersanen, and Paul Torremans, eds. *Global Copyright: Three Hundred Years Since the Statute of Anne, from 1709 to Cyberspace*. Cheltenham, UK: Edward Elgar, 2010.

Gervais, Daniel, ed. *Collective Management of Copyright and Related Rights*, 3rd ed. Alphen aan den Rijn, the Netherlands: Kluwer Law International, 2016.

Loewenheim, Ulrich, Matthias Leistner, and Ansgar Ohly, eds. *Urheberrecht: Kommentar*, 6th ed. Munich: C. H. Beck, 2019.

Schmidt, Manuela. "Friedrich Rösch – ein Vorkämpfer für die Rechte der Komponisten. Eine Hommage zum 80. Todestag." *Richard Strauss-Blätter* no. 55 (2006): 71–89.

"Tantiemen für Konzertaufführungen?" *Gewandhaus-Magazin* no. 51 (2006): 51–55.

"Von der Leipziger Anstalt zur Genossenschaft Deutscher Tonsetzer." In *Recht und Praxis der GEMA: Handbuch und Kommentar*, 3rd ed., edited by Harald Heker and Karl Riesenhuber, 5–12. Berlin: De Gruyter, 2018.

Walter, Michel M. and Silke von Lewinsky, eds. *European Copyright Law: A Commentary*. Oxford: Oxford University Press, 2010.

PART IV: PROFESSIONAL AND MUSICAL CONTEXTS

19 The Composer

Roth, Ernst. *The Business of Music: Reflections of a Music Publisher*. New York: Oxford University Press, 1969.

Schoolfield, George C. *The Figure of the Musician in German Literature*. New York: AMS Press, 1966.

Warfield, Scott. "Strauss and the business of music." In *The Cambridge Companion to Richard Strauss*, edited by Charles Youmans, 242–56. Cambridge: Cambridge University Press, 2010.

Youmans, Charles. *Mahler & Strauss: In Dialogue*. Bloomington: Indiana University Press, 2017.

20 The Conductor

Bowen, José Antonio, ed. *The Cambridge Companion to Conducting*. Cambridge: Cambridge University Press, 2003.
Holden, Raymond. *The Virtuoso Conductors*. New Haven, CT: Yale University Press, 2005.
Richard Strauss: A Musical Life. New Haven, CT: Yale University Press, 2012.
Martner, Knud. *Mahler's Concerts*. New York: The Overlook Press, 2010.
Trenner, Franz. *Richard Strauss: Chronik zu Leben und Werk*. Edited by Florian Trenner. Vienna: Verlag Richard Strauss, 2000.

21 The Orchestra

Carse, Adam. *The History of Orchestration*. London: Kegan, Paul, Trench, Trubner and Company, 1925. Reprinted by Dover Publications, 1964.
Corder, Frederick. *The Orchestra and How to Write for It*. London: Robert Cocks and Co., 1896.
Del Mar, Norman. *Anatomy of the Orchestra*. 2nd printing with revisions. Berkeley: University of California Press, 1983.
Lawson, Colin, ed. *The Cambridge Companion to the Orchestra*. Cambridge: Cambridge University Press, 2003.
Peyser, Joan, ed. *The Orchestra: Origins and Transformations*. New York: Scribner, 1986.
Warfield, Scott. "The Genesis of Richard Strauss's 'Macbeth'." Ph.D., University of North Carolina at Chapel Hill, 1995.

22 Program Music

Bonds, Mark Evan. *Absolute Music: The History of an Idea*. New York: Oxford University Press, 2014.
Eichner, Barbara. *History in Mighty Sounds: Musical Constructions of German National Identity 1848–1914*. Woodbridge, UK: The Boydell Press, 2012.
Kregor, Jonathan. *Program Music*. Cambridge: Cambridge University Press, 2015.
Shadle, Douglas. *Orchestrating the Nation: The Nineteenth-Century American Symphonic Enterprise*. New York: Oxford University Press, 2016.
Youmans, Charles. *Richard Strauss's Orchestral Music and the German Intellectual Tradition: The Philosophical Roots of Musical Modernism*. Bloomington: Indiana University Press, 2005.

23 Post-Wagnerian Opera

Frisch, Walter. *German Modernism: Music and the Arts*. Berkeley: University of California Press, 2005.

Gilliam, Bryan. *Rounding Wagner's Mountain: Richard Strauss and Modern German Opera.* Cambridge: Cambridge University Press, 2014.
Huebner, Steven. *French Opera at the Fin de Siècle: Wagnerism, Nationalism, and Style.* Oxford: Oxford University Press, 1999.
Kristiansen, Morten. "Strauss's Road to Operatic Success: *Guntram, Feuersnot,* and *Salome.*" In *The Cambridge Companion to Richard Strauss,* edited by Charles Youmans, 105–18. Cambridge: Cambridge University Press, 2010.
Young, Julian. *The Philosophies of Richard Wagner.* London: Lexington Books, 2014.

24 The Lied

Heinemann, Michael. "Generalprobe im Wohnzimmer: Zu Liedern von Richard Strauss," in *Öffentliche Einsamkeit: Das deutschsprachige Lied und seine Komponisten im frühen 20. Jahrhundert,* edited by Michael Heinemann and Hans-Joachim Hinrichsen, 37–48. Cologne: Dohr, 2009.
Petersen, Barbara. *Ton und Wort: The Lieder of Richard Strauss.* Ann Arbor: UMI Research Press, 1977.
Schmierer, Elisabeth. "Klavierlieder," in *Richard Strauss Handbuch,* edited by Walter Werbeck, 326-47. Stuttgart: Metzler, 2014.
Wason, Robert W. and Valerie Errante, eds. *Selected Songs of the Munich School, 1870–1920: Lieder for Soprano Voice and Piano by Alexander Ritter, Ludwig Thuille, Max Schillings, August Reuss, Walter Courvoisier, Walter Braunfels, and Richard Trunk.* Middleton: A-R Editions, 2010.

PART V: IN HISTORY

25 Modernism

Butler, Christopher. *Early Modernism: Literature, Music and Painting in Europe 1900–1916.* Oxford: Clarendon Press, 1994.
Downes, Stephen. *Music and Decadence in European Modernism: The Case of Central and Eastern Europe.* Cambridge: Cambridge University Press, 2010.
Franklin, Peter. *The Life of Mahler.* Cambridge: Cambridge University Press, 1997.
Hepokoski, James. "Fiery-pulsed Libertine or Domestic Hero? Strauss's Don Juan Reinvestigated." In *Richard Strauss: New Perspectives on the Composer and His Work,* edited by Bryan Gilliam, 135–75. Durham: Duke University Press, 1992.
"Round Table: Modernism and its Others," *Journal of the Royal Musical Association* 139, no. 1 (2014): 177–204.

26 Traditionalism

Carroll, Brendan G. *The Last Prodigy: A Biography of Erich Wolfgang Korngold.* Portland: Amadeus Press, 1997.

Hailey, Christopher. *Franz Schreker, 1878–1934: A Cultural Biography*. Cambridge: Cambridge University Press, 1993.

Kater, Michael H. *Composers of the Nazi Era: Eight Portraits*. New York: Oxford University Press, 2000.

Martin, Benjamin G. *The Nazi-Fascist New Order for European Culture*. Cambridge: Harvard University Press, 2016.

Moskovitz, Marc D. *Alexander Zemlinsky: A Lyric Symphony*. Woodbridge, UK: Boydell Press, 2010.

Walton, Chris. *Othmar Schoeck: Life and Works*. Rochester: University of Rochester Press, 2009.

27 World War I

Dennis, David B. *Beethoven in German Politics, 1870–1989*. New Haven: Yale University Press, 1996.

Jelavich, Peter. "German Culture in the Great War." In *European Culture in the Great War: The Arts, Entertainment, and Propaganda, 1914–1918*, edited by Aviel Roshwald and Richard Stites, 32–57. Cambridge: Cambridge University Press, 1999.

Levi, Erik. "Music in Modern German Culture." In *The Cambridge Companion to Modern German Culture*, edited by Eva Kolinsky and Wilfried van der Will, 233–55. Cambridge: Cambridge University Press, 1998.

Painter, Karen. *Symphonic Aspirations: German Music and Politics, 1900–1945*. Cambridge: Harvard University Press, 2007.

Watkins, Glen. *Proof through the Night: Music and the Great War*. Berkeley: University of California Press, 2002.

Weiner, Marc. *Undertones of Insurrection: Music and Cultural Politics in the Modern German Narrative*. 2nd ed. Oxford: Routledge, 2017.

28 Nazi Germany

Garberding, Petra. "'We Take Care of the Artist': The German Composers' Meeting in Berlin, 1934." Translated by Per Broman. *Music and Politics* 3, no. 2 (2009), 53–69.

Kater, Michael H. *Composers of the Nazi Era: Eight Portraits*. New York: Oxford University Press, 2000.

Martin, Benjamin G. *The Nazi-Fascist New Order for European Culture*. Cambridge: Harvard University Press, 2016.

Potter, Pamela M. "Strauss and the National Socialists: The Debate and Its Relevance." In *Richard Strauss: New Perspectives on the Composer and His Work*, edited by Bryan Gilliam, 93–113. Durham: Duke University Press, 1992.

Riethmüller, Albrecht. "Stefan Zweig and the Fall of the Reich Music Chamber President, Richard Strauss." In *Music and Nazism: Art under Tyranny*, edited

by Albrecht Riethmüller and Michael H. Kater, 269–91. Laaber: Laaber Verlag, 2004.
Splitt, Gerhard. "Richard Strauss und die Reichsmusikkammer – im Zeichen der Begrenzung der Kunst?" In *Die Reichsmusikkammer: Kunst im Bann der Nazi-Diktatur,* edited by Albrecht Riethmüller and Michael Custodis, 15–32. Cologne: Böhlau Verlag, 2015.
Walter, Michael. "Strauss in the Third Reich." In *The Cambridge Companion to Richard Strauss,* edited by Charles Youmans, 226–41. Cambridge: Cambridge University Press, 2010.

29 Lateness

Hottmann, Katharina. *"Die andern komponieren. Ich mach' Musikgeschichte!"* *Historismus und Gattungsbewusstsein bei Richard Strauss. Untersuchungen zum späteren Opernschaffen.* Tutzing: Hans Schneider, 2005.
Hutcheon, Linda and Michael Hutcheon. *Four Last Songs: Aging and Creativity in Verdi, Strauss, Messiaen, and Britten.* Chicago: University of Chicago Press, 2015.
May, Jürgen. "Last Works." In *The Cambridge Companion to Richard Strauss,* edited by Charles Youmans, 178–92. Cambridge: Cambridge University Press, 2010.
Satragni, Giangiorgio. "Strauss' späte Werke, der Mythos und das 20. Jahrhundert." In *Richard Strauss-Jahrbuch 2015,* edited by Günter Brosche and Walter Werbeck, 101–15. Wien: Hollitzer, 2017.
Strauss, Richard. *Späte Aufzeichnungen.* Edited by Marion Beyer, Jürgen May, and Walter Werbeck. Mainz: Schott, 2016.

30 Reception

Allen, Ann Taylor. *Satire and Society in Wilhelmine Germany: Kladderadatsch and Simplicissimus, 1890–1914.* Lexington: University Press of Kentucky, 1984.
Bekker, Paul. *Das deutsche Musikleben.* Berlin: Schuster & Loeffler, 1916.
Botstein, Leon, ed. "Richard Strauss and the Viennese Critics (1896–1924): Reviews by Gustav Schoenaich, Robert Hirschfeld, Guido Adler, Max Kalbeck, Julius Korngold, and Karl Krauss." Translated by Susan Gillespie. In *Richard Strauss and His World,* edited by Bryan Gilliam, 311–71. Princeton: Princeton University Press, 1992.
Kandel, Eric R. *The Age of Insight: The Quest to Understand the Unconscious in Art, Mind, and Brain – From Vienna 1900 to the Present.* New York: Random House, 2012.
Messmer, Franzpeter. "Musikstadt München: Konstanten und Veränderungen." In *München, Musenstadt mit Hinterhöfen: Die Prinzregentenzeit 1886–1912,* edited by Friedrich Prinz and Marita Krauss, 284–91. München: Beck, 1988.

PART VI: ARTIFACTS AND LEGACY

31 Publishers and Editions

Editions of letters and other documents appear on the online platform of the *Kritische Ausgabe der Werke von Richard Strauss*: www.richard-strauss-ausgabe.de.

Fetthauer, Sophie. *Musikverlage im 'Dritten Reich' und im Exil*. Hamburg: Bockel, 2004.

Hofer, Achim. "'Sie halten den Namen des Autors wohl für einen Schönheits-fehler' (Strauss): Die Korrespondenz zwischen Richard Strauss und dem Verlag C. F. Peters betreffend op. 57." *Richard Strauss-Jahrbuch 2016*, edited by Günter Brosche and Oswald Panagl, 5–40. Wien: Hollitzer, 2017.

Karbaum, Michael, "Strauss und die Genossenschaft Deutscher Tonsetzer." In *Richard Strauss Handbuch*, edited by Walter Werbeck, 29–34. Stuttgart: Metzler, 2014.

Ott, Alfons. "Richard Strauss und sein Verlegerfreund Eugen Spitzweg." In *Musik und Verlag: Karl Vötterle zum 65. Geburtstag am 12. April 1968*, edited by Richard Baum and Wolfgang Rehm, 466–75. Kassel: Bärenreiter, 1968.

Plesske, Hans-Martin. "'Wenn mich die Höhe der Honorarforderung auch überrascht hat': Leipzigs Musikverlage und ihr Anteil an den Erstausgaben von Gustav Mahler, Richard Strauss und Hans Pfitzner." *Jahrbuch der deutschen Bücherei* 14 (1978): 74–102.

Rahmer, Dominik. "Strauss und seine Verleger." In *Richard Strauss Handbuch*, edited by Walter Werbeck, 54–64. Stuttgart: Metzler, 2014.

32 Letters

See the Appendix.

33 In Performance

Böhm, Karl. *A Life Remembered: Memoirs*. Translated by John Kehoe. London: M. Boyars, 1992.

Heyworth, Peter. *Otto Klemperer: His Life and Times*. 2 Vols. Cambridge: Cambridge University Press, 1996.

Kristiansen, Morten. "The Works of Richard Strauss in the American Repertoire: A Preliminary Study." In *Richard Strauss: Der Komponist und sein Werk – Überlieferung, Interpretation, Rezeption*, edited by Sebastian Bolz, Adrian Kech and Hartmut Schick, 559–82. Munich: Allitera, 2017.

Lucas, John. *Thomas Beecham: An Obsession with Music*. London: Boydell, 2008.

Osborne, Richard. *Herbert von Karajan: A Life in Music*. London: Chatto & Windus, 1998.

Ryding, Erik and Rebecca Pechefsky. *Bruno Walter: A World Elsewhere*. New Haven: Yale University Press, 2001.

34 Influence

Bribitzer-Stull, Matthew. *Understanding the Leitmotif: From Wagner to Hollywood Film Music*. Cambridge: Cambridge University Press, 2015.

Cooke, Mervyn and Fiona Ford, eds. *The Cambridge Companion to Film Music*. Cambridge: Cambridge University Press, 2016.

Franklin, Peter. *Reclaiming Late-Romantic Music: Singing Devils and Distant Sounds*. Berkeley: University of California Press, 2014.

Lehman, Frank. *Hollywood Harmony: Musical Wonder and the Sound of Cinema*. Oxford: Oxford University Press, 2018.

35 *2001: A Space Odyssey* and Beyond

Agel, Jerome. *The Making of Kubrick's 2001*. New York: New American Library, 1968.

Gies, Stefan. "Zarathustras Odyssee durch die Medien: die Takte 1–20 der Strauss'schen Tondichtung in ihrem zweiten Dasein." In *Richard Strauss: Essays zu Leben und Werk*, edited by Michael Heinemann, Matthias Herrmann, and Hans John, 73–82. Laaber: Laaber-Verlag, 2002.

Krämer, Peter. *2001: A Space Odyssey*. London: Palgrave Macmillan, 2010.

Patterson, David. "Music, Structure and Metaphor in Stanley Kubrick's *2001: A Space Odyssey*." *American Music* 22, no. 3 (2004): 444–74.

Paulus, Irena. "Stanley Kubrick's Revolution in the Usage of Film Music: *2001: A Space Odyssey*. In *International Review of the Aesthetics and Sociology of Music* 40, no. 1 (2009): 99–127.

Schwam, Stephanie, ed. *The Making of 2001: A Space Odyssey*. New York: The Modern Library, 2000.

36 Scholarly Directions

See the list of dissertations provided in the chapter.

Appendix: Letters Bibliography

Claudia Heine and Adrian Kech

The following bibliography serves as further reading for Chapter 32. The list of publications is organized alphabetically by correspondent and then chronologically within each. Superscripts indicate editions, while superscripts in brackets indicate reprints.

Bahr, Hermann
Meister und Meisterbriefe um Hermann Bahr. Aus seinen Entwürfen, Tagebüchern und seinem Briefwechsel mit Richard Strauss, Hugo von Hofmannsthal, Max Reinhardt, Josef Kainz, Eleonore Duse und Anna von Mildenburg. Edited by Joseph Gregor. Wien: Bauer, 1947.
Bella, Johann L.
Zagiba, Franz. "Bella als Vorkämpfer des jungen Richard Strauss: Strauss' künstlerisches Credo in seinen Briefen an Bella." In *Johann L. Bella (1843–1936) und das Wiener Musikleben*, 46–66. Wien: Verlag des Notringes d. wiss. Verbände Oesterreichs, 1955.
Böhm, Karl
Richard Strauss – Karl Böhm: Briefwechsel 1921–1949. Edited by Martina Steiger. Mainz: Schott, 1999.
Bruch, Max
"Max Bruch und Richard Strauss im Briefwechsel über die sinfonische Fantasie Aus Italien op. 16." Edited by Claudia Valder-Knechtges. In *Aspetti musicali: Musikhistorische Dimensionen Italiens 1600 bis 2000 – Festschrift für Dietrich Kämper zum 65. Geburtstag.* Edited by Norbert Bolin, Christoph von Blumröder, and Imke Misch, 339–45. Köln: Dohr, 2001.
Bülow, Hans von
"Ein Brief Richard Strauss' an Hans von Bülow [vom 26. Mai 1885]" [Faksimile]. *Die Musik* 4 (1904/1905): H. 8: Beilage.
Briefe, Vols. 6–7. Edited by Marie von Bülow. Leipzig: Breitkopf & Härtel, 1907–08.
"Hans von Bülow / Richard Strauss: Briefwechsel." Edited by Willi Schuh and Franz Trenner. In *Richard Strauss Jahrbuch 1954*, 7–88. Bonn: Boosey & Hawkes, [1953].
Correspondence [of] Hans von Bülow and Richard Strauss. Edited by Willi Schuh. Translated by Anthony Gishford. London: Boosey & Hawkes, 1955.

Gregor, Joseph
Richard Strauss und Joseph Gregor: Briefwechsel 1934–1949. Edited by Roland Tenschert. Salzburg: Otto Müller, 1955.
"Strauss, Zweig and Gregor: Unpublished Letters." Edited by Kenneth Birkin. *Music & Letters* 56, no. 2 (1975): 180–95.
"Selections from the Strauss-Gregor Correspondence: The Genesis of Daphne." Translated by Susan Gillespie. In *Richard Strauss and His World*, edited by Bryan Gilliam, 237–70. Princeton: Princeton University Press, 1992.

Hartmann, Rudolf
Richard Strauss – Rudolf Hartmann: Ein Briefwechsel: Mit Aufsätzen und Regiearbeiten von Rudolf Hartmann. Edited by Roswitha Schlötterer. Tutzing: Schneider, 1984.

Hauptmann, Gerhart
"Gerhart Hauptmann – Richard Strauss: Briefwechsel." Edited by Dagmar Wünsche. *Richard Strauss-Blätter* no. 9 (1983): 3–39.

Hofmannsthal, Hugo von
Richard Strauss: Briefwechsel mit Hugo von Hofmannsthal. Edited by Franz Strauss. Berlin: Paul Zsolnay, 1926.
Correspondence between Richard Strauss and Hugo von Hofmannsthal, 1907–1918. Edited by Franz Strauss. Translated by Paul England. London: M. Secker, 1927.
Richard Strauss – Hugo von Hofmannsthal. Briefwechsel: Gesamtausgabe. Edited by Franz and Alice Strauss ([1]1952, [2]1955), Willi Schuh ([3]1964–[6]1990). Zürich: Atlantis, [1]1952, [2]1955, [3]1964, [4]1970, [5]1978. Munich and Mainz: Piper and Schott, [6]1990.
A Working Friendship: The Correspondence between Richard Strauss and Hugo von Hofmannsthal. Translated by Hanns Hammelmann and Ewald Osers, Introduction by Edward Sackville-West. New York: Random House, 1961. Reprint: New York: Vienna House, 1974. (Also: Hofmannsthal, Hugo von and Richard Strauss. *The Correspondence between Richard Strauss and Hugo von Hofmannsthal.* Translated by Hanns Hammelmann and Ewald Osers, Introduction by Edward Sackville-West, London: Collins 1961.) [these volumes use the text of the 2nd German edition of 1955]
Richard Strauss – Hugo von Hofmannsthal: Correspondance [French]. Edited by Willi Schuh. Translated by Bernard Banoun. Paris: Fayard, 1992.
Hugo von Hofmannsthal – Richard Strauss: Epistolario [Italian]. Edited by Willi Schuh. Translated by Franco Serpa. Milano: Adelphi, 1993.
Rihyaruto shutorausu hōfumansutāru ōfuku shokan zenshū [Japanese]. Edited by Willi Schuh. Translated by Yuji Nakajima. Tokyo, 2000.

Karpath, Ludwig
"Richard Strauss – Ludwig Karpath: Briefwechsel 1902–1933." Edited by Günter Brosche. *Richard Strauss-Blätter* no. 6 (1975): 2–29 and no. 7 (1976): 1–18.

Kerr, Alfred
"Der Briefwechsel zwischen Alfred Kerr und Richard Strauss: Erstveröffentlichung." Edited by Marc Konhäuser. *Richard Strauss-Blätter* no. 39 (1998): 34–51.

Kippenberg, Anton
"Richard Strauss und Anton Kippenberg: Briefwechsel." *Richard-Strauss-Jahrbuch 1959/60*, edited by Willi Schuh, 114–46. Bonn: Boosey & Hawkes, 1960.

Krauss, Clemens
Richard Strauss – Clemens Krauss: Briefwechsel. Edited by Götz Klaus Kende and Willi Schuh. München: Beck, ¹1963, ²1964.
Richard Strauss – Clemens Krauss: Briefwechsel, Gesamtausgabe. Edited by Günter Brosche. Tutzing: Schneider, 1997.

Krips, Josef
"Richard Strauss schreibt an Josef Krips." Edited by Götz Klaus Kende. *Richard Strauss-Blätter* no. 5 (1981): 34–47.

Lion, Karl
"Richard Strauss – Karl Lion: Briefwechsel." Edited by Maria Erdinger. *Richard Strauss-Jahrbuch 2012*, 103–253. Tutzing: Schneider, 2012.

Mahler, Gustav
Gustav Mahler – Richard Strauss: Briefwechsel, 1888–1911. Edited by Herta Blaukopf. Munich: Piper, ¹1980, ²1988.
Gustav Mahler – Richard Strauss: Correspondence, 1888–1911. Edited by Herta Blaukopf. Translated by Edmund Jephcott. London: Faber & Faber, 1984.
Gustav Mahler – Richard Strauss: Carteggio, 1888–1911 [Italian]. Edited by Herta Blaukopf. Translated by Artemio Focher. Mailand: SE, 1991.

Mautner Markhof, Manfred
"Richard Strauss – Manfred Mautner Markhof: Briefwechsel." Edited by Alice Strauss. *Richard Strauss-Blätter* no. 5 (1981): 5–23.

Nicodé, Jean Louis
"Richard Strauss und Jean Louis Nicodé im Briefwechsel." Edited by Alfons Ott. In *Quellenstudien zur Musik: Wolfgang Schmieder zum 70. Geburtstag*, edited by Kurt Dorfmüller and Georg von Dadelsen, 137–47. Frankfurt am Main: C. F. Peters, 1972.

Reichenberger, Hugo
"Richard Strauss – Hugo Reichenberger: Briefwechsel." Edited by Teresa Hrdlicka. *Richard Strauss-Blätter* no. 52 (2004): 12–66.

Ritter, Alexander
"Ten Letters from Alexander Ritter to Richard Strauss, 1887–1894." Edited by Charles Youmans. *Richard Strauss-Blätter* no. 35 (1996): 3–24.

Rolland, Romain
Richard Strauss et Romain Rolland: correspondance, fragments de journal. Edited by Gustave Samazeuilh. Paris: Michel, 1951.
Richard Strauss and Romain Rolland: Correspondence, Together with Fragments from the Diary of Romain Rolland and Other Essays and an Introduction by Gustave Samazeuilh. Edited and Annotated with a Preface by Rollo Myers. London: Calder & Boyars, 1968.
Richard Strauss – Romain Rolland: Briefwechsel und Tagebuchnotizen. Edited by Maria Hülle-Keeding. Berlin: Henschel, 1994.

Roth, Ernst
"Correspondence with Dr. Roth." Edited by George William Hopkins. *Tempo: A Quarterly Review of Modern Music* no. 98 (1972): 9–20.
Schalk, Franz
Richard Strauss – Franz Schalk: Ein Briefwechsel. Edited by Günter Brosche. Tutzing: Schneider, 1983.
Schillings, Max von
Richard Strauss – Max von Schillings: Ein Briefwechsel. Edited by Roswitha Schlötterer. Pfaffenhofen: W. Ludwig, 1987.
Schneiderhan, Franz
"Richard Strauss – Franz Schneiderhan: Briefwechsel." Edited by Günter Brosche. *Richard Strauss-Blätter* no. 43 (2000): 3–115.
Schoenberg, Arnold
"Richard Strauss und Arnold Schoenberg: Mit unveröffentlichten Briefen." Edited by Günter Brosche. *Richard Strauss-Blätter* no. 2 (1979): 21–28.
Schuch, Ernst von
Richard Strauss, Ernst von Schuch und Dresdens Oper. Edited by Friedrich von Schuch. Dresden: Verlag der Kunst, 1952. Leipzig: Breitkopf & Härtel ²1953.
Richard Strauss – Ernst von Schuch: Ein Briefwechsel. Edited by Gabriella Hanke Knaus. Berlin: Henschel, 1999.
"Neu entdeckte Briefe von Richard Strauss an Ernst von Schuch: Aus Dresdner Sammlungen." Edited by Ekaterina Smyka. *Richard Strauss-Jahrbuch 2012*, 65–102. Tutzing: Schneider, 2012.
Schuh, Willi
Richard Strauss: Briefwechsel mit Willi Schuh. Edited by Willi Schuh. Zürich: Atlantis, 1969.
Strauss, Franz and Strauss, Josephine
Richard Strauss: Briefe an die Eltern 1882–1906. Edited by Willi Schuh. Zurich: Atlantis, 1954.
Thuille, Ludwig
Richard Strauss und Ludwig Thuille: Briefe der Freundschaft 1877–1907. Edited by Alfons Ott. Munich: Walter Ricke, 1969.
Richard Strauss – Ludwig Thuille: Ein Briefwechsel. Edited by Franz Trenner. Tutzing: Schneider, 1980.
"Selections from the Strauss-Thuille Correspondence: A Glimpse of Strauss during His Formative Years." Translated by Susan Gillespie. In *Richard Strauss and His World.* Edited by Bryan Gilliam, 193–236. Princeton: Princeton University Press, 1992.
Tiessen, Heinz
"Richard Strauss und Heinz Tiessen: Briefwechsel." Edited by Dagmar Wünsche. *Richard Strauss-Blätter* no. 6 (1981): 23–47.
Tietjen, Heinz
"Richard Strauss und Heinz Tietjen: Briefe der Freundschaft." Edited by Dagmar Wünsche. *Richard Strauss-Blätter* no. 20 (1988): 3–150.

Wagner, Cosima
Cosima Wagner – Richard Strauss: Ein Briefwechsel. Edited by Franz Trenner with Gabriele Strauss. Tutzing: Schneider, 1978.

Walker, Edyth
"Edyth Walker: '... ich singe diesmal die Elektra ...' – Briefe der Sängerin." Edited by Dagmar Saval. *Richard Strauss-Blätter* no. 50 (2003): 131–48.

Wenzel, Cäcilie
"Richard Strauss to Cäcilie Wenzel: Twelve Unpublished Letters." Edited by J. Rigbie Turner. *19th-Century Music* 9, no. 3 (1986): 163–75.

Wolff, Karl
"Ein Brief von Richard Strauss." *Rheinische Musik-Zeitung*, 1, no 4 (1900): 37–38.

Wolzogen, Ernst von
"Der Vater des 'Überbrettl': Ernst von Wolzogen im Briefwechsel mit Richard Strauss." Edited by Stephan Kohler. *Jahrbuch der Bayerischen Staatsoper* 3 (1979/80): 100–20.

Wüllner, Franz
Richard Strauss und Franz Wüllner im Briefwechsel. Edited by Dietrich Kämper. Köln: Arno Volk, 1963.

Zweig, Stefan
Richard Strauss – Stefan Zweig. Briefwechsel. Edited by Willi Schuh. Frankfurt am Main: S. Fischer, 1957.
"Strauss, Zweig and Gregor: Unpublished Letters." Edited by Kenneth Birkin. *Music & Letters* 56, no. 2 (1975): 180–95.
A Confidential Matter: The Letters of Richard Strauss and Stefan Zweig, 1931–1935. Translated by Max Knight. Foreword by Edward E. Lowinsky. Berkeley: University of California Press, 1977.
Richard Strauss – Stefan Zweig: Correspondance, 1931–1936. Édition française établie, présentée et annotée par Bernard Banoun [French]. Edited by Willi Schuh. Translated by Nicole Casanova and Bernard Banoun. [Paris]: Flammarion, 1994.

Miscellaneous Correspondents
Der Strom der Töne trug mich fort: Die Welt um Richard Strauss in Briefen. Edited by Franz Grasberger, Franz Strauss, and Alice Strauss. Tutzing: Schneider, 1967.
Richard Strauss: Briefe aus dem Archiv des Allgemeinen Deutschen Musikvereins (1888–1909). Edited by Irina Lucke-Kaminiarz. Weimar: Böhlau, 1995.
Richard Strauss im Briefwechsel mit zeitgenössischen Komponisten und Dirigenten. Vol. 1: *Lieber Collega!* Edited by Gabriele Strauss. Berlin: Henschel, 1996. Vol. 2: *Ihr Aufrichtig Ergebener.* Edited by Gabriele Strauss and Monika Reger. Berlin: Henschel, 1998. Vol. 3: *Mit herzlichen Grüßen von Haus zu Haus.* Edited by Monika Reger. Berlin: Henschel, 2004.
"'Ihr aufrichtig ergebener Dr Richard Strauss': Briefe und Werkautographen von Richard Strauss in der Handschriftensammlung des Theatermuseums." Edited by Christiane Mühlegger-Henhapel. In *"Trägt die Sprache schon Gesang in sich ...": Richard Strauss und die Oper.* Edited by Christiane Mühlegger-Henhapel and Alexandra Steiner-Strauss, 183–201. St. Pölten, Austria: Residenz Verlag, 2014.

Index

CPSIA information can be obtained
at www.ICGtesting.com
Printed in the USA
BVHW050228070223
658039BV00014B/474